Price Indexes and Quality Change

Price Indexes and Quality Change

Studies in New Methods of Measurement

Edited by Zvi Griliches for the
Price Statistics Committee
Federal Reserve Board

Harvard University Press, Cambridge, Massachusetts, 1971

© Copyright 1971 by the President and Fellows of Harvard College
All rights reserved
Distributed in Great Britain by Oxford University Press, London
Library of Congress Catalog Card Number 72-152273
SBN 674-70420-7
Printed in the United States of America

Contents

Foreword by J. Charles Partee   vii

Editor's Preface   ix

1   Introduction: Hedonic Price Indexes Revisited   3
    Zvi Griliches

2   Taste and Quality Change in the Pure Theory of
    the True-Cost-of-Living Index   16
    Franklin M. Fisher and Karl Shell

3   Hedonic Price Indexes for Automobiles: An Econometric
    Analysis of Quality Change   55
    Appendix   82
    Zvi Griliches

4   Price and Quality Changes in Consumer Capital Goods:
    An Empirical Study   88
    Appendix A   117
    Appendix B   142
    Phoebus J. Dhrymes

5   International Price Comparisons by Regression Methods   150
    Appendix   176
    Irving B. Kravis and Robert E. Lipsey

6 Quality Bias in Price Indexes and New Methods of Quality Measurement 180
  Appendix 213
  Jack E. Triplett

7 Measuring Quality Changes and the Purchasing Power of Money: An Exploratory Study of Automobiles 215
  Appendix 235
  Phillip Cagan

8 The Measurement of Quality Change from Vintage Price Data 240
  Robert E. Hall

Bibliography
  I Price Indexes and Quality Change 275
  II Other Works Cited 279

Index 283

Foreword

The Federal Reserve System has long maintained an active interest in price developments and price research. This interest has embraced a wide range of issues—including, among others, the conceptual nature and statistical quality of existing price indexes, market structure, price measures as aids to forecasting, the relationship between price change and overall economic activity, and in recent years the type of analysis covered by the term "Phillips Curve"—that is, the relation between wages, prices, and unemployment. Over the years the System has fostered internal research on a number of these topics.

Much progress has been made in the past decade in improving the statistical underpinning of price analysis and in bettering understanding of some of the broader analytical issues posed above. Nonetheless, much remains to be done. In order to make a further contribution to the understanding of some of these issues and to stimulate research generally in the price area, the Board of Governors of the Federal Reserve System in early 1965 established a Committee on Prices and Price Measurement composed of a number of academic consultants. Professor Irving Kravis of the University of Pennsylvania served as Chairman and other members included:

Dorothy Brady (Pennsylvania)
Otto Eckstein (Harvard)
Franklin Fisher (M.I.T.)
Karl Fox (Iowa State)
Zvi Griliches (Harvard)

Lester Kellogg (Tryon)
Lawrence Klein (Pennsylvania)
Stanley Lebergott (Wesleyan)
Richard Lipsey (N.B.E.R.)
Alexander J. Yeats (FRB), Secretary

It was hoped that this Price Committee could make some progress in: delineating the conceptual issues as to which price measures are relevant to monetary policy; recommending whatever changes in data collection and indexing techniques are needed to produce more accurate measures of the price concepts relevant for monetary policy; stimulating research on the causes of price change and on the measurement of prices.

The present volume, *Price Indexes and Quality Change: Studies in New Methods of Measurement*, is in large part a product of the research stimulated by the FRB Price Committee. Under the editorship of Professor Zvi Griliches, this volume presents papers which were originally commissioned by the committee and also a number of selected earlier studies in this area. It is our hope that this collection of basic readings will serve to provide ready access to what has already been accomplished in this field and to stimulate further research on the theoretical and empirical problems involved in the measurement of price and quality change. The material provides an essential step toward the important, but difficult, goal of making adequate allowance for quality change in our interpretation of the significance of price change.

J. Charles Partee, Director
Division of Research and Statistics

Editor's Preface

The papers included in this volume were all commissioned by the Price Statistics Committee of the Federal Reserve Board (Fisher and Shell, Dhrymes, Triplett, and Hall) or were written by members of the committee (Griliches and Kravis-Lipsey), with the exception of two earlier seminal papers (Griliches 1961 and Cagan 1965), which originally appeared in rather inaccessible publications. The latter are reprinted with only minor editorial changes. Taken as a whole, this collection does, I think, represent fairly the state of the art. It does not, however, exhaust all of the work that has been done in this field. The bibliography that concludes this volume attempts to cover most of the work in this general area of research, as well as recording items cited in the text.

The papers in this volume fall roughly into three categories and are so organized: (1) A brief introduction on the state of the art by Griliches and a theoretical discussion of quality change and its implications for the construction of price index numbers by Fisher and Shell; (2) a series of papers outlining, applying, and extending the hedonic (regression) approach to price change measurement, starting with the early Griliches paper on automobiles, continuing with Dhrymes' extension of it to include individual manufacturer effects and use principle components to cope with the multicollinearity of the various characteristics, followed by the Kravis-Lipsey application of it to international price comparisons of durable goods, and closing with Triplett's discussion of the practical difficulties of implementing any such suggestions routinely; and (3) two papers on the use of secondhand market prices for the measurement of quality change: Cagan's 1965 paper on automobiles and Hall's synthesis of this and the hedonic price regression approach, analyzing pick-up truck prices, depreciation, and quality change. All of these papers raise as many questions as they answer, but this is true of any attempt to move forward on a problem as difficult and important as this one.

Zvi Griliches
Cambridge, Massachusetts, October 1970

Price Indexes and Quality Change

Zvi Griliches
Introduction:
Hedonic Price Indexes Revisited

A decade has passed since my first attempt to revive the "hedonic" multiple regression approach to the construction of price indexes.[1] While one cannot claim that it has taken the profession by storm (it is too imperfect and difficult a tool for that), there has, in the meantime, developed a reasonably large literature on the subject with a number of rather interesting applications. It has even infiltrated into some of the official government departments responsible for the work on price statistics.[2]

Most of this work has been empirical. Automobile prices attracted most of the attention with additional work reported by Fisher, Griliches, and Kaysen (1962), Griliches (1964), Cagan (1965), Cramer (1966), Triplett (1966), and Dhrymes (1967). Tractor prices were analyzed by Fettig (1963), electric apparatus by Dean and DePodwin (1961), house prices by Bailey, Muth, and Nourse (1963), Brown (1964), Musgrave (1969), and Yoshihara et al. (1970), diesel engines by Kravis and Lipsey (1969), refrigerators by Dhrymes (1967), and washing machines and carpets by

---

This work has been supported by a grant from the National Science Foundation and the Price Statistics Committee of the Federal Reserve Board. The paper appeared earlier in slightly different form ("Hedonic Price Indexes Revisited: Some Notes on the State of the Art," 1967, *Proceedings of the Business and Economics Statistics Section* [Washington: American Statistical Association], pp. 324–332).

Zvi Griliches is Professor of Economics, Harvard University.

1. Griliches 1961 and Adelman and Griliches 1961. The major earlier references are Court 1939 and Stone 1956.

2. See the articles by Nicholson 1967 and Musgrave 1969. This is also reflected in an unpublished Bureau of Labor Statistics memorandum by Thomas W. Gavett 1967b.

Gavett (1967a). There are also several studies dealing with other topics which could be interpreted as implying a "hedonic" price index: Barzel (1964) on steam power generators, Knight and Barr (1966) and Chow (1967) on computers, and Hanoch (1965) on people. Unfortunately, the theoretical base of such studies has not expanded greatly since the Adelman and Griliches article (1961). The idea of a commodity as a bundle of characteristics (dimensions or qualities) has been developed further by Lancaster (1966) and Muth (1966), but it has not produced any new implications for the construction of price indexes. More important has been the development of the concept of various types of technical change (embodied, factor-augmenting, etc.) in the production function and growth literature. The implications of this literature for the construction of price indexes have been derived and extended in an important paper by Fisher and Shell (1967) included in this volume. A similar approach was used by Hall (1968) to derive measures of quality change from secondhand market data.

In this brief paper I shall first comment on regression analyses of prices as they are practiced today, then explore in some detail the promise and difficulties associated with the use of secondhand market prices for the measurement of quality change, make some observations on the current state of practice in the official price indexes, and conclude with a comment on difficulties with the concept of "quality change" itself.

The "hedonic," or, using a less value-loaded word, characteristics approach to the construction of price indexes is based on the empirical hypothesis (or research strategy) which asserts that the multitude of models and varieties of a particular commodity can be comprehended in terms of a much smaller number of characteristics or basic attributes of a commodity such as "size," "power," "trim," and "accessories," and that viewing the problem this way will reduce greatly the magnitude of the pure new commodity or "technical change" problem, since most (though not all) new "models" of commodities may be viewed as a new combination of "old" characteristics. In its parametric version, it asserts the existence of a "reasonably well-fitting" relation between the prices of different models and the level of their various but not too numerous characteristics. If one views the commodity as an *aggregate* of individual components or characteristics, there is no reason to expect that this relationship between the overall price of the bundle and the level or quantity of the various characteristics will remain constant. Both the relative and the absolute prices of the various components may change.

Hedonic Price Indexes Revisited

In practice the following questions arise:

1. What are the relevant characteristics?
2. What is the form of the relationship between prices and characteristics?
3. How does one estimate the "pure" price change from such data?

There isn't much that one can say in general about the first question—it is very much an empirical matter—except to note that most of the studies included in this volume do quite well with some combination of "size" and "power" variables. I would like to warn, however, against the use of variables which are not direct characteristics of the commodity (or a transformation of them) but an outcome of the market experiment. I have in mind here such things as the use by Brown of the purchaser's income in explaining house prices, and the use by Dhrymes (in the earlier version of his work) of total quantities produced to explain relative automobile prices. The latter variable is an *outcome* of the encounter of consumers with commodities of different qualities and price. The characteristics theory would predict that models which have more "quality" per dollar will sell better, but this is a characteristic of the market, not of the commodity. I'll admit that there is an identification problem here, but I don't believe that it is relevant for the derivation of characteristic prices to be used in the construction of a "purer" price index.[3]

The Dhrymes and Triplett papers do remind us, however, of a problem overlooked in most of the previous studies, including my own. A characteristic and its price are important only to the extent that they capture some relevant fraction of the market. Most of the analyses have used unweighted data on models, specifications, and prices. But at any point of time some manufacturers may offer models with characteristics in undesirable combinations and at "unrealistic" (from the consumer's point of view) relative prices. Such models will not sell very well and hence should also not be allowed to influence our analyses greatly. There is no good argument except simplicity for the one-vote-per-model approach to regression analysis. It is true that market shares by detailed characteristics are not easy to come by, but some scattered data are available and more of them should be used.

The form of the relationship is again an empirical matter. Most of the investigators settle after some experimentation for a semi-logarithmic relationship between prices and characteristics, implying a rising supply

---

3. Nor did Dhrymes use it for this purpose. His interest was in testing the homogeneity of the relationship across manufacturers.

price per characteristic unit.[4] Such experimentation, however, is usually conducted without the help of a relevant statistical framework. I would like therefore to draw attention to an article by Box and Cox (1964) which does provide the appropriate methodology for choosing between different functional forms.

There are several ways of constructing a "pure" price index from such data. The particular way chosen will depend both on the kind of price index one wants and on the type of data that one has. The first, and the one most directly in the usual price index spirit, is to use the regression equations *only* to estimate the *"prices"* of the relevant characteristics, using these in turn in the construction of a more detailed quantity-of-characteristics index and the associated price-of-characteristics index. To evade the usual Laspeyres and Paasche problem, let me proceed for a while via Divisia indexes (see Jorgenson and Griliches 1967 for an application of such indexes in a different context, and Richter 1966 for a proof of their optimality). Also, since data on characteristics are more readily and frequently available, let us start from a change in the quantity-of-characteristics index per particular model, defined as

$$\frac{dQ_i}{Q_i} = \sum_j w_j \frac{dq_j}{q_j},$$

where Q_i is the quality index for the ith model of the product, q_j is the level of the jth characteristic, and w_j is the value share of that characteristic in the total price of the (aggregate) commodity, $w_j = p_j q_j$ (and hence also $\sum w_j dq_j/q_j = \sum p_j dq_j$). The pure price change is then estimated simply as the rate of change of observed price minus the rate of the change of "quality" per commodity unit:

$$\frac{d\pi_i}{\pi_i} \equiv \frac{dP_i}{P_i} - \frac{dQ_i}{Q_i}.$$

The total pure price index for the whole class of such commodities is $d\pi/\pi = \sum v_i (d\pi_i/\pi_i)$, where v_i is the value share of the ith model in the aggregate consumption or sales of this class ($v_i = p_i n_i$, where n_i is the number of units sold or consumed). This approach calls for relatively recent and often changing "price" weights. Since such statistics come to us in discrete intervals, we are also faced with the usual Laspeyres-Paasche

---

4. See the Kravis-Lipsey paper included in this volume for a detailed discussion of this problem.

Hedonic Price Indexes Revisited

problem. The oftener we can change such weights, the less of a problem it will be. In practice, while one may want to use the most recent cross-section to derive the relevant price weights, such estimates may fluctuate too much for comfort as the result of multi-collinearity and sampling fluctuations. They should be smoothed in some way, either by choosing $w_i = \frac{1}{2}[w_i(t) + w_i(t+1)]$, or by using "adjacent year" regressions in estimating these weights.

This approach focuses on the estimation of quality change due to a change in a particular set of dimensions and characteristics, assuming either that the other "left out" aspects of quality are not correlated with the included ones, or, if they are, that this correlation also persists into the future. It does not pretend to accomplish everything, to adjust for all quality change. But half a loaf should be better than none.

The alternative approach, first used by Court, is to interpret the coefficient of a time dummy variable(s) in a combined two (or several) years cross-section regression of prices on specifications as a direct estimate of the pure price change. The justification for this is very simple and appealing: We allow as best we can for all of the major differences in specifications by "holding them constant" through regression techniques. That part of the average price change which is not accounted for by any of the included specifications will be reflected in the coefficient of the time dummy and represents our best estimate of the "unexplained-by-specification-change average price change." I used this approach extensively in the first half of my own early paper on this subject (included in this volume), but I am much less satisfied with it now. Besides the fact that it imposes a common set of implicit specification prices on several periods and is not well articulated with the rest of the index number literature, it is very much subject to the vagaries of sample selection. Most of the workers in this area, including myself, tried to get as large a cross-section in any year as possible, not worrying too much about the overall comparability of any two cross-sections. As a result of this, depending on the propensity for publishing such data and the changing proclivities of manufacturers to proliferate different model variants, actual cross-sections used vary significantly in sample size from year to year. This would not matter if all of the observed price variance were just due to the variables considered. Then all points would be on the line, and the different models included or excluded in a particular year would be just different versions of the same thing. But in practice there are "model effects" that persist. Consider an equation of the form

$$\log p_{it} = a + \sum b_k x_{kit} + v_t + e_i,$$

where x_{kit} stands for the quantity of the kth dimension in the ith model in year t, v_t is the common "year" or "pure" price change effect, and e_i is a "model" effect, the effect of other left-out qualities, assumed to be independent of calendar time and the other x's. If one uses two adjacent cross-sections and they do not contain all the same i's in the two years, even if the b's remain unchanged, the estimate of the time dummy coefficient will be unbiased *only* if $\sum e_n$ for the "new" models just equals $\sum e_o$, the sum of the individual effects of the "old" models no longer appearing in the new sample. But this would be true only if the "included dimensions" exhausted all there was or they were perfectly correlated with the left-out variables. For example, consider a new year in which we suddenly include both the Volkswagen and Mercedes-Benz models among our standard cars. Since these are more expensive per unit of size than the regular American cars, we shall suddenly show a rise in price or a decline in quality. But what has actually happened is a change in the mix of our sample. That this may be a serious problem can be seen from the proliferation of Packard and Studebaker models just before their disappearance. The problem could be reduced somewhat if these regressions were weighted by total sales of the various models, but in any case one needs here to worry much more about the comparability of the samples than if one were only interested in the estimates of some of the slope coefficients (and not the year constants). Without further analysis of whether changing the size and composition of the various cross-sections makes much of a difference, one should not interpret the time dummy estimates presented by myself and Triplett for automobiles as unbiased estimates of the pure-price change. This stricture does not apply, however, to the specific quality indexes constructed for a particular fixed sample of cars using the estimated dimensions weights, which appear later in my paper.

The time dummy approach does have the advantage, if the comparability problem can be solved, of allowing us to ignore the ever-present problem of multi-collinearity among the various dimensions. Using it, we may not care that in one year the coefficient of weight is high and horsepower is low while in another year these coefficients reverse themselves, as long as the two coefficients taken together hold the *joint* effect of weight and horsepower constant. But even here, we should use a weighted regression approach, since we are interested in an estimate of a weighted average of the pure-price change, rather than just an unweighted average over all possible models, no matter how peculiar or rare.

The idea that one ought to be able to measure quality differences with the help of prices of used items must have been in the air for quite a while. It appears first in Burstein's paper (1961), but Cagan (1965, reprinted in

Hedonic Price Indexes Revisited

this volume) was the first to present actual estimates based on such an approach. The basic idea is extremely simple: We can observe today both 1970 and 1969 Chevrolet cars being sold in the market. The price of the two differs because (a) the 1969 car is one year older than the 1970 one and (b) because the 1970 model may be better (or worse) than the 1969 one. If we can assume that the rate of "aging" is independent of calendar time, and if we could somehow find out what it is, we could derive the implied premium of 1970 over 1969 cars (provided that this relative premium does not change with age). Consider the price of used machines or cars of model (or manufacturer) j (such as Chevrolet) in year t (say 1970) of vintage (model year) v (e.g., 1968), or equivalently of age $h = t - v$. The basic hypothesis can then be written as follows:

$$P_{tvj} = P_t Q_{tvj},$$

when P_t is the overall average price per unit of constant quality machine, and Q_{tvj} are the units (quantity) of "carness" or "machinery" still embodied in year t, in machine type j of vintage v. It is assumed that

$$Q_{(t+1)vj} = d_{hj} Q_{tvj},$$

where d is a depreciation factor (one minus the depreciation rate) which is independent of calendar time or vintage (this is what Hall calls a "stationarity" assumption) but may depend on age (h) and make (j). Moreover, we assume that we can write

$$Q_{t,v,j} = T_v Q_{t-1,v-1} e^{u_{vj}}.$$

That is, the quantity (or quality) of a new model in year t, relative to the previous vintage (when new), is composed of an average improvement factor T over all models, and a factor special to the particular model and vintage $e^{u_{vj}}$, and this relative superiority is constant and independent of age or calendar time. This is a very strong assumption about the character of technical or quality change, stating that any new version of model j can be expressed as so many units more or less than the old version of j, this premium once established being fixed and independent of everything else. This means, technically, that all quality change is of the factor- or product-augmenting type. Fisher and Shell call this the "repackaging" case. To reiterate, it implies that the relative superiority of one version of a commodity over the other is independent of market conditions, relative supplies of the two versions, and age.[5]

---

5. In addition, unless we can assume that the depreciation rate is independent of age ($d_h = d$), i.e., exponential depreciation at a fixed rate, we cannot assume that these relationships (relative model prices) are independent of the interest rate. This important point is made by Hall (1968), but I shall not pursue it further here.

If we can observe a number of different vintages being sold at the same time, we can form logarithms of price ratios which given our assumptions will equal

$$\ln P_{tvj} - \ln P_{t(v-1)j} = \ln T_v + \ln d_{hj} + u_{vj} - u_{v-1,j}.$$

Given a number of vintages per year, a reasonably large number of models and makes, and several years' worth of observations, there should be enough degrees of freedom to estimate most of the parameters of interest.[6]

The appropriate approach here is via the use of dummy variables for age (d's), make, and vintage. Note, however, that for estimation purposes one must impose some constraints of the form $\sum \ln T_v = \sum \ln d_{hj} =$ constant, and hence *in general one cannot separate the effect of an average rate of quality improvement (obsolescence) from the average effect of aging (depreciation)* on the basis of such data.[7] Only if one assumes that in some period(s) there was no improvement in quality $T_v \equiv 1$, which is the procedure adopted by Cagan, can one get an unambiguous estimate of d and hence also estimates of T for other periods. But Cagan's numbers are also consistent with lower average depreciation rates and higher rates of quality change. The only thing that can be estimated unambiguously from such data is the *change in the rate of change of quality improvement*, but that may be interesting enough by itself.

The major advantage of using secondhand market prices to measure quality change lies in freeing us from the necessity of choosing and specifying a limited list of commodity characteristics and estimating their relative contributions. Such lists are never complete and such estimates are never perfect. It is bought, however, only at the cost of very specific assumptions about the nature of quality change and a fundamental identification problem. It cannot really supplant the hedonic index approach. The latter is at least needed to arbitrate the assertion that $T_v = 1$ for a particular pair of vintages allowing the identification of the

---

6. One would, however, expect the residuals from such equations (the $u_{vj} - u_{v-1, j}$'s) to be negatively correlated, and this should be taken into account in the estimation procedure. In particular, some smoothing is in order. It is unfortunate, for example, that Cagan ends his analysis with the 1959–1960 comparison and a large negative "residual." A rough computation indicates that if his data were extended to 1960–1961, they'd show a positive residual for that year, largely canceling the earlier negative one and leading to a higher overall estimated rate of quality change for the whole period.

7. These difficulties of identification are explored in greater detail in Hall's 1968 paper and in the paper included in this volume.

Hedonic Price Indexes Revisited

rest of the parameters.[8] Moreover, by not insisting that the relative prices (weights) of the various characteristics remain constant (and independent of other variables), the hedonic index approach can adapt itself and remain valid for a much wider range of types of quality changes.

The power of the approach outlined in the previous section can be illustrated by using it to evaluate some recent official procedures. "It is standard procedure for the BLS [Bureau of Labor Statistics] to adjust for quality when measuring price changes for the Consumer Price Index and the Wholesale Price Index" (Stotz 1966, p. 178). This statement has a somewhat strange but welcome ring to participants of the old debates on this topic. I welcome the increased attention given to quality change by the BLS, but I am concerned that by basing such adjustments largely on data furnished by manufacturers and on "producer costs" it may wind up overestimating "quality change," accepting as "improvements" expenditures which consumers may not interpret as such. For example, the reported improvement in "quality" for the basket of cars priced by the CPI was about 0.8 percent between the 1965 and 1966 models of these cars and 1.9 percent between 1966 and 1967 models (Stotz 1966 and Commissioner Ross's statement of November 23, 1966). If this conclusion is correct, then it should be true that 1967 cars will be considered more valuable than 1966 cars were relative to the 1966 models. Using Cagan's approach, the basket of cars described by Stotz (1966), used car prices given by National Automobile Dealers' Association (for November 1967 and 1966), and rough relative weights based on model sales for 1966 from *Ward's Automotive Reports*, one must conclude that there is no evidence in the used car market that "quality change" occurred at a higher rate between 1967 and 1966 than between 1966 and 1965 (see Table 1.1 for details). The overall numbers are small, such calculations are rough, and the differences may not be significant and shouldn't be taken too seriously. Nevertheless, unless the BLS presents a clearer and more detailed description of how it actually makes these adjustments, (an appeal to the confidentiality of manufacturers' data and the opinions of engineering experts doesn't really help much here), doubts about the "quality" of such quality

---

8. Hall, in his paper in this volume, uses the hedonic approach to estimate the no-change point implicitly by defining it as no change in any of the listed characteristics. His approach, however, assumes that all of the characteristics (qualities) depreciate at the same rate. This assumption appears to be contradicted by the results of hedonic regressions using secondhand prices reported in the earlier Griliches paper (see Table 3.10, p. 78, this volume). The implied prices (coefficients) of the various characteristics decline with age but at different rates.

Table 1.1. Prices of the CPI Cars in the Used Car Market[a]

	Model Year				Ratios			Approximate weights (8)
	November 1967		November 1966					
Model and make	1967 (1)	1966 (2)	1966 (3)	1965 (4)	(1)/(2) (5)	(3)/(4) (6)	(5)/(6) (7)	
Chevelle Malibu, 2 dr. sport cp.	2340	1895	2160	1685	1.2348	1.2819	0.9633	0.08
Chevrolet Impala, Super Sport, 2 dr. hard top	2730	2235	2580	2090	1.2215	1.2344	0.9895	0.30
Ford Mustang, 2 dr. hard top	2350	1875	2220	1785	1.2533	1.2437	1.0077	0.12
Ford Galaxie 500, 2 dr. hard top	2540	2060	2420	1930	1.2330	1.2539	0.9833	0.19
Plymouth Fury III, 4 dr. sedan	2440	1990	2355	1900	1.2261	1.2395	0.9892	0.06
Pontiac Catalina, 4 dr. sedan	2610	2135	2510	2075	1.2225	1.2096	1.0107	0.10
Rambler Rebel-Classic 770, 4 dr. sedan	2155	1670	1965	1595	1.2904	1.2320	1.0474	0.06
Volkswagen 113, 2 dr. sedan	1590	1345	1510	1310	1.1822	1.1527	1.0256	0.09

[a] An index of the *rate of change* of quality change: $\sum (7) \times (8) = 0.997$

SOURCE: Cols. (1)–(4): *Used Car Guide,* November 1966 and 1967 issues. Col. (8): *Ward's Automotive Reports,* 1967.

All cars are V-8 models except for Rambler (6 cyl.) and VW (4 cyl.). Rambler Rebel in 1967, Classic 1966, 1965.

adjustments and their objectivity will remain. I assume that the BLS is doing a good job, and I believe that it will do an even better job in the future, but I would appreciate much more detailed information on how it is actually done.

This is not the place nor is there time to go into all the intricacies of utility theory and associated price index problems, but it is worthwhile to point out that we are living in a complicated world and that it is both unrealistic and unnecessary to expect that one number, "the" price index, can summarize adequately all the changes that occur. Economists will often define a "price-of-living" index by the question: "How much [more] income is required [relatively] *today* to make me just indifferent between

Hedonic Price Indexes Revisited

facing yesterday's budget constraint [with yesterday's money income and prices] and a budget constraint defined by today's prices and the income in question?" (Fisher and Shell 1967, see p. 19 below). Implicitly, this question assumes that any change in consumer behavior can be factored into a "real income" effect (the reciprocal of the price index) and a substitution effect, and that *this is all there is to that*. But many other things, all of which may affect the level of utility achieved with a given money income, may be changing at the same time. It is then a question of *definition* and research strategy whether we want to lump them all into one concept of "the" price index.

Schematically and purely definitionally, let us visualize the following set of equations summarizing the tastes of a consumer and the constraints and opportunities facing him:

$$U = U(S)$$
$$S = F(X, Z, t_s, E)$$
$$Y = W(t_y) = PX$$
$$t_s + t_y \leq T, Z \leq \bar{Z}$$

where $U(S)$ is the utility indicator of a stream of services S, $F(X, Z, t_s, E)$ is the "production function" of such services using purchased inputs X, non-market inputs Z, time t_s, and affected by uncontrollable environment factors E. Money income y is a function of time spent at work and in turn constrains the total value of purchased commodities PX, where P is our "price" index of goods purchased. Finally, we have the constraints on time and non-market commodities (the levels of the latter could in turn be correlated with income, as in the case of fringe benefits).[9]

Unfortunately, the distinction between the U and S function, while illuminating, is not very operational. Moreover, it can be shown that an important class of changes in S can be equally well represented by changes in the "quantities" of X. This is true for quality changes of the commodity augmenting type, the "repackaging" case, where either representation will describe the facts. If we could get measures of the changing utility efficiency of some goods, we would want to do so, because it would be an interesting piece of information of major economic significance. Whether or not we would want to incorporate them into our measure of the "price" index is then a purely definitional rather than substantive issue. It depends on what the particular "price" index purports to measure.

---

9. See Becker 1965, Lancaster 1966, and Muth 1967 for further elaboration of such framework.

Most economists would agree that they would like the "price" index to be a "price-of-living or of utility" indicator. Many government statisticians in charge of producing actual price indexes will reply that they *cannot* achieve this and that therefore they should not even try, but should concentrate instead on some more "objective" index of "transaction" prices and/or allow only for those "quality" changes which are based on "production" costs. The fact that "truth" cannot be achieved doesn't mean that one shouldn't strive to do so, though I sympathize with the position that it is better to measure well something definite than to do a very poor job on a more interesting but also more nebulous concept. Nevertheless, I would deny the contention that "transaction" units or "production" costs are much more definitive concepts. In general, they too make little sense without some appeal to utility considerations.

Consider the simple example of a box of crackers of an unchanged size and price. If its contents (in terms of ounces of crackers per box) have declined, the statistician will usually record (correctly, I believe) a rise in the price of crackers. But the "transaction" unit is a "box," it is priced as a "box," and most consumers don't know or notice the exact number of ounces per box. Nevertheless, the statistician will usually decide that the relevant unit is an ounce of crackers, not the box, even if crackers are not sold by the ounce. Why? Because he believes that the ounce of crackers is a more relevant *utility unit*, that the consumer is ultimately interested in crackers and not in the package they come in.[10] Without an appeal to utility considerations, he wouldn't know what to do in this and many other cases. With this fact established, it is only fair to let the statistician haggle about its price, since bringing utility considerations into the measurement of commodities will prove to be a much harder task in some cases (such as medical service) than in others. This doesn't mean, however, that he shouldn't want to do it if he could.

Nor are "production costs" an adequate guide to quality changes without a check of their utility implications. There may be changes that cost more, such as antipollution devices for automobiles, which are "quality changes" in some sense, but not the relevant one. From the point of view of the individual consumer, if he were not willing to buy these devices on his own, their introduction by law represents a form of tax (in kind) rather than a rise in his utility. This should be recorded as a rise in price, not a fall. It may lead to externalities, possibly to an overall improvement of his environment (E), and hence to an indirect rise in his

---

10. This is not to imply that "packaging" is irrelevant to the consumer, only that in this context it is a second-order consideration.

Hedonic Price Indexes Revisited

utility, which then could be perhaps represented by a decline in the "real price" of air, but that is a different matter.[11]

Nor should we ignore "costless" changes if we can measure them. If the consumer is in fact buying "horsepower," and if a design change makes it possible to deliver more horsepower from the same size and "cost" engine, then the price of horsepower to the consumer has fallen *and he is better off.*[12] There always remains the question, how do we know what the consumer is buying? What *are* the relevant units? "Hedonic" price indexes are one way of answering this question. The critical property of such price indexes is that when prices (and units) are given by such a "hedonic index for the commodities [models] within a group, all such commodities have marginal rates of transformation vis-a-vis commodities outside the group that move in proportion to each other. Insofar as this property is substantiated by empirical evidence, [such] adjustment . . . amounts to correcting an error of aggregation" (Jorgenson and Griliches 1967, p. 260). In simpler words, this means that we look for such units that would allow us the most *concise* and stable explanation of reality, one that is based on a smaller number of variables (than the almost infinite number of various varieties of commodities) and in terms of which the demand relations, the relations between prices and quantities purchased, are more stable, explain a larger fraction of the observed variance of prices and quantities, and require the introduction of a smaller number of ad hoc parameters, trends, or shift variables. At this level of generality, such a statement is neither a fact nor a theorem, but rather a methodological prejudice, a prejudice about what is likely to be the most fruitful way of approaching such problems and organizing our knowledge about consumer behavior and the economy at large.

---

11. Alternatively one could view it as a deterioration in his environment, the same as a colder winter that requires him to purchase more fuel to achieve a given level of satisfaction. In such a case, one may not record a rise in the "price" of living, even though there has clearly occurred a rise in the "cost" of living.

12. Gavett's discussion of this point (1967a, pp. 18–19) is confusing because he does not recognize that one could interpret such a change as a decline in price per corrected unit, and hence as a downward shift in the relevant supply function. The increase in total utility he observes is not the consequence of an increase in total consumption of the good at an unchanged price (since this couldn't happen with a fixed budget constraint) but is rather due to a fall in the relevant price.

2.

Franklin M. Fisher and Karl Shell
Taste and Quality Change in the Pure Theory of the True Cost-of-Living Index

1. Introduction

The standard theory of the true cost-of-living index gives a rather uncomfortable treatment to taste and quality changes (including the introduction of new goods). The consumer is assumed to have always had an unchanging indifference map, complete with axes for all new goods of whose potential existence he in fact was not aware before their introduction. Similarly, quality change is treated either as an introduction of a new good or as a simple repackaging of an old one equivalent to a price reduction.[1] Yet the justification for the latter procedure has never been satisfactorily set forth, while the former one meets with many of the same difficulties as does the treatment of new goods itself.

If the treatment of new goods and quality change is less than fully satisfactory, however, the treatment of taste change is nonexistent. The assumption of an unchanging indifference map even defined over non-

---

This research was supported by the Federal Reserve Board Committee on Prices and Price Measurement. The authors are indebted to Paul Samuelson and Robert Summers for helpful discussions, but they retain responsibility for error. The paper first appeared in *Value, Capital, and Growth: Essays in Honour of Sir John Hicks,* 1968, ed. J. N. Wolfe (Edinburgh: University of Edinburgh Press) and is reprinted by permission of the publisher.

Franklin M. Fisher is Professor of Economics, Massachusetts Institute of Technology, and Karl Shell is Associate Professor of Economics, Wharton School of Finance and Commerce, University of Pennsylvania.

1. An exception is the theory of hedonic price indices, where a quality change is regarded as providing a new bundle of old underlying attributes. See Court 1939, Griliches 1961, Lancaster 196β, and Stone 1956.

Taste and Quality Change

existent goods is apparently crucial for a theory which is often erroneously thought to answer the question: How much would it cost in today's prices to make the consumer just as well off as he was yesterday? This question cannot be answered without resorting to an arbitrary intertemporal weighting of utilities. Yet taste changes do occur, and the cost-of-living index is often carelessly thought to be designed to answer that question (*Price Statistics* 1961, pp. 51–59; Hofsten 1952).

This paper begins by arguing that the difficulty is due only to a misinterpretation of the theory of the true cost-of-living index. That theory does not in fact seek to answer the question posed above, nor does it make intertemporal comparisons of utility. Indeed, we observe that such a question can never be answered and such comparisons never made because they have no operational content. Incautious application of the theory has avoided facing up to this by the use of an apparently appealing but completely arbitrary and untestable hidden assumption which does no apparent harm when tastes are constant but which breaks down utterly when tastes do change.

That assumption, however, is not part of the theory, and the question which the theory does answer retains its meaning whether or not tastes are constant. The pure theory of the cost-of-living index, rigorously interpreted, accommodates taste changes quite comfortably.

Accordingly, we then go on to consider a case of parametrizable taste change in full detail. That case can be given the interpretation of consumers learning more about the properties of a recently introduced good. We derive the consequences for index number construction of such a circumstance.

Moreover, the rigorous formulation of the theory involved in the treatment of taste change aids also in the treatment of new goods and of quality change. It does so in two ways. First, the formally acceptable but practically uncomfortable assumption that the consumer has always known about unavailable goods and qualities disappears. Second, by focusing attention on a proper question, the analysis of new goods and quality change becomes relatively straightforward. While it is true in principle that (unlike the case of taste change) the same analysis could be carried out without so rigorous a formulation (given the assumption of unchanging tastes for nonexistent goods), that formulation makes it very clear what is involved. Asking the right question is a good part of obtaining the answer.

Thus the last two sections of the paper discuss the treatment of new goods and of quality change respectively and show what kind of information is needed for the handling of these problems in a satisfactory manner.

2. The Theory of the True Cost-of-Living Index and Intertemporal Comparisons of Welfare

As indicated, a frequently encountered view of the true cost-of-living index is that it is designed to answer the question: "What income would be required to make a consumer faced with today's prices just as well off as he was yesterday when he faced yesterday's income and yesterday's prices?" The difficulty that is presented by taste changes in answering this question is immediately apparent. What is meant by "just as well off as he was yesterday" if the indifference map has shifted?

Yet reflection on this issue shows that the same difficulty appears even if tastes do not change. While it is apparently natural to say that a man whose tastes have remained constant is just as well off today as he was yesterday if he is on the same indifference curve in both periods, the appeal of that proposition is no more than apparent. In both periods, the man's utility function is determined only up to a monotonic transformation; how can we possibly know whether the level of true utility (whatever that may mean) corresponding to a given indifference curve is the same in both periods? The man's efficiency as a pleasure-machine may have changed without changing his tastes.

Indeed, we have no more justification for saying that a man on the same indifference curve at two different times is equally well off at both than we do for saying that two men who happen to have the same indifference map are equally well off if they have the same possessions. Both statements are attractive for reasons of simplicity, and both are completely without any operational content whatsoever. One never steps into the same river twice, and the comparison between a man's utility now and his utility yesterday stands on precisely the same lack of footing as the comparison of the utilities of two different men.

Thus, a consideration of the problem of taste change on this interpretation of the theory of the true cost-of-living index merely makes explicit a problem that is apparently there all the time. If that theory were really founded upon intertemporal comparisons of utility of the type described, then that theory would be without foundation.[2]

In fact, however, the theory of the true cost-of-living index makes no such comparisons, and rigorous statements of that theory have avoided

---

2. Intertemporal comparisons which do not involve the same set of consumers at both times or geographical comparisons also sharply point up the problem. Following this testament to our ordinalist purity, it is only fair to remark that if the results of our work

Taste and Quality Change

them. Such statements run as follows: "Given an indifference map, we compare two *hypothetical* situations, A and B. We ask how much income the consumer in B would require to make him just indifferent between facing B's prices and facing A's prices with a stated income." Note that the question of whether the consumer has the same utility in A as in B never arises. So long as we remain on this level of abstraction, the point in time and space at which the consumer has the indifference map used in the comparison may be A or it may be B or it may be any other *single* point different from both of these.

In practice, however, the cost-of-living index is meant to compare two real situations rather than two hypothetical ones, and A and B become, for example, yesterday and today, respectively. In this case, it is natural to take the indifference map to be used as the one in force at either A or B,[3] and if tastes have not changed so that the two maps are the same, it is easy to slip into the erroneous (but in this case harmless) usage of saying that what are compared are the relative costs of making the consumer at B just as well off as he was at A. If the indifference maps differ, however, such a slip is dangerous, and it must never be forgotten that the viewpoint from which the comparison is made is not necessarily identical with either A or B.

Thus, the true cost-of-living index is supposed to represent a comparison between two opportunity or constraint loci, not between two utility levels. The first constraint locus is that given by yesterday's income and prices —it is yesterday's budget constraint. The second is a budget constraint defined by today's prices but with income a parameter. The true cost-of-living index does not answer the question: "How much income would it take today to make me as well off as I was yesterday with yesterday's budget constraint?" That question is unanswerable. A similar-seeming question which *can* be answered is: "How much income is required *today* to make me just indifferent between facing yesterday's budget constraint and facing a budget constraint defined by today's prices and the income in question?" The latter question refers to a choice which can in principle be posed; the former does not.

---

are to shed light on the construction of a cost-of-living index for a society or even a class within that society, the existence of a "representative consumer" must be assumed. In general, to draw welfare conclusions from aggregate price and quantity data requires interpersonal utility comparisons. For a full discussion of this point, see Samuelson 1947.

3. Yet this is not inevitable. One can ask how the cost of living in the United Kingdom changed as seen with American tastes or how a man of today would view nineteenth-century price changes.

Note further that the question just posed retains its meaning even if tastes have changed between yesterday and today. It is a question posed entirely in terms of today's tastes and involves a comparison of present and past *constraints*, not a comparison of present and past utilities. As it were, we replace the question: "Were you happier when young than you are now?" with the question: "Would you like to live your youth over again, having the tastes you do now?" The latter question may seem more fanciful than the former, but it is the one which is operationally meaningful.

It is evident, however, that a second question can also be posed, the answer to which may differ from that to the question just suggested if tastes in fact change. That question is: "What income would have been required *yesterday* to make you just indifferent between facing yesterday's budget constraint and facing a budget constraint defined by today's prices and the income in question?" This is the same question as before from the vantage of yesterday's tastes rather than today's. It is equally meaningful, but, we shall argue below, not as interesting.[4]

If tastes do not change, then the answers to the two questions coincide. In this case also, it is obvious that the required income is precisely that income which would place the consumer today on the same indifference curve as he achieved yesterday. Thus, in the case of no taste change, the cost-of-living index implied by the answers to our questions is precisely that given by the erroneous application of the traditional theory. As indicated in the introduction, however, even in the case of no taste change the advantage of a rigorous formulation is more than aesthetic, since, by focusing attention on a choice between alternative constraints, such a formulation aids in the treatment of problems such as the incorporation of new goods or quality change into the cost-of-living index.

What about the case of taste change, however, in which we have asked two parallel but different questions which (in this case) have two different answers in general? It seems clear that when intertemporal problems are involved, the asymmetry of time makes the question asked assuming today's tastes more relevant than the equally meaningful question asked

---

4. As already observed, there is a further set of questions in which the tastes are neither those of today nor those of yesterday but are those of a wholly different third situation. For some purposes, these are quite interesting questions to ask, but we shall have nothing to say about them directly in this paper. When the indifference map used in the comparison is one not tied to the situations to be compared, then, of course, we are in the situation envisaged in existing theoretical treatments.

Taste and Quality Change

assuming yesterday's tastes.[5] That this is so may be seen from the following example.

Consider two alternative time paths of prices with the same initial values. In the first, path A, the cost-of-living index considered from the point of view of yesterday's tastes rises, while that considered from the point of view of current tastes stays constant or falls; in the second, path B, the reverse is true. It is clear that the consumer will be better off in every period under path A than under path B, or, equivalently, that in every period, the cost-of-living is higher on path B than on path A. Faced with a choice, rational policy should prefer path A to path B.[6] Indeed, every practical question which one wants the cost-of-living index to answer is answered with reference to current, not base-year tastes. Succinctly, if the prices of goods no longer desired rise and those of goods newly desired fall, a cost-of-living index should fall, not rise. The question of how a man with base-year tastes would view the matter is an operationally meaningful one; it is not a terribly relevant one, however, save insofar as it casts light on the cost of living viewed with current tastes.

This argument has an immediate corollary. The general practice in the construction of consumer price indices is to use Laspeyres indices with base-period quantity weights rather than Paasche indices with current weights. In the case of no taste change, a frequently encountered proposition is that a Laspeyres index overstates price rises and a Paasche index understates them, because of the inadequate treatment afforded substitution effects.[7] If tastes change, however, and if we agree that it is the

---

5. In the case of international or interregional comparisons, both questions have equal interest. The fact that the answers may be quite different is then an inevitable consequence of the fact that people differ. The answer to the question: "How much income would just make an American with income 100 willing to face British prices?" is not the same as that to the question: "How much income would make an Englishman indifferent between continuing to face British prices and facing American prices with an income of 100?" Both questions are equally interesting, but they are obviously different. There *is* generally no one answer to both questions and no point in attempting to construct a single index which answers both. One way of looking at the analysis of the next section is as a demonstration of the way in which the answers to the two questions are related if British and American tastes differ in the particular way parametrized in that section.

6. Note, however, that a policy choice made at the start of the process which did not foresee the taste changes would opt for path B. This is very similar to the myopia problem considered by Strotz 1955–1956.

7. In fact, this proposition is not true if price and income changes are large. This is because of yet another ambiguity in comparing today and yesterday that we have not discussed. The theory of the true cost-of-living index compares the expenditures required yesterday and today to reach a particular indifference curve on a stated indifference map. But *which* indifference curve is to be used? The natural choices are the indifference

current-taste cost-of-living in which we are interested, a Laspeyres index loses much of its meaning. That index is a relevant upper bound for a true cost-of-living index with base-year tastes; it need not be such a bound for a true cost-of-living index with current tastes. A Paasche index, on the other hand, retains its property of being a lower bound on the current-tastes index (but may lose it for the base-year-taste index). When tastes change, Laspeyres and Paasche indices cease to become approximations to the same thing and become approximations to different things. As we have just seen, it is the Paasche index which approximates the relevant magnitude; the Laspeyres index becomes less relevant.

Indeed, such relevance as is retained by a Laspeyres index occurs only if taste changes take place in such a way as to make a base-year-taste index differ from a current-taste index in some specific way. If one is willing to specify *how* tastes change and to parametrize that specification, one may obtain results on how a Laspeyres index should be adjusted. This is done for a specific class of cases in the next section. If one is not willing to make such a specification, but believes that important taste changes have taken place, one should put more reliance on a Paasche index and less on a Laspeyres than has traditionally been done.[8]

---

curve tangent to yesterday's budget constraint and that tangent to today's. If the indifference map is not homothetic, however, a true cost-of-living index based on the first of these curves (Index A) will not generally coincide with that based on the second (Index B). Yet a moment's consideration reveals that it is Index A which is bounded from above by a Laspeyres index and Index B which is bounded from below by a Paasche index. Unless either the indifference map is homothetic (or obeys other special conditions) or price and income changes are sufficiently small to make Indices A and B close together, there is no reason why the Laspeyres index must lie above Index B or the Paasche index below Index A. Further, both A and B are equally valid and interesting indices.

In this paper, we have, for convenience, concentrated on Index A, that corresponding to the indifference curve tangent to yesterday's budget constraint. Most of our results are equally applicable to Index B, that corresponding to the indifference curve tangent to today's budget constraint. When reading statements about the bounds set by Paasche and Laspeyres indices, however, the discussion of this footnote should be kept in mind. The text implicitly includes the assumption that Index A and Index B do in fact coincide, and we have proceeded on the assumption that in fact the index under discussion is known to be bounded by the Paasche and Laspeyres indices for the case of no taste change. Without that assumption, statements about such bounds apply as statements about the relationship of the bounding index (Laspeyres or Paasche) to the appropriate true cost-of-living index (A or B). We have tried not to overburden the exposition by being explicit about this save in this footnote.

For a discussion of these problems see Hofsten 1952, pp. 28–29, or Malmquist 1953, pp. 221–223.

8. Note that the implication is not that the true index lies closer to a Paasche index than to a Laspeyres. One does not know this. What one does know is that the Paasche

Taste and Quality Change

Before closing this section, it may be well to formalize the question which, we have argued, the true cost-of-living index is designed to answer. Given base-period prices of goods $\hat{p}_1, \hat{p}_2, \ldots, \hat{p}_n$, base-period income $\hat{y}$, current prices of goods $p_1, p_2, \ldots, p_n$, the problem is to find that income y such that the representative consumer is *currently* indifferent between facing current prices with income y and facing base-period prices with base-period income. The true cost-of-living index is then $(y/\hat{y})$.

Let $u(\cdot)$ be an ordinal utility function derived from the representative consumer's current preference map. The problem reduces to solving for the non-negative values $x_1, x_2, \ldots, x_n$, that minimize the expression

$$(2.1) \qquad y = p_1 x_1 + p_2 x_2 + \cdots + p_n x_n,$$

where x_i ($i = 1, 2, \ldots, n$) is the amount of the ith good that would be purchased at current prices and income y, subject to the requirement that

$$(2.2) \qquad u(x_1, x_2, \ldots, x_n) = u(\hat{x}_1, \hat{x}_2, \ldots, \hat{x}_n).$$

$\hat{x}_i$ ($i = 1, 2, \ldots, n$) is the amount of the ith good that currently would be purchased if the consumer faced base-period prices with base-period income. That is non-negative $\hat{x}_1, \hat{x}_2, \ldots, \hat{x}_n$ are chosen to maximize utility

$$(2.3) \qquad u(\hat{x}_1, \hat{x}_2, \ldots, \hat{x}_n)$$

subject to the budget constraint

$$(2.4) \qquad \hat{y} \geq \hat{p}_1 \hat{x}_1 + \hat{p}_2 \hat{x}_2 + \cdots + \hat{p}_n \hat{x}_n.$$

It may be noted that a more compact formulation can be given in terms of the indirect utility function (Houthakker 1951, 1952, pp. 157–163). Thus, let $\phi(p_1, p_2, \ldots, p_n, y)$ be the indirect utility function, so that $\phi(p_1, p_2, \ldots, p_n, y)$ is the maximal value of $u(x_1, x_2, \ldots, x_n)$ subject to $\sum_i^n p_i x_i = y$. The cost-of-living index is $(y/\hat{y})$, where y is the solution to $\phi(p_1, p_2, \ldots, p_n, y) = \phi(\hat{p}_1, \hat{p}_2, \ldots, \hat{p}_n, \hat{y})$. We have not used this formulation in what follows, since taste changes seem to be parametrizable more easily in terms of the direct than in terms of the indirect utility function and because we shall later work with more complicated constraints. However, the properties of the indirect utility function may be useful for future work in this area.

---

puts a lower bound on changes in the true index, while a Laspeyres fails to have a known relation to it. The asymmetry between Paasche and Laspeyres indices when tastes change is observed by Malmquist 1953, p. 211.

3. Taste Change

Consumers' tastes change for a variety of reasons, some of which are so mysterious to the ordinary economist that he is unlikely to offer much in the way of a systematic understanding. But certain instances of taste change possess a more systematic structure. For example, it may be known to be the case that a recently introduced electrical appliance, say, increases monotonically in desirability through time during the period in which consumers are learning about the usefulness of the appliance. In such a case, one unit of the appliance in a later year may afford the same service as more than one in an earlier year because of the increase in consumer information but with no physical change in the good itself.

Certain goods seem to suffer similar losses in desirability through time. Dairy products, for which publicity about their possible relationship to certain circulatory diseases has been increasing through time, might be considered to have suffered a systematic decline in desirability to consumers.

These examples raise the important question of just what we mean by a taste change as opposed to a quality change. To take a slightly different idealized case, suppose that consumers suddenly learn to use a certain fuel more efficiently, getting a certain number of BTU's out of a smaller quantity of fuel. If the relevant axis on the indifference map is the amount of fuel *purchased*, then there has been a taste change; if it is the number of BTU's gained from such fuel, there has not been a taste change but a quality change—a change in the opportunities available to consumers. The change can be consistently treated in either way, but the two treatments will differ. When the phenomenon is treated as a quality change, the true cost-of-living index will decline; when it is analyzed as a taste change, this will not be the case. The decision turns on whether the cost of living should be said to decrease just because consumers are better at consuming. If we are concerned with the delivery to the consumer of certain "basic satisfactions," a quality change is involved; this is an extension of the position taken in the construction of hedonic price indices. If, on the other hand, we are concerned with the valuation of opportunities *as available in the market*, then treatment of the change as being one of tastes is more appropriate. Both positions are tenable and both can lead to uncomfortable results if pushed to absurdity. (Suppose on the one hand that the new technique is discovered and popularized by fuel sellers. Suppose, on the other, that there is no change in the technology of fuel use but that people decide they now prefer a lower temperature in their houses.) The present section treats taste changes, the quality change case which is similarly parametrizable being treated in section 5.

Taste and Quality Change

In this section, the case in which taste change may be parametrized as solely good augmenting is treated in detail. A taste change is said to be good-augmenting if and only if the preference maps can be represented by a utility function whose ith argument is a function of the amount of purchases of the ith good and of the level of some taste change parameter.[9] Following the terminology employed in capital theory, we might call a taste change which is independent of any change in the qualities of the goods a disembodied taste change. In this section, the effect of such taste change upon the value of the true cost-of-living index is studied. We derive results in terms of the parameters of the demand functions which are, in principle, capable of being estimated from market data.

For convenience, assume that only one good, say the first, experiences an own-augmenting disembodied taste change. (Immediate generalization of the results to the case where more than one of the n goods experience own-augmenting disembodied taste changes is discussed at the end of this section.) Let the representative consumer's utility function be given by $u(bx_1, x_2, \ldots, x_n)$, where b is the parameter representing first-good-augmenting taste change and x_i ($i = 1, 2, \ldots, n$) is the amount of the ith good that is purchased.[10] Also assume that $u(\cdot)$ is an increasing, twice differentiable, strictly quasi-concave function which is defined over the non-negative orthant of an n-dimensional space.[11] For the purposes of this section we also assume that all relevant maxima and minima are given

---

9. We treat this case as being the simplest one to analyze. Further, the particular parametrization used not only appears in the theory of technological change but also reappears in the analysis of quality change given below as a result rather than an assumption. Of course, the present section is largely meant as an example of what can be done if an explicit model of taste change is adopted. The necessity for further work is obvious.

10. Such cases as these may be somewhat more general than the sort of learning effect example given above and continued below. Thus, suppose that the first and second commodities in some sense serve the same needs, so that the utility function can be written as $v(g(bx_1, x_2), x_3, \ldots, x_n)$. Then a change in b might be interpreted as a change in the relative efficiency of the first two commodities in serving those needs, as perceived by the consumer. (Of course, the special form of the utility function in this case has implications for the true cost-of-living index beyond those developed below for the more general case considered in the text.) $u(\cdot)$ serves as a utility function for current *and* base-period tastes. If taste change is solely first good augmenting then the units of b can always be chosen such that the first argument can be written as x_1 in the base period. (Also notice for this section $u(\cdot)$ is a function of n arguments. This notation is inconsistent with that of later sections but no confusion should follow.)

11. If ψ is a scalar-valued function of the vector w, then $\psi(\cdot)$ is said to be (strictly) quasi-concave if for each scalar ξ the set $\{w: \psi(w) \geqq \xi\}$ is (strictly) convex. See Arrow and Enthoven 1961.

by interior solutions to the first-order conditions. Corner solutions are treated in Section 4.

We now turn to the formal analysis of the problem. If with current tastes the representative consumer faces base-period income $\hat{y}$ and base-period prices $\hat{p}$ where $\hat{p}$ is an n-dimensional column vector defined by $\hat{p}' = (\hat{p}_1, \hat{p}_2, \ldots, \hat{p}_n)$, his purchases would have been given by the column vector $\hat{x}$ which is defined by $\hat{x}' = (\hat{x}_1, \hat{x}_2, \ldots, \hat{x}_n)$. $\hat{p}_i$ and $\hat{x}_i$ ($i = 1, 2, \ldots, n$) are respectively the base-period price of the ith good and the amount of the ith good that *would have been* purchased if he had faced the base-period constraints with current tastes. $\hat{x}$ is found by solving the system of first-order conditions:

$$(3.1) \quad \begin{matrix} \hat{p}'\hat{x} \\ b\hat{u}_1 \\ \hat{u}_2 \\ \vdots \\ \hat{u}_n \end{matrix} - \begin{pmatrix} \hat{y} \\ \hat{\lambda}\hat{p} \end{pmatrix} = 0,$$

where $\hat{u}_i$ ($i = 1, 2, \ldots, n$) denotes the derivative of $u(\cdot)$ with respect to its ith argument evaluated at the point $\hat{x}$. $\hat{\lambda}$ is a non-negative scalar Lagrange multiplier which has the (cardinal) interpretation of the current marginal utility of income when prices are evaluated at $\hat{p}$ and income is $\hat{y}$.

Next we solve for that income y that makes the individual currently indifferent between his current constraints and his base-period constraints. y is defined by

$$(3.2) \quad p'x - y = 0,$$

where p is the column vector of current prices, $p' = (p_1, p_2, \ldots, p_n)$, where p_i ($i = 1, 2, \ldots, n$) is the current price of the ith good. x is the column vector of purchases, $x' = (x_1, x_2, \ldots, x_n)$, that minimizes y subject to $u(bx_1, x_2, \ldots, x_n) = u(b\hat{x}_1, \hat{x}_2, \ldots, \hat{x}_n)$. Constrained minimization of y implies that

$$(3.3) \quad \begin{matrix} u \\ bu_1 \\ u_2 \\ \vdots \\ u_n \end{matrix} - \begin{pmatrix} \hat{u} \\ \lambda p \end{pmatrix} = 0,$$

where u_i ($i = 1, 2, \ldots, n$) denotes differentiation of $u(\cdot)$ with respect to its ith argument evaluated at x, $\hat{u}$ denotes $u(b\hat{x}_1, \hat{x}_2, \ldots, \hat{x}_n)$, and λ is a non-negative Lagrange multiplier.

Taste and Quality Change

We are interested in how the true cost-of-living index $(y/\hat{y})$ is affected by taste change. Thus, it is necessary to develop the total derivative of y with respect to b. Base-period income $\hat{y}$, base-period prices $\hat{p}$, and current prices p are the given data of the problem. We evaluate $(\partial y/\partial b)$ in steps.

Lemma 3.1. $\quad \left(\dfrac{\partial y}{\partial b}\right)_{u = \hat{u} \text{ const.}} = \dfrac{-p_1 x_1}{b}.$

Proof. Total differentiation of (3.3) with respect to b yields:

(3.4)
$$\begin{bmatrix} 0 & bu_1 & u_2 & \cdots & u_n \\ p_1 & b^2 u_{11} & bu_{12} & \cdots & bu_{1n} \\ p_2 & bu_{21} & u_{22} & \cdots & u_{2n} \\ \vdots & \vdots & \vdots & & \vdots \\ p_n & bu_{n1} & u_{n2} & \cdots & u_{nn} \end{bmatrix} \begin{bmatrix} -\dfrac{\partial \lambda}{\partial b} \\[4pt] \dfrac{\partial x}{\partial b} \end{bmatrix} + \begin{bmatrix} x_1 u_1 \\ u_1 + bx_1 u_{11} \\ x_1 u_{12} \\ \vdots \\ x_1 u_{1n} \end{bmatrix} = 0,$$

where u_{ij} ($i, j = 1, 2, \ldots, n$) denotes partial differentiation of u_i with respect to its jth argument and $(\partial x/\partial b)$ denotes the column vector $(\partial x_1/\partial b, \partial x_2/\partial b, \ldots, \partial x_n/\partial b)'$. Denote the nonsingular $(n + 1) \times (n + 1)$ matrix in (3.4) by H. Then:

(3.5)
$$\begin{bmatrix} -\dfrac{\partial \lambda}{\partial b} \\[4pt] \dfrac{\partial x}{\partial b} \end{bmatrix} = -H^{-1} \begin{bmatrix} x_1 u_1 \\ u_1 + bx_1 u_{11} \\ x_1 u_{12} \\ \vdots \\ x_1 u_{1n} \end{bmatrix}$$

But from (3.2) and (3.3)

(3.6)
$$\left(\frac{\partial y}{\partial b}\right)_{u=\hat{u} \text{ const.}} = p' \left(\frac{\partial x}{\partial b}\right) = (0 \mid p') \begin{bmatrix} -\dfrac{\partial \lambda}{\partial b} \\[4pt] \dfrac{\partial x}{\partial b} \end{bmatrix}$$

$$= -(0 \mid p') H^{-1} \begin{bmatrix} x_1 u_1 \\ u_1 + bx_1 u_{11} \\ x_1 u_{12} \\ \vdots \\ x_1 u_{1n} \end{bmatrix}$$

in view of (3.5). By (3.3), the first row in H is equal to λ times $(0 \mid p')$ so by the definition of the matrix inverse we have that

$$(3.7) \qquad \left(\frac{\partial y}{\partial b}\right)_{u=\hat{u} \text{ const.}} = \frac{-x_1 u_1}{\lambda} = \frac{-p_1 x_1}{b}$$

by (3.3), which proves the lemma.

Following the practice in capital theory, a fruitful way to understand Lemma 3.1 is to proceed by measuring the purchases of the various goods in (utility) efficiency units. Let x^*, the vector of purchases *measured in efficiency units*, be defined by

$$(3.8) \qquad x^{*\prime} = (x_1^*, x_2^*, \ldots, x_n^*) = (bx_1, x_2, \ldots, x_n).$$

Since the corresponding vector of *prices per efficiency unit* is $(p_1/b, p_2, \ldots, p_n)$, income y can be written as

$$(3.9) \qquad y = (p_1/b, p_2, \ldots, p_n) x^*.$$

Holding x^* fixed, differentiating (3.9) with respect to b yields

$$(3.10) \qquad \left(\frac{\partial y}{\partial b}\right)_{x^* \text{ const.}} = \frac{-p_1 x_1}{b} = \left(\frac{\partial y}{\partial b}\right)_{u=\hat{u} \text{ const.}}$$

by Lemma 3.1, if x^* and b are such that the system (3.3) is satisfied. Thus the effect on y along a constant utility surface of a first-order change in the taste parameter b is the same as the effect on y, holding the amount of purchases measured in efficiency units constant, of a first-order change in the taste parameter b.[12]

Now define $(\partial \hat{x}/\partial b)$ to be the column vector with ith entry $(\partial \hat{x}_i/\partial b)$ and let $(\partial \hat{u}/\partial \hat{x})$ be the column vector with ith entry $(\partial u/\partial x_i)$ evaluated at $\hat{x}$.

Lemma 3.2. $\left(\dfrac{\partial \hat{u}}{\partial \hat{x}}\right)' \left(\dfrac{\partial \hat{x}}{\partial b}\right) = 0.$

Proof. Totally differentiating (3.1) with respect to b yields

$$(3.11) \qquad \begin{pmatrix} 0 & \hat{p}_1 & \hat{p}_2 & \cdots & \hat{p}_n \\ \hat{p}_1 & b^2 \hat{u}_{11} & b\hat{u}_{12} & \cdots & b\hat{u}_{1n} \\ \hat{p}_2 & b\hat{u}_{21} & \hat{u}_{22} & \cdots & \hat{u}_{2n} \\ \vdots & \vdots & \vdots & & \vdots \\ \hat{p}_n & b\hat{u}_{n1} & \hat{u}_{n2} & \cdots & \hat{u}_{nn} \end{pmatrix} \begin{pmatrix} -\dfrac{\partial \hat{\lambda}}{\partial b} \\ \\ \dfrac{\partial \hat{x}}{\partial b} \end{pmatrix} + \begin{pmatrix} 0 \\ \hat{u}_1 + b\hat{x}_1 \hat{u}_{11} \\ \hat{x}_1 \hat{u}_{12} \\ \vdots \\ \hat{x}_1 \hat{u}_{1n} \end{pmatrix} = 0.$$

---

12. Equation (3.10) is an instance of the class of envelope theorems frequently encountered in the constrained minimization (and maximization) problems of economics. For a discussion of envelope theorems, see Samuelson 1947, pp. 34–35.

Taste and Quality Change

The $\hat{u}_{ij}$ ($i, j = 1, 2, \ldots, n$) are the cross partials defined previously but evaluated at $\hat{x}$. Let $\hat{J}$ denote the nonsingular matrix in (3.11). Then from (3.1) and (3.11)

$$(3.12) \quad \left(\frac{\partial \hat{u}}{\partial \hat{x}}\right)'\left(\frac{\partial \hat{x}}{\partial b}\right) = \hat{\lambda}(0 \mid \hat{p}') \begin{pmatrix} -\dfrac{\partial \hat{\lambda}}{\partial b} \\ -\dfrac{\partial \hat{x}}{\partial b} \end{pmatrix}$$

$$= -\hat{\lambda}(0 \mid \hat{p}')\hat{J}^{-1} \begin{pmatrix} 0 \\ \hat{u}_1 + b\hat{x}_1\hat{u}_{11} \\ \hat{x}_1\hat{u}_{12} \\ \vdots \\ \hat{x}_1\hat{u}_{1n} \end{pmatrix},$$

which equals zero because $(0 \mid \hat{p}')$ is the first row in $\hat{J}$. Lemma 3.2 is an "envelope theorem" where the change in $\hat{u}$ due to a first-order change in b (*ceteris paribus*) is exactly equal to the change in $\hat{u}$ due to first-order change in b when $\hat{x}$ is allowed to vary optimally (*mutatis mutandis*).

Lemma 3.3. $\left(\dfrac{\partial y}{\partial \hat{u}}\right) = \dfrac{1}{\lambda} > 0.$

Lemma 3.3 taken with Lemma 3.2 has the familiar interpretation that λ is the current marginal utility of income when prices are evaluated at p and income is y.

Proof. Total differentiation of (3.2) with respect to $\hat{u}$ yields

$$(3.13) \quad H \begin{pmatrix} -\dfrac{\partial \lambda}{\partial \hat{u}} \\ -\dfrac{\partial x}{\partial \hat{u}} \end{pmatrix} = \begin{pmatrix} 1 \\ 0 \\ \vdots \\ 0 \end{pmatrix},$$

where $(\partial x/\partial \hat{u})$ is an n-dimensional column vector with ith entry $(\partial x_i/\partial \hat{u})$. Differentiating (3.2) with respect to $\hat{u}$ and substituting from (3.13) yields

$$(3.14) \quad \frac{\partial y}{\partial \hat{u}} = p'\left(\frac{\partial x}{\partial \hat{u}}\right) = (0 \mid p')H^{-1}\begin{pmatrix} 1 \\ 0 \\ \vdots \\ 0 \end{pmatrix} = \frac{1}{\lambda},$$

because the first row in H is equal to $\lambda(0 \mid p')$.

From (3.1)–(3.3), total differentiation of y with respect to the parameter b gives

$$(3.15) \quad \frac{\partial y}{\partial b} = \left(\frac{\partial y}{\partial b}\right)_{u=\hat{u}\text{ const.}} + \left(\frac{\partial y}{\partial \hat{u}}\right)\left[\hat{x}_1\hat{u}_1 + \left(\frac{\partial \hat{u}}{\partial \hat{x}}\right)'\left(\frac{\partial \hat{x}}{\partial b}\right)\right].$$

Theorem 3.1. $\dfrac{\partial y}{\partial b} = \dfrac{p_1 x_1}{b}\left(\dfrac{\hat{x}_1 \hat{u}_1}{x_1 u_1} - 1\right).$

Proof. Substitute the results of Lemmas 3.1–3.3 into equation (3.15) and then simplify by using equations (3.1) and (3.3) to establish the theorem.

Substituting from (3.1) and (3.3), (3.15) can be rewritten as

$$(3.16) \quad \frac{\partial y}{\partial b} = \frac{\hat{x}_1 \hat{u}_1 - x_1 u_1}{\lambda}.$$

Notice that the numerator of the RHS of (3.16) is the *ceteris paribus* increase in current utility when facing base-period prices minus the *ceteris paribus* increase in current utility when facing current prices, due to a first-order increase in the value of b. By Lemma 3.2, we recognize the numerator of the RHS of (3.16) as the additional compensation in units of utility required to keep the consumer indifferent between base-period and current constraints when b changes. Since Lemma 3.3 allows λ the interpretation of the marginal utility of income, the full fraction on the RHS of (3.16) gives the same additional compensation in money units.[13]

Corollary 3.1. If $p = \hat{p}$, then $\left(\dfrac{\partial y}{\partial b}\right) = 0.$

Proof. The corollary is an immediate consequence of Theorem 3.1. The corollary is obvious from consideration of the definition of the true cost-of-living index. After all, if $p = \hat{p}$ then $y = \hat{y}$ for all values of b.

Since we know that $(\partial y/\partial b)$ is zero when current prices equal base-period prices, in order to study the effect of taste change on the true cost-of-living index it is natural to investigate the qualitative behavior of $(\partial y/\partial b)$ when prices are displaced from $\hat{p}$. In particular, we want to derive results concerning the sign of $(\partial y/\partial b)$ for values of p different from $\hat{p}$. To do this, it is convenient to define $z(p) = x_1 u_1$ and to study the effects of price changes upon $z(p)$.

---

13. Note that there are two effects. An increase in b makes it cheaper today to attain a given utility level, but it also raises the utility level which would have been achieved with yesterday's income and prices. If we were analyzing quality change rather than taste change, only the former effect would be present.

Taste and Quality Change

Lemma 3.4. $\dfrac{\partial u_1}{\partial p_1} = \dfrac{u_1}{\lambda}\dfrac{\partial \lambda}{\partial p_1} + \dfrac{u_1}{p_1}$, and

$$\dfrac{\partial u_1}{\partial p_i} = \dfrac{u_1}{\lambda}\dfrac{\partial \lambda}{\partial p_i} \text{ for } i = 2, \ldots, n.$$

Proof. From (3.3) we have that

$$\dfrac{\partial u_1}{\partial p_i} = \dfrac{1}{b}\dfrac{\partial(\lambda p_1)}{\partial p_i} \text{ for } i = 1, 2, \ldots, n.$$

The lemma follows immediately.

Lemma 3.5. $\dfrac{1}{\lambda}\left(\dfrac{\partial \lambda}{\partial p_i}\right) = -\left(\dfrac{\partial x_i}{\partial y}\right)_{p \text{ const.}}$, for $i = 1, 2, \ldots, n.$

Proof. Total differentiation of (3.3) with respect to p_i yields

(3.17) $\begin{pmatrix} -\dfrac{\partial \lambda}{\partial p_i} \\ \dfrac{\partial x}{\partial p_i} \end{pmatrix} = H^{-1} \begin{pmatrix} 0 \\ \vdots \\ 0 \\ \lambda \\ 0 \\ \vdots \\ 0 \end{pmatrix}$,

where $\left(\dfrac{\partial x}{\partial p_i}\right)$ is a column vector with ith entry $(\partial x_i/\partial p_i)$. The column vector on the RHS of (3.17) has λ for its $(i + 1)$st entry with all other entries zero. Therefore

(3.18) $\dfrac{1}{\lambda}\left(\dfrac{\partial \lambda}{\partial p_i}\right) = -(1 \ 0 \ \cdots \ 0)H^{-1}\begin{pmatrix} 0 \\ \vdots \\ 0 \\ 1 \\ 0 \\ \vdots \\ 0 \end{pmatrix}$,

where the unit in the column vector in (3.18) appears in the $(i + 1)$st entry. The LHS of (3.18) is thus shown to be equal to minus the element in the first row and $(i + 1)$st column of H^{-1} which in turn is equal to minus the element in the first row and $(i + 1)$st column of the matrix J^{-1} where J is defined by

$$J = \begin{pmatrix} 0 & p_1 & p_2 & \cdots & p_n \\ p_1 & b^2 u_{11} & b u_{12} & \cdots & b u_{1n} \\ p_2 & b u_{21} & u_{22} & \cdots & u_{2n} \\ \vdots & \vdots & \vdots & & \vdots \\ p_n & b u_{n1} & u_{n2} & \cdots & u_{nn} \end{pmatrix}.$$

This follows because only the first rows of H and J differ and they only differ by a scalar multiple. Consideration of the evaluation of inverses by the adjoint method shows that except for their first entries the first rows of H^{-1} and J^{-1} must be equal. Substituting J^{-1} for H^{-1} in (3.18) and transposing both sides yields

$$(3.19) \quad \frac{1}{\lambda}\left(\frac{\partial \lambda}{\partial p_i}\right) = -(0 \cdots 0 \ 1 \ 0 \cdots 0) J^{-1} \begin{pmatrix} 1 \\ 0 \\ \vdots \\ 0 \end{pmatrix}$$

because J^{-1} is a symmetric matrix.

If the first equation in the system (3.3) is replaced by equation (3.2) and the resulting system is totally differentiated with respect to y holding prices constant, then we have

$$(3.20) \quad J \begin{pmatrix} -\frac{\partial \lambda}{\partial y} \\ \hline \frac{\partial x}{\partial y} \end{pmatrix}_{p \text{ const.}} = \begin{pmatrix} 1 \\ 0 \\ \vdots \\ 0 \end{pmatrix},$$

where $(\partial x/\partial y)$ is a column vector with ith entry $(\partial x_i/\partial y)$. It follows immediately from (3.20) that

$$(3.21) \quad \left(\frac{\partial x_i}{\partial y}\right)_{p \text{ const.}} = (0 \cdots 0 \ 1 \ 0 \cdots 0) J^{-1} \begin{pmatrix} 1 \\ 0 \\ \vdots \\ 0 \end{pmatrix},$$

where the unit in the row vector on the RHS of (3.21) appears in the $(i + 1)$st entry. The lemma follows after combining (3.19) and (3.21).

Next define the elasticity of demand for the ith good with respect to the first price by

$$\eta_{i1} = \left(\frac{p_1}{x_i}\right)\left(\frac{\partial x_i}{\partial p_1}\right)_{y \text{ const.}}$$

for $i = 1, 2, \ldots, n$.

Taste and Quality Change

Lemma 3.6. If $z(p) = x_1 u_1$, then

$$\frac{\partial z}{\partial p_1} = \frac{x_1 u_1}{p_1} \{\eta_{11} + 1\} \quad \text{and}$$

$$\frac{\partial z}{\partial p_i} = \frac{x_i u_1}{p_1} \eta_{i1}, \quad i = 2, \ldots, n.$$

Proof. By Lemmas 3.4 and 3.5

$$\frac{\partial z}{\partial p_1} = u_1 \left[\left(\frac{\partial x_1}{\partial p_1}\right)_{u = \bar{u}\,\text{const.}} - x_1 \left(\frac{\partial x_1}{\partial y}\right)_{p\,\text{const.}} + \frac{x_1}{p_1} \right] \quad \text{and}$$

(3.22) $$\frac{\partial z}{\partial p_i} = u_1 \left[\left(\frac{\partial x_1}{\partial p_i}\right)_{u = \bar{u}\,\text{const.}} - x_1 \left(\frac{\partial x_i}{\partial y}\right)_{p\,\text{const.}} \right], \quad i = 2, \ldots, n.$$

Because substitution effects are symmetric, in (3.22), $(\partial x_1/\partial p_i)_{u=\bar{u}\,\text{const.}}$ can be replaced by $(\partial x_i/\partial p_1)_{u=\bar{u}\,\text{const.}}$. Application of Slutsky's theorem then yields

$$\frac{\partial z}{\partial p_1} = u_1 \left[\left(\frac{\partial x_1}{\partial p_1}\right)_{y\,\text{const.}} + \frac{x_1}{p_1} \right] \quad \text{and}$$

(3.23) $$\frac{\partial z}{\partial p_i} = u_1 \left(\frac{\partial x_i}{\partial p_1}\right)_{y\,\text{const.}}, \quad i = 2, \ldots, n.$$

Using the definition of the η_{i1} in (3.23) and rearranging completes the proof of the lemma.

We must now agree on some terminology. We shall call the demand for the first good *price elastic (price inelastic)* if $\eta_{11} < (>) -1$. Next, we shall call the ith good a *gross substitute (gross complement)* for the first good if $\eta_{i1} > (<) 0$ ($i = 2, \ldots, n$). Note that this relation is not symmetric; the ith good can be a gross substitute for the first good while the first good is a gross complement for the ith good. This, of course, is due to income effects. The symmetric substitution relationships defined by the substitution terms in the Slutsky equation we shall refer to as those of *net substitutes* or *net complements*.

Theorem 3.2. (A) Suppose $p_i = \hat{p}_i$ for $i = 2, \ldots, n$. If the demand for the first good is price elastic, then $(\partial y/\partial b)$ has the same sign as $(p_1 - \hat{p}_1)$. If that demand is price inelastic, then $(\partial y/\partial b)$ and $(p_1 - \hat{p}_1)$ have opposite signs. If $\eta_{11} = -1$, then $(\partial y/\partial b) = 0$.

(B) Suppose $p_i = \hat{p}_i$ for $i = 1, \ldots, n$ and $i \neq j \neq 1$. If the jth good is a gross complement for the first good, then $(\partial y/\partial b)$ has the same sign as $(p_j - \hat{p}_j)$. If the jth good is a gross substitute for the first good, then

$(\partial y/\partial b)$ and $(p_j - \hat{p}_j)$ have opposite signs. If $\eta_{j1} = 0$, then $(\partial y/\partial b) = 0$.

(C) If $p_i = k\hat{p}_i$, $i = 1, 2, \ldots, n$, where k is a positive constant, then $(\partial y/\partial b) = 0$.

Proof. (A) and (B) follow directly from Theorem 3.1, Corollary 3.1, and Lemma 3.6.

(C) Totally differentiating z with respect to k yields

$$(3.24) \qquad k\frac{\partial z}{\partial k} = u_1 x_1 + u_1 \sum_1^n p_i \left(\frac{\partial x_i}{\partial p_1}\right)_{y\text{ const.}}$$

by Lemma 3.6 since $k(\partial p_i/\partial k) = p_i$ by hypothesis. But from (3.2), $\sum_1^n p_i (\partial x_i/\partial p_1)_{y\text{ const.}} = -x_1$. Theorem 3.2 (C) follows from Theorem 3.1 and Corollary 3.1.

Notice that Theorem 3.2 (A) is a *global* result (i.e., it is a result that holds for all values of p_1) when the sign of $(\eta_{11} + 1)$ is independent of the value of p_1. Likewise, Theorem 3.2 (B) is a global result when the sign of η_{j1} is independent of the value of p_j. Theorem 3.2 (C) is an extension of Corollary 3.1. If current prices are all k times base-period prices then the income that makes the consumer currently indifferent between current constraints and base-period constraints is equal to k times base-period income regardless of the value of b.[14]

Theorem 3.2 has important practical implications and may be interpreted as follows. Suppose first that all prices except the jth are the same in the two periods ($1 \leq j \leq n$). If tastes did not change ($b = 1$), the only change in the cost-of-living index would be due to the change in the value of the jth price from $\hat{p}_j$ to p_j and would, of course, be in the same direction. Assuming b to be increasing through time, if $(\partial y/\partial b)$ has the same sign as $(p_j - \hat{p}_j)$, the effect of the taste change is to magnify the effect of the change in p_j. One can express this by saying that the jth good ought to receive increased weight in the index because of the taste change. Similarly, if $(\partial y/\partial b)$ and $(p_j - \hat{p}_j)$ have opposite signs, the effect of the taste change reduces the effect of the change in p_j and the jth good ought to

---

14. More complicated theorems can be derived from Theorem 3.1, Corollary 3.1, and Lemma 3.6 (or from Theorem 3.2 using the chain property of the true cost-of-living index). For example, we know that if demand for the first good is price elastic and its price has risen ($p_1 > \hat{p}_1$) and if we know that prices have risen for all goods that are gross complements for the first and have fallen for all goods that are gross substitutes for the first good, then we know that $(\partial y/\partial b) > 0$ (assuming, of course, that for the relevant values of prices, all goods other than the first remain either gross complements or gross substitutes for the first good. The assumption that the sign of $\eta_{j1}, j = 2, \ldots, n$, or of $(\eta_{11} + 1)$ does not change when prices change is implicit in much of the discussion that follows.)

Taste and Quality Change

receive a decreased weight. Since we can always analyze a change in more than one price (for our purposes) as a series of individual price changes (because of the definition of the true cost-of-living index), these conclusions are not restricted to cases in which only one price changes between the two periods considered. Thus, Theorem 3.2 suggests that in practice, when computing a cost-of-living index, the recently introduced good should receive more weight (less weight) if demand for it is price elastic (price inelastic) than it would in a price index that does not allow for taste change. Similarly the prices of the goods that are gross complements for the recently introduced good should receive more weight and gross substitutes less weight than they would be given in a traditional price index.

Under certain conditions, such as homotheticity of the utility function $u(\cdot)$, we know that the true cost-of-living index $(y/\hat{y})$ is such that

$$(3.25) \qquad \left(\frac{p'x}{\hat{p}'x}\right) \leq \left(\frac{y}{\hat{y}}\right) \leq \left(\frac{p'\hat{x}}{\hat{p}'\hat{x}}\right)$$

because the price indices on the left and the right do not account for substitution effects. The price index on the left of (3.25) is the (current weight) Paasche index. If tastes have not changed, the price index on the right is equal to the (base-period weight) Laspeyres index, since in that case the vector $\hat{x}$ is equal to the vector $\tilde{x}$, an n-dimensional column vector with ith entry $\tilde{x}_i$ denoting the quantity of the ith good actually purchased during the base period. Since the vector $\hat{x}$ is not observed while the vector $\tilde{x}$ is observed, it is of interest to know the relationship of the Laspeyres index $(p'\tilde{x}/\hat{p}'\tilde{x})$ to the unobserved index $(p'\hat{x}/\hat{p}'\hat{x})$. This is the purpose of the next theorem.

Theorem 3.3. (A) $\dfrac{\partial \hat{x}_1}{\partial b} = \dfrac{-\hat{x}_1}{b}(1 + \eta_{11})$

(B) $\dfrac{\partial \hat{x}_i}{\partial b} = \dfrac{-\hat{x}_i}{b}\eta_{i1}, \quad i = 2, \ldots, n.$

Proof. Theorem 3.3 can be easily proved by appropriate manipulation of equation (3.11). It is more interesting, however, to analyze the problem when purchases are measured in efficiency units. Let $\hat{x}_1^* = b\hat{x}_1$ be the amount of the first good purchased (measured in efficiency units) when prices are $\hat{p}$. $\hat{p}_1^* = (\hat{p}_1/b)$ is the price per efficiency unit of the first good. The equilibrium amounts of purchases measured in efficiency units depend only upon prices per efficiency unit and income $\hat{y}$. For $\hat{p}_1^*$ fixed, the amounts of equilibrium purchases are independent of the values of b and $\hat{p}_1$. Therefore we conclude that

$$(3.26) \quad \left(\frac{\partial \hat{x}_1^*}{\partial b}\right)\left(\frac{\partial b}{\partial \hat{p}_1^*}\right)_{\hat{p}_1 \text{ const.}} = \left(\frac{\partial \hat{x}_1^*}{\partial \hat{p}_1}\right)\left(\frac{\partial \hat{p}_1}{\partial \hat{p}_1^*}\right)_{b \text{ const.}} \quad \text{and}$$

$$(3.27) \quad \left(\frac{\partial \hat{x}_i}{\partial b}\right)\left(\frac{\partial b}{\partial \hat{p}_1^*}\right)_{\hat{p}_1 \text{ const.}} = \left(\frac{\partial \hat{x}_i}{\partial \hat{p}_1}\right)\left(\frac{\partial \hat{p}_1}{\partial \hat{p}_1^*}\right)_{b \text{ const.}}, \quad i = 2, \ldots, n.$$

Using the definitions of $\hat{x}_1^*$, $\hat{p}_1^*$, and η_{11} in (3.26) yields (A). Using the definitions of $\hat{p}_1^*$ and η_{i1} in (3.27) yields (B). The price elasticities of demand η_{i1}, $i = 1, 2, \ldots, n$, in (A) and (B) are evaluated at $\hat{p}$, $\hat{x}$, and $\hat{y}$.

Again consider the case in which the first good has been recently introduced and thus the value of b has been increasing through time. Theorem 3.3 tells us, e.g., that if the price of the recently introduced good has fallen ($\hat{p}_1 > \not{p}_1$) and the demand for the first good is price elastic while the prices of all goods that are gross complements (gross substitutes) for the first good are falling (rising), then $(\hat{p}'\tilde{x}/\hat{p}'\tilde{x}) > (\hat{p}'\hat{x}/\hat{p}'\hat{x})$. In this special case, therefore, the value of the true cost-of-living index lies between the values of the Paasche and Laspeyres price indices (subject, of course, to the qualifications discussed in footnote 7). This result can also be deduced from Theorem 3.2 because in this special case $(\partial y/\partial b) < 0$.

Theorem 3.3 reinforces Theorem 3.2. It tells us that had current tastes been in force during the base period, purchases of gross complements for the recently introduced good would have been greater and purchases of gross substitutes less than was actually the case. Similarly, the demand for the good itself would have been greater (less) if its demand is price elastic. It follows that in constructing a Laspeyres price index, the price of the recently introduced good should receive more weight (less weight) if demand for it is price elastic (price inelastic). Similarly the prices of goods that are gross complements (gross substitutes) for the recently introduced good should receive more weight (less weight). Theorem 3.2 assures us that similar weight changes should be made in a true cost-of-living index (a Paasche index, of course, needs no such corrections).[15]

We have stated Theorem 3.2 (and interpreted Theorem 3.3) in qualitative terms to give them some practical usefulness. In practice, one might

---

15. It may be thought that these results are obvious. It is natural to expect, for example, that in the situation being analyzed substitutes for the first good will decline in importance and complements will increase. While it is clear that one should indeed expect this as part of the intuitive meaning of "substitutes," however, it is not at all clear to us that one would automatically apply such intuition to *gross* substitutes rather than to *net* substitutes or to substitutes defined in yet some different way.

Taste and Quality Change

very well be willing to say that a taste change of the sort described (a change in b) has occurred, but it is unlikely that one would be willing to say by how much b has changed. Obviously, if such information were somehow available, our lemmas would yield precise quantitative results.

Theorems 3.1–3.3 can be extended to include cases where more than one good has experienced an own-augmenting taste change. For example, consider the case in which the first two goods have been recently introduced so that the preference maps can be represented by the utility function $u(b_1 x_1, b_2 x_2, x_3, \ldots, x_n)$ where b_1 and b_2 have been increasing through time. In constructing a cost-of-living index, prices of those goods that are gross complements (gross substitutes) for *both* of the recently introduced goods should receive more weight (less weight). If demand for the first good is elastic and demand for the second is inelastic, if the first and second goods are gross substitutes for each other, and if $(b_1/b_2) > 1$ in the current period while $(b_1/b_2) = 1$ during the base period, then the first good should receive more weight and the second good less weight.

Before closing this section, we may briefly ask a second-order question. Do the effects described in Theorem 3.2 get larger with larger price changes or do they decrease as price changes increase? This question is of some interest if attention is to be paid to such effects in practice. Since, as in Theorem 3.2, it suffices to look at one price change at a time, we may answer it by examining $(\partial^2 y / \partial b\, \partial p_j)(j = 1, \ldots, n)$.

Define the *net* price elasticity of demand η_{j1}^n by

(3.28) $$\eta_{j1}^n = \left(\frac{p_j}{x_1}\right)\left(\frac{\partial x_1}{\partial p_j}\right)_{u = \hat{u}\text{ const.}}, \quad j = 1, \ldots, n.$$

Lemma 3.7 $$\frac{\partial^2 y}{\partial b\, \partial p_1} = (1/p_1)(\partial y/\partial b)\{\eta_{11}^n + 1\} - \left(\frac{\hat{x}_1 \hat{u}_1}{b u_1}\right)(\eta_{11} + 1)$$

and $$\frac{\partial^2 y}{\partial b\, \partial p_j} = (1/p_j)(\partial y/\partial b)\eta_{j1}^n - \left(\frac{\hat{x}_1 \hat{u}_1 x_j}{b x_1 u_1}\right)\eta_{j1} \quad j = 2, \ldots, n.$$

Proof. This follows immediately from Theorem 3.1 and Lemma 3.6.

We may now state:

Theorem 3.4 (A) Suppose that $p_i = \hat{p}_i$, $i = 2, \ldots, n$. For p_1 sufficiently close to $\hat{p}_1 (\partial^2 y/\partial b \partial p_1)$ is positive if the demand for the first good is elastic and negative if it is inelastic. Further, if $\eta_{11}^n \geqq -1$, the same statement holds for all $p_1 > \hat{p}_1$; if $\eta_{11}^n \leqq -1$, it holds for all $p_1 < \hat{p}_1$.[16]

---

16. As before, it is implicitly assumed that we remain in ranges of prices in which the elasticity stays on the same side of minus unity and substitute-complement relationships are not reversed.

(B) Suppose that $p_i = \hat{p}_i$ for $i = 1, \ldots, n$ and $i \neq j \neq 1$. For p_j sufficiently close to $\hat{p}_j$, $(\partial^2 y/\partial b \partial p_j)$ is positive if the jth good is a gross complement for the first good and negative if the jth good is a gross substitute for the first good. Further, if the two goods are *net* substitutes (or if $\eta_{j1}^n = 0$), the same statement holds for all $p_j > \hat{p}_j$; if they are *net* complements (or if $\eta_{j1}^n = 0$), it holds for all $p_j < \hat{p}_j$.

Proof. The statements about sufficiently small price changes follow from Lemma 3.7 and Corollary 3.1. The remaining statements follow from Lemma 3.7 and Theorem 3.2.

Thus, for all cases which can be definitely determined, the second-order effects being examined reinforce the first-order ones already treated. The effects of taste change on proper weights in the cost-of-living index are bigger for bigger price changes. For example, we have already seen in Theorem 3.2 that the weight given a gross complement for the first good should be increased on account of the taste change. We now see that for small changes in the price of that complement this effect gets bigger the bigger the price change, and that this remains true globally if the goods are also net complements and the price of the good in question has fallen. Similarly, if the jth good is a gross substitute for the first good, the weight given the jth good should be decreased as a result of the taste change. The amount of decrease should be greater, the higher is p_j above $\hat{p}_j$, provided that the two goods are net substitutes as well.[17]

4. New Goods and Other Corner Solutions

In the previous section, we restricted our analysis of taste change to cases where the relevant maxima and minima are given by interior solutions to the first-order conditions. This section is devoted to a general analysis of the treatment of corner solutions in the cost-of-living index. The problem of this type that is most frequently encountered in practice is the problem of "new goods." For our purposes, a new good is one that is purchased in positive amount during the current period but for which base-period purchases were zero. The opposite case of "disappearing goods," where purchases of the disappearing goods were positive in the base period but are zero in the current period, is also of practical interest.

---

17. If the first good is not inferior, certain cases are ruled out. Thus, in this case, the jth good must be a net substitute for the first good if it is also a gross substitute. Similarly, if the demand for the first good is inelastic, η_{11}^n must be greater than -1.

Taste and Quality Change

Using the vector form of the notation developed in (2.1)–(2.4), the problem is to find that income y that makes the representative consumer currently indifferent between facing current prices p with income y and facing base-period prices $\hat{p}$ and base-period income $\hat{y}$. Formally the problem is to solve for a non-negative vector of purchases x such that:

(4.1) $$\left(\frac{\partial u}{\partial x}\right) - \lambda p \leq 0,$$

where $(\partial u/\partial x)$ is a column vector with ith entry $(\partial u/\partial x_i)$, $i = 1, 2, \ldots, n$,

(4.2) $$x'\left[\left(\frac{\partial u}{\partial x}\right) - \lambda p\right] = 0,$$

(4.3) $$x \geq 0 \quad \text{and} \quad \lambda \geq 0.$$

x is constrained by $u(x) = u(\hat{x})$ or simply

(4.4) $$u - \hat{u} = 0,$$

where $\hat{x}$ solves the system:

(4.5) $$\left(\frac{\partial \hat{u}}{\partial \hat{x}}\right) - \hat{\lambda}\hat{p} \leq 0,$$

where $(\partial \hat{u}/\partial \hat{x})$ denotes the vector $(\partial u/\partial x)$ evaluated at $\hat{x}$,

(4.6) $$\hat{x}'\left[\left(\frac{\partial \hat{u}}{\partial \hat{x}}\right) - \hat{\lambda}\hat{p}\right] = 0,$$

(4.7) $$\hat{\lambda}(\hat{y} - \hat{p}'\hat{x}) = 0,$$

(4.8) $$\hat{x} \geq 0 \quad \text{and} \quad \hat{\lambda} \geq 0.$$

Income y is defined by

(4.9) $$y - p'x = 0,$$

and $(y/\hat{y})$ is the true cost-of-living index.[18]

---

18. The systems (4.1)–(4.4), (4.9), and (4.5)–(4.8) are the well-known conditions of Kuhn-Tucker-Lagrange (KTL). The assumption of nonsatiation of consumption guarantees that if (4.1)–(4.9) are solved for y then $(y/\hat{y})$ is the true cost-of-living index. The proof of the optimality of KTL for quasi-concave programming problems with nonsatiation is given in Arrow and Enthoven 1961, pp. 783–788. Nonsatiation also implies that the equilibrium values of λ and $\hat{\lambda}$ are positive.

Inequation (4.1) and equation (4.2) imply that if for any $k = 1, 2, \ldots, n$, $(\partial u/\partial x_k) < \lambda p_k$, then $x_k = 0$. A similar implication is drawn from (4.5) and (4.6). λ and $\hat{\lambda}$ are scalar Lagrange multipliers. In (4.7), if we assume nonsatiation in consumption then the budget constraint holds with equality.

Now assume that the kth good is a new good; that is, $x_k > 0$ with $(\partial u/\partial x_k) = \lambda p_k$ and $\tilde{x}_k = 0$, where $\tilde{x}_k$ is the *actual* amount of the kth good that was purchased during the base period. If tastes have not changed, then $\hat{x}_k = \tilde{x}_k = 0$. The difficulty in this case is that there is no recorded base-period market price for the kth good. In the case of no taste change, the computation of the true cost-of-living index which allows for corner solutions is straightforward. If, for example, the kth good is a new good, the restriction $\hat{x}_k = 0$ is added to the system (4.1)–(4.9) leaving the value of $\hat{p}_k$ as an unknown to be determined in solving the new system. Or equivalently, the system (4.1)–(4.9) is solved for y after assigning to $\hat{p}_k$ any value greater than or equal to the demand reservation price (the lowest price at which demand for the kth good is zero) including the supply reservation price (the highest price at which supply of the kth good is zero) which in some sense is the price that consumers actually faced during the base period.

Note, however, that in the base-period constrained utility maximization problem, the demand reservation price itself is the maximizing value of the shadow multiplier associated with the constraint $\hat{x}_k = 0$, since by definition the demand reservation price is what the representative consumer is willing to pay per unit (locally) for a relaxation of the constraint $\hat{x}_k = 0$.[19]

As stated in Section 2, it is a well-known proposition in the traditional theory of index numbers (Hofsten 1952, pp. 28–29) (where it is assumed that tastes and qualities are unchanging and that all goods are purchased in positive amounts) that under certain conditions the Laspeyres (base-period weighted) price index $(p'\hat{x}/\hat{p}'\hat{x})$ bounds the true cost-of-living index from above, while the Paasche (current-period weighted) price index $(p'x/\hat{p}'x)$ bounds the true cost-of-living index from below. In the case with new goods, it is obvious that the Laspeyres index bounds the true index from above and is independent of the assignment of base-period price weights to the new goods. If we allow for the complication of new goods, however, the Paasche price index is a lower bound upon the true cost-of-living index only if we assign to the new goods base-period prices

---

19. Arrow 1958, p. 85 discusses the use of demand reservation prices in the construction of a cost-of-living index.

Taste and Quality Change

greater than or equal to the demand reservation prices. Note, however, that of all such Paasche indices, the largest (and therefore in a sense the greatest lower bound on the true cost-of-living index) is the index in which new goods purchases are weighted by their demand reservation prices. (The analysis for disappearing goods is similar and is left to the reader.)

Thus, if they are known, it is the demand reservation prices themselves which should be used to weight new-goods purchases in the construction of a Paasche index and not simply some arbitrary prices equal to or greater than the demand reservation prices. In particular, *supply* reservation prices are not relevant if the demand reservation prices are known.

This is a natural result if we recall that the demand reservation price measures (locally) the value to the base-period consumer of the relaxation of the constraint stating that the good in question is unavailable. It is the shadow price of that constraint. It is thus the demand reservation price which affects how much income the consumer would be willing to give up to relax that constraint. How much income he would in fact be technologically required to give up to accomplish such relaxation (the supply reservation price) is not directly germane to a theory which runs in terms of indifferent positions. If the demand reservation price is known, the supply reservation price is not relevant.

There remains the difficult practical question as to how one knows the values of demand reservation prices. To ascertain them in general might require a rather detailed demand analysis which might not be available. There are some special circumstances, however, in which demand reservation prices may be less difficult to determine. Suppose that it was known that during a period for which closely spaced, time-series data are available the supply reservation price of a certain good is falling. With constant tastes and qualities and all other prices constant, the price at which the good was first marketed would then be the demand reservation price. Also, since the supply reservation price is never less than the demand reservation price, supply reservation prices can be used for new goods in the Paasche index and the latter will retain its property as lower bound on the true index (but see footnote 7).

In order to study the effects of new goods on the true cost-of-living index when tastes are changing, the previous analysis can be combined with the analysis of Section 3. If, for example, the first good is a new good that has experienced a positive own-augmenting taste change, if the price of the first good has fallen while all other prices have remained constant, and if demand for the first good is elastic, then by Theorems 3.2 and 3.3 the value of the true cost-of-living index is below the value of the Laspeyres index for whatever base-period prices are assigned to the new good. The

Paasche index is known to be a lower bound for the true cost-of-living index if and only if the new good is assigned a base-period price greater than or equal to its demand reservation price (subject to the qualification discussed in footnote 7).

5. Quality Change

In this section, we take up the problem of quality change.[20] In practice, quality change is handled in the consumer price index (when it is handled at all) by assuming that an improvement in quality in a given good is equivalent to a price reduction in that good. For some cases of quality change, this is obviously the appropriate general treatment. If widgets are sold by the box and twenty widgets now are packed into the same size box as previously held ten, it is clear that this is equivalent to a halving of the price of widgets. Somewhat more generally, if one new widget delivers the same services as two old ones, this may also be considered to be simply a repackaging of widgets and thus equivalent to a price reduction.

Quality change may take other forms than that of simply augmenting the services of just that good whose quality has changed, however, and a simple adjustment of the price of that good may not suffice to account for that quality change in a cost-of-living index. Indeed, we show that such a price adjustment made independently of the amount of all goods purchased is an appropriate one if *and only if* the only effect of quality change is of the good-augmenting type just considered. Then and only then can quality change be considered a simple repackaging of the good in question.

Furthermore, while an adjustment in the price of the quality-changing good can always be made to suffice *locally* (that is, for given purchases of all goods), in general, the price adjustment which must be made will depend on all prices and purchases of all commodities and not simply on the physical characteristics of the quality change. If the new and the old qualities of the good sell in positive amount on the same (perfect) market,

---

20. We have already discussed the problem of deciding whether to treat a given change as one in quality or one in tastes. There is a less basic decision as to whether a change in quality should be treated as such or as the appearance of a new good and the disappearance of an old one. This decision (unlike the former one) is largely a matter of convenience. In this section, we assume that it has been made in favor of retaining the same name (or subscript) for a good before and after the change, i.e., in favor of treating the change as one in the quality of a given good.

Taste and Quality Change

then all the information needed to make the appropriate *local* price adjustment for the quality change is of course coded in the difference in the prices of the two varieties. The extension of the same price adjustment to other (perhaps later) situations, however, when other prices change or other related qualities are introduced is appropriate, as stated, only in the pure repackaging case. If the two varieties do not coexist in the same (perfect) market, then even such a local price adjustment must be made to depend explicitly on the quantities of all goods purchased and not simply on physical characteristics, save in the pure repackaging case.[21]

In circumstances other than the simple repackaging case, then, we show that the simplest adjustment of the cost-of-living index may be an adjustment in the price of one or more goods *other than the one whose quality has changed*. While part of the effects of any quality change may well be to augment the services of the quality-changing good, there are likely to be other effects as well and here more than one price change is required.

Thus, for example, suppose that there is a quality change in refrigerators. If this change simply makes one new refrigerator deliver the services of some larger number of old ones, then the simplest price adjustment in the cost-of-living index is indeed an adjustment in the price of refrigerators. On the other hand, if that quality change also increases the enjoyment obtained from a quart of ice cream, then an adjustment in refrigerator price will not suffice; an adjustment in the price of ice cream is also called for. Indeed, if the *only* effect of a refrigerator quality change is to augment the enjoyment obtained from ice cream, then the simplest adjustment is one made *only* in the price of ice cream, even though the quality change takes place in refrigerators. In this case, an adjustment in the price of refrigerators can be made to suffice; the magnitude of that adjustment, however, will depend on the quantities demanded of all goods. An adjustment in the price of ice cream will also suffice; the magnitude of that adjustment, however, will only depend on the quantity of ice cream and the quantity of refrigerators.

---

21. The use of hedonic price indices (see the references in footnote 1) is the most sophisticated way now known of using such market information to obtain price adjustments for quality change. It should come as no surprise that the extension of the results of hedonic price index investigations outside the sample period in which the market observations are made is strictly appropriate only in the repackaging case. The theory of hedonic price indices treats a new quality of a given good as a repackaging of a bundle of underlying attributes. Only if the attributes enter the utility function through the "package," rather than directly, will hedonic price index adjustments be more than locally appropriate. Obviously, to say this is not to disparage the usefulness of hedonic price indices in practice.

Now, of course, this is fairly easy to see in the case of this example. Refrigerators are not directly consumed, rather, they are used as an intermediate good in the production of certain consumption goods, including cold ice cream. Thus, one can argue, since refrigerator services do not enter the utility function directly, the cost of using refrigerator services is but part of the price of the foodstuffs concerned, and an improvement in refrigerator quality ought clearly to be accounted for in the prices of just those particular foodstuffs affected. If that quality improvement only changes ice cream enjoyment, then the true quality improvement is in refrigerated ice cream. An adjustment in the price of refrigerated ice cream, however, is most easily done by adjusting the price of ice cream (assuming all ice cream to be refrigerated); an adjustment in the price of refrigerators, on the other hand, affects the cost of consuming other refrigerated foodstuffs as well. Thus, in this simple example, adjustment of the price of ice cream can be made much more simply than adjustment of the price of refrigerators to achieve the same result in the cost-of-living index.

In fact, this is quite a good way to look at the matter and at our results, even if refrigerator services do appear in the utility function directly, as is the case in some treatments[22] and as would certainly be the analogous case in treatments of other examples. In this case, refrigerators should *still* be looked on as an intermediate good, affecting the enjoyment of foodstuffs and also the enjoyment of its own services. As before, it is those "final" goods whose enjoyment is affected by the quality change whose prices should be adjusted to obtain the simplest equivalent change in the cost-of-living index. The fact that one of those "final" goods happens to have the same name and to be consumed in fixed proportions with the intermediate good does not change this statement. If this is borne in mind throughout, the interpretation of our results will be relatively straightforward.

We now turn to the formal analysis of the problem. The current (twice differentiable) utility function is given by:

$$(5.1) \qquad u = u(x_1, \ldots, x_n, b) \equiv u(x, b),$$

where b is a parameter measuring quality change in the first good, with

---

22. For many purposes it is simpler to regard refrigerator services as entering the utility function directly than it is to leave them out. Consumer theory deals with goods traded in the market place, not with later composites of them made up by consumers (such as home-refrigerated ice cream). In any case, to say that refrigerators enter directly rather than through other goods is a matter of notation at the level of abstraction of most treatments of consumer theory.

Taste and Quality Change

$b = 1$ being the case of no quality change.²³ As quality change is to take place in the first good, it is natural to assume:

(5.2) $$u_b(0, x_2, \ldots, x_n, b) \equiv 0,$$

where the subscript denotes differentiation with respect to b. However, we shall not make direct use of this property.²⁴

As before, in the base period, the consumer has income $\hat{y}$ and faces prices $\hat{p}$. He is also constrained in that period by only being able to purchase a quality of the first commodity for which $b = 1$. The purchases which are made under these conditions are $\hat{x}$, and the corresponding utility level is:

(5.3) $$\hat{u} = u(\hat{x}, 1).$$

The constraints of the present period are defined by some $b \neq 1$ and prices p. The income at which the consumer would be just indifferent between the two sets of constraints is y, and the true cost-of-living index is $y/\hat{y}$. y is thus defined as:

(5.4) $$y = p'x,$$

where x is given as the solution to the problem:

(5.5) Minimize y subject to $u(x, b) = \hat{u}$.

x thus satisfies:

(5.6) $$u(x, b) - \hat{u} = 0$$
$$u_i - \lambda p_i = 0 \quad (i = 1, \ldots, n),$$

where λ is a Lagrange multiplier and is the marginal utility of income.²⁵

---

23. There is no reason other than one of convenience why b has to be a scalar. Quality change may take place in more than one attribute of the first good, in which case b would be replaced by $(b_1, \ldots, b_k)$ and the analysis would be essentially unchanged.

24. It may be noted that the present problem differs from that of taste changes discussed in section 3 above in that the change in the utility function is "embodied" in the first good rather than being "disembodied." The parallel to models of embodied and disembodied technical change in production functions is obvious, extending the well-known parallel between the theory of the utility-maximizing consumer and the theory of the cost-minimizing firm. Indeed, some of the results of this section also parallel some of the results in the analysis of such models. We shall return to this in a later footnote.

25. We assume that $u(\cdot)$ is a strictly quasi-concave function of its first n (non-negative) arguments and restrict our attention to interior minima.

Given $\hat{p}$ and $\hat{y}$, therefore, y is a function of p and b, and we may write:

(5.7) $$y = y(p, b).$$

Suppose now that we wish to take account of the quality change by a suitable change in the price of the first good. We thus seek a p_1^*, such that:

(5.8) $$y(p_1^*, p_2, \ldots, p_n, 1) = y(p_1, \ldots, p_n, b).$$

For $b = 1, p_1^* = p_1$. As b changes from unity, p_1^* will change. Differentiating (5.8) totally with respect to b and rearranging, we have:

(5.9) $$\frac{\partial p_1^*}{\partial b} = \frac{\partial y/\partial b}{\partial y/\partial p_1^*}.$$

We must therefore investigate $\partial y/\partial b$ and $\partial y/\partial p_1^*$.

Lemma 5.1. $\partial y/\partial b = -u_b/\lambda$.

Proof. Differentiate (5.6) totally with respect to b, obtaining

(5.10) $$\begin{bmatrix} 0 & u_1 & \cdots & u_n \\ p_1 & u_{11} & \cdots & u_{1n} \\ \vdots & \vdots & & \vdots \\ p_n & u_{n1} & \cdots & u_{nn} \end{bmatrix} \begin{bmatrix} -\partial \lambda/\partial b \\ \overline{\partial x/\partial b} \end{bmatrix} = - \begin{bmatrix} u_b \\ u_{1b} \\ \vdots \\ u_{nb} \end{bmatrix},$$

where $\partial x/\partial b$ is an n-component vector whose ith element is $\partial x_i/\partial b$.

Denote the first matrix on the left by D. Then

(5.11) $$\begin{bmatrix} -\partial \lambda/\partial b \\ \overline{\partial x/\partial b} \end{bmatrix} = -D^{-1} \begin{bmatrix} u_b \\ u_{1b} \\ \vdots \\ u_{nb} \end{bmatrix}.$$

Now,

(5.12) $$\begin{aligned} \partial y/\partial b = p'(\partial x/\partial b) &= (0 \mid p') \begin{pmatrix} -\partial \lambda/\partial b \\ \overline{\partial x/\partial b} \end{pmatrix} \\ &= \frac{1}{\lambda}(0, u_1, \ldots, u_n) \begin{pmatrix} -\partial \lambda/\partial b \\ \overline{\partial x/\partial b} \end{pmatrix} \end{aligned}$$

in view of (5.6).

However, $(0, u_1, \ldots, u_n)$ is the first row of D and the lemma now follows immediately from (5.11) and (5.12).[26]

---

26. Note that the result is just that which would be obtained ignoring the effects of b on x. Thus a small unit increase in b raises u by u_b which allows a decrease in expenditure by u_b/λ, since $1/\lambda$ is the marginal cost of a unit of utility. As in the analogous case in section 3 (and as in the lemma which follows), this is an envelope theorem.

Taste and Quality Change

Lemma 5.2. $\partial y/\partial p_1 = x_1$.

Proof. Differentiate (5.6) totally with respect to p_1, obtaining:

(5.13) $$\begin{pmatrix} -\partial \lambda/\partial p_1 \\ \overline{\partial x/\partial p_1} \end{pmatrix} = D^{-1} \begin{matrix} 0 \\ \lambda \\ 0 \\ \vdots \\ 0 \end{matrix},$$

where $\partial x/\partial p_1$ is the n-component vector whose ith element is $\partial x_i/\partial p_1$.

(5.14) $\partial y/\partial p_1 = x_1 + p'(\partial x/\partial p_1) = x_1 + \dfrac{1}{\lambda}(0, u_1, \ldots, u_n)\begin{pmatrix} -\partial \lambda/\partial b \\ \overline{\partial x/\partial b} \end{pmatrix}.$

The lemma now follows as before, since, $(0, u_1, \ldots, u_n)$ is the first row of D.

Thus, $\partial y/\partial p_1 = x_1$. Similarly, if we substitute p_1^* for p_1 and write x_1^* for the corresponding amount of the first commodity purchased, $\partial y/\partial p_1^* = x_1^*$. It is thus clear that as long as $x_1^* \neq 0$, p_1^* is a uniquely defined function of b (given the other elements of p). Since, at $b = 1$, $p_1^* = p_1$ no matter what the values of the other elements of p and the elements of x are, p_1^* will be independent of any subset of those elements if and only if $\partial p_1^*/\partial b$ is so independent. We therefore concentrate on the latter quantity. To avoid a burdensome notation, we always take that derivative at $b = 1$; only notational changes would be required to perform the analysis at an arbitrary b.

Combining Lemmas 5.1 and 5.2 with (5.9) and evaluating at $b = 1$, we have:

Lemma 5.3. $\dfrac{\partial p_1^*}{\partial b} = \dfrac{-p_1 u_b}{x_1 u_1}.$

Proof. This follows immediately from the two preceding lemmas and (5.6).

Thus we have evaluated the adjustment which must be made in p_1 to give a result equivalent to the quality change involved in a change in b. Clearly, such an adjustment can be made (as long as $x_1 \neq 0$). That adjustment depends in general, however, on all the elements of x. Thus, in the general case, the adjustment cannot be made independent of knowledge of all purchases and the way they affect (u_b/u_1).[27] It is natural to ask

---

27. If the new and old varieties of the first good coexist on the same (perfect) market, however, their relative prices will code all the information needed for local adjustment. See the discussion above.

under what circumstances the adjustment can be made without such knowledge or, equivalently, under what circumstances an adjustment made from market data in a given situation will retain validity when that situation changes.

Theorem 5.1. (A) A necessary and sufficient condition for $\partial p_1^*/\partial b$ to be independent of $x_2, \ldots, x_n$ is that it be possible to write the utility function in the form:

(5.15) $\quad u(x, b) = F(g(x_1, b), x_2, \ldots, x_n) \equiv F(g^*(x_1, b)x_1, x_2, \ldots, x_n)$

for some choice of continuously differentiable functions F and g.[28] We write $g(x_1, b) \equiv g^*(x_1, b)x_1$ for ease of interpretation.

(B) A necessary and sufficient condition for $\partial p_1^*/\partial b$ to be independent of *all* the elements of x (including x_1) is that (5.15) hold with g in the form:

(5.16) $\qquad g(x_1, b) = x_1 h(b) \quad$ or $\quad g^*(x_1, b) = h(b)$

for some choice of the function h. (This is the pure repackaging case.)

Proof. (A) By Lemma 5.3, a necessary and sufficient condition for $\partial p_1^*/\partial b$ to be independent of $x_2, \ldots, x_n$, is that u_b/u_1 be so independent. This is equivalent to (5.15) by a well-known theorem of Leontief (1947a, p. 364; 1947b).

(B) In view of Lemma 5.3 and (A), a necessary and sufficient condition for $\partial p_1^*/\partial b$ to be independent of all the elements of x is that (5.15) hold and that, in addition, $u_b/x_1 u_1$ be independent of x_1. This means that it is necessary and sufficient that there exist a function $\phi(b)$ such that:

(5.17) $$\frac{g_b}{g_1} = \frac{u_b}{u_1} = -x_1 \phi(b).$$

Now consider a curve in the $x_1 - b$ plane along which g is constant—an indifference curve of g. This is defined by:

(5.18) $$g(x_1, b) = \bar{g}.$$

Differentiating (5.18) totally with respect to b and rearranging:

(5.19) $$dx_1/db = -\frac{g_b}{g_1} = x_1 \phi(b)$$

along that curve. Thus:

(5.20) $$d \log x_1 = \phi(b) db.$$

---

28. It is natural to take $g(x_1, 1) = x_1$, i.e. $g^*(x_1, 1) = 1$, but this is not required for our results.

Taste and Quality Change

Integrating:

(5.21) $$\log x_1 = \log \mu(b) + \log c,$$

where $\mu(b)$ is an integral of $\phi(b)$, and c is an arbitrary constant. In other words:

(5.22) $$\frac{x_1}{\mu(b)} = c$$

is the equation of the indifference curve defined in (5.18).

Now, we can clearly replace g in (5.15) by any monotonic transformation of it, adjusting the result by redefining F. Thus we can choose the scale on which g is measured and can do so in such a way as to make $\bar{g} = c$ without changing anything else. If we do this, however, the theorem follows immediately from (5.18) and (5.22), with $h(b) = 1/\mu(b)$.

Some remarks on the theorem are now in order.

First, as observed, part (B) of the theorem is the repackaging case. In this case, it might appear more natural to have b appearing in place of $h(b)$. $h(b)$ appears because the scaling of b is arbitrary. There is no reason not to measure quality change in this case in units of h rather than in units of b, in which case the more natural-appearing result is obtained.

Second, part (B) shows that the repackaging case is the *only* case in which the quality change is equivalent to a *simple* adjustment in the price of the first commodity. Any other case requires knowledge of the elements of x. Another way of putting this is to say that in any other case the adjustment in p_1 will be different at different points in the commodity space.

Third, part (A) shows that, even if we are willing to let the adjustment in p_1 depend on the quantity of the first good purchased, the class of quality changes in the first good which can be so handled is not really much widened. The only generalization is, in effect, to move to a sort of variable repackaging in which the amount of repackaging is allowed to depend on x_1. As soon as a quality change in the first commodity enters in a more general way—for example, by affecting other commodities—an equivalent adjustment in p_1 depends on other elements of x.[29]

---

29. The situation is very similar to that in models of embodied technical change in which a capital aggregate is to be formed or the effect of technical change removed by the use of a quality-corrected capital index, that is, by adjusting the prices of capital goods of different vintages. Under constant returns, technical change must be capital augmenting, analogous to part (B) of the theorem. Under a generalized form of constant returns in which the production functions are homogeneous of degree one in labor and some function of capital, technical change must be capital-altering, a kind of change analogous to the variable repackaging of part (A) of the theorem. See Fisher 1965.

Finally, if the conditions of part (A) hold, the dependence of the adjustment on the level of p_1 is of a very simple kind, given x_1. The *percentage* adjustment in p_1 which must be made is dependent only on x_1 in this case, since, given x_1, p_1 enters only multiplicatively in $\partial p_1^*/\partial b$. A similar remark applies to all later results in this section.

Theorem 5.1 can be generalized to give the conditions under which quality change is equivalent to an adjustment in p_1 which depends only on selected elements of x. Thus:

Theorem 5.2. (A) For any $m = 1, \ldots, n-1$, a necessary and sufficient condition for $\partial p_1^*/\partial b$ to be independent of $x_{m+1}, \ldots, x_n$, is that it be possible to write the utility function in the form:

$$u(x, b) = F(g(x_1, \ldots, x_m, b), x_2, \ldots, x_n)$$
(5.23)
$$\equiv F(g^*(x_1, \ldots, x_m, b)x_1, x_2, \ldots, x_n)$$

for some choice of continuously differentiable functions F and g.[30]

(B) For any $m = 1, \ldots, n-1$, a necessary and sufficient condition for $\partial p_1^*/\partial b$ to be independent of x_1 and $x_{m+1}, \ldots, x_n$ is that (5.23) hold with g in the form:

(5.24)
$$g(x_1, \ldots, x_m, b) = x_1 h(x_2, \ldots, x_m, b) \quad \text{or}$$
$$g^*(x_1, \ldots, x_m, b) = h(x_2, \ldots, x_m, b),$$

for some choice of a function h.

Proof. The proof of part (A) follows again from Leontief's theorem. That of part (B) is the same as that given for part (B) of Theorem 5.1, save that the indifference variety of g is taken at fixed values of $x_2, \ldots, x_m$. The values of $x_2, \ldots, x_m$ then become parameters of $\mu(b)$.

Unfortunately, while this generalization allows us to handle a wider variety of quality change than that covered in Theorem 5.1, it still leaves us in the case of repackaging of the first commodity (although the extent of repackaging is now allowed to depend on the quantities of other commodities). It does not touch the case in which a quality change in the first commodity affects other commodities by augmenting their services, for example, the case of refrigerators and ice cream mentioned above being a case in point. This leads us to abandon the notion that simple adjustments in the price of the good whose quality has changed are likely to be generally

---

30. It is natural to take $g(x_1, \ldots, x_m, 1) = x_1$, i.e. $g^*(x_1, \ldots, x_m, 1) = 1$, but this is not required for our results.

Taste and Quality Change

effective and to ask whether for some quality changes adjustments in *other* prices might not be more appropriate.

Accordingly, we next examine an extreme case in which only an adjustment in the price of the second commodity is called for. There is an asymmetry in the problem. It was reasonable to ask under what conditions an adjustment in p_1 can be made independent of x_2; it is not reasonable to ask under what conditions an adjustment in p_2 can be made independent of x_1. The quality change is embodied in the first commodity and the consumer cannot take advantage of it without purchasing that commodity [see (5.2), for example]. It is reasonable to ask under what circumstances an adjustment in p_2 can be made independent of the other elements of x, however, and this we shall do.

We thus replace (5.8) by:

(5.25) $\qquad y(p_1, p_2^*, p_3, \ldots, p_n, 1) = y(p_1, \ldots, p_n, b).$

It is clear that the argument leading to Lemma 5.3 shows:

Lemma 5.4. $\quad \dfrac{\partial p_2^*}{\partial b} = \dfrac{-p_2 u_b}{x_2 u_2}.$

We have immediately:

Theorem 5.3. (A) A necessary and sufficient condition for $\partial p_2^*/\partial b$ to be independent of $x_3, \ldots, x_n$ is that it be possible to write the utility function in the form:

(5.26) $\qquad u(x, b) = F(x_1, g(x_1, x_2, b), x_3, \ldots, x_n)$

$\qquad\qquad\quad \equiv F(x_1, g^*(x_1, x_2, b)x_2, x_3, \ldots, x_n)$

for some choice of continuously differentiable functions F and g.[31]

(B) A necessary and sufficient condition for $\partial p_2^*/\partial b$ to be independent of $x_3, \ldots, x_n$ *and* x_2 is that (5.26) hold, with g in the form:

(5.27) $\quad g(x_1, x_2, b) = x_2 h(x_1, b) \quad$ or $\quad g^*(x_1, x_2, b) = h(x_1, b)$

for some choice of a function h.

Proof. (A) follows from Lemma 5.4 and Leontief's theorem. (B) is proved as before, noting that x_1 is a parameter of the appropriate indifference curve of g in the $x_2 - b$ plane.

This is an interesting case. Whereas what was interesting about Theorem 5.1 was the necessity of the conditions, what is interesting here is

---

31. It is natural to take $g(x_1, x_2, 1) = x_2 = g(0, x_2, b)$, i.e. $g^*(x_1, x_2, 1) = 1 = g^*(0, x_2, 1)$, but this is not required for our results.

sufficiency. Looked at in this way, the theorem tells us that if quality change in good one augments the services of good *two*, then a simple adjustment in the price of the latter good is called for. Once again, an adjustment can be made in this case in the price of good one, but Theorem 5.1 assures us that the adjustment will not be a simple one; it will depend on all commodity purchases. The simple adjustment is one in the price of the second good which is not the good whose quality has changed. If the only effect of a quality change in refrigerators is to make ice cream taste better, the simple adjustment which should be made is in the price of ice cream, not the price of refrigerators. The magnitude of that adjustment will depend on the quantity of refrigerators, and it may also depend on the quantity of ice cream (which is reasonable when one supposes that the effect depends on the ice cream–refrigerator ratio), but, unlike an adjustment in the price of refrigerators, it does not depend on the quantities of other goods.

Such polar cases, however, are too simple. In practice, quality change, even if it takes the relatively simple form of augmenting the services of certain goods, is unlikely merely to augment the services of only one good. A better refrigerator affects goods other than ice cream. Clearly, from Theorems 5.1 and 5.3, a simple adjustment in a single price will not suffice in such circumstances.

Fortunately, however, simple adjustments in more than one price will suffice, and this can be done by using our results simultaneously for more than one good. Thus, suppose that the utility function can be written in the form:

$$(5.28) \quad u(x, b) = F(g^1(x_1, b), g^2(x_1, x_2, b), \ldots, g^n(x_1, x_n, b))$$
$$\equiv F(g^{*1}(x_1, b)x_1, g^{*2}(x_1, x_2, b)x_2, \ldots, g^{*n}(x_1, x_n, b)x_n)$$

for some choice of continuously differentiable functions, F and $g^1, \ldots, g^n$. This is the case in which every good is augmented, but, if $g^1(x_1, x_i, b) = x_i g^{*i}(x_1, x_i, b) = 1$ for all b, then the augmentation of the ith good is zero (and similarly for the first good). This case contains all those turned up in Theorems 5.1 and 5.3; generalization along the lines of Theorem 5.2 is left to the reader.[32]

Since g^1 is to reflect the augmentation of the first commodity itself, it is

---

32. It is natural to take $g^1(x_1, 1) = x_1$ and $g^i(x_1, x_i, 1) = x_i = g^i(0, x_i, b)$ ($i = 2, \ldots, n$), i.e. $g^{*1}(x_1, 1) = 1$ and $g^{*i}(x_1, x_i, 1) = 1 = g^{*i}(0, x_i, b)$ ($i = 2, \ldots, n$), but this is not required for our results.

Taste and Quality Change

obviously reasonable to assume that $g_1^1 \neq 0$.[33] Actually, we need only assume that x_1 is uniquely determined given b and g^1, i.e., that there exists a function ϕ, such that:

(5.29) $$x_1 = \phi(g^1(x_1, b), b).$$

With this assumption, our previous results enable us to handle this relatively general case.

Theorem 5.4. If quality change satisfies (5.28) and (5.29), its effect on the true cost-of-living index can be equivalently represented as a set of price adjustments. The percentage adjustment in the first price depends at most on the amount of the first commodity; the percentage adjustment in the ith price ($i = 2, \ldots, n$) depends at most on the amount of the first and ith commodities.[34]

Proof. In view of (5.29), every g^i ($i = 2, \ldots, n$) can be written as a function of g^1, x_i, and b. Thus:

(5.30) $$g^i(x_1, x_i, b) = h^i(g^1, x_i, b) \quad (i = 2, \ldots, n).$$

We shall break up the effect of a change in b into its effects on the various commodities, as follows. Let the b appearing as an argument of g^1 be denoted b_1; let the b appearing as an argument of h^i be denoted b_i ($i = 2, \ldots, n$). We shall begin with all the b_i equal to unity and shall change them to their common post-quality-change value, denoted $\bar{b}$, one at a time.

Thus, set all the $b_i = 1$, save b_1 and consider the effect of changing b_1 from unity to $\bar{b}$. By (5.30), b_1 enters the utility function only through g^1, and hence the condition of (A) of Theorem 5.1 is satisfied. It follows that the effect of b_1 on y can be equivalently represented as an adjustment in p_1. That adjustment (in percentage terms) depends only on x_1 and not on the other elements of x. Further, in view of Lemma 5.3, that adjustment does not depend on the values of the b_i ($i = 2, \ldots, n$), so there is no need to remake it when we change those values.

Now move b_2 from unity to $\bar{b}$, keeping $b_1 = \bar{b}$ and $b_i = 1$ ($i = 3, \ldots, n$). With b_1 fixed, g^1 depends only on x_1, so that h^2 depends only on x_1, x_2, and b_2. It is clear that the condition of (A) of Theorem 5.3 is satisfied, so

---

33. If $g_1^1 = 0$ in some open neighborhood in the $x_1 - b$ plane in which $g_b^1 \neq 0$, then b enters the utility function in that neighborhood in some way other than by augmenting the services of the commodities.

34. If g^i takes the form of (B) of Theorem 5.3, only dependence on the first commodity is involved; if g^1 takes the form of (B) of Theorem 5.1, the percentage adjustment in p_1 is a constant.

that the effect of the change in b_2 can be equivalently represented as an adjustment in p_2. That adjustment (in percentage terms) depends at most on x_1 and x_2, and, as before, is independent of the values of the b_i ($i = 3, \ldots, n$).

Next, move b_3 and adjust p_3. This adjustment is independent of the other b_i ($i = 4, \ldots, n$) and also independent of b_2. Proceeding in this way, we account for all effects of the quality change and the theorem is proved.

Thus any quality change in the first good, every effect of which can be represented as an augmentation of the services of some good[35] can be handled by adjusting in the cost-of-living index the prices of every good whose services are so augmented and *only* the prices of those goods. In the simplest case of this, given in (5.28), those adjustments (taken in percentage terms) depend at most on the quality of the first good purchased, and possibly on the purchased quantity of the good in question. These price adjustments can be made independently. More complicated cases along the lines of Theorem 5.2 can also be handled. Only in the very simplest of all cases, where only the first good itself is augmented, will a change in the price of the good whose quality has changed be sufficient. (Even then, unless the augmentation is constant, the price change will depend on the quantity of the first good that is purchased.) An adequate treatment of quality change in cost-of-living indices must pay attention to cross-good effects.[36]

---

35. This is quite general in the small, but not in the large.

36. Is it really much more difficult to say, for example, how the introduction of larger, more powerful cars affects the enjoyment of the services of other prestige items than it is to say how such introduction affects the enjoyment of the services of cars? Both evaluations seem hard to make, but the second one is made in practice. Admittedly, however, the second evaluation can be made implicitly through the use of market data if new and "old" (but not necessarily used) cars sell on the same perfect market. Even then, as we have seen, that adjustment will generally only suffice while that market situation lasts.

3.

Zvi Griliches
Hedonic Price Indexes for Automobiles: An Econometric Analysis of Quality Change

1. Introduction and Summary

"If a poll were taken of professional economists and statisticians, in all probability they would designate (and by a wide majority) the failure of the price indexes to take full account of quality changes as the most important defect in these indexes."[1] In spite of its potential importance, there is almost no published empirical work devoted explicitly to this problem. The only available book that deals with problems raised by changes in quality reaches essentially defeatist conclusions (Hofsten 1952).

The main purpose of this paper is to investigate a relatively old, simple, and straightforward method of adjusting for quality change and find out whether (a) this method is feasible and operational, and (b) whether the results are promising and different enough to warrant the extra investment. It is standard practice in the price index industry to adjust for those quality changes to which a price can be attached. The appearance of automatic transmissions on the market at $200 extra will not raise the price of automobiles in the conventional indexes (except those of the U.S. Department of Agriculture) even though eventually almost all cars are sold with it and the base price incorporates it as "standard equipment."

From *The Price Statistics of the Federal Government*, 1961, General Series, No. 73 (New York: National Bureau of Economic Research). Also published as U.S. Congress, Joint Economic Committee, *Government Price Statistics, Hearings*, 87th Congress, 1st Session, Part I, Jan. 24, 1961 (Washington, D.C.: Government Printing Office). Reprinted by permission of the author.

1. *Price Statistics* 1961, p. 35.

However, only a few of the observed quality changes come in discrete lumps with an attached price tag. Most of the changes are gradual and are not priced separately. Nevertheless, many dimensions of quality change can be quantified (e.g., horsepower, weight, or length for automobiles); a variety of models with different specifications can be observed being sold at different prices at the same time; using multiple regression techniques on these data one can derive implicit prices per unit of the chosen additional dimension of the commodity; and armed with these "prices" one can proceed to adjust the observed price per "average item" for the changes that have occurred in its specification. There are many technical problems to be solved, but the main idea is quite simple: Derive implicit specification prices from cross-sectional data on the price of various "models" of the particular item and use these in pricing the time series change in specifications of the chosen (average or representative) item.[2] Alternatively, one can interpret the procedure as answering the question of what the price of a new combination of specifications (or qualities) of a particular commodity would have been in some base period in which that particular combination was not available, by interpolating or extrapolating the apparent relationship of price to these specifications for models or varieties of the "commodity" that were available in that period. This latter interpretation avoids some of the more metaphysical problems involved in the notion of "quality" and "quality change."

In this paper I investigate the relationship of automobile prices in the U.S. to the various dimensions of an "automobile" in 1937, 1950, and 1954 through 1960. A limited number of specifications or dimensions explain a very large fraction of the variance of car prices (as among different models) in any one of these years. Due to the high intercorrelation between some of these dimensions, there is some instability in the estimated "implicit prices" (the coefficients) of the dimensions. Also, there appears to have been a very substantial secular decline in the "price" of some of these dimensions (e.g., horsepower). Thus, estimates of the actual price change (after the quality change adjustments are made) differ markedly depending on whether they are based on beginning or end period weights. If we value the quality changes at their 1950 "implicit prices," we find that all the apparent increase in car prices between 1950 and 1960 can be explained by quality improvements, the hedonic price index actually falling during 1950–1960. Valued at 1960 implicit quality prices, these

---

2. As far as I know, this procedure was first suggested by A. T. Court 1939. A more recent exposition is given by R. Stone 1956.

Hedonic Price Indexes for Automobiles

same quality changes account for a little over half of the apparent price increase over this period. Over the whole period since 1937, the CPI may be overestimating the rise in automobile prices by at least a third. Since the CPI is a Laspeyres index, the appropriate quality adjustment should also be based on "base" (beginning) period weights. If this is done, about three-fourths of the rise in automobile prices in the CPI since 1937 could be attributed to quality improvements.

Some limitations of this type of approach are explored in the last part of the paper and, in light of these, it is not yet recommended that such adjustments should be made routinely as part of the price index computations. Continuous studies of this sort, however, covering a wide range of commodities, would be of great value. They could provide us with estimates of the order of magnitude of the possible upward drift in the official price indexes due to their inability to cope adequately with the ever-present quality change problem. Moreover, they would spot for the price data collecting agencies what appear to be the more relevant dimensions or specifications of a commodity, providing them with a better basis for judging which specifications should be controlled in the pricing process.

2. Theoretical Considerations

It is impossible to deal here with all the index number problems raised by the changing quality of commodities.[3] Since we are interested in the effect of quality change on measured prices and price indexes, our first job is to find what relationship, if any, there is between the price of a particular commodity and its "quality."

Most commodities, particularly consumer and producer durables, are sold in many varieties or models. Thus at any one time we can observe a population of prices—p_{it}—where i is the index of varietal designation (e.g., No. 2 corn, or a Chevrolet Impala four-door hardtop with a V-8 engine) and t stands for the time period of observation. The reason why these different varieties or models sell at different prices must be due to some differences in their properties, dimensions, or other "qualities," real or imaginary. Thus we can write p_{it} as a function of a set of "qualities" X,

---

3. The reader is referred to the literature on this problem, and in particular to Hofsten 1952 and to Stone 1956; see also Adelman and Griliches 1961.

and some additional small, and hopefully random, factors measured by the disturbance u.

(1) $$p_{it} = f_t(x_{1it}, x_{2it}, \ldots, x_{kit}, u_{it}).$$

These qualities do not necessarily have to be numerical. Given a sufficient number of observations, we can use variables which take the value one if the item possesses the particular quality and zero if it does not and derive the average contribution of this "quality" to the price of the item. Nor do they have to be desired for their own sake. It will suffice if they are well correlated with some more basic dimension which may be more difficult to measure. For example, for many commodities, and at least over some range, "size" and "capacity" are very important qualities. They are, however, quite elusive and difficult to measure. On the other hand, they can often be approximated quite well by variables such as volume, weight, or length, even though none of these "proxy" dimensions may be desirable per se.

The existence and usefulness of such a function is an empirical rather than theoretical question.[4] To estimate such a function we have to make additional assumptions about the number and kind of relevant qualities and the form in which they affect the price of the product. There is no a priori reason to expect price and quality to be related in any particular fixed fashion. This again is an empirical question. In this study, I have used the semilogarithmic form, relating the logarithm of the price to the absolute values (pounds, inches, etc.) of the qualities:

(2) $$\log p_{it} = a_0 + a_1 x_{1it} + a_2 x_{2it} + \cdots + u_{it}.$$

This choice was based on an inspection of the data and the convenience of this particular formulation.[5] Other forms, e.g., linear, or linear in the logarithms, may however be more appropriate in a study of other commodities and qualities.

Assuming that the equation can be estimated with enough precision, it can be used to estimate the value of certain quality changes in the base period. Moreover, one can use it to estimate the price of a new bundle of qualities which may not have been available in this period, provided that the new bundle differs only quantitatively in its "qualities" from the previously available items and does not contain some new, previously

---

4. It can always be made into a tautology by specifying enough factors or qualities.

5. If natural logarithms are used, an "a" coefficient will provide an estimate of the percentage increase in price due to a one-unit change in the particular quality, holding the level of the other qualities constant.

Hedonic Price Indexes for Automobiles

unknown or unavailable qualities. Even if the new item possesses some previously unknown qualities, the equation can be used to estimate the change in price due to changes in the subset of quantifiable qualities, and half a loaf may be better than none.

An equation of this type can be computed for each period for which we have enough observations to do it. If the results are not the same in different periods, and they are unlikely to be so, we are faced with the general index number problem of changing weights. The implicit prices we obtain will depend on the particular period or periods chosen as "weight" or reference periods, and Laspeyres' and Paasche's indexes may diverge sharply. If the periods are not too far apart and the weight pattern not too different, we can estimate the average price change directly by assuming that the equation holds well enough in both periods except for the change in the additional variable "time".

(3) $$\log p_{it} = a_0 + a_1 x_{1it} + a_2 x_{2it} + \cdots + a_d D + u_{it}$$

where D is a variable that is zero in the first period and one in the second.[6] The coefficient a_d provides us with an estimate of the average percentage increase in price of these models or varieties between the two periods, holding the change in any of the measured quality dimensions constant. If we want to impose the same set of weights on more than two cross sections, this can be achieved by specifying additional "time" or "dummy" variables, taking the value one in their reference period and the value zero in all other periods. The necessary number of such variables is one less than the number of cross sections that are being estimated together. The resulting coefficients measure the percentage change in the average price, holding qualities constant, with the average price for the earliest cross section being the base of measurement.

Having estimated such equations, instead of adjusting the prices or price indexes directly, we can first define an index of quality change and use that to adjust the official indexes. Consider a particular variety of a commodity, say a Plymouth Savoy four-door sedan with a six-cylinder engine, whose qualities may have changed over some time period. Then the quality change measure g is defined as

$$g_{1i}^0 = \frac{\hat{P}_{i1}}{\hat{P}_{i0}} \quad \text{where } \hat{P}_{i0} = f_0(x_{1i0}, \ldots),$$

and $\hat{P}_{i1} = f_0(x_{1i1}, \ldots)$.[7] That is, the p's are each predicted prices for variety i on the basis of estimated equation f_0, one for the combination of

---

6. This was the procedure followed by Court 1939.
7. The designation g is borrowed from Hofsten 1952.

qualities this variety had in period 0 and the other for the combination of qualities it has in period 1. More simply g_1^0 measures the percentage increase in price predicted by the function f_0 on the basis of the change in the level of different qualities (the x's) between the two periods. Of course, if we had used the estimated function for the second period, f_1, or a price quality function for some other period, we would have gotten a somewhat different measure. For a larger number of varieties, or models, these g's can be aggregated into a quality change index, using the same weights that are used in aggregating their prices in the price index. To get at the adjusted "real" change in prices, we would "deflate" the observed price index by the estimated quality change index.[8]

$$\text{"true price index"} = \frac{\text{observed price index}}{\text{quality change index}} = \frac{P_1}{P_0} \bigg/ \frac{\hat{P}_1}{\hat{P}_0} = \frac{P_1/\hat{P}_1}{P_0/\hat{P}_0}.$$

Note that this "quality change" index is based only on those "qualities" for which a price is being paid or exacted, and only to the extent of the price differential. If these price differentials are "phony" or "too high" or "too low" from some omniscient point of view, the index will not take this into account. In fact, it may not take into account some aspects of "quality" which may be important, and incorporate other "imaginary" qualities such as brand names whose "superiority" over unbranded items would be denied by many people. Thus, if we observe that garments bearing one union label sell on the average at a 5-percent higher price than comparable unlabeled items, and also that garments bearing the labels of three different unions sell for 15 percent more than comparable unlabeled items, we would predict that if a similar garment were available with two union labels, it would probably sell for about 10 percent more than the unlabeled items. And we would use this in calculating our price index (or price relative) for the two-label garment, even though we are morally certain (and supported in this by extensive test laboratory findings) that there is no "real" quality difference among all these items. We would do this since we are answering only a relatively modest question: What would the price have been if it were available? And not: Would consumers be "right" in paying this particular price, or for that matter the price of any other item? Once raised, the doubt whether the evidence of the marketplace reflects adequately, if at all, the "true" marginal

---

8. Compare this with Adelman 1960, where the quality change index is defined additively rather than multiplicatively. Ideally the varietal prices should be deflated individually before they are aggregated into an overall price index. Only for geometrically weighted indexes will the ratio of the two equal the "true" index exactly.

Hedonic Price Indexes for Automobiles

utility of different items or qualities to the consumer can be turned against any other price or commodity. It is not a problem peculiar to the measurement of "quality."

While it is not necessary for our purposes, it would be nice, however, if these quality indexes represented something "real" and not just the mistakes and idiosyncrasies of manufacturers' pricing policies. There are two possible sources of evidence on this point. The first, which will be explored to some extent at the end of the paper, is the evidence of second-hand markets. Do different qualities command approximately similar relative prices in the used market, a market which could be considered to be more competitive than the market for new items? If they do, this would indicate that consumers are still willing to pay these differentials even when they are not imposed by manufacturers. A second and more stringent test, which will not be pursued here, could have been made by investigating what happens to the sales of varieties or brands if their prices are too high or too low relative to their quality content. Given an estimated price-quality equation for a particular period, the estimated residual for a specific model or brand could be interpreted as a measure of over or under pricing relative to the quality content of this model. If, with the help of these residuals, we were able to predict reasonably well the market share experience of different models or brands, i.e., "over priced" items losing and "under priced" items gaining, this would provide strong support for the correctness of our price-quality equation and its interpretation.

3. The Sample and the Variables

The analysis of price-quality relationships reported below is based on data for U.S. passenger four-door sedans for the years 1937, 1950, and 1954 through 1960. In each of these years an attempt was made to collect price and specification data for all models and brands for which such data were easily available.[9] Since these calculations were viewed as being exploratory, no special attempts were made to assure completeness of coverage,

---

9. The 1937 price and specification data for new 1937 automobile models are taken from the Sept.–Oct. 1937 issue of the *Red Book*. The 1950 model data are from the Nov. 15, 1956, issue of the *Red Book*. For 1954 through 1960 the data are taken from various issues of *Used Car Guide*. For 1955 through 1958 the data are from the February issue of the corresponding year. For 1954 models, the figures are taken from the July 1959 issue; for 1959 models, from the January 1959 issue; and for 1960 models, from the December 1959 issue. Data on power brakes come from various issues of *Ward's Automotive Reports*.

nor were the model observations weighted by their relative importance in the market. The number of observations in each cross section varies from a low of 50 in 1937 to a high of 103 in 1958.

The new car prices used throughout this study are factory-delivered "suggested" (list) retail prices, at approximately the beginning of the model year.[10] Unfortunately, there are no published data on actual transaction prices for a wide range of models. Discounts from list prices may have varied over time, and this will make it somewhat difficult to compare our results with the CPI, since the CPI has tried to take discounts into account, at least since 1954. Only to the extent that relative discounting is correlated with some of our quality dimensions will the use of list prices lead to any special bias in the estimates of the quality coefficients. This same difficulty would not be present if an official government agency were doing such a study. The WPI actually collects the manufacturers' wholesale price to dealers for most automobile models. Similarly, it should not prove difficult to expand the CPI sample, at least once a year, to include a wider range of models.

No adjustment was made for any changes in minor equipment items that became standard equipment at some later point in time, such as directional signals or electric clocks.[11] Major items, such as automatic transmissions, power steering, and power brakes were treated by defining independent variables that took the value of one if the item was "standard equipment" on a particular model and zero if it was not.

The major numerical "quality" variables used in this study are horsepower (advertised brake horsepower), weight (shipping), and length (wheelbase for 1937 and 1950, and overall from 1950 on). In addition, "dummy" variables, i.e., variables that take the value of one if the particular model possesses this particular "quality" and zero if it does not, are defined for the following "qualities": V-8 engine or not, hardtop or not, automatic transmission as standard equipment or not, power steering as standard equipment or not, power brakes as standard equipment or not, and for 1960 models whether a car is a "compact" or not. Note that some of these variables do not measure the consequence of having a particular item of equipment as much as they stratify and control for the type of car on which such equipment is "standard" (included in its base price). Thus, for example, the variable for power steering effectively

---

10. Factory-advertised delivered price includes only standard equipment, federal excise tax, and dealer handling and preparation charges. Transportation and state or local taxes are not included.

11. The possible consequences of this omission are explored briefly in the appendix to this chapter.

Hedonic Price Indexes for Automobiles

identifies most of the large luxury cars that differ from other cars in other ways besides sheer size or the presence of power steering as standard equipment.

A variety of variables for which no convenient data are available was not included in the calculations. Most important of these are the various "performance" variables: gasoline mileage, acceleration, handling ease, durability, and styling. Scattered data already exist on some of these qualities, and I am sure that it would not prove very difficult to collect more and include such variables explicitly in a similar price-quality analysis. Variables reflecting the level of "workmanship" associated with a particular car and variables accounting for small design changes, such as the substitution of an alternator for the generator, were also omitted for lack of data. Nor were brand or manufacturer differentials taken into account. In fact, as far as the numerical qualities that are included in the analysis are concerned, they could probably all be interpreted as different aspects of one underlying quality "size" or "capacity."

Table 3.1. Characteristics of the Cross Sections Used in This Study: U.S. Passenger Four-Door Sedans—1937, 1950, and 1954–1960

Years	Number of Models	Average (Geometric) Price	Average Horse-power	Average Shipping Weight in Pounds	Average Length in Inches	
					Wheelbase	Overall
1937	50	$1,183	109	3,506	122	—
1950	72	2,113	115	3,533	122	205.7
1954	65	2,360	141	3,452	—	205.0
1955	55	2,281	166	3,429	—	205.4
1956	87	2,594	200	3,616	—	207.5
1957	95	2,785	226	3,696	—	208.9
1958	103	3,054	252	3,835	—	211.6
1959	87	3,180	251	3,907	—	213.7
1960	78	2,800	211	3,606	—	208.6

SOURCE: See footnote 9 for sources of data.

The characteristics of the sample are summarized in Table 3.1. Note the sharp increase in horsepower per car since 1950, due to a large extent to the introduction of the V-8 engine, and the lengthening of cars which reached its peak in 1959. The drop in the average price and specification level of cars in 1960 is due mainly to the introduction of the "compacts" and the decline in the number of high- and medium-priced models on the market.

4. The Regression Results

It is impossible to reproduce here the very large number of multiple regressions that were computed for different years and different combinations of years and independent variables. Due to the very high multicollinearity between the three numerical "qualities" chosen for analysis (see Table 3.2) there was substantial instability in the coefficient estimates

Table 3.2. First-Order Correlation Coefficients: r

Between	Year					
	1960	1959	1957	1954	1950	1937
H and log P	0.89	0.85	0.85	0.89	0.84	0.88
W and log P	0.90	0.92	0.95	0.88	0.87	0.92
L and log P	0.77	0.75	0.84	0.81	0.91	0.88
H and W	0.85	0.82	0.90	0.92	0.76	0.80
H and L	0.72	0.75	0.79	0.73	0.74	0.84
W and L	0.92	0.86	0.85	0.87	0.83	0.92

H = Horsepower.
W = Weight.
L = Length, overall, except wheelbase in 1937.
log P = logarithm of list price.

for some of the years. Usable estimates were obtained only for years in which there was some independent variation along the three numerical quality dimensions, and for combinations of years where the larger number of observations allowed us to determine the separate coefficients with greater precision.

Regression estimates for selected years are summarized in Table 3.3. Table 3.4 summarizes a set of regressions utilizing two adjacent annual cross sections each and introducing an explicit variable to estimate the average price change holding quality change constant. It also presents the estimated coefficients of the overall regression for 1954–1960, lumping all of the seven (1954 through 1960) cross sections together and allowing them to differ from each other in level but not in slope.

Hedonic Price Indexes for Automobiles

Table 3.3. Coefficients of Single Year Cross-Sectional Regressions Relating the Logarithm of New U.S. Passenger Car Prices to Various Specifications, Selected Years[a]

	Model Year					
				1950		
Coefficients of	1960	1959	1957	(1)	(2)	1937
H	0.119	0.118	0.117	0.365	0.585	0.867
	(0.029)	(0.029)	(0.030)	(0.110)	(0.133)	(0.181)
W	0.136	0.238	0.135	0.111	0.145	0.388
	(0.046)	(0.034)	(0.010)	(0.066)	(0.096)	(0.078)
L	0.015	−0.016	0.039	0.192	0.147	−0.009
	(0.017)	(0.015)	(0.013)	(0.026)	(0.045)	(0.078)
V	−0.039	−0.070	−0.025	−0.054	−0.091	−0.023
	(0.025)	(0.039)	(0.023)	(0.032)	(0.040)	(0.060)
T	0.058	0.027	0.028	—	—	—
	(0.016)	(0.019)	(0.012)	—	—	—
A	0.003	0.063	0.114	—	—	—
	(0.040)	(0.038)	(0.025)	—	—	—
P	0.225	0.188	0.078	—	—	—
	(0.037)	(0.041)	(0.030)	—	—	—
B	—	—	0.159	—	—	—
			(0.026)	—	—	—
C	0.048	—	—	—	—	—
	(0.039)					
R^2	0.951	0.934	0.966	0.892	0.835	0.904

[a] While the original computations were all done with logarithms to the base 10, the results in this table are converted to natural logarithms (to the base e) as an aid to interpretation. The resulting coefficients, if multiplied by a hundred, measure the percentage impact on price of a unit change in a particular specification or "quality," holding the other qualities constant. The numbers in parentheses are the calculated standard errors of the coefficients. For 1950 regression (2) and 1937: length of wheelbase rather than overall length.

H = Advertised brake horsepower in 100's.
W = Shipping weight in thousand pounds.
L = Overall length, in tens of inches.
V = 1 if the car has a V-8 engine; = 0 if it has a 6-cylinder engine.
T = 1 if the car is a hardtop; = 0 if it is not.
A = 1 if automatic transmission is "standard" equipment (included in the price); = 0 if not.
P = 1 if power steering is "standard"; = 0 if not.
B = 1 if power brakes are "standard"; = 0 if not.
C = 1 if the car is designated as a "compact"; = 0 if not.
R^2 = Coefficient of multiple correlation squared.

Table 3.4. Coefficients of Regressions of the Logarithms of Price on Various "Qualities": U.S. Passenger Cars, Two Years Taken Together, and All the Seven Years, 1954 through 1960[a]

Coefficients of	Model Years							
	1954–1960	1959–1960	1958–1959	1957–1958	1956–1957	1955–1956	1954–1955	1937–1950
H	0.056	0.114	0.062	0.040	0.095	0.091	0.241	0.538
	(0.013)	(0.018)	(0.025)	(0.026)	(0.028)	(0.055)	(0.059)	(0.108)
W	0.249	0.212	0.285	0.271	0.211	0.241	0.009	0.328
	(0.021)	(0.029)	(0.034)	(0.038)	(0.039)	(0.056)	(0.060)	(0.053)
L	0.023	−0.006	−0.018	0.007	0.045	0.053	0.082	0.108
	(0.007)	(0.011)	(0.013)	(0.013)	(0.011)	(0.015)	(0.016)	(0.039)
V	0.010	−0.059	−0.026	0.005	−0.037	−0.043	−0.031	−0.093)
	(0.013)	(0.023)	(0.031)	(0.026)	(0.020)	(0.031)	(0.024)	(0.035)
T	0.023	0.040	0.030	0.024	0.022	0.018	—	—
	(0.009)	(0.013)	(0.012)	(0.013)	(0.010)	(0.018)	—	—
A	0.090	0.034	0.070	0.075	0.058	0.079	0.236	—
	(0.016)	(0.027)	(0.030)	(0.026)	(0.021)	(0.028)	(0.037)	—
P	0.088	0.206	0.125	0.113	0.089	0.062	0.035	—
	(0.017)	(0.028)	(0.040)	(0.030)	(0.023)	(0.029)	(0.038)	—
B	0.109	—	0.115	0.162	0.138	0.098	−0.045	—
	(0.016)	—	(0.038)	(0.028)	(0.019)	(0.029)	(0.045)	—
C	0.157	0.052	—	—	—	—	—	—
	(0.031)	(0.031)	—	—	—	—	—	—
D	—	−0.023	0.005	0.027	0.027	0.020	−0.093	0.527
	—	(0.011)	(0.014)	(0.012)	(0.011)	(0.018)	(0.020)	(0.027)
D_1	−0.044	—	—	—	—	—	—	—
	(0.015)	—	—	—	—	—	—	—
D_2	−0.015	—	—	—	—	—	—	—
	(0.014)	—	—	—	—	—	—	—
D_3	0.019	—	—	—	—	—	—	—
	(0.015)	—	—	—	—	—	—	—
D_4	0.044	—	—	—	—	—	—	—
	(0.016)	—	—	—	—	—	—	—
D_5	0.044	—	—	—	—	—	—	—
	(0.016)	—	—	—	—	—	—	—
D_6	0.023	—	—	—	—	—	—	—
	(0.016)	—	—	—	—	—	—	—
R_2	0.922	0.943	0.915	0.929	0.945	0.924	0.904	0.916

[a] See notes to Table 3.3 for the definition of most of the variables.

$D = 1$ in the second of two periods being estimated together; $= 0$ in the first. The coefficient of D can be interpreted as the percentage change (if it is multiplied by 100) in the average price of cars between the two periods, holding all the qualities constant. Thus, e.g., for 1937–1950, the estimated "true" price change is approximately 53 percent.

Hedonic Price Indexes for Automobiles

Table 3.4. (*continued*)

$D_1 = 1$ in 1955; $= 0$ in other years.
$D_2 = 1$ in 1956; $= 0$ in other years.
$D_3 = 1$ in 1957; $= 0$ in other years.
$D_4 = 1$ in 1958; $= 0$ in other years.
$D_5 = 1$ in 1959; $= 0$ in other years.
$D_6 = 1$ in 1960; $= 0$ in other years.

The coefficients of these variables measure the average percentage change in price holding quality constant as of 1954. Thus for 1960, it indicates that since 1954 the average price holding quality constant increased only by about 2 percent and that, moreover, this increase is not significantly different from zero. To get the estimated percentage change between two adjacent years, one has, in this case, to take the difference between the two coefficients. Thus, e.g., the 1954 through 1960 equation estimates the average percentage change in price between 1957 and 1958 as 1.5 (4.4–1.9), against a 2.7 estimate given by the equation for 1957–1958 alone.

Since our dependent variable is the logarithm of price, the resulting regression coefficients can be interpreted as the estimated percentage change in price due to a unit change in a particular "quality," holding the other qualities constant. Thus, for example, the results for the 1960 cross section (column 1 in Table 3.3) imply that the following was true, on the average, for the 1960 model cars and their list prices. An increase of 10 units in horsepower, ceteris paribus, would result on the average in a 1.2-percent increase in the price of a car (with a standard error of 0.3 percent). An increase of 100 pounds in the weight of a car was associated with a 1.4-percent increase in price. An increase of 10 inches in the length of a car, holding the other qualities constant, was associated with a 1.5-percent increase in the price of the car (but was not significantly different from zero at conventional significance levels). A V-8 engine, holding horsepower, weight, etc., constant was associated with a 4-percent lower price than a six having comparable characteristics.[12] A "hardtop" was on the average 6 percent more expensive than other comparable ("soft top"?) models. Holding other "qualities" constant, the inclusion of an automatic transmission as "standard equipment" was not associated with any significant price increase. The presence of power steering as "standard equipment" led to a 22-percent higher price over comparable models.[13] The cars designated as "compacts" were selling for about 5

---

12. There was very little overlap in horsepower between the sixes and the V-8's in the sample. What the coefficient measures, actually, is the fact that higher horsepower levels could be achieved at a price-horsepower relationship for six-cylinder engine cars. For more on this, see the text below.

13. This is more related to the "luxuriousness" of these models than to the presence of power steering per se.

percent more than other cars, holding other "quality" differences constant, but again, this premium was not significantly different from zero.

If we look now across the rows of Tables 3.3 and 3.4, several things are worth noting. The fit of these equations is quite good. With the help of a few numerical and shift variables, we manage to explain most of the time 90 or more percent of the variance of the logarithm of car prices in a particular year or set of years, even though the range of our sample extends from Ramblers to Cadillacs.[14] The coefficient of "weight" is almost always significantly different from zero, at conventional levels, and its magnitude remains relatively stable from cross section to cross section. The coefficient of horsepower is also statistically significant in a large fraction of cases, but varies somewhat more in magnitude around a downward trend. The coefficient of length is perhaps the most unstable of all the estimated coefficients, being very large and significant in 1950, declining rapidly in the middle fifties, and becoming insignificant and sometimes negative by 1958 and in subsequent years. This is partly the result of the generally very low variability of "length" in the sample (its coefficient of variation was only about 4 percent, on the average) and the very marked increase in the length of the lower priced cars since 1957.

Looking at the coefficients of the shift or "dummy" variables representing the presence or absence of certain "qualities," perhaps the most interesting result is the consistently negative sign attached to the coefficient of the V-8 versus six-cylinder engine variable. It is true that most of the time this coefficient is not significantly different from zero, but the consistency in sign from period to period is both surprising and instructive. While we know that a V-8 engine costs about $100 more than a six on a "comparable" car, this is not what is meant by "comparable" in the context of our equations. What the coefficient says is that if we hold horsepower and the other variables constant, a V-8 is cheaper by about 4 percent. Since the "comparable" cars are likely to differ much only in horsepower, and since there is very little overlap in the sample between the horsepower levels achieved by six-cylinder engines and the horsepower generated by the V-8's, what this coefficient is really saying is that higher horsepower levels can be achieved more cheaply if one shifts to V-8 engines than would be estimated by extrapolating the price-horsepower relationship for the six-cylinder engines alone. It is a measure of the decline in the "price" per horsepower as one shifts to V-8's even though the total expenditure on horsepower goes up.

---

14. This does not mean, necessarily, that we are able to predict the price for any one particular car very well. The average standard error of regression for these equations is around 8 percent.

Hedonic Price Indexes for Automobiles

The coefficient of the "hardtop" variable is reasonably stable over time, indicating a premium of around 3 to 4 percent for this type of car. The coefficient of the "automatic transmission included in the price" variable is always positive, but varies substantially from time to time. The coefficients of the "power steering" and "power brakes standard equipment" variables are usually very significant and relatively large in size.[15] It is quite apparent that what they measure is not so much the presence or absence of these particular equipment items, as the presence of many other "luxuriousness" attributes associated with cars on which these items are "standard equipment." In a sense, these shift variables take care of some of the nonlinearity in the relationship of the logarithm of price to numerical qualities such as weight or horsepower. Usually the high-medium and high-priced cars are priced somewhat higher than would be predicted just by extrapolating the price-horsepower (or length or weight) relationship from the lower price range. Allowing the cars having power steering, power brakes, or automatic transmission as standard equipment, to have separate constant terms, brings these cars "into line" and reduces the possible bias in the estimated price-quality relationship for the numerical qualities.

5. Price and Quality Indexes for U.S. Automobiles

A. *Hedonic Price Indexes for the Sample as a Whole*

As we have noted already in our discussion of Table 3.4, the results presented there provide us with an estimate of the average price change that occurred between two periods in the list prices of automobiles, holding all the specified qualities constant. This is comparable to the deflation of the change in the price of the average car in the sample by a quality index with "average" rather than base or end period weights. These "average" weights are derived from the coefficients of the regression that provides the best fit simultaneously to data for two years, a regression that imposes the same price-quality relationship (slope) on both years, but allows them to differ in level. The weights are used then to adjust for the change in the specifications of the average car in the sample that has occurred between the two periods.

---

15. The power brakes variable is not included in the years when all (or almost all) the models on which power steering is "standard equipment" also have power brakes included in their price. Note that in those years the estimated coefficient of power steering alone equals approximately the sum of the two coefficients in the other years.

The resulting price indexes are summarized in Table 3.5 and compared to the Wholesale Price Index "Passenger Cars" component. The comparison with the WPI is more appropriate for two reasons. First, it is the only one of the official indexes that covers all passenger cars rather than just a few selected makes and models, and second, it is based on manufacturer prices to dealers whose relationship to the list prices used in this study has remained approximately constant over time. Unfortunately, the comparison is imperfect in the sense that the WPI is a weighted index of car prices, with weights based on the market shares of various makes (in some base period?), while our list price index is an unweighted average of all makes and models.[16] Relative to the WPI, our index gives too much weight to the high and medium priced cars.

Table 3.5. U.S. Cars: Percentage Change in Various Price Indexes, Selected Years

Model Year	List Prices			WPI[c]
	Average Car in Sample[a]	Hedonic Price Index Based on[b]		
		Estimated Adjacent Two-Period Weights	Estimated Average 1954 through 1960 Weights	
1937–1950	79.0	52.7	—	83.0
1954–1955	−3.3	−9.3	−4.4	2.7
1955–1956	13.7	2.0	2.9	4.1
1956–1957	7.7	2.7	3.4	4.7
1957–1958	9.6	2.7	2.5	0.6
1958–1959	3.6	0.5	0.0	5.1
1959–1960	−11.9	−2.3	−2.1	0.1
1954–1960	18.7	−4.2[d]	2.3	19.7

[a] Percentage change in the geometric average of all list prices in the sample.

[b] Computed from Table 3.4.

[c] From various BLS releases. For 1937 and 1950 models, price as of December of the previous year. For 1954 models, price as of January 1954. For all subsequent model years, price as of November of the preceding calendar year.

[d] Computed by multiplying all the estimated 2-year price relatives.

16. Different makes are weighted, in a sense, by the number of models of each make included in the sample. This mitigates the problem somewhat since the more popular makes are likely to have a larger number of models on the market, but does not solve it.

Hedonic Price Indexes for Automobiles

If we disregard these reservations, or limit the implications to our sample only, the results presented in Table 3.5 attest strongly to the importance of "quality" change. About one-third of the price change between 1937 and 1950 and almost all of the price increase between 1954 and 1960 is attributable to changes in a few selected specifications. If we use a chain-link index for the 1954–1960 period, adjusting the 1954–1955 price change by a quality index with average 1954–1955 weights, adjusting the 1955–1956 price change by a quality index with 1956–1957 weights, and so on, we actually come to the conclusion that the average 1960 car in our sample was cheaper than the 1954 average car, once some of the appropriate quality adjustments are made. If we use average 1954–1960 weights derived from the joint multiple regression equation for all seven cross sections, we do indicate a small price rise for the 1954–1960 period (2.3 percent) but we cannot reject the hypothesis that actually there was no real change in price over the period as a whole.

B. *Quality and Price Indexes for the "Lower Priced Three"*

Since two of the most important automobile price indexes (the automobile components of the CPI and of the Prices Paid by Farmers Index of the USDA) are based on prices for the "low priced three" makes—Chevrolet, Ford, and Plymouth—it is of some interest to develop quality and quality-adjusted price indexes that are restricted to this particular group of cars.[17] An attempt will be made to approximate a quality index appropriate to the group of cars priced by the CPI. Since it is impossible, from the published material alone, to discover all the details of the pricing and specification procedure used by the CPI, we cannot reproduce it exactly, adding only our quality adjustments.[18] In principle, however, our methods can be applied directly to the CPI data by the BLS, allowing a more firm estimate of the possible "quality bias" in the index.

The specification and list price history of the "average" Chevrolet, Ford, and Plymouth in the sample is presented in Table 3.6. Some attempt is made at weighting the different makes by including only two Plymouth models in this sample versus three models each for Chevrolet and Ford cars. Also, the specification and price history of six-cylinder engine cars and V-8 engine cars is recorded separately. Since the CPI switched over

---

17. The USDA index also includes one Buick model. The CPI will probably introduce "compact" cars into its calculations in the fall of 1960.

18. It is not clear which models within a make are being priced; what weights, if any, are attached to each model and make; whether the index averages price relatives for each model or make, or takes the relative of the average price of these models; and so forth. See also the Appendix for additional discussion of the CPI.

in 1956 from pricing six-cylinder cars to pricing the V-8 models of these same cars, we shall follow suit by computing separate indexes for each type of car and linking them at 1956.[19]

Table 3.6. Specifications and List Prices of the Average[a] "Low Priced Three" Car

Year	Horsepower	Weight (Pounds)	Length Wheelbase	Length Overall	Price[b]
Six-Cylinder Engines					
1937	81	2,756	112	196.0	$ 703
1950	94	3,099	116	196.1	1,521
1954	111	3,149	—	195.8	1,795
1955	120	3,129	—	198.7	1,839
1956	135	3,172	—	199.7	1,938
1957	139	3,255	—	203.6	2,140
1958	142	3,349	—	206.6	2,275
1959	138	3,448	—	209.6	2,415
1960	141	3,539	—	211.5	2,425
V-8 Engines					
1955	163	3,185	—	198.7	1.939
1956	176	3,246	—	199.7	2,039
1957	184	3,354	—	203.6	2,240
1958	210	3,440	—	206.6	2,390
1959	202	3,525	—	209.6	2,533
1960	190	3,615	—	211.5	2,537

[a] Average for 3 Chevrolets, 3 Fords, and 2 (the 2 lower priced series) Plymouth models, except in 1937 and 1950. The 1937 sample consists of 2 Chevrolets, 2 Plymouths, and 3 8-cylinder Fords. The 1950 sample consists of 4 Chevrolets, 2 Fords, and 2 Plymouths. The 8-cylinder Fords in 1937 were included to raise the sample size to approximately the same levels as in the subsequent years. Since these 8's (not V-8's) had a lower list price than comparable 6's in 1937, their inclusion, if anything, will bias the quality indexes downward.

[b] Arithmetic average.

Table 3.7 presents some of the weights used in aggregating these "qualities." It is immediately apparent that the computed quality indexes will differ substantially depending on which set of weights is used. To

---

19. Alternatives to this linking procedure are discussed below.

Hedonic Price Indexes for Automobiles

provide historical perspective, this table also records weights derived by Court in his earlier study of the same problem. The weights reproduced in this table and additional weights taken from Table 3.4 are used in constructing the set of quality indexes summarized in Table 3.8.

Table 3.7. Estimated Quality Weights or "Prices": Percentage Change in the Price of Cars as the Result of a Unit Change in Selected "Qualities," in Selected Years

	Percentage Change in Price per—		
Years	10-Unit Change in Horsepower	100-Pound Change in Weight	One-Inch Change in Length[a]
1930 to 1935[b]	5.5	5.7	0.31
1935 to 1937[b]	5.3	5.8	0.01
1937 to 1939[b]	7.1	3.0	0.15
1937[c]	8.7	3.9	−0.09
1950 (2)[c]	5.8	1.5	1.47
1950 (1)[c]	3.6	1.1	1.92
1957[c]	1.2	1.4	0.39
1959[c]	1.2	2.4	−0.16
1960[c]	1.2	1.4	0.15
1954 through 1960[d]	0.6	2.5	0.23

[a] Wheelbase length, 1935 through 1950 (2), overall length therafter.
[b] From Court 1939, p. 111.
[c] From Table 3.3.
[d] From Table 3.4.

The quality indexes measure how much higher the price of the particular car (or the average price of a particular class of cars) would have been, in the weight period, if its specifications had changed by the same amount as they did between the two periods that are being compared. Using beginning period weights, we find that "quality per car" practically doubled since 1937, with most of the increase occurring since 1950. Using end period weights, the indicated increase is only about 37 percent, which is still quite substantial. Using chain-link weights, or average 1954–1960 weights, produces intermediate results. Since the CPI is a Laspeyres based fixed weight index, with the latest set of weights being based on the 1950 Consumer Expenditure Survey, the "beginning period" weighted quality index is the most appropriate deflator for it. From a theoretical

Table 3.8. Quality Indexes for the "Low-Priced Three" (6-cylinder engines to 1956, V-8's thereafter)

	Percentage Change			
Period	Beginning Period Weights[a]	Adjacent Year Weights[b]	1954 through 1960 Weights[c]	End Period Weights[d]
1937 to 1950	24.3	22.7	—	18.7
1950 to 1960	61.0	—	18.7	15.1
1937 to 1960[e]	100.1	—	—	36.6
1950 to 1954	6.1	—	2.2	2.3
1954 to 1955	9.3	5.7	0.7	—
1955 to 1956	8.1	2.9	2.2	—
1956 to 1957	12.4	4.8	4.1	—
1957 to 1958	16.9	3.4	4.4	—
1958 to 1959	4.3	1.4	2.3	—
1959 to 1960	0.6	0.3	2.0	—
1954 to 1960	51.7	20.0	16.1	12.4

[a] 1937 weights for the 1937–1950 comparison and 1950(1) weights for all the subsequent comparisons. For example, the 1937–1950 figure is arrived at by multiplying the change in the average specifications given in Table 3.6, by the 1937 weights given in Table 3.7 and adding them together (8.7 × 1.3 + 3.9 × 3.43 − 0.1 × 4.0 = 24.3).

[b] Weights from Table 3.4, i.e., the 1954–1955 comparison uses average 1954–1955 weights, and so on. The figure for 1954–1960 is the product of all the paired year comparisons.

[c] Weights from Table 3.4.

[d] 1950(2) weights for the 1937–1950 comparisons and 1960 weights for the 1950–1960 and 1954–1960 comparisons.

[e] Derived by adding 100 each to the first 2 rows, multiplying, and substracting 100.

point of view, the chain-link index with its frequently changing weights is probably the best single measure of quality change.

Before proceeding to "deflate" the CPI by our quality indexes we have to convince ourselves that it is legitimate to do so. Since our indexes were derived from list prices, we have first to compare the CPI to an unadjusted list price index for the same makes and models. Such a comparison is presented in the first two columns of Table 3.9. It is apparent that the list prices and the CPI moved fairly closely together until 1954. Since 1954 the CPI has risen much less than the list prices of comparable cars (or the comparable WPI index, see Table 3.5). It is not exactly clear how and

Hedonic Price Indexes for Automobiles

Table 3.9. The "Low Priced Three" (Sixes to the 1956 Model Year, V-8's Thereafter): Percentage Changes in Price—List Prices, the CPI, and the CPI Adjusted for Quality Change

Years	List Prices Unadjusted[a]	CPI Unadjusted[b]	CPI Adjusted for Quality Change Using[c]			
			Beginning Period Weights	Adjacent Year Weights	1954 through 1960 Weights	End Period Weights
1937–1950	116.0	101.3	61.2	64.1	—	69.2
1950–1960	58.5	31.3	−18.4	—	10.6	14.1
1937–1960	242.4	161.3	30.6	—	—	91.3
1950–1954	18.0	18.0	11.2	—	15.5	15.3
1954–1955	2.5	−1.7	−10.0	−8.0	−2.4	—
1955–1956	5.4	−0.9	−8.3	−3.7	−3.0	—
1956–1957	9.9	5.1	−6.5	0.3	1.0	—
1957–1958	6.7	4.2	−10.9	0.8	−0.2	—
1959–1960	0.2	0.1	−0.2	−0.2	−1.9	—
1954–1960	34.4	11.3	−26.6	−7.8	−4.1	−1.0

[a] Computed from Table 3.7.

[b] From BLS Bulletin No. 1256 and various CPI releases. For 1937 and 1950 as of March of the same year; for 1954 as of January 1954; for subsequent years as of November of the preceding year.

[c] Computed by dividing the figures in the second column by the appropriate entry from Table 8 (adding first 100 to each and subtracting 100 from the result).

why this happened, and the problem is explored in greater detail in the Appendix. In part this may be due to the BLS beginning to ask for discounts in 1954; in part to absolute or relative declines in transportation costs and the cost of various attachments which were not included in the list prices. Be this as it may, unless the recent divergence between list prices and the CPI index is somehow associated with one or the other of our quality dimensions, these indexes are still appropriate deflators for the CPI. They would be inappropriate if either relative discounting were associated with some of the quality dimensions, e.g., higher horsepower cars being discounted disproportionately, or if the CPI had, in collecting its prices, linked out the particular horsepower, weight, and length increases we have used in constructing the quality indexes. Since we have no reason to believe that either is true, deflation of the CPI by these indexes appears to be warranted.

The results of deflating the changes in the CPI by the appropriate entries from Table 3.8 are presented in Table 3.9. For the 1937–1950 period about a third of the price rise can be attributed to quality change no matter which set of weights we use.[20] In the 1950–1954 period the role of quality change appears to have been minor, unless we weight it by 1950 weights. All weights point to the conclusion that "real" automobile prices fell rather than rose during 1954–1960.[21] Using beginning period (1950) weights, the fall was around one-quarter. Using end period (1960) weights, the fall was very small, indicating roughly no change in "real" automobile prices. For the 1937–1960 period as a whole, quality change accounted for about one-third (using end period weights) to about three-fourths (using beginning period weights) of the recorded price change in the CPI. These results are quite tentative and subject to various limitations to be discussed below. Nevertheless, if we realize that we have only scratched the surface as far as quality adjustments are concerned, considering only a very limited and narrow class of "qualities," the conclusion is inescapable that the lack of adequate quality adjustments has resulted in a very serious upward bias in the official automobile price indexes.[22]

6. Additional Tests, Limitations, and Conclusions

A. *The Evidence of the Used Car Market*

One of the problems associated with the use of list prices in this study is the extent to which they may just represent pricing mistakes by manufacturers at some point in time. A manufacturer may overprice or underprice a particular innovation, and there is nothing in our method that would

---

20. Loosely speaking. Since the quality index is defined multiplicatively, there is no unique way of decomposing a given price change into additive "quality" and "pure" price change components. With 1937 = 100, the CPI stood at 201 in 1950, the beginning period weighted quality index at 124, and the "adjusted" CPI at 161. $1.25 \times 1.61 \approx 2.01$. The "role" of quality in change could be measured as

$$\frac{24}{101}, \quad \text{or} \quad \frac{101 - 61}{101} = \frac{40}{101}, \quad \text{or as} \quad \frac{\frac{1}{2}(24 + 40)}{101}.$$

The last procedure leads to the "one-third" statement in the text. On this problem see the note by Levine 1960.

21. If we had deflated the list price index instead of the CPI, we would have shown some price rise for the 1954–1960 period with all but the 1950 set of weights.

22. And in the CPI as a whole. Adjusting the overall CPI for quality change in only *one* commodity—automobiles (applying 1950 quality weights to the 1950–1960 changes in specifications and using the 1950 weight of automobiles in the index—3.7 percent) —results in a reduction of the index from 125.6 (in November 1959) to 123.7 (1947–1949 = 100). Over 7 percent of the increase in the CPI since 1947–1949 may be due just to the changing quality of one commodity.

Hedonic Price Indexes for Automobiles

catch it. Of course, if we had sales data broken down by makes, models, and attachments, an appropriate weighting of the original data would go a long way toward the solution of this problem. In the meantime, however, we may want to investigate the prices of these cars. The prices of used cars are not tied any more to the manufacturers' list prices and are set, presumably, more directly by the "market."

Since a used and a new car are not exactly the same commodity, we should not expect a perfect agreement between estimates of "quality prices" from these two different sets of data. In particular, as cars age, one might expect that some of the "qualities" depreciate much faster than others. Nevertheless, relatively "new" used cars should be reasonably good substitutes for new cars and their prices should reflect similar quality differentials.

Table 3.10 compares the results of using used prices instead of list prices for selected cross sections. For the 1960 models the used prices are for approximately 6-month-old cars. For the other cross sections they are for a little over one-year-old cars. As can be seen by comparing the coefficients of the "new" and "used" regressions respectively, the difference between the two are relatively minor and usually well within the range of their respective standard errors. Thus, the quality weights that could be derived from the regressions using the prices of 1-year-old cars are roughly similar to those that we obtain using new car (list)prices.[23]

B. *Reliability*

One of the advantages of the approach outlined above is the possibility of computing confidence intervals for the quality indexes or the quality adjusted price indexes. For each new combination of specifications we can compute not only its predicted price in some base period but also the "prediction interval," the probable range of the error of prediction based on the goodness of the fit of the equation and the distance of the new specifications from their mean values. Since this computation is somewhat laborious and since time was limited, no such calculations were actually performed.[24] Some insight, however, into the possible magnitude of such

---

23. There are some minor differences that foreshadow the results that would be found if we were to use prices of 3-, 4-, 5-, and 6-year-old cars in our analysis. The relative price of horsepower falls somewhat with age, while the coefficient of weight remains stable or rises somewhat. The discount on V-8's turns to a premium with age. The premium on "hardtops" rises. The "automatic transmission" premium depreciates very rapidly. In general the results for 5- and 6-year-old used cars look quite different from those reported here. They will be described elsewhere.

24. But they present no problem, in principle. See Mood 1950 and Chow 1960.

Table 3.10. A Comparison of Price-Quality Regression Coefficients of New and Used Cars[a]

Coefficients of	Model Year 1960		Model Year 1959		Model Year 1957		Model Year 1954			
	New	Used in 1960	New	Used in 1960	New	Used in 1958	New	Used in 1955	Used in 1956	Used in 1957
H	0.052 (0.009)	0.040 (0.011)	0.058 (0.011)	0.029 (0.015)	0.051 (0.013)	0.042 (0.015)	0.149 (0.038)	0.067 (0.038)	0.057 (0.038)	0.052 (0.050)
W	0.063 (0.009)	0.069 (0.011)	0.090 (0.013)	0.112 (0.017)	0.059 (0.017)	0.053 (0.020)	0.084 (0.032)	0.126 (0.032)	0.122 (0.032)	0.118 (0.042)
L	— —	— —	— —	— —	0.017 (0.006)	0.024 (0.007)	— —	— —	— —	— —
V	−0.017 (0.010)	−0.011 (0.021)	−0.035 (0.015)	−0.030 (0.020)	−0.011 (0.010)	−0.011 (0.012)	−0.022 (0.015)	0.024 (0.015)	0.035 (0.015)	0.049 (0.020)
T	0.026 (0.007)	0.039 (0.008)	0.011 (0.008)	0.028 (0.011)	0.012 (0.005)	0.047 (0.006)	— —	— —	— —	— —
A	— —	— —	— —	— —	0.050 (0.011)	0.026 (0.013)	— —	— —	— —	— —
P	0.102 (0.011)	0.094 (0.013)	0.104 (0.014)	0.077 (0.018)	0.034 (0.013)	0.001 (0.015)	0.037 (0.030)	0.091 (0.029)	0.123 (0.030)	0.145 (0.038)
B	— —	— —	— —	— —	0.069 (0.011)	0.095 (0.014)	— —	— —	— —	— —
R^2	0.950	0.919	0.934	0.872	0.966	0.948	0.828	0.854	0.854	0.793

[a] The results differ from those presented in Table 3.3 in two ways. First, they exclude variables which turned out to be insignificant in the particular years such as length or "automatic transmissions." Second, they are presented as computed, using logarithms to the base 10. To make them comparable to the results in Tables 3.3 and 3.4, all the coefficients and standard errors should be divided by 0.4343 ($\log_{10} e$).

The used prices in 1960 are taken from the July issue of *Used Car Guide*. For all other years they are taken from the February issues of the *Guide*.

Hedonic Price Indexes for Automobiles

an interval can be obtained by examining the standard error of regression (the standard deviation of the residuals from the equation). The average error of "prediction" for any *one* particular car is quite large. It varies from about 5 percent in 1957 to about 8 percent in 1950 for single year cross sections, from about 6 percent for the 1956–1957 combined regression to about 9 percent in the 1958–1959 regression, and is about 8 percent for the overall 1954 through 1960 regression. This figure is applicable if we want to predict the price of a particular make and model. We are interested, however, in predicting the *average* price for the three "low-priced" makes. In our case this is an average of eight models and the error of predicting an average goes down, approximately and under suitable conditions, as the square root of the number of items. Thus, the average residual for this group of cars as a whole is only about a third ($\sqrt{8} = 2.8$) of the individual errors quoted above. It would be even smaller if we had computed a weighted regression, since the three "low-priced" makes would probably account for about 60 percent of the weights.

C. *Shifting Supply Conditions and Tastes*

To the extent that shifting supply conditions or changing tastes change the relative "price" of a particular quality we are back to the classical index number problem of changing weights. Not much can be done about this in practice except to shorten the timespan of comparison, compute base and end period weighted indexes, and hope that they are not too far apart. In our case, the more striking examples of such changes are the rapid decline in the "price" of horsepower with the introduction of the V-8's and the fall in the "price" of length.

The CPI in switching to the pricing of V-8's in 1956 linked them to the previously priced six-cylinder engine cars without allowing the index to rise or fall as the result of this substitution, and we have followed suit in the calculation of our indexes. If we use contemporary weights (e.g., for 1955–1956) this is about right. Our estimates of the horsepower coefficients are based on a sample that includes V-8's and thus it is not surprising that the increase in horsepower weighted by its coefficient comes close to the difference in price.[25] For the "low-priced three," if we use the horsepower and weight difference between the sixes and the V-8's in 1956 and weight them with 1955–1956 quality prices, we predict that comparable V-8's should cost about 6 percent more. Actually, they were only 5.5 percent

---

25. A V-8 engine has usually 50 more horsepower units than a comparable "six" and costs about $100 more. Since our horsepower coefficient during this period is around 1 percent per 10 horsepower units, we would predict a 5 percent higher price. But 5 percent on a $2,000 car is $100.

more expensive. Using the 1959 horsepower differences between these cars and 1959–1960 weights we predict a 9-percent price differential against the observed 5 percent.[26] This agrees with our finding for the sample as a whole that the V-8's were about 3 or more percent cheaper than would be predicted from an extrapolation of the price-horsepower relationship for six-cylinder engine cars.

The introduction of the V-8's represented a decline of a few percentage points in the "real" price of cars that is not caught by the linking procedure. But this is only an "economies of scale" effect along a given relationship, and does not represent the total possible contribution of the V-8 engine. In fact, the appearance of the V-8 on the market in substantial quantities brought the whole level of horsepower "prices" down. Thus, if we were to value the V-8 at 1950 horsepower "prices," when there were only a few V-8 engine cars in the sample, we would estimate it to be a 15-percent "more car" (to have a 15-percent higher "quality" index) as against only a 5-percent increase in its price. The very fact of the rapid rise of the V-8 to market dominance would indicate that it was somewhat "underpriced" relative to the sixes. This is also supported by the used car price-quality regressions. In a large number of cases, the negative coefficient (discount) of the V-8 variable observed for new car prices turns into a positive coefficient (premium) once these cars get to the used car market.

Another problem is created by our use of proxy variables, of dimensions that may not be desirable per se, but which are correlated with other, more difficult to measure, but basically more desired dimensions. Weight, for example, is unlikely to be desired very much for its own sake. Rather, it is a proxy for "size." The relationship between price and weight may involve, however, other things besides "size," and the relationship between weight and the underlying desired characteristics may change over time. Our weight coefficients are derived on the basis of the difference in price between the cheap and the expensive cars, but the "large" cars may be expensive for reasons other than just "size." We have tried to control this by introducing a variety of dummy variables such as power steering and

---

26. This brings out an additional problem associated with the linking procedure. The additional cost of a V-8 engine has remained approximately constant at $100 while the absolute price of cars increased. Thus a price index based on six-cylinder engine cars would rise somewhat faster than the V-8 based index. The inclusion of attachments in the pricing procedure may lead to an underestimate of the price rise of the attachmentless car if, as appears to have happened recently, attachment prices do not rise as much as the price of the "basic" unit or at all. To the extent that a substantial fraction of cars is bought without them, this could bias the index.

Hedonic Price Indexes for Automobiles

automatic transmissions which are standard equipment on the more expensive cars.[27] This prevents these cars from exerting an undue influence on the price-weight relationship for the sample as a whole. Alternatively, we could have computed separate estimates for different groups of cars; for example, the "low," "medium," and "high" priced cars. Still another approach would have been to estimate "comparable" prices for different models by subtracting from the more expensive cars the estimated "value" of most of the attachments and features not available on the lower priced cars. Since many of these are listed as "extras" for other cars, one could probably go some distance in "standardizing" prices.

The basic method would of course be seriously compromised if the relationship between any one of the measured dimensions and the more basic "real" qualities were to change from one period to the next. For example, suppose all cars were, after a given date, made of an aluminum alloy which halved their weight, but absolute and relative prices did not change. This change in weight would increase the apparent price of weight and reduce its level per car while in fact nothing may have happened except for a change in units of measurement. If we did not know what had happened, we would have mistaken this weight change for a quality change. But in practice this should not present an insuperable problem. We usually know enough about what is happening in a particular market and to a particular product to be able to make some adjustments for it. More important, such changes are unlikely to be sudden and all inclusive. Aluminum cars will probably sell for several years together with more "old-fashioned" cars, and we shall be able, by the use of dummy variables or other techniques, to detect the difference between these cars and build it into our equations.[28]

D. *Suggestions for Further Research and Conclusions*

It is obvious that our investigation is only illustrative of a promising line of attack on the quality change problem. There are more than just a half-dozen dimensions to an automobile and they may not interact in any

---

27. This is one reason why these estimated coefficients should not be used directly in estimating the "value" of a particular attachment. We know that power steering and brakes come to about $130, which is far from the 20 percent or so increase in price indicated by their coefficients. The main purpose of these variables is not to estimate the price of these attachments, which we know, but to reduce the possible bias in our slope estimates for the numerical qualities by allowing different groups of cars to differ in the position or intercept of these slopes.

28. The next few years will provide a good test of this assertion. One of the 1961 model year cars is already using an aluminum block engine.

simple linear fashion.[29] Further work along these lines would include the introduction and testing of a number of additional "qualities"; an examination of the residuals from the various non-linearities; use of weighted regressions, where different cars would be weighted according to their importance in the market; division of the sample into separate subgroups to test hypotheses about the linearity of the various price-quality relationships; use of actual transaction prices instead of list prices in the analysis; and the extension of this type of analysis to a variety of other commodities such as trucks, refrigerators, and cameras.[30]

Continuous studies of the present type by the price collecting agencies should prove of great value. First, they would eventually perfect the method enough so that it could be used routinely in the computation of the official indexes. Second, they would provide them with much more information on the various dimensions of a commodity, allow the use of a more sophisticated linking procedure, and isolate the qualities or dimensions which appear to be most important. Third, the availability of such information is also likely to lead to a more useful specification of commodities for price collection purposes. And finally, such studies, if done for a wide enough range of commodities, could provide an estimate of the probable upward drift of the price indexes due to their inability to control adequately for many of the constantly occurring quality changes.

Appendix to Chapter 3
The Official Automobile Price Indexes

There are three official automobile price indexes: The "new automobiles" component of the CPI, the "passenger cars" component of the WPI, and the automobile component of the Prices Paid Index of the U.S. Department of Agriculture. The CPI new automobile price index is a retail price index for Chevrolet, Ford, and Plymouth sedans with V-8 engines (sixes before 1956 except Ford), automatic transmissions (since 1956), and other

---

29. For evidence on how complicated a machine an automobile really is and for the many changes that actually occurred in it since the 1930's, see the history of the Plymouth and its specifications summarized in *Administered Prices*, pp. 3655–3665 and 3734–3749.

30. A study of wheel tractor prices along these same lines is in progress.

Hedonic Price Indexes for Automobiles

minor items such as extra trim, radio and heater, gasoline and antifreeze. The WPI is a wholesale (manufacturer to dealer) index of car prices, presumably covering all or most makes and models weighted by some base period production. The Agricultural Marketing Service index, which is not published separately, is based on a mail survey of prices paid by farmers for six-cylinder Chevrolets, Fords, and Plymouths, and for V-8 Chevrolets, Fords, Plymouths, and Buicks. Average prices paid for six-cylinder cars and for V-8's are published separately each quarter in *Agricultural Prices*. Again, it is not clear how the different makes and models are weighted, and what weights are used in aggregating state data into national averages.

Of the three indexes, the AMS stands alone in not specifying exactly what attachments are included in the model being priced. The CPI explicitly deals with the items that are being priced with the car and adjusts for changes in "extras." The WPI presumably prices the "standard equipment" car and adjusts for major changes in what is being considered as standard. The AMS, however, has collected prices paid by farmers for specified models and makes "together with the usual equipment bought by farmers." It has tried to control for some aspects of size by comparing similar "price lines" of each make in different years, and has priced V-8's and sixes separately, but its failure to specify other attachments allows the index to drift upward as the result of farmers shifting to the purchase of more heavily equipped cars, cars that include radios and heaters, automatic transmissions, power steering and brakes, and other extras. That this drift is serious is indicated by the fact that the difference between the average six- and eight-cylinder car priced by the AMS which stood at $200 in 1947–1949 increased to $660 by November 1959. Since the price of V-8's and Buicks probably did not increase as much, percentage-wise, as the price of the "low-priced-three" sixes, most of this increase must be due to the increasing number of attachments bought with the more expensive cars.

Percentage changes in these indexes are tabulated in Table 3A.1. for selected periods and are compared to changes in a list price index of the "low-priced-three" makes. Note that in almost all of the comparisons, the AMS prices rise more than all the other indexes, including the list price one. This is another indication of the upward drift in the AMS index as the result of its relatively loose specification policy. Looking at the other indexes, we note that the movements to 1954 are roughly similar, with the WPI rising somewhat less than the CPI and the list price index. The main divergence between these indexes comes in the 1954–1958 model year

Zvi Griliches

Table 3A.1. A Comparison of Official Indexes and List Prices for U.S. Cars: Percentage Change, Selected Periods

				List Prices	
Period	WPI[a]	CPI[b]	AMS[c]	Unadjusted[d]	Adjusted for Minor Equipment Changes[e]
1937–1950	83.0	101.0	129.0	116.0	—
1947–1949 to January 1954	20.6	29.7	32.7	18.0[f]	16.9
January 1954 to November 1954	2.7	−1.7	2.2[g]	2.5	—
November 1954 to November 1955	4.1	−0.9	3.8[h]	5.4	—
November 1955 to November 1956	5.7	5.1	5.4	9.9	—
November 1956 to November 1957	0.6	4.2	5.4	6.7	—
November 1957 to November 1958	5.1	4.2	11.8	6.0	—
November 1958 to November 1959	0.1	0.1	3.0	2.0	—
January 1954 to November 1959	19.7	11.3	33.6	34.4	—
1947–1949 to November 1959 (1960 models)	44.3	44.3	68.4	58.6[f]	—
January 1954 to November 1957	13.8	6.7	29.8	26.7	21.6

[a] See Table 3.6.
[b] See Table 3.7.
[c] Sixes before November 1955, V-8's thereafter; the V-8's include Buick Special in addition to the "low-priced three." From various issues of *Agricultural Prices*. The 1937–1950 comparison is based on an unpublished index used to deflate farmers' expenditures on automobiles.
[d] From Table 3.7: The "low-priced three." The model year is assumed to start in November of the previous calendar year.
[e] Adjusting list prices for differences in minor equipment items included in the price, such as directional signals and electric clocks, based on data from *Administered Prices*, pp. 3548–3549, 3622–3626, and 3730–3733. Also, including automatic transmissions in the list prices as of 1956.
[f] Beginning with 1950 models.
[g] January 1954 to January 1955.
[h] January 1955 to November 1955.

period, with the CPI rising substantially less than either the WPI or list prices. It is not too surprising that the WPI rose less than the list price index for the lower priced makes. About half of its weight is given to medium and higher priced cars which have risen less percentagewise than

Hedonic Price Indexes for Automobiles

the lower priced makes.[31] The sharp divergence between the CPI and list prices during 1954–1958 is, however, surprising and requires explanation.

A reconciliation of the two series is seriously hampered by the lack of a detailed description of how the CPI is actually computed. There is no published information on whether the index is a ratio of the average price for these makes or an average of their price relatives; what weights, if any, are used in averaging the price data for different makes and models; which models of a given make are being priced in a particular year and to what models they are being compared in the previous year; and what quality changes were "linked-in" or "out," and when and how.[32] The list price index was constructed in such a way as to approximate the CPI closely.[33] It differs from the CPI in that it does not adjust for changes in minor equipment items, it does not include transportation costs, state and local taxes, and minor accessories sold with the car, and it does not allow for changes in the discount from list prices.

It is possible to adjust the list prices for some of the minor equipment changes using more detailed price data presented in the Kefauver Hearings (*Administered Prices*). This will reduce the rise in list prices somewhat (see the last column of Table 3.10), but it still leaves a very substantial difference between the CPI and list prices (or the WPI) unexplained. Some of this difference could be due to the inclusion in the CPI of various "trim" items, transportation costs, and taxes, which may have remained constant or risen less than the price of the "basic" (stripped) car. Still it could not explain it all—the actual difference is too large for that.

Another source of this difference could lie in the fact that the CPI started in 1954 to collect data on discounts offered by retailers. But even this is unlikely to explain much of the difference between the two series. Assume that before 1954 the CPI did not include discounts, that it does so since 1954, and that no linking was done to account for this. We know that list prices went up by about a third during 1954–1960, that the spread

---

31. Between 1954 and 1958 the prices of Buicks, Pontiacs, Mercurys, and Dodges advanced relatively less (about 15 percent) than the prices of Chevrolets, Fords, and Plymouths (which rose 23 percent). Compare also with Table 3.5.

32. Many of these problems could have been settled by a consultation with BLS personnel and an examination of their records. Unfortunately, previous commitments, deadlines, and distance prevented this from being accomplished in time.

33. It differs from the CPI in that before 1956 it prices only six-cylinder engine cars (except in 1937) whereas the CPI priced eight-cylinder Fords throughout, and it does not include automatic transmissions in its price, which the CPI has done since 1956.

between the price to the dealer and the list price remained at approximately the same percentage level (24 percent) throughout the period, and that during the same period the CPI rose only 11 percent. Consider the following arithmetic example: A representative car cost $1,350 wholesale in 1954, listed for $1,800 at retail, with the dealer's margin being $450. No discount was given in 1954. The same type of car lists for $2,400 in 1960 (a rise of 33 percent) and costs the dealer $1,800. If the actual retail price had risen only 11 percent, to $1,998, the dealer's return would have dropped from $450 to $198 per car, or from a 25 to an 8 percent margin. This seems to be too big a drop in the return to dealers in a period of rising prices to be plausible.

An additional explanation for this divergence has been suggested by John M. Blair, who was also puzzled by it (*Administered Prices*, pp. 4000–4002). He has argued that since the BLS agent first asks for the list price and then separately for the magnitude of the discount, the difference between the two may not equal the actual price charged. It is said to have been common practice during 1955–1958 for dealers to "pack the price," i.e., to quote a discount that was not calculated from the list price but from some higher figure. Subtracting this "unrealistic" discount figure from the list price would lead to a downward bias in the estimated price actually paid by consumers. But this should be a transitory phenomenon. Once eliminated, as it apparently has been in the most recent years, it should have led to a comparably higher rise in the CPI. This has not happened.

The final possibility is that the CPI has been much more thorough in its quality adjustments than is reflected in the published literature. That is, it could have been argued in some year, for example, that "this year's cheapest Ford model is equivalent in size, trim, and horsepower to last year's medium-priced Ford." The only detailed description of automobile price in the CPI suggests this possibility by saying:

> ... the automobile retail price indexes have been designed to measure solely the trend of prices paid by city workers for automobiles of as nearly fixed quality as possible ... Therefore, prices are collected for automobiles which are regarded as most nearly equivalent to the cars priced in the preceding year. [Mack 1955]

But then the next sentence reduces the probability of this by stating:

> Equivalent quality of new cars has been assured to a great extent by specifying as a basis of pricing the same make and body style, the *same or equivalent price series*, and the same number of cylinders as the car which was priced in the preceding year. [Emphasis supplied.]

Hedonic Price Indexes for Automobiles

Thus, it appears quite unlikely that the CPI has linked out the type of horsepower, weight, and length changes used in constructing our quality indexes. If this is true, then it is quite probable that, for some unknown reason, the CPI underestimated the rise in new car prices (given its own definition) between 1954 and 1958.[34]

---

34. See Triplett, 1970b, for further discussion of this point. Much of the difference *was* apparently due to the use of discounted prices by the CPI without any linking out of the shift from list to transaction prices. (Note added in 1971).

4.

Phoebus J. Dhrymes
Price and Quality Changes in Consumer Capital Goods: An Empirical Study

1. Introduction

This paper reports on the findings of an investigation designed to determine whether it is feasible to correct, routinely, for quality in the price of certain consumer capital goods by the methods suggested by Court (1939) and more recently by Griliches (1961) and Fisher, Griliches, and Kaysen (1962).

If it is feasible to do so, then we can easily construct price indices "corrected for quality change" and in this fashion provide a clearer indication of the true character of price movements. Price indices uncorrected for "quality" changes may seriously under- or overstate the extent of price movement. Of course, we should declare at the outset that by "quality" we shall mean the set of identifiable characteristics exhibited by a given product. In this study we are dealing with automobiles and refrigerators. "Quality" in the case of the former means, for example, the weight, length, brake horsepower, and so forth, exhibited by a given model. In the case of the latter it means the height, weight, depth, freezer compartment capacity, and so on, of the given refrigerator. Although it would be desirable, it is still not possible, due to lack of data, to include in the measurement of quality the durability or frequency of repair record or economy of operation of an automobile or a refrigerator.

The author wishes to express his thanks to the editor of this volume and his readers for several helpful suggestions. He also wishes to acknowledge the very able research assistance of Mr. Fu-chen Lo, who carried out all computations.

Phoebus J. Dhrymes is Professor of Economics, Wharton School of Finance and Commerce, University of Pennsylvania.

Price and Quality Changes

Studies of this type are not new, as we have remarked above. What will particularly engage us is the examination of the question of homogeneity in the price behavior of various manufacturers. This is a problem of some consequence in the automobile industry, where well over 90 percent of total car sales is accounted for by the output of three manufacturers. If the price decision-making processes of any two manufacturers are appreciably different, then it is clear that in attempting to "correct for quality" one must pay due attention to the division of the market by such manufacturers. Moreover, it would be inadmissible, under such circumstances, to estimate the pricing equation from a single cross section in which several manufacturers are represented. Rather, we should estimate each manufacturer's decision rule separately. This is a problem that, unfortunately, has received little attention in the current literature.

2. The Samples

The automobile sample is, in principle, an exhaustive one for a certain subuniverse of models. The data were obtained from *Ward's Automotive Reports* or *Automotive Industries*.[1] In selecting models for inclusion the following criteria were employed:

a. Exclude sports cars, hardtops, convertibles, and station wagons.
b. Include all 2- and 4-door models except deluxe versions of a given model not differing from the basic version in cylinders, weight, length, piston displacement, or horsepower.

Notice that the criterion in (b) refers to *standard equipment*. Whenever data ambiguities arose, the relevant manufacturer was contacted. The samples cover six years: 1953, 1957, 1961, 1962, 1963, and 1964. Two of the manufacturers provided corrections over the entire period, while one provided corrections for only one year.

The refrigerator sample was mainly obtained from *1966 Home Appliance Blue Book* and various issues of *Mart* magazine. By and large we used the entire set available from such publications. Some manufacturers were underrepresented, or only incomplete information was available for their products. In such cases they were contacted directly and some information was solicited. Most responded. This sample covers the period 1950–1965.

---

1. The sample was collected in the first instance by I. Kravis and R. Lipsey; I am indebted to them for making it available to me.

In the automobile sample we deal with 912 models (observations).[2] In the refrigerator sample we deal with 632 models (observations) of which Frigidaire accounts for 132, GE for 144, Hotpoint for 54, Kelvinator for 80, Philco and RCA 38 each, and Westinghouse for 52. Other manufacturers represented are Admiral (9), Amana (4), Gibson (8), and others.

It is useful at this juncture to examine briefly the evolution of the automobile and refrigerator characteristics that are dealt with in this paper. (Appendix A to this chapter presents the data in Tables A.1–A.33. It also lists all the symbols and variables used.)

In considering the tables of mean characteristics (Tables A.1 through A.6),[3] one must bear in mind that these represent *unweighted* means, because the basic sample observations consist of the models produced by the various manufacturers. No attempt has been made to weight observations, say, by the relevant volume of sales.

Looking at Tables A.1, A.2, and A.3, we see that the average price of sample models for Manufacturer 1 has increased only slightly between 1953 and 1964. For Manufacturer 2 the average price has remained fairly constant between 1961 and 1964, while for Manufacturer 3 the mean price has actually *declined* between 1953 and 1964, as indeed was the case for most of this period. We should caution the reader that this does not necessarily mean that, say, the price of a Cadillac or a Lincoln Continental or an Imperial has remained constant or declined over the 11-year period. Rather it could, and does, mean that relatively more models are being produced which are intermediate in size and/or fall in the intermediate and lower price category. In this connection it is noteworthy that the average weight and length of models have *declined for all manufacturers* over the sample period.

Although past studies have consistently interpreted increased weight and length as indicating higher "quality," it is of course not clear that this is so in the usual sense of the term. Thus, improvements in metallurgy could render cars of otherwise comparable attributes lighter; this could rightly be considered an improvement in the quality of the product, since a heavy automobile simply consumes more gasoline and beyond a certain point offers no additional benefits in terms of freedom from vibration and other discomforts.

On the other hand, displacement and especially horsepower have appreciably increased over the sample period. This is in general true of

---

2. Since some data were provided by automobile manufacturers on a confidential basis, we shall not identify manufacturers by name.

3. Unless otherwise indicated, all tables whose number is prefixed by A will appear in Appendix A.

Price and Quality Changes

all manufacturers. The proportion of 8-cylinder models has increased appreciably over the sample period as well, while the proportion of 4-door models and models having automatic transmission as standard equipment has slightly declined.

What does all this mean in terms of the evolution of the "quality" of the average model? Of course the first issue is, what does one mean by "quality"? In this study, as in previous investigations of this type, one means the weight, length, displacement, and other identifiable characteristics as exhibited in the list of variables in Appendix A. Each such variable carries a positive weight in determining quality. Thus, for example, an increase in weight or length indicates an increase in quality, while a decrease in these two characteristics (or any one of them) would indicate a reduction in quality. In terms of this definition of quality, the historical experience of the decade presents for all three manufacturers a rather mixed record, although, in the ordinary usage, it is doubtful whether one would accept the proposition that a larger and heavier car is necessarily one of improved quality.

But in this context it is clear that the apparent stability of average model prices will not allow us to assert that the price of automobiles has been relatively stable, because the tables strongly suggest that the average model produced in 1953 is appreciably different from that produced in 1964.

These rough generalizations become entirely transparent when we look at Table A.4, which gives the mean characteristics for the entire sample. We see that the average price has declined by $40.00 between 1953 and 1964. This decline, however, has not been steady. The average price, in fact, rose appreciably above the 1953 level in 1957 and 1963. On the other hand, when one recalls that the consumer price index has increased by 16 percent over the sample period, we see that even without taking into account quality changes, automobile prices have declined in some "real" (relative) sense, beyond the magnitude indicated by the table.

The average weight has declined by 400 pounds and the average length by about 5 inches. Displacement has increased by about 19 cubic inches or roughly 7 percent over the 1953 level. Brake horsepower, on the other hand, has undergone a phenomenal increase—from 137.4 in 1953 to 204.9 in 1964. In the case of both displacement and horsepower, the peak was reached in 1957, before the American automobile industry responded to the inroads of European manufacturers in the domestic market. The bulk of the horsepower increase took place between 1953 and 1957, and is of course a symptom of the great horsepower (technical) revolution of the early and middle fifties. The nature of this technical revolution is easily perceived in the relation between displacement and brake horsepower as indicated in the table.

The fraction accounted for by 4-door models has slightly declined over the period, while the fraction of 8-cylinder models has increased noticeably. Finally, the fraction of models equipped with automatic transmission as standard equipment has markedly declined, while that with power steering has declined in recent years.

Turning now to refrigerators (Tables A.5 and A.6), it should be noted that since the number of manufacturers is relatively large, at least relative to the number of automobile manufacturers, it is not useful to give a summary of mean characteristics by manufacturer for each year, because the mean will be based on a rather small number of models. Instead, in Table A.5 we give a summary, by year, covering all manufacturers, while in Table A.6 we give a summary for the larger manufacturers covering *all* the years of our sample. Obviously the tables convey different types of information. Thus, Table A.5 gives some information on the evolution of the average refrigerator model over the years; Table A.6, on the other hand, may serve to give an indication of the extent to which manufacturers have tended to specialize in different types of products.

From Table A.5 we see that average refrigerator price has increased substantially over the sample period, although the rather irregular behavior of the series might suggest that part of this phenomenon might be related to the differing model composition of our sample from year to year.

By and large we see that over the period 1950–1964 the average refrigerator has become larger (from 8 to 14 cubic feet in capacity); its freezing compartment capacity has increased from 0.8 to 3.8 cubic feet; its height has increased by about 5 inches; and its width about 1 inch. These dimensional changes are not sufficient to account for the capacity increase remarked on above; they indicate, of course, substantial improvement in the technology of refrigerator manufacturing, especially as it pertains to the thickness of the "walls" needed to insure proper insulation of the unit. I suppose one would regard an increase in capacity as an improvement in the quality of the product; given this, however, one would think that an increase in the width or depth of the model would not be so considered. However, viewing the dimensional and capacity measures together, the tables strongly suggest that, in this aspect at least, there has been a considerable improvement in the quality of the average model over our sample period. Thus, it is an interesting question to ask: To what extent do "quality" improvements account for the price increases noted earlier?

Price and Quality Changes

3. Empirical Findings

A. *Generalities*

The attempt to relate the price of a commodity to its various identifiable characteristics is of great potential significance for the construction of "quality corrected" price indices. Such problems have been dealt with by Court (1939), Griliches (1961), Fisher, Griliches, and Kaysen (1962), and more recently by Lancaster (1966) in a somewhat different context. The approach of Court, Griliches, and Fisher, Griliches, and Kaysen has been entirely empirical; it was their objective to obtain estimators of the coefficients in a (typically linear or log linear) function connecting the (list) price of automobiles and various identifiable characteristics. In such an investigation, however, particularly with reference to automobiles, two questions are of great importance. If we seek to establish a relation between list price and identifiable characteristics, is this to be interpreted as representing the consumers' evaluation of the features displayed by the commodity, as a cost plus markup equation, or perhaps as something else?

The second and related question is whether this function is the same for all manufacturers. If not, it would appear that we ought to take into account the market shares of various manufacturers in constructing "quality corrected" price indices. In addition, if we regard the established function as a cost plus markup relation, then the estimated coefficients reflect the manufacturers' evaluation of each characteristic *as well as their pricing policies; they do not necessarily indicate a market evaluation of "quality" contributions made by the enumerated physically identifiable characteristics.* Thus, unless we conclude that all manufacturers' pricing functions are statistically indistinguishable and unless we can interpret their coefficients as representing consumer (market) evaluations of the quality content of the identifiable characteristics, we cannot, strictly speaking, construct "quality corrected" price indices routinely in the manner suggested by Court (1939) and Griliches (1961).

A subsidiary issue to the above is the following: What mathematical form best describes such pricing equations? This is a problem not specifically related to the current investigation, in that it is one that occurs in all empirical work in which the model under consideration is not sharply specified by some well-grounded theoretical construct.

Here, we shall consider three possible alternatives: the linear, semilog, and double log forms, and shall examine the empirical findings for automobiles and refrigerators in the context of the questions just raised.

Finally, we shall, as an exercise, obtain the implications of the scheme presented above by decomposing actual price changes over the sample period for automobiles and refrigerators into a "quality effect" and a "pure price effect"; the former will measure the increase in the mean price of sample models *due solely* to changes in the mean sample characteristics between the two years in question; the latter, conceptually, would measure the component that is *solely* due to a change in price not "compensated" by a change in quality. Of course the two components will sum up to the *actual price change* between the two years in question and thus, given the "quality effect," we can always derive the "pure price effect" *residually* and vice versa.

B. *Automobiles*

At the risk of some repetition, let us note that our automobile sample consists of six cross sections, one each for the years 1953, 1957, 1961, 1962, 1963, and 1964. The basic observations consist of the *standard* models produced by each of the three major manufacturers; for reasons of confidentiality we shall term them Manufacturers 1, 2, and 3. Thus, essentially, for each year (except 1953 and 1957 in which we have no information on one manufacturer) we have *three subsamples*—one for each manufacturer. This affords us an opportunity to test the hypothesis of homogeneity in the pricing functions of the three manufacturers. It should be noted that the earlier studies of Court, Griliches, and Fisher, Griliches, and Kaysen did not consider this aspect of the problem, presumably because they did not have the requisite data. The statistical tools needed for this aspect of our investigation are developed in Appendix B.[4]

In Tables A.7, A.8, and A.9 we give the coefficients of the linear, semilog, and double log regressions for Manufacturer 1; in Tables A.10, A.11, and A.12, similar information for Manufacturer 2; and in Tables A.13, A.14, and A.15, for Manufacturer 3. From all these tables it is apparent that generally the semilog and double log forms perform somewhat better than the linear form, insofar as our criterion is the comparison between the coefficients of determination of the linear form and the antilog $R^2(R^{*2})$ of the semilog and double log forms. The two measures of fit differ generally in their second decimal, although for the years 1963 and 1964 there is really very little difference, and thus there exists only a tenuous basis of discriminating among the three forms insofar as Manufacturers 2 and 3 are concerned. Indeed, for Manufacturer 2 there is little basis for

---

4. It may be convenient for the reader to take a look at this appendix before proceeding to the discussion following. The motivation of the procedure and the notation would thus become much clearer.

Price and Quality Changes

differentiating among the three forms for the entire sample at our disposal (1961 through 1964).

Comparing the semi- and double log forms for all three manufacturers, we find that generally there is little basis for discriminating on the basis of their coefficients of determination, although numerically the semilog form yields slightly higher statistics.

Since the difference between the two R^2 is the difference in the residual variances from the two forms (in reverse order) scaled by the sample variance of the dependent variable, which is common to both cases, this statistic is only slightly different from the one required by Cox's test (1961, 1962). But the magnitude of such differences is seen from the tables to be so slight that it would be rather superfluous to employ a formal test of discrimination. Since previous investigators in this field have chosen to use the semilog form, we shall follow the same practice in our subsequent analysis; however, this has mainly tradition to recommend it.

Although the usefulness of Tables A.7 through A.15 is essentially exhausted by the remarks above, we shall point out here two aspects which are pertinent to the proper reading of these and subsequent tables. First, for purposes of computational convenience the units of the several variables have been chosen as follows: Price is stated in 10^2 dollars, weight in 10^2 pounds, length in 10 inches, displacement in cubic inches, brake horsepower at 3800 revolutions per minute. Of course the variables C, DOR, ATR, PS are dummy variables assuming the value 1 if the given model is equipped respectively with 8 cylinders, 4 doors, automatic transmission, and power steering, and zero otherwise.

Thus, if one wishes to convert the coefficients of a regression equation to numbers corresponding to the "natural" units of these variables as stated in Tables A.1–A.4, then one ought to make the appropriate corrections. The numbers in parentheses are always t-ratios, and these are, of course, independent of the units in which the variables are measured. A second observation is that the variables weight, length, displacement, and brake horsepower are highly collinear in our samples. This explains why the variable displacement is omitted from the regressions presented in Tables A.7 through A.15. Suppressing one variable in order to mitigate the consequences of collinearity is, of course, an unsatisfactory way of coping with the problem and we shall correct this below.

We should also note that we do not always report a coefficient for PS (power steering). This is so because the sample *did not always contain models which were equipped with* PS *but not with automatic transmission.* This is especially relevant for Manufacturers 2 and 3, where every model equipped with *PS* was *also equipped* with *ATR*. The converse, however, was not always true. Thus, there is an ambiguity in interpreting the coefficient of *ATR*. A reasonable, but not entirely accurate, interpretation of it would be to regard it as an estimator of the *sum* of the true coefficients of *PS* and *ATR*.

Thus, to summarize this segment, on the basis of the results just discussed, it was determined that:

a. The semilog form is to be chosen over the linear and double log forms, and
b. In view of the serious collinearity of the weight, length, displacement, and brake horsepower variables, a subset of their principal components should be used as explanatory variables.

In connection with (b) it should be remarked that this collinearity probably does not solely arise from a fairly exact (technical) relation amongst these variables (for a *given* model). Remembering that, for example, the semilog and double log forms do almost equally well in "explaining" (the log of) price, we can infer that *different* models (observations) do not differ very much in the identifiable physical characteristics noted above, so that our sample gives information about a relatively small subset of the (hypothetical) price surface. Hence, if we interpret the semilog and double log forms as approximations to the "true" but "very complicated" price surface, it is to be expected that over a small region a linear and loglinear form will be about equally good approximations.

The fact that the data are rather clustered is easily borne out by examining the coefficients of variation of the explanatory variables for the various manufacturers. In the interest of brevity such statistics are omitted. Thus, the results obtained so far might well be rather sensitive to the sample with which we are working. On the other hand, our sample in principle covers almost the universe of standard models so that it is difficult to see how one can overcome the problems mentioned above by further sampling. The use of principal components to overcome this difficulty does, perhaps, require some explanation. A consequence of multicollinearity is that it is impossible to identify the coefficients of individual variables with much precision. Omitting a variable or two is clearly an unsatisfactory way of approaching the problem.

Multicollinearity indicates that the "independent information" conveyed by the sample is not accurately indexed by the *number of variables*

Price and Quality Changes

at our disposal. The implication is that we can express substantially the same information in *fewer dimensions*. This can be given a more precise interpretation. We recall that in ordinary regression analysis what we try to do is to account for the variations of the dependent variable in terms of variations in the independent (or explanatory) ones. Now, suppose that we can form a few linear combinations of the explanatory variables which exhaust (or nearly so) the variability of the latter. Then we have accounted for the movement of the explanatory variables and, hopefully, have reduced the dimensionality of the problem by using a smaller number of linear combinations than there are explanatory variables. This certainly would be desirable. It is the case that principal components are linear combinations of the explanatory variables; these linear combinations are mutually uncorrelated, and they are so constructed that the sum of their variances is equal to the sum of the variances of the original variables. The interested reader may find a good exposition of certain aspects of principal component theory in Kendall (1957).

Pursuant to conclusion (b) above, our first step was to obtain for each manufacturer, for each year, the principal components of the variables weight, (W) length (L), displacement (DIS), and brake horsepower (BHP). Since, in general, principal components are sensitive to the units of measurement, we have used *standardized deviates* of the variables. Thus, principal components were in fact obtained from the *correlation matrix* of the four variables and *not* from their *covariance matrix*. This, of course, standardizes the units in which the variables are measured.

In Tables A.16, A.17, A.18, and A.19 we give respectively the characteristic roots and vectors defining the principal components of weight, length, displacement, and brake horsepower for Manufacturers 1, 2, and 3, and for the total sample over the years 1953, 1957, 1961, 1962, 1963, and 1964.

Certain interesting results emerge from these tables. In nearly all cases the two largest roots account for over 97 percent of the sum of the four roots. This would imply that the first two components account for nearly all the variation in these four characteristics. The "independent information" content of the four variables is individually rather small.

Further, it is apparent that computational inaccuracies involved in obtaining the last two principal components are likely to be rather considerable, because the last two roots are small and thus their associated characteristic vectors could be wildly unreliable. Typically the smallest root is only one-hundredth of the largest.

Thus, we can define only two principal components with confidence, and for this reason we employ, in subsequent regressions, the first two *principal components* as explanatory variables.[5] In this connection, it is rather remarkable that for all manufacturers and for all years the first principal component accounts from about 83 percent to 89 percent of the variation in the four variables, so that the contribution of the second component is somewhat marginal.

Finally, there does not appear to be sufficient pattern similarity in the characteristic vectors over the years or across manufacturers to suggest convincingly a factor analytic interpretation of the results exhibited in the tables. For a given year corresponding characteristic vectors for Manufacturers 2 and 3 appear to be somewhat similar; on the other hand, those of Manufacturer 1 are rather appreciably different. Of course, it is not entirely clear what one is to understand, statistically, by significant differences in the characteristic vectors of correlation matrices.

That a factor analytic interpretation of the results is a somewhat strained exercise is suggested by Table A.19, in which the relevant vectors are defined on the basis of the pooled sample, year by year. While from 1953 and 1957 it would appear that the first two components weight heaviest the variables weight (W) and length (L), this is not so for 1961 through 1964 in which the weight attached to L is considerably diminished. The second component weights most heavily length and attaches a *negative* weight to DIS and BHP. But the orders of magnitude of these two weights are so small as to leave some doubt whether the two components weight DIS and BHP differently.

Thus, our principal components transformations are best regarded as a statistical means of reducing the dimensionality of the data and reducing the incidence of collinearity.

The regressions using the first two principal components (denoted by Z_1 and Z_2) of weight, length, displacement, and brake horsepower are given in Tables A.20, A.21, A.22 for Manufacturers 1, 2, 3 respectively, and are based on the semilog form. The statistic R^{*2} (antilog R^2) has no significance in this context and is presented only as an indication of how well the regression "explains" price.

Consider first, for each year, the first column of Table A.20. We observe that both components have "significant" coefficients and that invariably

---

5. While using only these two components appears to be a highly efficient way of coping with the problem of multicollinearity, it must not be thought that the problem is thereby "solved," i.e., that we can now identify the coefficients of all the individual variables. Obviously, only a noncollinear sample can accomplish this. Our procedure merely ensures that in using the information conveyed by all four variables we discard as little as possible while at the same time closely approximating identification of individual coefficients.

Price and Quality Changes

such coefficients are positive. The size of these coefficients, however, does not appear to remain constant over time, or, for that matter, to change in any systematic way.

The dummy variables C and DOR are, by and large, insignificant except for 1961. DOR is also significant for 1964. The interpretation of this result is essentially that when all other variables are accounted for, the effect on price of having 6 cylinders is not appreciably different from that of having 8 cylinders, and the effects of having 2 or 4 doors are indistinguishable.

On the other hand, ATR and PS are nearly always significant. A comparison with Table A.8 shows that with the exception of 1953 the R^{*2} statistics of the two types of regression are only slightly different, so that little explanatory power is lost by dropping the last two principal components.

Considering Table A.21, we notice several differences between Manufacturer 2 and Manufacturer 1. In the case of the former the second principal component is "insignificant" for 1963 and 1964, while C is never significant, and DOR is significant only for 1962 and 1963. As for Manufacturer 1, for Manufacturer 2 ATR is always significant.

Finally, comparing R^{*2} in Tables A.21 and A.11, we see that absolutely no explanatory power is lost by not using the last two principal components.

Turning now to Table A.22 (Manufacturer 3), we see that while the coefficient of the first principal component uniformly has a significant coefficient whose value, after 1961, has remained relatively stable, the coefficient of the second component is rather erratic and generally insignificant.

The difference between this manufacturer and the other two is quite considerable in the behavior of the coefficients of C and DOR. For this manufacturer they appear to be, by and large, significantly different from zero and negative. Remembering the definition of these two dummy variables, their coefficients are to be interpreted as the contrasts of the two effects (of having 8 or 6 cylinders and 4 or 2 doors). Thus, the coefficient of C measures the difference of the contribution to the price of the model of its having 6 or 8 cylinders. A significant negative coefficient, as in the case here, means that the model would have been *more expensive* for given *DIS, BHP if it had 6 cylinders* than if *it had 8*. This, technically, is a perfectly reasonable result, because it is technically simpler to attain a given horsepower with more cylinders than with fewer. Similarly, a negative coefficient for DOR means that given all other pertinent characteristics the model would have been more expensive had it featured 2 doors. This, however, does not appear to have any technical basis. It probably merely means that relatively higher priced models are manufactured with 2 doors rather than 4.

Finally, a comparison of Tables 22 and 14 clearly shows that in terms of the statistic R^{*2} little explanatory power, if any, is sacrificed by the omission of the last two principal components of W, L, DIS, and BHP.

In connection with the results for all three manufacturers, we should again remind the reader that the units in which the four variables above enter the principal components are those of *standardized deviates*. This then should explain the consistent differences in the constant terms of Tables A.8, A.11, A.14 and A.20, A.21, A.22.

To introduce some comparability between the results of the two groups of tables, we include Table A.24 in which we "translate" the coefficients of the two principal components into the implied coefficients for W, L, DIS, BHP.

We note that the principal components are defined, in this context, by

(1) $$Z_i = a_{1i} \frac{W - \overline{W}}{s_W} + a_{2i} \frac{L - \overline{L}}{s_L} + a_{3i} \frac{DIS - \overline{DIS}}{s_{DIS}}$$
$$+ a_{4i} \frac{BHP - \overline{BHP}}{s_{BHP}}, \quad i = 1, 2$$

where e.g., $\overline{W}$ means the sample mean of Weight (W), and s_W its sample standard deviation.

In the various regressions we have the term $b_1 Z_1 + b_2 Z_2$. But then we can write

(2) $$b_1 Z_1 + b_2 Z_2 = (b_1 a_{11} + b_2 a_{12}) \frac{W - \overline{W}}{s_W}$$
$$+ (b_1 a_{21} + b_2 a_{22}) \frac{L - \overline{L}}{s_L}$$
$$+ (b_1 a_{31} + b_2 a_{32}) \frac{DIS - \overline{DIS}}{s_{DIS}}$$
$$+ (b_1 a_{41} + b_2 a_{42}) \frac{BHP - \overline{BHP}}{s_{BHP}}.$$

Now, the coefficients b_1, b_2 can be obtained from Tables A.20, A.21, A.22, while the a_{ij}—the elements of the appropriate characteristic vectors defining the principal components—can be obtained from Tables A.16, A.17, A.18.

Price and Quality Changes

In Table 24 we give the quantities appearing in parentheses in equation (2). These, then, are comparable to the coefficients appearing in Tables A.8, A.11, and A.14 except for the obvious difference in units and the fact that, there, we had arbitrarily suppressed the variable *DIS*.

While we cannot deduce any firm conclusions on the basis of Table A.24—since little can be inferred concerning the "significance" of the coefficients there exhibited or of differences among these coefficients and those exhibited in Tables A.16, A.17, A.18—nonetheless it is interesting to note from Table A.24 that the implied coefficients of W and L are always positive and that this is nearly so for the coefficients of *DIS* and *BHP* as well. This is in contrast to the results of Tables A.16, A.17, A.18, in which some of the corresponding coefficients have a negative sign, occasionally significantly so.

In the preceding we sought to establish the nature of the functional dependence between price and various identifiable characteristics of automobiles. At this stage it becomes proper to ask: Does our investigation support the hypothesis that such relationships represent the market (consumer) evaluation of the features embodied in the various models? If so, then the coefficients of the variables in the equation under consideration would indicate the consumer evaluation of the features exhibited by the model; thus, we could obtain an implicit market valuation of quality changes wrought as model characteristics evolve over the years.

Now, if the relations truly reflect market evaluation, then we would expect similar features to be similarly evaluated across manufacturers. Formally, this aspect can be tested by the procedures indicated in Appendix B. In this connection we should note that although the formalities of that test are impeccable, we must be aware of certain types of specification errors when we apply it in the present context. Thus, it should be obvious that there are several characteristics of the product that are important in determining its price which, however, have not been entered in the equation, for example, the frequency of repair record of the various models. If specification errors are serious the results of the test above will be open to some doubt. Despite this caveat, there unfortunately does not exist any other alternative than to proceed with the formal aspects of the test, given the data at our disposal.

A second consideration in testing whether the estimated relationships represent market evaluation is to test for the "significance" of the variable *MOD*. We remind the reader that this represents the number of units of a given basic model produced by a manufacturer in a given model year. Under the hypothesis above, such a variable ought not to have a coefficient significantly different from zero.

From Tables A.20, A.21, A.22 we can infer the implications of this second consideration. We see that MOD has a significant and negative coefficient for 1961, 1962, 1963 in the case of Manufacturer 1, and 1963 for Manufacturer 2; for Manufacturer 3 it has a significant negative coefficient in 1961 and a significant *positive* coefficient in 1963 and 1957.

Although it is not entirely clear what interpretation one is to make of a *positive* coefficient, it is clear that a *negative* coefficient could well indicate a "trade off" between quantity and price in the market strategy of an oligopolistic firm, an interpretation that is not compatible with the hypothesis considered here. While the results just noted may be somewhat suggestive, they are certainly not conclusive. A much more promising approach to the problem of elucidating the nature of the estimated price regressions lies in testing the statistical hypothesis that the parameters in the price equations of the three manufacturers are identical. Indeed, unless there is substantial product differentiation (no doubt nurtured by the advertising policies of oligopolistic firms), one would not expect consumers to make substantially different evaluations of similar features because of their differing manufacturing origin.

To this effect we require the regression based on the pooled sample which is given in Table A.23. A comparison even of R^2 of Table A.23 and the corresponding statistics of Tables A.20, A.21, A.22 strongly implies rejection of the hypothesis, since the fit is unquestionably poorer with the pooled sample.[6]

By inspection, it is also obvious that the point estimators presented there are perceptibly different from those obtained for the three manufacturers.

The information needed to carry out the test developed in Appendix B is given in Table 4.1. The results of the table leave no doubt that in all instances we should reject the hypothesis of homogeneity of the price equations.

A similar test was carried out using, in the regressions, the variables W, L, BHP, the results being entirely similar to those of Table 4.1. In addition, the hypothesis that the pricing equations for Manufacturers 2 and 3 are identical was tested and rejected. In the interest of brevity we omit the supporting empirical results.

It may not be unreasonable, despite the evidence above, to inquire whether the hypothesis might be accepted that the slope coefficients of the three manufacturers are the same and the results given in Table 4.1 merely

---

6. The test is obviously to be carried out with respect to the regressions, reported in Tables A.20, A.21, A.22, which do *not* include MOD as an explanatory variable.

Price and Quality Changes

Table 4.1. Test Statistics for Homogeneity of Pricing Equations, Manufacturers 1, 2, 3, Based on Tables A.20, A.21, A.22, A.23

Year	Test Statistic	Distribution	Critical Point at 5%	1%
1953	4.7149	$F_{6,50}$	2.30	3.28
1957	19.6989	$F_{7,83}$	2.10	2.87
1961	19.6623	$F_{14,171}$	1.75	2.14
1962	12.1383	$F_{14,157}$	1.75	2.14
1963	9.1371	$F_{12,173}$	1.80	2.30
1964	18.6659	$F_{12,174}$	1.80	2.30

reflect the fact that it is only the constant terms that differ amongst the three manufacturers.

To this effect we have run the pooled regression (corresponding to that exhibited in Table A.23) with dummy variables reflecting the individual manufacturers. In fact, we have estimated the contrasts, or differences, in the "effects" between the other two manufacturers and the first. The contrasts are uniformly significant and negative. Also, a test similar to that exhibited in Table 4.1 still rejects the homogeneity hypothesis. These results are given in Table 4.2. For economy of space the new pooled regressions are not given.

The conclusion, then, seems inescapable that we cannot regard such equations as furnishing information about "consumer evaluation" of the

Table 4.2. Test Statistics for Homogeneity of Slope Coefficients of Pricing Equations between Manufacturers 1, 2, and 3

Year	Test Statistic	Distribution	Critical Point at 5%	1%
1953	3.5576	$F_{5,50}$	2.40	3.40
1957	18.3140	$F_{6,83}$	2.21	3.04
1961	4.9712	$F_{12,171}$	1.80	2.25
1962	5.7564	$F_{12,157}$	1.81	2.26
1963	5.6465	$F_{10,173}$	1.89	2.42
1964	6.2402	$F_{10,174}$	1.89	2.42

"quality content" of various identifiable characteristics of the product (automobile).

Two other aspects of the investigation should be reported. First, there is the question as to whether the estimation of these three pricing equations is efficient; or equivalently, whether the error terms of the three equations are uncorrelated. We should note that in this connection one should be very careful about the meaning of the test implied, because there is no "natural" way of ordering observations in a cross-sectional sample. Perhaps a very useful way of looking at the ordering problem is to order observations through ranking by the magnitude of the dependent variable. Thus, what we should be testing is, roughly speaking, whether the residual variations in the pricing of Chevrolets, Fords, and Plymouths are correlated. A test of this hypothesis based on the correlation matrix of the residuals from the three equations resulted in rejection.

Secondly, the hypothesis that for a given manufacturer the parameters of the pricing equations are invariant over a 2-year interval was also rejected.

Of course this last result is a rather expected one, since in a world of flexible prices there is no reason to expect that the "price attached" to a given physical characteristic of an automobile should remain constant from year to year. Again the supporting empirical results are omitted in the interest of brevity.

Before we conclude this section, certain other aspects of our results should be clearly brought out. Our findings point to considerable instability in the year-to-year estimates of the price relation. Thus, even if we settle on the semilog as the relevant functional form and even if we confine ourselves to a single manufacturer, parameter estimates still vary appreciably from cross section to cross section.

All these considerations tend toward rejection of the hypothesis that the estimated price relation represents the consumers' (market) evaluation of the features embodied by an automobile model. Of course, it is always possible to rationalize such results in the framework above by building into the preferences of individuals a bias relative to one manufacturer or another, but this is rather transparent.

Now the negative aspect of our findings is clear enough; we must, however, still ask: What *is* the meaning of such estimated price relation? I personally would prefer to think of the estimated coefficients of such relations as the manufacturer's own evaluation of the model's features in the context of his own price-quantity selling strategy—remembering that we deal essentially with an oligopolistic market and that the oligopolist may well be "satisficing" his profits on a cost-plus-markup basis.

Price and Quality Changes

C. *Refrigerators*

The composition of our refrigerator sample is given in Table A.26. The contrast in the composition of the automobile and refrigerator samples is evident from a comparison of Tables A.26 and A.25, the latter containing information on the automobile sample. It should be apparent from the two tables that it is not possible to carry out the same sort of analysis with respect to refrigerators. We recall that the theoretical underpinnings of the analysis in the previous section imply that at a given point in time we may, by observing variations in the characteristics exhibited by various models, "explain" their price variations and thereby assign an implicit valuation to these characteristics. This argues for a *cross-sectional sample*. If one is prepared to argue that one manufacturer's models are substantially undifferentiated from those of another except for differences in identifiable characteristics, and *if* such characteristics are identically valued as between different manufacturers, then one can use a cross-sectional sample over various manufacturers. Certainly from 1954 onward we have sufficient observations to carry out such an investigation. However, our experience with automobiles has indicated that the pricing relation may *not* be homogeneous among manufacturers. If this is so, then the effective size of subsamples becomes simply the number of observations per cell in Table A.26, and this is rarely of a magnitude that would encourage one to continue along this line.

In dealing with the problem we have followed two approaches. First, assuming that the pricing equation for each manufacturer is homogeneous over time except for an element associated with time, we have, for each manufacturer adequately represented in our sample, pooled observations *over the sample period* and have introduced in the regression *time as an explanatory variable*. If the relation is semilog or double log, then this seems to imply that we view the valuation of each component as *invariant* with respect to time, but the latter by its mere passage increases or decreases price by a constant percentage (for given characteristics). Of course, the role of time here is to index not only the incidence of technical progress, which in general will serve to reduce costs and thus possibly price, but also the behavior of the economic system in general and the price level in particular which, over the sample period, could only have served to increase appliance prices. In addition to this we have pooled observations over all manufacturers *for each year*. This is the type of sample other researchers have customarily worked with. We shall comment on the results below when we consider the empirical findings.

As in the case of automobiles, we first examine the question of the appropriate functional form. By and large the same results emerge, namely, the linear form is generally less satisfactory, while there is really little to choose from, statistically, between the semi- and double log forms. In the interest of brevity we shall not produce all the relevant empirical findings, thus confining ourselves to a comparison of the semi- and double log forms in the case of the two manufacturers having the largest representation in our sample—Frigidaire and GE. This is exhibited in Tables A.27 and A.28. It is apparent that differences in the standard error of the estimate and coefficient of determination between the two forms are rather negligible, and statistically we are offered little guidance as to which is the more appropriate form. Largely due to ease of interpretation of the resulting coefficients, but also due to conversations we had with industrial cost "engineers," we have chosen to conduct the remainder of our investigation in terms of the double log form.

It will be noticed from the tables that the cubic footage capacity of the unit is not entered as our explanatory variable. The reason for its absence lies in the collinearity of the variables CF, FCF, H, W^*, and D. Of course one might argue that given the dimensional variables H, W^*, and D, the total capacity of the unit is almost uniquely determined, so that CF is indeed superfluous. This, however, does neglect the fact that since the variables reflect *exterior* measurements, the technology of proper insulation plays a significant role in determining the capacity of the unit, which is an interior measure, via the required thickness of its walls. For this reason it was deemed proper to operate with the principal components of (the logarithms of) CF, FCF, H, W^*, and D. The characteristic roots and vectors defining these principal components are given in Table A.29. The table discloses some interesting features. First, the size of the largest characteristic root is not similar over all manufacturers nor is its relation to the remaining roots. One is tempted to interpret this as indicative of substantial differences in the model mix produced by various manufacturers. We observe that this was not so for automobiles.

On the other hand, such a conclusion should be tempered by the realization that the incidence of observations varies from manufacturer to manufacturer, so that for some we have many observations at the early years of our samples while for others we may have few, if any.

Another interesting feature is that the incidence of collinearity is not as severe here as it was in the case of automobiles. No doubt this is in part a reflection of the differing time profile of the two samples. A consequence of this fact is that we have, typically, at least four meaningfully defined principal components. In particular, note that while the first characteristic root accounts for 49.7 percent and 51.6 percent of the sum of all roots for Hotpoint and Kelvinator respectively, it accounts for 72.0

Price and Quality Changes

percent and 72.2 percent for RCA and Philco respectively. Also, the smallest root accounts for 0.7 percent and 1.2 percent of the sum of all roots for RCA and Frigidaire respectively, but 3.3 percent for Kelvinator.

No reasonable generalization can be offered regarding the characteristic vectors given in the table. For Frigidaire the first component (vector) weights most heavily depth (D), height (H), and width (W^*) — in that order. On the other hand the order for the first component in RCA is H, W^*, and cubic footage (CF), D being assigned a *negative weight*. Thus, as in the case of automobiles, no meaningful factor analytic interpretation can be assigned to the principal components so determined. They are best regarded as a means of reducing the dimensionality of the data and of coping with problems of multicollinearity, which had led to the suppression of the variable CF from the regressions exhibited in Tables A.27 and A.28. Retaining all principal components of the (continuous) variables CF, FCF, H, W^*, and D, we first tested for homogeneity of the pricing equation of the major manufacturers represented in our sample (Frigidaire, GE, Hotpoint, Kelvinator, Philco, RCA, and Westinghouse).

The technique is exactly the same as that employed in the previous section, and the (dummy) variables included in the regression were, beyond the principal components, $D1$, $D8$, $D13$, $D19$, $D21$, $D22$, and *time*. In the interest of brevity, these derived regressions are not presented. The relevant test statistic is F-distributed with 84 and 440 degrees of freedom. The critical values at 5 percent and 1 percent levels of the significance are respectively 1.35 and 1.54. The test statistic obtained was $F^* = 7.3391$, and thus the homogeneity hypothesis is unambiguously rejected.

Next it appeared that several manufacturers might be *pairwise* homogeneous. In a homogeneity test involving Frigidaire and GE, the test statistic was $F^* = 6.5479$, and thus the hypothesis was again rejected, the statistic being F-distributed with 14 and 248 degrees of freedom.

Testing Philco and RCA for homogeneity one obtains $F^* = 2.3775$; the statistic is now F-distributed with 14 and 48 degrees of freedom. The critical values at the 10-percent, 5-percent and 1-percent levels of significance are respectively 1.88, 2.26, and 3.24. Thus the hypothesis can be rejected at the 10-percent and 5-percent levels of significance but *not* at the 1-percent level.

Testing Hotpoint and Westinghouse, one obtains $F^* = 1.2371$; the test statistic is now F-distributed with 14 and 78 degrees of freedom. Here the hypothesis is unambiguously accepted.

Several other pairwise tests could have been carried out, but rejection of the homogeneity hypothesis appeared to be a foregone conclusion simply by inspection of the regression results. For this reason the test formality was dispensed with. In connection with these tests we should observe that the rejection of homogeneity for Frigidaire and GE is rather important, because both are very well represented in our sample; and, as may be seen from Table A.26, their time profile is rather similar, although GE has relatively more models at the earlier years of the sample.

The ambiguity in the rejection of homogeneity for Philco and RCA is somewhat surprising, because RCA is represented in our sample only for 1957–1965, while Philco is represented over the entire period.

The acceptance of the homogeneity hypothesis between Hotpoint and Westinghouse is significant in that the time profile of the two samples is similar.

By and large such results are consistent with the formulation of the estimation scheme which implies that for given characteristics, time has a proportional effect, neutral with respect to the characteristics.

Finally, in Table A.30 we present the (double log) regressions for major manufacturers, using the first four principal components of the variables CF, FCF, H, W^*, and D.

We note that the first component is uniformly "significant" and has a positive coefficient; the second component is not uniformly "significant," and for RCA its coefficient is "significant" but *negative*. Components three and four are only occasionally "significant," and their coefficients are of either sign. Incidentally, when used as an explanatory variable, the fifth component turned out to be nearly uniformly "insignificant"; since its computational accuracy was in doubt and its usefulness as an explanatory variable questionable, it was omitted in obtaining the regression results summarized in Table A.31.

An interesting feature of these results is the uniform significance of time (T) and the negative sign of its coefficient. Perhaps here a word of explanation is necessary. The original form of the hypothesized equation is $\ln P = \alpha_0 + \sum_{i=1}^{s} \alpha_i D_i + \beta_0 T + \sum_{i=1}^{k} \beta_i y_i$ where the y_i's stand for the continuous variables CF, FCF, H, W^*, D; the D_i's denote the various dummy variables; and T time. Now time is measured as 1, 2, and so on, depending on the first year for which observations are available. It is clear, then, that if we are dealing with a short series in terms of time, the estimator of β_0 would tend, for that reason, to be higher. This will explain the magnitude of the time coefficient in the RCA regression. Otherwise the time coefficient lies between 0.022 and 0.0455. What interpretation can we give to this? Well, the result indicates that for *given physical characteristics* the price of the average model has been declining at the rate,

Price and Quality Changes

say, of about 3 percent per annum. But this is a price movement that occurs for "standardized" quality. Thus, it comes close to being a price movement *corrected* for quality, and the coefficient of T may be identified with the "pure price" behavior of refrigerators over the sample period.

In particular, from Table A.5 we see that while the nominal price of the average model (for all manufacturers) has increased from $284.30 in 1950 to $363.60 in 1965, or by about 30 percent, *in fact, the price of refrigerators corrected for "quality" change has been declining at an approximate overall rate of 2.7 percent*. Hence a price index based on the nominal price of models would have given an erroneous view of the process. Some caution, however, is needed in this context. First, Table A.30 shows that the "pure price" component of refrigerators as indexed by the coefficient of time T is not uniform across manufacturers, so that the 2.7-percent figure mentioned above represents a rough judgment. Strictly speaking, one can speak only about the "pure price" behavior of individual manufacturers.

Second, this downshift, induced by the passage of time to some (perhaps considerable) extent, represents the mix of models *produced* by the manufacturers. Thus, in obtaining the result each model is given *equal weight*. If a price index were to be constructed, presumably individual models should be *weighted by their volume of sales*. Further, we have no guarantee that for each year our sample exhausts the models produced by the various manufacturers. Indeed for some years we know that it definitely does not. To the extent that the process of observation (model) selection for inclusion in the sample is not random, it is conceivable that a more complete sample might yield somewhat different results.

Associated with the results of Table A.30 are those given in Table A.31. The coefficients presented in Table A.31 are obtained from those given in Table A.30, mutatis mutandis, by the procedure indicated in equations (1) and (2) of the previous section.

The visual impression of the table confirms the rejection of the homogeneity hypothesis in the pricing behavior of the various manufacturers, since the implied coefficients of the variables CF, FCF, H, W^*, and D vary widely amongst manufacturers. Of course this visual impression is never a substitute for a (tolerably) rigorous procedure since some of the principal components in Table A.30 carry "insignificant" coefficients, and confidence intervals on the elements of the characteristic vectors defining the principal components could not be easily established. One very interesting aspect of Table A.31 is the nearly uniform negativity of the coefficient of depth (D) across manufacturers. This is not an unreasonable result, since the deeper a unit is, the less desirable it might be considered (due to inaccessibility of some of its parts), and thus manufacturers allow for that in their pricing behavior. In general the inhomogeneity of the price equations across manufacturers seems to lend support to the view that the estimated equations are cost plus markup (pricing) relations; thus, we cannot interpret the coefficients of the variables as indicating the consumer evaluation of the feature connoted by the corresponding variable.

Finally, referring again to Table A.30, the estimated coefficients of the dummy variables indicate that meat drawers ($D1$) add perceptibly to the price of the unit, as does the presence of shelves in the freezer compartment ($D8$). Whether shelves are sliding ($D13$) does not appear to be significant for most manufacturers. The presence or absence of automatic defrosting ($D20$) or other frostless features ($D21$) seems quite generally to contribute appreciably to the price of the unit.

4. Quality Component of Price Movements: Some Implications

If one were to lay aside for the moment one's qualms about the data, the approach, and the results, what inferences could one obtain concerning the "quality" and "pure price" components of observed price changes with respect to automobiles and refrigerators, and to what use can such information be put?

If we think of an actual price change as consisting solely of two components, a "quality" and a "pure price" one, then in the context of our sample we need determine independently only one; the other may be obtained residually.

In the case of refrigerators, the "pure price" component may be obtained directly as the coefficient of T in the regression presented in Table A.30. Thus, for example, we may infer that the "quality corrected" price of refrigerators produced by GE has been declining at an annual rate of 2.26 percent. The difference between the actual relative price change of average models for any two (consecutive) years and 2.26 percent would represent the price equivalent of the quality change in the average model between these two years. Thus, in the framework of the analysis of the refrigerator sample, the problem of "quality correction" of price movements is rather easy to cope with.

Turning to automobiles, however, we see that we are dealing with a number of cross sections in which the "general" price and cost conditions are held constant so that variations in price from model to model "truly" reflect the cost (or price) evaluation of the model's various identifiable

Price and Quality Changes

characteristics. Of course, there is always a residual due to characteristics which are not quantifiable or for some other reason we have not taken into account.

Thus, the coefficient of weight (W), for example, indicates the contribution to price of a unit increase in weight and so on. Whether this is the consumer's evaluation of this feature or the manufacturer's desired cost plus markup relation is another matter on which we have commented earlier.

If we estimate in year t a relation of the form

(3) $$\ln P = \sum_{i=1}^{n} \hat{\beta}_{it} x_i^t$$

where the x_i's denote the various identifiable characteristics of automobiles, and if we evaluate the function in (3) at the vector of mean characteristics for the year j, then we have

(4) $$\ln P_{jt} = \sum_{i=1}^{n} \hat{\beta}_{it} \bar{x}_i^j$$

which gives the (log of) price of an automobile with characteristics $\bar{x}_i^j$, $i = 1, 2, \ldots, n$, valued at year t "weights." Of course such an automobile, in general, cannot be produced since, for example, it may be characterized by 0.05 automatic transmission (ATR) or 0.22 doors (DOR)—meaning that 5 percent of the models produced in year j were equipped with automatic transmission and 22 percent had four doors.

On the other hand this exercise will give us some indication of the price of the average model produced in year j, if it were produced at year t.

If we have a number of cross sections, so that $j = 1, 2, \ldots, k$, then the quantities $\ln P_{jt}$ give a series on the (log of the) price of the average model over the length of the sample period at "constant price weights" of their characteristics. We can then interpret $\ln P_{jt}$ as the (log of the) standardized cost or price (based on year t weights) of "quality" embodied in the average model of successive years.

Now, what is the meaning of

(5) $$\ln P_{tt} = \sum_{i=1}^{n} \hat{\beta}_{it} \bar{x}_i^t?$$

Well, it is the standardized cost (or price) of "quality" embodied in the average model of year t. Thus

(6) $$c_{jt} = \ln P_{jt} - \ln P_{tt}$$

is the standardized cost equivalent (in relative terms) of "quality" change between years j and t. On the other hand,

$$(7) \qquad c_{jt}^* = \ln P_{jj} - \ln P_{tt}$$

is the actual change in the average price of models (here average means geometric average) between years j and t. Another way to interpret c_{jt}^* of (7) is as the relative rate of change in the price of the average car produced in years j and t *under contemporary cost conditions*. Since (7) thus represents some actual relative change in average model prices, we may define the "pure price" component of price changes as

$$(8) \qquad \bar{c}_{jt} = c_{jt}^* - c_{jt} = \ln P_{jj} - \ln P_{jt}.$$

We define, then, c_{jt} and $\bar{c}_{jt}$ respectively as the "quality" and "pure price" components of an actual (relative rate of) price change.

Now, it is apparent that this is not the only way one can define "quality" and "pure price" components of observed price change. Thus, let

$$(9) \qquad \ln P_{jt}^* = \sum_{i=1}^{n} \hat{\beta}_{ij} \bar{x}_i^t$$

where β_{ij} are the coefficients of the price equation as estimated for the jth cross section, and the $\bar{x}_i^t$ represent the mean characteristics of models in the tth year (cross section). The quantities $\ln P_{jt}^*$ give the evaluation of a standard model, defined by the vector of mean characteristics $(\bar{x}_1^t, \bar{x}_2^t, \ldots, \bar{x}_n^t)'$, with weights based on the regression in the jth cross section. Varying j, then, we obtain the (log of the) price of the average model of year t were it to be produced under the conditions of year j. Thus we have the evolution of price over time for *given* "quality." Clearly

$$(10) \qquad \bar{d}_{jt} = \ln P_{jt}^* - \ln P_{tt}$$

indicates the "pure price" component of actual price change between years j and t since it gives the relative rate of change in the price of a standardized product between years j and t. The relative change in (average) model prices between years j and t is given of course by $\bar{c}_{jt}^*$ of (7). Thus the "quality" component of price change is simply

$$(11) \qquad d_{jt} = c_{jt}^* - \bar{d}_{jt} = \ln P_{jj} - \ln P_{jt}^*.$$

Thus the two sets of measures of "quality" and "pure price" components correspond roughly to the notions of "price" and "quantity" weighted indices. In particular, c_{jt} gives the "quality" component of price change

Price and Quality Changes

between years j and t based on valuing a *changing* model at *fixed* pricing conditions, while d_{jt} gives the same information based on valuing a *fixed* model at *varying* pricing conditions.

In Tables A.32 and A.33 we give the results of applying this scheme of decomposition to the automobile sample. The difference between the two tables lies in the fact that in Table A.32 we take the actual relative (average) price change as the difference in the *logarithms of the geometric mean of model prices*, while in Table A.33 we take the relevant actual price change to be the difference in the *logarithms of the mean model price* between any two years. Clearly the latter is the more appealing measure of average price change. The former has only statistical convenience to recomm d it, since under that scheme $\ln P_{tt}$ *is also the sample mean of the logarithms of model prices in year t*. If one were to conduct a test of some hypothesis on the quantities $\bar{c}_{jt}$ and d_{jt}, then this fact will induce an appreciable simplification.

From Table A.32 we see that the (geometric) average price of models has risen approximately 13.9 percent between 1953 and 1961 for Manufacturer 1, and has fallen 4.1 percent for Manufacturer 3. A decomposition of these changes based on a *varying* model ($c_{1953, 1961}$, $\bar{c}_{1953, 1961}$) would indicate, however, a "pure price" component amounting to approximately a price reduction of 48 percent and a "quality" component approximately equivalent to an increase in price by 62 percent for Manufacturer 1. For Manufacturer 3 the nominal price fall of approximately 4.1 percent between 1953 and 1961 can be decomposed (on the basis of a varying model) into a "quality" component equivalent to (approximately) a reduction in price by 63 percent and a "pure price" component accounting for a 59 percent increase in price. Roughly speaking, for this manufacturer, "quality" has fallen between 1953 and 1961, so that if we correct for this aspect, average price has "really" risen by 59 percent and not the nominal 4.1 percent. If we base this decomposition on a *fixed* model (i.e., we consider $d_{1953, 1961}$, $\bar{d}_{1953, 1961}$) the qualitative results are similar although the numerical magnitudes will differ somewhat. Essentially the same conclusions will be obtained if we consider Table A.33, in which we operate with the relative rate of change of (arithmetic) mean model price (in lieu of geometric mean price).

But perhaps it is a bit more meaningful to consider the more recent experience of 1961–1964.

Again considering first Table A.32, we see that for Manufacturer 1, while nominal mean price has risen by 2.1 percent and 3.3 percent between 1961 and 1962 and between 1961 and 1963, respectively, and fallen by 1.6 percent between 1961 and 1964, the "quality" component

$(c_{j, 1961})$ indicates a change equivalent to a reduction in price by 14.1 percent, 21.2 percent, and 7.4 percent respectively between 1961 and 1962, 1963, and 1964. Thus, over this period "quality" was declining.

Conversely, the "pure price" component $(\bar{c}_{j, 1961})$ indicates an increase in price by 16.9 percent, 24.3 percent, and 5.8 percent respectively between 1961 and 1962, 1963, and 1964.

Based on Table A.33 the corresponding figures are $(c_{j, 1961})$ reductions by 14.8 percent, 21.2 percent, 7.4 percent as between 1961 and 1962, 1963, and 1964 respectively; also the "pure price" components indicate a price increase of 18.2 percent, 25.9 percent, 7.1 percent respectively between 1961 and 1962, 1963, and 1964. The results are qualitatively similar if we consider a decomposition based on a fixed model, that is, if we consider the $d_{j, 1961}$ and $\bar{d}_{j, 1961}$ of Tables A.32 and A.33.

For Manufacturer 2, if we again consider the $c_{j, 1961}$ and $\bar{c}_{j, 1961}$ of Tables A.32 and A.33, what appears to be a nominal price decline over the period 1961–1964 (the $c^*_{j, 1961}$ of the tables) is inaccurate in that if we compensate for the "reduction" of "quality" we must conclude that auto prices have risen.

This, however, is decidedly *not so* for Manufacturer 3. Table A.32 shows a nominal price reduction of 1.2 percent, 0.1 percent, and 1.7 percent respectively between 1961 and 1962, 1961 and 1963, and 1961 and 1964. However, the decompositions of the table show a "quality" component equivalent to a price increase of 12.1 percent, 5.5 percent between 1961 and 1962 and 1963 respectively; between 1961 and 1964 the "quality" component implies a price reduction of 5.5 percent.

Having allowed for the behavior of "quality," the table implies price reductions of 13.3 percent and 5.6 percent between 1961 and 1962 and 1963, and a price increase of 3.8 percent between 1961 and 1964. From Table A.33 the "quality" component implies a price increase of 12.1 percent, 5.5 percent and a price reduction of 5.5 percent respectively between 1961 and 1962, 1963, and 1964. Similarly the "pure price" component implies a price reduction of 12.9 percent, 6.3 percent and a price increase of 4.0 percent between 1961 and 1962, 1963, and 1964 respectively. Similar results will be obtained if we consider instead a decomposition based on a *fixed* model, i.e., if we examine the $d_{j, 1961}$ and $\bar{d}_{j, 1961}$ of Tables A.32 and A.33.

While the nature of the calculations above is such that the results are affected by the type of models a manufacturer chooses to produce, irrespective of how well they sell in the market, nonetheless the exercise serves to bring forth the point that, on the basis of our sample at least,

Price and Quality Changes

the relative influence of "quality" and "pure price" effects on nominal model prices is not uniform among all manufacturers. While this might tend to discourage the routine application of the aggregative approach to the problem of "quality" corrected price indices, one could use the coefficients of our estimated regressions—or some more refined version of them—as weights to be attached to variations in the characteristics of models produced by the various manufacturers. In fact, if one knew the volume of sales for each observation (model) in one year, then one could compute a weighted mean characteristic vector. Using this and applying the decomposition scheme above, we could obtain "quality" corrected price indices for each manufacturer. Aggregating over manufacturers according to their market share, one would then determine a marketwide index of quality corrected price. Unfortunately we do not have the requisite information in our sample.

5. Summary and Conclusions

In this paper we have examined the feasibility of correcting for quality in the construction of price indices. The basic premise of such an attempt is that a given product is characterized by a number of attributes and that its price is related to the nature of these attributes. Thus, by fixing time and observing members of a (basic) class of products exhibiting varying (but basically similar) attributes, we may arrive at an implicit valuation of such attributes. As time goes by, the (class of) commodities may experience price variations. These variations may be due to increased relative scarcity (or related to a generally rising price level) or to changing attributes or both. However, if we have a measure of the "value" of such attributes, we may correct for this aspect, thus obtaining a truer measure of the product's price variations. We have considered in particular the case of automobiles and refrigerators.

Previous investigators have sought to solve the problem in connection with automobiles by obtaining a cross-sectional sample of models produced by various manufacturers (for a given year) and then regressing list price on the various attributes of the model such as Weight, Length, and so on. In this context we raised the following issues:

1. What functional form best describes the relation between price and attributes?
2. Is this price-attribute relation homogeneous among manufacturers?

3. How are the coefficients of such a relation best described: as the consumer (market) implicit evaluation of such attributes, or do the coefficients reflect the manufacturer's price strategy so that the estimated relation is best described as a cost-plus-markup equation?
4. Is it feasible to construct routinely "quality corrected" price indices?
5. What do the empirical results indicate about the intrinsic price movements of such commodities, taking "quality" into account?

In the case of automobiles it is possible to give at least a tentative answer to all these questions. If we confine our attention to the linear, semilog, and double log forms in connection with (1), we find that while the semi- and double log forms are comparable, the semilog does slightly better in "explaining" the data in the case of automobiles. The estimated list price–attribute relations are not homogeneous among the three manufacturers represented in our sample. A statistical test clearly rejects the homogeneity hypothesis.

The previous result and the fact that the list price is used as the dependent variable strongly suggest that the estimated regressions are best interpreted as cost-plus-markup relations, and thus the coefficients of the various attributes are best viewed as the manufacturer's evaluation of their role in his overall price strategy.

It is clear that because of the heterogeneity of pricing behavior, it is not permissible to use a cross-sectional sample comprising more than one manufacturer. Thus, in making "quality corrections" one ought to take into account the division of the market. The empirical results strongly indicate that having "corrected for quality" in the context of this analysis, the price behavior of the various manufacturers has been rather different. In this framework, models of Manufacturer 3 have experienced a price decline over the period 1961 through 1963 and a price increase between 1963 and 1964. On the other hand, for Manufacturers 1 and 2, we observe an appreciable and consistent price increase over the period 1961 through 1964.

Finally there is considerable instability in coefficient estimates from cross section to cross section, even when we confine ourselves to a given manufacturer.

In the case of refrigerators, because of the nature of the sample, the same detailed analysis was not possible. The question of homogeneity of price behavior cannot be posed in the same unambiguous terms as in the case of automobiles. Within the limitations thus imposed on our analysis we find a slight preference for the double log form, an inhomogeneity in

Price and Quality Changes

the price behavior of the major manufacturers represented in our sample, although some manufacturers exhibit *pairwise* homogeneity. In this case we cannot strongly dispute the interpretation that the estimated price–attribute regression yields coefficients which, to some extent, measure the consumer evaluation of the product's attributes.

Correcting for quality we find that prices of refrigerators have been declining over the period 1950–1965. While the rate of decline is not uniform amongst all manufacturers, it tends to be in the neighborhood of 3 percent per annum.

Even in the case of refrigerators, however, it does not yet appear feasible routinely to construct "quality corrected" price indices by using the coefficients of the attributes of the product estimated on the basis of a sample encompassing all manufacturers.

Tentatively, the average rate of "quality corrected" price decline alluded to above may be used to obtain an indication of the extent to which "quality improvement" has taken place. But still the analysis in both cases leaves many issues unsettled. With the advent of more complete samples, it may be possible to give more definitive answers to the problems examined in this paper. Unfortunately this is not quite so yet.

Appendix A to Chapter 4

Symbols and Variables

P = price in current dollars (for both automobiles and refrigerators)
W = weight, in pounds
L = length, in inches
DIS = displacement, in cubic inches
BHP = brake horsepower, at 3800 revolutions per minute
MOD = production (in units of 100) of relevant basic model.
DOR = dummy variable; 1 if model has 2 doors, zero otherwise (automobiles only)
C = dummy variable; 1 if model has 8 cylinders, zero otherwise
ATR = dummy variable; 1 if model has automatic transmission as standard equipment, zero otherwise

PS = dummy variable; 1 if model has power steering as standard equipment, zero otherwise
Z_i = principal components of W, L, DIS, BHP; $i = 1, 2$
Const = estimated constant term
SDev = standard deviation of residuals
R^2 = multiple correlation coefficient squared
R^{*2} = squared correlation coefficient of the antilogs of the predicted values with the original values of the dependent variable

Refrigerators only

CF = cubic footage capacity of model, in cubic feet
FCF = freezer cubic footage capacity of model in cubic feet
H = height, in inches
W* = width, in inches
D = depth, in inches
D1 = dummy variable; 1 if model has meat drawer, zero otherwise
D3 = dummy variable; 1 if model has egg shelves, zero otherwise
D4 = dummy variable; 1 if model has butter shelf, zero otherwise
D7 = dummy variable; 1 if model has shelves in freezer door, zero otherwise
D8 = dummy variable; 1 if model has shelves in freezer compartment, zero otherwise
D9 = dummy variable; 1 if model has ice ejector, zero otherwise
D13 = dummy variable; 1 if model has sliding shelves, zero otherwise
D14 = dummy variable; 1 if model has swing-out shelves, zero otherwise
D18 = dummy variable; 1 if model has semiautomatic defrosting, zero otherwise
D19 = dummy variable; 1 if model has automatic defrosting, zero otherwise
D20 = dummy variable; 1 if automatic defrosting is available in the freezer compartment but not in fresh foods section, zero otherwise
D21 = dummy variable; 1 if model is completely frostless, zero otherwise
D22 = dummy variable; 1 if model has two doors, zero otherwise
T = arithmetic time trend (1950 = 1)
Z_i = principal components of CF, FCF, H, W^*, D; $i = 1, 2, 3, 4$

Price and Quality Changes

Table A.1. Mean Characteristics of Models of Manufacturer 1

Year	P	W	L	DIS	BHP	MOD	DOR	C	ATR	PS
1953	2,462.80	3,655.7	209.39	274.228	142.406	62.091	0.469	0.594	0.250	0
1957	2,682.80	3,664.8	207.13	319.838	237.631	76.794	0.354	0.862	0.323	0.108
1961	2,709.80	3,550.7	206.49	311.427	237.973	91.692	0.146	0.876	0.213	0.101
1962	2,794.60	3,424.3	203.94	296.872	221.973	109.363	0.216	0.811	0.230	0.122
1963	2,822.10	3,435.5	206.05	305.971	236.624	120.869	0.200	0.824	0.153	0.153
1964	2,683.00	3,335.0	205.32	298.155	215.238	131.450	0.262	0.643	0.119	0.119

Table A.2. Mean Characteristics of Models of Manufacturer 2

Year	P	W	L	DIS	BHP	MOD	DOR	C	ATR	PS
1961	2,299.20	3,467.5	207.83	270.831	185.343	83.129	0.343	0.543	0.029	0.029
1962	2,259.70	3,170.3	202.50	236.618	150.078	90.351	0.373	0.490	0.020	0.020
1963	2,223.30	3,185.4	201.93	232.888	148.560	106.946	0.380	0.520	0.020	0.020
1964	2,239.70	3,179.5	199.25	253.386	162.750	123.439	0.341	0.568	0.023	0.023

Table A.3. Mean Characteristics of Models of Manufacturer 3

Year	P	W	L	DIS	BHP	MOD	DOR	C	ATR	PS
1953	2,513.70	3,610.8	207.90	263.620	132.067	28.207	0.167	0.400	0.400	0.033
1957	2,580.50	3,661.6	210.99	304.344	227.313	41.519	0.281	0.750	0.188	0.156
1961	2,297.80	3,356.5	206.16	293.809	223.132	28.369	0.221	0.632	0.015	0.015
1962	2,275.40	3,025.2	199.28	290.132	224.302	26.189	0.226	0.585	0.019	0.019
1963	2,299.80	3,164.6	204.13	304.250	234.339	37.546	0.196	0.607	0.018	0.018
1964	2,261.10	3,142.2	203.21	298.620	220.350	46.018	0.250	0.656	0.016	0.016

Table A.4. Mean Characteristics of All Manufacturers Combined

Year	P	W	L	DIS	BHP	MOD	DOR	C	ATR	PS
1953	2,487.40	3,633.9	208.67	269.1	137.403	45.695	0.323	0.500	0.323	0.016
1957	2,649.10	3,663.7	208.41	314.7	234.227	65.157	0.330	0.825	0.278	0.124
1961	2,489.10	3,466.7	206.62	297.8	221.198	67.704	0.208	0.729	0.109	0.057
1962	2,486.80	3,232.7	202.16	277.6	202.067	79.151	0.264	0.652	0.107	0.062
1963	2,512.20	3,290.6	204.41	286.3	212.901	92.795	0.246	0.681	0.079	0.079
1964	2,441.20	3,235.0	203.23	288.02	204.901	101.130	0.277	0.630	0.063	0.063

Table A.5. Mean Characteristics, Refrigerators, All Manufacturers, 1950–1965

Year	P	CF	FCF	H	W*	D	D1	D3	D4	D7	D8	D9	D13	D14	D18	D19	D20	D21	D22
1950	284.30	8.438	0.930	58.730	29.407	27.817	0.522	—	0.261	—	0.098	—	0.270	0.066	0.131	0.279	0.213	—	0.213
1951	317.80	8.545	1.145	58.232	29.215	28.220	0.100	0.250	0.200	—	—	—	0.103	0.051	0.128	0.256	0.128	—	0.103
1952	371.30	8.796	1.263	58.926	29.811	28.983	0.522	—	0.609	—	—	—	—	—	0.200	0.200	0.300	—	0.300
1953	365.00	9.220	1.310	56.685	29.325	29.145	0.400	—	0.500	0.200	—	—	—	—	0.043	0.522	0.217	—	0.217
1954	340.50	9.493	1.349	58.122	28.972	29.103	0.308	0.564	0.615	—	—	—	—	—	—	—	—	—	0.100
1955	367.90	10.197	1.810	59.426	29.475	29.754	0.213	0.836	0.738	0.066	—	—	—	—	—	0.100	0.100	—	0.100
1956	375.10	10.783	1.856	59.375	29.022	30.267	0.552	0.690	0.793	0.155	0.224	—	0.397	0.052	0.207	—	0.130	—	0.130
1957	407.00	10.911	2.042	60.306	29.365	28.474	0.593	0.926	0.815	0.296	0.259	0.111	0.259	0.111	0.222	0.224	0.379	—	0.121
1958	417.90	11.790	2.470	62.488	29.491	29.135	0.545	0.970	0.939	0.424	0.333	0.212	0.364	0.152	—	—	0.593	—	0.259
1959	376.90	11.811	2.176	61.752	29.816	28.308	0.438	0.938	0.938	0.406	0.156	—	0.219	0.156	—	—	0.667	—	0.424
1960	483.10	12.879	2.940	64.072	31.088	28.255	0.526	1.0	1.0	0.711	0.395	0.053	0.395	0.132	—	0.031	0.469	0.031	0.406
1961	392.40	12.384	2.677	63.367	30.183	27.971	0.289	0.974	0.868	0.526	0.289	0.158	0.474	0.053	—	—	0.474	0.395	0.763
1962	356.00	12.764	2.546	61.892	29.973	28.290	0.256	0.977	0.814	0.419	0.186	—	0.372	0.070	0.023	—	0.368	0.316	0.553
1963	411.40	12.909	3.114	62.621	30.543	27.878	0.306	0.919	0.871	0.726	0.387	0.048	0.468	0.081	—	—	0.233	0.256	0.419
1964	421.60	13.641	3.179	62.122	31.588	28.761	0.486	1.000	0.892	0.703	0.351	0.135	0.432	0.081	—	—	0.194	0.532	0.726
1965	363.60	14.244	3.787	63.610	31.488	28.872	0.551	1.000	0.962	0.859	0.423	0.141	0.551	0.038	—	—	0.351	0.432	0.703
																	0.218	0.667	0.859

Price and Quality Changes

Table A.6. Mean Characteristics by Major Manufacturers, 1950–1965

	Frigidaire	GE	Hotpoint	Kelvinator	Philco	Westinghouse
P	385.500	335.800	398.700	377.100	355.900	370.500
CF	11.955	10.366	12.577	11.783	11.218	11.882
FCF	2.417	1.797	3.021	2.488	2.096	2.604
H	62.056	58.827	62.453	59.747	62.461	62.658
W*	30.017	28.776	31.794	30.817	29.417	30.351
D	29.123	28.224	28.308	28.654	28.470	28.635
D1	0.515	0.238	0.519	0.362	0.158	0.385
D3	0.932	0.610	0.907	0.800	0.658	0.904
D4	0.856	0.733	0.852	0.775	0.605	0.731
D7	0.439	0.314	0.537	0.375	0.263	0.423
D8	0.258	0.124	0.241	0.212	0.105	0.192
D9	0.220	—	—	—	0.026	0.096
D13	0.409	0.352	0.389	0.362	0.263	0.346
D14	—	0.010	0.074	—	—	—
D18	0.076	—	—	0.125	—	0.077
D19	0.045	0.086	0.074	0.087	0.053	0.096
D20	0.333	0.395	0.315	0.262	0.342	0.369
D21	0.280	0.152	0.333	0.200	0.132	0.231
D22	0.447	0.390	0.593	0.400	0.368	0.462

Table A.7. Manufacturer 1 Coefficients of $P = \sum_{i=1}^{n} \alpha_i x_i$

	1953	1957	1961	1962	1963	1964
W	4.3160	0.6271	0.7334	0.6687	1.1463	2.3761
	(9.5188)	(2.2392)	(1.1225)	(0.9084)	(2.3259)	(5.0071)
L	−2.1676	3.2186	0.7270	0.8133	−0.0580	−3.0911
	(−3.3243)	(2.1373)	(0.2556)	(0.2747)	(−0.0286)	(−2.0186)
BHP	−0.1488	0.0046	−0.0216	−0.0132	−0.0195	−0.0536
	(2.8283)	(0.3184)	(−1.5951)	(−0.9264)	(−1.4870)	(−2.7925)
C	−3.5014	0.0630	3.2898	0.7103	−0.4321	−0.2475
	(−1.7843)	(0.0429)	(1.4189)	(0.3248)	(−0.2021)	(−0.1282)
DOR	0.6207	0.7638	−3.3208	−2.1740	−1.333	−0.4378
	(0.4617)	(0.7935)	(−1.7888)	(−1.1483)	(−0.6133)	(−0.3012)
ATR	−0.0569	2.0671	0.2600	1.6752	14.8170	12.8294
	(−0.0172)	(1.9114)	(0.1103)	(0.6783)	(5.0939)	(4.0471)
PS	—	14.6412	21.9994	20.4848	—	—
	—	(5.3212)	(6.8753)	(5.5202)	—	—
Const	−64.7726	−66.4767	−13.4943	−11.5916	−7.0253	21.3308
	(−4.2597)	(−2.5917)	(−0.3557)	(−0.3088)	(−0.2562)	(1.1056)
SDev	3.2952	3.2685	5.8372	6.3090	6.3635	5.4571
R^2	0.9380	0.8956	0.7594	0.7645	0.7480	0.8083

Table A.8. Manufacturer 1 Coefficients of $\ln P = \sum_{i=1}^{n} \beta_i x_i$

	1953	1957	1961	1962	1963	1964
W	0.0960	0.0211	0.0236	0.0141	0.0260	0.0470
	(11.5748)	(3.4646)	(2.0309)	(1.1844)	(3.0288)	(6.5597)
L	−0.0361	0.1135	−0.0175	0.0269	0.0031	−0.0421
	(−3.0133)	(3.4695)	(−0.3465)	(0.5625)	(0.0866)	(−1.8205)
BHP	−0.0009	0.0004	−0.0000	0.0002	0.0000	−0.0005
	(−0.9083)	(1.3826)	(−0.0511)	(1.0401)	(0.1622)	(−1.6339)
C	−0.0259	0.0175	0.0940	0.0310	0.0023	−0.0172
	(−0.7179)	(0.5477)	(2.2826)	(0.8800)	(0.0620)	(−0.5882)
DOR	−0.0052	0.0009	−0.0554	−0.0492	−0.0323	−0.0198
	(−0.2100)	(0.0429)	(−1.6807)	(−1.6115)	(−1.0058)	(−0.9014)
ATR	−0.0004	0.0688	0.0372	0.0642	0.3683	0.3175
	(−0.0066)	(2.9303)	(0.8895)	(1.6115)	(7.2838)	(6.6312)
PS	—	0.2920	0.4788	0.4518	—	—
	—	(4.8848)	(8.4295)	(7.5501)	—	—
Const	0.4958	−0.0543	2.6432	2.1008	2.2636	2.6064
	(1.7767)	(−0.0974)	(3.9244)	(3.4708)	(4.7475)	(8.9441)
SDev	0.0605	0.0710	0.1036	0.1017	0.1106	0.0824
R^2	0.9783	0.9409	0.8708	0.8987	0.8782	0.9272
R^{*2}	0.9490	0.9120	0.8160	0.8300	0.8280	0.8920

Table A.9. Manufacturer 1 Coefficients of $\ln P = \sum_{i=1}^{n} \gamma_i \ln x_i$

	1953	1957	1961	1962	1963	1964
W	4.2710	0.7624	−0.4288	−0.5785	0.3404	1.2541
	(12.0477)	(3.2095)	(−0.9814)	(−1.3845)	(1.0163)	(4.1285)
L	−1.0222	2.3618	2.6286	2.8708	1.1402	−0.4126
	(−3.8359)	(3.3434)	(2.2386)	(2.7401)	(1.3532)	(−0.6875)
BHP	−0.2853	0.0864	0.0725	0.1233	0.0495	−0.0691
	(−1.9283)	(1.1552)	(1.1573)	(2.2741)	(0.9841)	(−0.9875)
C	−0.0700	0.0135	0.0800	0.0160	−0.0014	−0.0111
	(−1.8647)	(0.3927)	(1.6557)	(0.4362)	(−0.0346)	(−0.3130)
DOR	0.0069	0.0005	−0.0662	−0.0621	−0.0352	−0.0321
	(0.2818)	(0.0212)	(−1.9206)	(−1.9882)	(−1.0007)	(−1.2446)
ATR	−0.0072	0.0693	0.1043	0.1066	0.4574	0.4285
	(−0.1257)	(2.8809)	(2.3944)	(2.6778)	(9.2364)	(8.4763)
PS	—	0.3254	0.5445	0.5377	—	—
	—	(5.5660)	(9.9204)	(10.2867)	—	—
Const	−7.6759	−7.1952	−3.7127	−4.0940	−1.6925	0.4286
	(−7.3191)	(−4.3643)	(−1.7115)	(−2.2302)	(−1.0883)	(0.4313)
SDev	0.0596	0.0725	0.1086	0.1040	0.1204	0.0967
R^2	0.9789	0.9383	0.8581	0.8940	0.8557	0.8998
R^{*2}	0.9530	0.9070	0.8050	0.8170	0.7840	0.8230

Price and Quality Changes

Table A.10. Manufacturer 2 Coefficients of $P = \sum_{i=1}^{n} \alpha_i x_i$

	1961	1962	1963	1964
W	0.1800	0.2890	0.0838	0.2178
	(1.2051)	(3.7598)	(0.10011)	(1.7281)
L	0.6200	0.3555	0.7748	−0.1283
	(0.8883)	(1.1301)	(2.2654)	(0.2770)
BHP	0.0055	0.0100	0.0177	0.0302
	(1.0826)	(2.5543)	(3.4125)	(3.4122)
C	0.8817	0.1430	0.2018	−0.9373
	(1.4488)	(0.4381)	(0.5584)	(−1.4503)
DOR	−0.5981	−0.4365	−0.5332	−0.5405
	(−1.3498)	(−1.8255)	(−2.0495)	(−1.5718)
ATR	29.1958	26.3342	30.1319	27.0397
	(14.2712)	(23.6564)	(26.2204)	(16.3925)
Const	1.7975	4.3049	0.7812	8.0980
	(0.1830)	(0.9686)	(0.1593)	(1.3426)
SDev	1.1298	0.7668	−0.8402	1.0417
R^2	0.9663	0.9802	0.9771	0.9704

Table A.11. Manufacturer 2 Coefficient of $\ln P = \sum_{i=1}^{n} \beta_i x_i$

	1961	1962	1963	1964
W	0.0101	0.0131	0.0040	0.0099
	(1.5571)	(3.9910)	(1.0846)	(1.9344)
L	0.0260	0.0202	0.0399	0.0104
	(0.8654)	(1.5063)	(2.6613)	(0.5535)
BHP	0.0002	0.0004	0.0007	0.0011
	(0.9628)	(2.1413)	(2.9973)	(3.1938)
C	0.0381	0.0112	0.0162	−0.0262
	(1.4415)	(0.8027)	(1.0207)	(−1.000)
DOR	−0.0262	−0.0194	−0.0260	−0.0241
	(−1.3595)	(−1.9041)	(−2.2829)	(−1.6312)
ATR	0.7141	0.6130	0.6324	0.6002
	(7.9993)	(12.9370)	(14.5485)	(8.9816)
Const	2.1535	2.2125	2.0369	2.3876
	(5.0407)	(11.6959)	(9.4825)	(9.7715)
SDev	0.0491	0.0326	0.0368	0.0422
R^2	0.9348	0.9671	0.9547	0.9506
R^{*2}	0.9670	0.9820	0.9780	0.9730

Table A.12. Manufacturer 2 Coefficients of $\ln P = \sum_{i=1}^{n} \gamma_i \ln x_i$

	1961	1962	1963	1964
W	0.2565	0.3651	0.0464	0.2270
	(1.2685)	(2.8404)	(0.3261)	(1.1138)
L	0.5308	0.3410	0.8029	0.3492
	(0.8768)	(1.0842)	(2.4347)	(0.8184)
BHP	0.0549	0.0885	0.1560	0.2052
	(1.0617)	(2.1347)	(2.9036)	(2.2658)
C	0.0359	0.0003	−0.0036	−0.0395
	(1.2465)	(0.0171)	(−0.1710)	(−0.9931)
DOR	−0.0274	−0.0215	−0.0265	−0.0264
	(−1.4129)	(−1.9506)	(−2.2198)	(−1.6626)
ATR	0.7621	0.6701	0.7785	0.7019
	(10.5582)	(14.5589)	(16.4173)	(11.0821)
Const	0.2865	0.3763	−0.2620	0.2449
	(0.2296)	(0.5880)	(−0.3811)	(0.3076)
SDev	0.0499	0.0355	0.0385	0.0476
R^2	0.9329	0.9610	0.9504	0.9372
R^{*2}	0.9660	0.9790	0.9760	0.9660

Table A.13. Manufacturer 3 Coefficients of $P = \sum_{i=1}^{n} \alpha_i x_i$

	1953	1957	1961	1962	1963	1964
W	2.8211	2.9080	0.7842	0.9982	0.6593	0.6182
	(10.6977)	(11.6323)	(2.0674)	(3.9563)	(4.4160)	(4.7442)
L	−3.7597	−3.5407	−1.2987	−1.3251	−0.3104	−0.3146
	(−3.5512)	(−3.7437)	(−1.1197)	(−1.6370)	(−0.6323)	(−0.7416)
BHP	−0.1746	−0.0251	0.0188	0.0133	0.0161	0.0093
	(−2.5957)	(−1.7378)	(3.0746)	(4.0149)	(6.0858)	(2.9218)
C	5.5465	−1.0860	−0.8306	−1.7927	1.9719	−0.7457
	(1.7204)	(−0.8335)	(−2.2458)	(−3.3794)	(−3.1714)	(−1.6989)
DOR	0.5038	1.6447	−0.6083	−0.6195	−0.4786	−0.6257
	(0.3812)	(2.8222)	(−1.3862)	(−1.8573)	(−1.2938)	(−2.0652)
ATR	2.1328	−2.2800	9.1287	7.6353	7.7370	8.8206
	(1.9665)	(−1.8912)	(6.4486)	(6.9986)	(6.9916)	(7.6839)
Const	21.3402	0.5256	20.4210	16.9946	5.8497	8.0488
	(1.4504)	(0.0342)	(1.6446)	(1.8495)	(0.9225)	(1.5028)
SDev	2.3375	1.3073	1.2399	0.9203	0.9959	0.9169
R^2	0.9445	0.9752	0.8445	0.9329	0.9161	0.9197

Price and Quality Changes

Table A.14. Manufacturer 3 Coefficients of $\ln P = \sum_{i=1}^{n} \beta_i x_i$

	1953	1957	1961	1962	1963	1964
W	0.0589	0.0625	0.0326	0.0371	0.0257	0.0233
	(12.3258)	(8.7924)	(2.1242)	(3.4000)	(4.0250)	(4.1050)
L	−0.0053	−0.0369	−0.0456	−0.0296	−0.0025	0.0032
	(−0.2752)	(−1.2728)	(−0.9701)	(−0.8669)	(0.1177)	(0.1753)
BHP	−0.0010	0.0004	0.0008	0.0006	0.0007	0.0004
	(−0.8228)	(0.9680)	(3.0696)	(3.9707)	(5.8905)	(2.9258)
C	0.0457	−0.0833	−0.0706	−0.0638	−0.0716	−0.0219
	(0.7812)	(−2.0829)	(−2.1366)	(−2.7867)	(−2.6954)	(−1.1472)
DOR	0.0029	0.0281	−0.0296	−0.0321	−0.0235	−0.0316
	(0.1195)	(1.5685)	(−1.6637)	(−2.2304)	(−1.4888)	(−2.3957)
ATR	0.0579	−0.0476	0.2599	0.1939	−0.2265	−0.2719
	(2.9421)	(−1.2855)	(4.5307)	(4.1165)	(−4.7904)	(−5.4990)
Const	1.2394	1.4863	2.8488	2.4964	2.1501	2.2389
	(4.6448)	(3.1518)	(5.6617)	(6.2918)	(7.9362)	(9.5940)
SDev	0.0424	0.0401	0.0502	0.0397	0.0426	0.0400
R^2	0.9830	0.9779	0.8487	0.9270	0.9131	0.9144
R^{*2}	0.9860	0.9840	0.8530	0.9330	0.9160	0.9190

Table A.15. Manufacturer 3 Coefficients of $\ln P = \sum_{i=1}^{n} \gamma_i \ln x_i$

	1953	1957	1961	1962	1963	1964
W	2.7351	3.0165	0.8497	1.5304	0.9802	0.9189
	(10.8580)	(8.7280)	(1.6910)	(4.6699)	(4.0459)	(4.6002)
L	−0.7247	−1.5556	−0.7762	−1.7386	−0.5487	−0.4002
	(−1.3657)	(−2.2142)	(0.7763)	(−2.5654)	(−1.1055)	(−0.9733)
BHP	−0.6030	0.0237	0.1600	0.1259	0.1577	0.0834
	(−2.5677)	(0.1838)	(2.5885)	(3.2677)	(4.4921)	(2.2343)
C	0.1735	−0.0930	−0.0582	−0.0942	−0.0978	−0.0406
	(2.1552)	(−1.5096)	(−1.5525)	(−3.5375)	(−3.1141)	(−1.7737)
DOR	0.0191	0.0425	−0.0361	−0.0273	−0.0238	−0.0300
	(0.6482)	(2.2313)	(−1.9211)	(−1.8349)	(−1.4239)	(−2.2533)
ATR	0.0730	−0.0455	0.3187	0.2439	0.2433	0.2707
	(3.1780)	(−1.1542)	(5.5681)	(5.4054)	(4.9607)	(5.5825)
Const	−1.5336	−2.9475	1.6785	2.4932	0.6152	0.7404
	(−1.4448)	(−2.0672)	(1.1446)	(2.2625)	(0.7277)	(1.0781)
SDev	0.0514	0.0425	0.0536	0.0405	0.0449	0.0399
R^2	0.9750	0.9752	0.8276	0.9243	0.9034	0.9145
R^{*2}	0.9760	0.9810	0.8320	0.9320	0.9070	0.9190

Table A.16. Characteristic Roots and Vectors Associated with the Principal Components of W, L, DIS, and BHP: Manufacturer 1

	1953				1957			
Characteristic roots	3.3101	0.5865	0.0791	0.0243	3.4650	0.3513	0.1007	0.0830
Percent of sum of all roots	82.8	97.4	99.4	100.0	86.6	95.4	97.9	100.0
Characteristic vectors	0.0190	0.0003	0.0260	0.0136	0.0136	0.0154	0.0159	0.0090
	0.0436	−0.0948	−0.0247	−0.0107	0.0912	0.0793	−0.1223	−0.0570
	0.0024	0.0016	−0.0029	0.0022	0.0013	−0.0012	0.0010	−0.0017
	0.0023	0.0015	0.0001	−0.0035	0.0010	−0.0011	−0.0005	0.0013

	1961				1962			
Characteristic roots	3.4167	0.4634	0.0949	0.0250	3.5949	0.3300	0.0536	0.0215
Percent of sum of all roots	85.4	97.0	99.4	100.0	89.9	98.1	99.5	100.0
Characteristic vectors	0.0085	0.0071	0.0026	0.0220	0.0080	0.0069	0.0045	0.0108
	0.0434	0.0446	0.0098	−0.0591	0.0390	0.0389	0.0016	−0.0542
	0.0007	−0.0004	−0.0011	0.0000	0.0006	−0.0004	−0.0010	0.0002
	0.0006	−0.0009	0.0007	−0.0001	0.0006	−0.0008	0.0066	−0.0002

	1963				1964			
Characteristic roots	3.5747	0.3377	0.0535	0.0342	3.5590	0.3745	0.0445	0.0220
Percent of sum of all roots	89.4	97.8	99.1	100.0	89.0	98.3	99.5	100.0
Characteristic vectors	0.0077	0.0066	0.0008	0.0113	0.0090	0.0058	0.0140	0.0005
	0.0382	0.0402	0.0152	−0.0505	0.0396	0.0539	−0.0476	−0.0052
	0.0006	0.0009	−0.0009	−0.0001	0.0007	−0.0006	−0.0002	0.0010
	0.0005	−0.0007	0.0006	0.0000	0.0007	−0.0007	−0.0001	−0.0010

Table A.17. Characteristic Roots and Vectors Associated with the Principal Components of W, L, DIS, and BHP: Manufacturer 2[a]

	1961				1962			
Characteristic roots	3.2598	0.6360	0.0900	0.0143	3.5291	0.3971	0.0586	0.0152
Percent of sum of all roots	81.5	97.4	99.6	100.0	88.2	98.2	99.6	100.0
Characteristic vectors	0.0156	0.0102	0.0228	0.0061	0.0118	0.0055	0.0177	0.0064
	0.0808	0.1141	−0.1047	−0.0057	0.0605	0.0922	−0.0657	09.0087
	0.0011	−0.0008	0.0000	−0.0016	0.0009	−0.0006	0.0001	−0.0013
	0.0012	−0.0013	−0.0006	0.0015	0.0011	−0.0012	−0.0008	0.0013
	1963				1964			
Characteristic roots	3.4898	0.4264	0.0714	0.0125	3.4347	0.4964	0.0577	0.0113
Percent of sum of all roots	87.2	97.9	99.7	100.0	85.9	98.3	99.7	100.0
Characteristic vectors	0.0130	0.0059	0.0208	0.0005	0.0130	0.0084	0.0198	0.0026
	0.0680	0.1066	−0.0726	−0.0095	0.0587	0.0824	−0.0720	−0.0098
	0.0009	−0.0008	−0.0004	0.0013	0.0010	−0.0010	−0.0004	0.0014
	0.0012	−0.0012	−0.0004	−0.0017	0.0013	−0.0013	−0.0001	−0.0019

[a] Years 1953 and 1957 not applicable.

Table A.18. Characteristic Roots and Vectors Associated with the Principal Components of W, L, DIS, and BHP: Manufacturer 3

	1953				1957			
Characteristic roots	3.4288	0.4647	0.0585	0.0481	3.6057	0.3201	0.0595	0.0148
Percent of sum of all roots	85.7	97.3	98.8	100.0	90.1	98.1	99.6	100.0
Characteristic vectors	0.0173	0.0104	0.0233	0.0128	0.0203	0.0126	0.0317	0.0041
	0.0780	0.1084	−0.0902	−0.0293	0.1255	0.1728	−0.1486	−0.0039
	0.0023	−0.0018	0.0009	−0.0032	0.0017	−0.0015	−0.0002	−0.0025
	0.0028	−0.0032	−0.0024	0.0031	0.0013	−0.0014	−0.0005	0.0018

	1961				1962			
Characteristic roots	3.4782	0.4964	0.0156	0.0097	3.4329	0.5328	0.0179	0.0165
Percent of sum of all roots	87.0	99.4	99.8	100.0	85.8	99.1	99.6	100.0
Characteristic vectors	0.0180	0.0111	0.0169	0.0214	0.0216	0.0127	0.0298	0.0137
	0.650	0.0895	−0.0371	−0.0715	0.0839	0.1118	−0.1023	−0.0188
	0.0009	−0.0007	−0.0011	0.0005	0.0009	−0.0007	0.0002	−0.0013
	0.0008	−0.0009	0.0007	−0.0008	0.0007	−0.0008	−0.0005	0.0008

	1963				1964			
Characteristic roots	3.3807	0.5486	0.0568	0.0139	3.3903	0.5339	0.0571	0.0197
Percent of sum of all roots	84.5	98.2	99.7	100.0	84.8	98.1	99.5	100.0
Characteristic vectors	0.0192	0.0108	0.0270	0.0117	0.0173	0.0097	0.0243	0.0108
	0.0801	0.1173	−0.0964	−0.0173	0.0687	0.1017	−0.0794	−0.0229
	0.0008	−0.0006	0.0002	−0.0012	0.0008	−0.0006	0.0002	−0.0011
	0.0007	−0.0007	−0.0005	0.0007	0.0007	−0.0008	−0.0006	0.0008

Price and Quality Changes

Table A.19. Characteristic Roots and Vectors Associated with the Principal Components of W, L, DIS, and BHP: Total Sample

	1953				1957			
Characteristic roots	3.3130	0.5294	0.1032	0.0544	3.4306	0.3927	0.1185	0.0583
Percent of sum of all roots	82.8	96.1	98.6	100.0	85.8	95.6	98.5	100.0
Characteristic vectors	0.0128	0.0022	0.0204	0.0013	0.0114	0.0086	0.0169	0.0047
	0.0391	0.0742	−0.0323	−0.0005	0.0697	0.0888	−0.0859	−0.0231
	0.0016	−0.0012	−0.0008	−0.0023	0.0010	−0.0010	0.0002	−0.0014
	0.0018	−0.0014	−0.0011	0.0024	0.0008	−0.0008	−0.0004	0.0011

	1961				1962			
Characteristic roots	3.3257	0.5608	0.0610	0.0525	3.3857	0.5260	0.0515	0.0368
Percent of sum of all roots	83.1	97.2	98.7	100.0	84.6	97.8	99.1	100.0
Characteristic vectors	0.0068	0.0052	0.0045	0.0092	0.0061	0.0049	0.0079	0.0043
	0.0328	0.0387	−0.0301	0.0324	0.0300	0.0344	−0.0402	−0.0072
	0.0005	−0.0003	0.0006	−0.0004	0.0004	−0.0003	0.002	−0.0006
	0.0004	−0.0005	−0.0005	0.0002	0.0005	−0.0005	−0.0002	0.0006

	1963				1964			
Characteristic roots	3.4204	0.4772	0.0655	0.0370	3.4136	0.4849	0.0779	0.0236
Percent of sum of all roots	85.5	97.4	99.1	100.0	85.3	97.5	99.4	100.0
Characteristic vectors	0.0061	0.0051	0.0084	0.0031	0.0067	0.0052	0.0098	0.0023
	0.0306	0.0347	−0.0417	−0.0040	0.0294	0.0369	−0.0384	−0.0045
	0.0004	−0.0003	0.0001	−0.0006	0.0004	−0.0004	0.0000	−0.0006
	0.0004	−0.0004	−0.0001	0.0004	0.0005	−0.0005	−0.0002	0.0006

Table A.20. Parameter Estimates of $\ln P = \sum_{i=1}^{n} \alpha_i x_i$
Using First Two Principal Components of W, L, DIS, and BHP: Manufacturer 1

	1953		1957		1961	
Z_1	1.2796	1.1890	0.7921	1.0048	0.5552	0.6655
	(5.7533)	(4.9589)	(12.3830)	(6.2300)	(7.4765)	(8.5820)
Z_2	0.2997	0.12962	0.6717	0.5973	0.5120	0.5288
	(1.7607)	(1.7404)	(3.0793)	(2.6868)	(2.5948)	(2.8382)
C	−0.1549	−0.1839	0.0194	0.0085	0.1013	0.0395
	(−1.9009)	(−2.1286)	(0.5453)	(0.2368)	(2.3559)	(0.8843)
MOD	—	−0.0008	—	0.0008	—	−0.0008
	—	(−1.0087)	—	(1.4344)	—	(−3.3244)
DOR	−0.0341	−0.0541	−0.0044	−0.0030	−0.0678	−0.0795
	(−1.1075)	(−1.1076)	(−0.2122)	(−0.1461)	(−2.0626)	(−2.5458)
ATR	0.0514	0.0759	0.0729	0.0667	0.0605	−0.0038
	(0.4300)	(0.6225)	(3.0837)	(2.8047)	(1.6595)	(−0.0958)
PS	—	—	0.2864	0.2642	0.5152	0.4742
	—	—	(4.4958)	(4.0663)	(9.4191)	(8.9349)
Const	0.2706	0.5627	−0.2961	−0.8741	1.8101	1.7740
	(0.4387)	(0.8259)	(−0.6582)	(−1.4544)	(8.7061)	(9.0265)
R^2	0.9102	0.9103	0.9393	0.9405	0.8665	0.8811
SDev	0.1230	0.1231	0.0719	0.0717	0.1053	0.9940
R^{*2}	0.8400	0.8300	0.9110	0.9140	0.8180	0.8350

	1962		1963		1964	
Z_1	0.6772	0.6920	0.8341	0.8410	0.7788	0.7831
	(9.1810)	(9.5890)	(10.4298)	(10.7620)	(8.4375)	(8.7750)
Z_2	0.4568	0.4649	0.7151	0.6361	0.6698	0.6708
	(2.2322)	(2.3319)	(3.1206)	(2.8073)	(3.5142)	(3.4932)
C	0.0350	0.0065	0.0060	−0.0211	−0.0080	−0.0085
	(0.9699)	(0.1737)	(0.1566)	(−0.5329)	(−0.2307)	(−0.2415)
MOD	—	−0.0004	—	−0.0004	—	0.0000
	—	(−2.1514)	—	(−2.2065)	—	(0.1108)
DOR	−0.0571	−0.0546	−0.0407	−0.0371	−0.0501	−0.0496
	(−1.8654)	(−1.8280)	(−1.2363)	(−1.1519)	(−2.0704)	(−2.0006)
ATR	0.0669	0.0410	0.4244	0.3941	0.4569	0.4571
	(1.7924)	(1.0723)	(9.6218)	(8.7220)	(10.2066)	(10.1356)
PS	0.4849	0.4656	—	—	—	—
	(9.5996)	(9.3110)	—	—	—	—
Const	1.9058	1.9531	1.5360	1.6570	1.4062	1.3970
	(10.0725)	(10.5238)	(7.2213)	(7.7143)	(7.1602)	(6.5115)
R^2	0.8943	0.8997	0.8704	0.8764	0.9042	0.9030
SDev	0.1039	0.1012	0.1141	0.1114	0.0946	0.0952
R^{*2}	0.8240	0.8250	0.8210	0.8190	0.8390	0.8370

Price and Quality Changes

Table A.21. Parameter Estimates of $\ln P = \sum_{i=1}^{n} \beta_i x_i$
Using First Two Principal Components of W, L, DIS, and BHP: Manufacturer 2

	1961		1962		1963		1964	
Z_1	0.2843	0.2844	0.4649	0.4648	0.3553	0.3635	0.4672	0.4574
	(6.0602)	(6.0607)	(15.2269)	(15.3417)	(12.0568)	(12.8023)	(11.6788)	(11.3482)
Z_2	0.1644	0.1467	0.1746	0.1389	0.0841	0.0536	−0.0587	−0.0495
	(2.2418)	(1.9423)	(2.9546)	(2.1469)	(1.3305)	(0.0663)	(−0.6133)	(−0.5216)
C	0.03339	0.0327	0.0041	0.0020	0.0057	0.0110	−0.0370	−0.0366
	(1.2108)	(1.1654)	(0.2821)	(0.1388)	(1.0554)	(0.7694)	(−1.4400)	(−1.4385)
MOD	—	−0.0002	—	−0.0001	—	−0.0002	—	−0.0002
		(−0.9829)		(−1.3011)		(−2.2742)		(−1.3152)
DOR	−0.0277	−0.0257	−0.0202	−0.0185	−0.0245	−0.0241	−0.0223	−0.0181
	(−1.4755)	(−1.3625)	(−1.9625)	(−1.7998)	(−2.2306)	(−2.2923)	(−1.6522)	(−1.3176)
ATR	0.7513	0.7356	0.6740	0.6602	0.7281	0.7003	0.6446	0.6314
	(13.9703)	(13.1070)	(18.3516)	(17.3931)	(17.5933)	(16.9162)	(13.2924)	(12.8671)
Const	1.9355	1.9903	1.8994	1.8725	2.1267	2.1924	2.2256	2.2528
	(12.2350)	(13.1070)	(19.5910)	(17.7006)	(17.8161)	(18.6301)	(19.6220)	(19.7188)
R^2	0.9366	0.9365	0.9662	0.9666	0.9569	0.9606	0.9536	0.9545
SDev	0.0484	0.0485	0.0331	0.0328	0.0359	0.0343	0.0409	0.0405
R^{*2}	0.969	0.969	0.982	0.983	0.979	0.981	0.975	0.976

Table A.22. Parameter Estimates of $\ln P = \sum_{i=1}^{n} \alpha_i x_i$
Using First Two Principal Components of W, L, DIS, and BHP: Manufacturer 3

	1953		1957		1961	
Z_1	0.8507	1.0882	0.8440	1.1650	0.5705	0.5529
	(8.6733)	(16.1416)	(9.9034)	(12.2652)	(8.4326)	(8.5050)
Z_2	0.5593	0.8365	−0.0890	0.5403	−0.1859	−0.1881
	(2.5844)	(6.2591)	(−0.3951)	(2.5128)	(−1.8589)	(−1.9676)
C	0.0083	0.0124	−0.1936	−0.1423	−0.0746	−0.0707
	(0.1164)	(0.2937)	(−2.7593)	(−2.6658)	(−2.3010)	(−2.2790)
MOD	—	0.0060	—	0.0045	—	−0.0030
	—	(6.8095)	—	(4.6782)	—	(−2.6185)
DOR	−0.0008	−0.0132	0.0055	0.0133	−0.0403	−0.0393
	(−0.0177)	(−0.4874)	(0.1962)	(0.6363)	(−2.5099)	(−2.5580)
ATR	0.0627	0.0736	0.0780	−0.0345	0.2870	0.2329
	(1.6100)	(3.2071)	(1.5932)	(−0.7903)	(5.4549)	(4.2844)
Const	−0.5739	−1.9946	0.0845	−3.5835	2.1683	2.2975
	(−2.0821)	(−7.5488)	(0.1248)	(−3.8434)	(14.9110)	(15.5763)
R^2	0.9379	0.9785	0.9422	0.9679	0.8534	0.8661
SDev	0.0811	0.0477	0.0648	0.0483	0.0495	0.0473
R^{*2}	0.9160	0.9760	0.9340	0.9720	0.8350	0.8730

	1962		1963		1964	
Z_1	0.5820	0.5756	0.6093	0.6110	0.5045	0.5046
	(11.5956)	(10.8241)	(10.6150)	(10.4193)	(12.3195)	(12.2160)
Z_2	−0.0689	−0.0693	−0.0586	−0.0531	0.0706	0.0750
	(−1.0403)	(−1.0380)	(−0.8524)	(−0.7074)	(0.9165)	(0.9039)
C	−0.0676	−0.0656	−0.0703	−0.0705	−0.0222	−0.0216
	(−2.6789)	(−2.5331)	(−2.4823)	(−2.4646)	(−1.0563)	(−1.0093)
MOD	—	−0.0005	—	−0.0002	—	0.0002
	—	(0.3990)	—	(−0.1905)	—	(0.1496)
DOR	−0.0380	−0.0379	−0.0292	−0.0296	−0.0384	−0.0385
	(−2.5245)	(−2.4967)	(−1.7818)	(−1.7744)	(−2.8837)	(−2.9626)
ATR	0.2246	0.2197	0.2569	0.2613	0.3101	0.3151
	(4.7615)	(5.4681)	(5.4431)	(4.9308)	(7.2031)	(5.7518)
Const	1.7243	1.7561	1.7017	1.6765	1.8063	1.7890
	(10.3475)	(9.4359)	(10.0823)	(7.7753)	(13.3298)	(9.9967)
R^2	0.9174	0.9159	0.9027	0.9008	0.9084	0.9068
SDev	0.0423	0.0426	0.0450	0.0455	0.0413	0.0417
R^{*2}	0.9250	0.9230	0.9070	0.9050	0.9130	0.9110

Price and Quality Changes

Table A.23. Parameter Estimates of $\ln P = \sum_{i=1}^{n} \beta_i x_i$
Using First Two Principal Components of W, L, DIS, and BHP: Total Sample

	1953	1957	1961	1962	1963	1964
Z_1	1.1548	0.5713	0.4255	0.3793	0.5087	0.3341
	(12.2921)	(8.7491)	(6.3296)	(9.1623)	(10.9613)	(9.1496)
Z_2	−0.2233	−0.3936	−0.3833	−0.3460	−0.4456	−0.3099
	(−9.8170)	(−8.7852)	(−5.8484)	(−9.0145)	(−11.0311)	(−7.1672)
C	−0.1550	−0.0728	−0.0063	0.0116	−0.0253	0.0048
	(−2.9272)	(−1.8053)	(−0.1706)	(0.5023)	(−1.0456)	(0.2086)
DOR	−0.0570	0.0113	−0.0178	−0.0278	−0.0221	−0.0494
	(−1.5116)	(0.4661)	(−0.7241)	(−1.5316)	(−1.1762)	(−2.7416)
ATR	0.0344	0.0559	0.2207	0.1090	0.5813	0.6744
	(0.7423)	(1.7819)	(5.0916)	(3.2126)	(19.1285)	(18.9996)
PS	—	0.4303	0.3979	0.5640	—	—
	—	(8.9476)	(6.8841)	(13.2314)	—	—
Const	−0.0959	2.1036	2.8231	2.9091	2.8653	2.9368
	(−0.3903)	(17.9220)	(61.0672)	(98.9721)	(90.5156)	(81.2396)
R^2	0.8795	0.8700	0.7520	0.8440	0.8322	0.7976
SDev	0.1284	0.1023	0.1261	0.0999	0.1051	0.1093

Table A.24. Coefficients Implied for W, L, DIS, BHP from Tables A.20, A.21, A.22

Manufacturer 1	W	L	DIS	BHP
1953	0.02440	0.02738	0.00355	0.00352
1957	0.02111	0.12551	0.00022	0.00005
1961	0.00835	0.04693	0.00018	−0.00013
1962	0.00857	0.04411	0.00022	0.00004
1963	0.01114	0.06061	0.00021	−0.00008
1964	0.01089	0.06694	0.00014	0.00008
Manufacturer 2				
1961	0.00611	0.04173	0.00018	0.00013
1962	0.00645	0.04422	0.00031	0.00030
1963	0.00512	0.03313	0.00025	0.00033
1964	0.00558	0.02259	0.00053	0.00068
Manufacturer 3				
1953	0.02053	0.12698	0.00095	0.00059
1957	0.01601	0.09054	0.00157	0.00122
1961	0.00821	0.02044	0.00064	0.00062
1962	0.01170	0.04113	0.00057	0.00046
1963	0.01107	0.04193	0.00052	0.00047
1964	0.00943	0.04190	0.00036	0.00030

Table A.25. Number of Observations by Model Year and Manufacturer, Automobiles

Year	Manuf. 1	Manuf. 2	Manuf. 3	Total
1953	32	—	30	62
1957	65	—	32	97
1961	89	35	68	192
1962	74	51	53	178
1963	85	50	56	191
1964	84	44	64	192
Total	429	180	303	912

Table A.26. Number of Observations by Model Year and Manufacturer, Refrigerators

Year	Admiral	Amana	Coldspot	Coolridge	Crosley	Frigidaire	GE	Gibson	Hotpoint	Kelvinator	Montgomery Ward	Norge	Philco	RCA	Westinghouse	International Harvester	Leonard	Total
1950	1		1	1	1		9	1	1	1	1	1	4		1			23
1951					1		9		1	4			3		1	1		20
1952	1	1	3		1	10		1	2	1		1	1		1			23
1953			2				6		2									10
1954	1	1			11	1	7		9	7			1		1			39
1955					8	12	8		6	7			10		8		2	61
1956	2	1	2		9	12	8		3	7	2	10	2					58
1957						12	4			11				10				37
1958	1	1				9	6			1		1	1	6	7			33
1959		1				7	10	2	1			1		8	2			32
1960	1	1	1			9	10	1	1	1		1	1	10	1			38
1961						11	9						11		7			38
1962						10	10	1	2	10		1	1	1	7			43
1963		1	1			12	13	1	13	10		2	1	1	7			62
1964						14	9			14								37
1965	2	1				22	16	2	16	3	1	2	2	2	9			78
Total	9	4	9	1	35	132	144	8	54	80	5	20	38	38	52	1	2	632

Price and Quality Changes

Table A.27. Estimates of Parameters in $\ln P = \sum_{i=1}^{n} \alpha_i x_i$ (Semilog); $\ln P = \sum_{i=1}^{n} \beta_i \ln x_i$ (Double Log): Frigidaire

	Semilog	Double Log
FCF	−0.0180	−0.0276
	(−0.704)	(0.412)
H	0.0152	0.5473
	(3.603)	(2.565)
W	0.0197	0.5138
	(2.734)	(2.529)
D	−0.0193	−0.9238
	(−2.636)	(−3.717)
D1	0.0622	0.0741
	(1.834)	(2.112)
D3	0.0797	−0.0750
	(−1.1339)	(−1.164)
D4	0.0688	0.1029
	(1.459)	(2.122)
D7	−0.0429	−0.0953
	(−0.280)	(−0.623)
D8	0.1409	0.1149
	(2.600)	(2.473)
D9	0.0215	0.0228
	(0.529)	(0.536)
D13	0.2002	0.2015
	(4.945)	(4.803)
D14	0	0
D18	0.0915	0.1010
	(1.842)	(1.897)
D19	0.2679	0.2901
	(4.078)	(4.281)
D20	0.2375	0.2501
	(5.281)	(5.397)
D21	0.3584	0.3566
	(6.063)	(5.817)
D22	0.0545	0.867
	(0.370)	(0.576)
R^2	0.8669	0.8760
SDev	0.1389	0.1340

Table A.28. Estimates of Parameters in $\ln P = \sum_{i=1}^{n} \alpha_i x_i$ (Semilog); $\ln P = \sum_{i=1}^{n} \beta_i \ln x_i$ (Double Log): GE

	Semilog	Double Log
FCF	−0.0023	0.0165
	(−0.125)	(0.444)
H	0.0025	0.0855
	(0.924)	(0.626)
W*	0.0462	1.1234
	(8.314)	(7.294)
D	−0.0166	−0.9343
	(−3.037)	(−5.011)
D1	0.0395	0.0413
	(1.361)	(1.417)
D3	−0.0870	−0.0950
	(−2.589)	(−2.792)
D4	0.0371	0.0605
	(0.969)	(1.578)
D7	−0.1728	−0.2301
	(−2.922)	(−3.935)
D8	0.2350	0.2237
	(5.574)	(5.472)
D9	−0.1774	−0.1895
	(−1.336)	(−1.414)
D13	−0.0153	−0.0133
	(−0.313)	(−0.269)
D14	0.1912	0.1996
	(3.948)	(4.048)
D18	−0.0363	−0.0337
	(−0.473)	(−0.433)
D19	0.2276	0.2420
	(4.600)	(4.839)
D20	0.1568	0.1508
	(2.610)	(2.493)
D21	0.2798	0.2896
	(4.074)	(4.184)
D22	0.2259	0.2482
	(3.327)	(3.754)
R^2	0.8999	0.8981
SDev	0.1260	0.1272

Price and Quality Changes

Table A.29. Characteristic Roots and Vectors Associated with the Principal Components of CF, FCF, H, W^*, and D for Selected Manufacturers and Entire Sample

	Frigidaire						GE					
Characteristic roots	3.4026	0.8597	0.3851	0.2910	0.0615		3.3576	1.0755	0.3313	0.1709	0.0647	
Percent of sum of roots	68.1	85.2	92.9	98.8	100.0		67.2	88.7	95.3	98.7	100.0	
Characteristic vectors (appears below corresponding root)	0.1936	0.0653	0.0285	0.0231	0.3071		0.1314	0.0006	0.0809	0.0609	0.1885	
	0.0704	0.0248	−0.0935	0.0784	−0.0470		0.0564	0.0203	0.0193	0.0606	−0.0672	
	0.4501	0.0113	0.7213	0.2308	−0.3709		0.2683	−0.1286	0.1713	−0.4044	−0.1294	
	0.3985	0.1009	−0.1392	−0.4800	−0.2073		0.3850	−0.0590	−0.7182	−0.0479	0.0556	
	0.5841	−2.3268	−0.2518	0.0027	0.1500		−0.0849	1.4204	0.0347	0.4399	−0.0935	
	Hotpoint						Kelvinator					
Characteristic roots	2.4834	1.2492	0.9963	0.1896	0.0815		2.5809	1.1796	0.6291	0.4460	0.1643	
Percent of sum of roots	49.7	74.7	94.6	98.4	100.0		51.6	75.2	87.8	96.7	100.0	
Characteristic vectors (appears below corresponding root)	0.3529	0.0508	0.0035	0.0779	0.4433		0.1218	0.0489	0.1200	0.1495	0.0858	
	0.1387	0.0119	−0.0036	0.1229	−0.1334		0.1087	0.0214	0.0078	−0.0162	−0.1492	
	0.3834	−0.4769	−0.3949	−0.5595	−0.1490		0.2488	0.5180	−0.4899	−0.1185	0.2427	
	0.2360	0.9248	−0.0102	−0.5677	−0.1941		0.3013	−0.2240	0.1366	−0.4194	0.2402	
	−0.6391	0.7248	−2.8694	0.8830	0.2920		−0.4718	0.9876	0.9114	−0.6196	−0.0870	

Table A.29 (continued)

	Philco					RCA				
Characteristic roots	3.6091	0.8971	0.2592	0.1538	0.0808	3.6010	0.7471	0.3671	0.2480	0.0368
Percent of sum of roots	72.2	90.1	95.3	98.4	100.0	72.0	87.0	94.3	99.3	100.0
Characteristic vectors (appears below corresponding root)	0.3806	0.1110	0.0640	0.5459	0.3636	0.6009	0.3159	0.2492	0.3764	0.9075
	0.1530	0.0125	0.0991	0.0384	−0.2392	0.1436	0.0826	−0.2322	−0.1538	0.0025
	1.2728	0.5172	0.9900	−1.7553	0.9706	1.4452	−0.5468	1.9823	−1.5328	—
	1.0860	0.0643	−1.9785	−0.4132	−0.1877	0.8373	0.4069	1.1649	−0.7694	−0.7042
	0.5553	−2.5871	0.2098	−0.0801	0.2914	−0.8687	2.3963	−0.0967	0.6141	−0.4794

	Westinghouse					Total				
Characteristic roots	3.0820	0.9913	0.5619	0.2639	0.1009	2.830	1.0358	0.6025	0.3054	0.1935
Percent of sum of roots	61.6	81.5	92.7	98.0	100.0	57.3	78.0	90.0	96.1	100.0
Characteristic vectors (appears below corresponding root)	0.3897	0.0101	0.2000	0.0736	0.5725	0.0749	0.0059	0.0086	0.0546	0.1018
	0.1244	−0.0247	0.0582	−0.1836	−0.0809	0.0333	−0.0044	0.0026	0.0315	−0.0414
	1.5155	−0.4888	0.5639	1.9175	−1.4666	0.1632	0.0778	0.2083	−0.2145	−0.0272
	0.6240	0.0562	−1.3572	−0.0389	0.0534	0.1529	−0.0479	−0.2612	−0.1540	−0.0050
	0.3653	3.0898	0.2768	0.1017	−0.4129	−0.0181	0.6486	−0.1670	0.0651	−0.0449

Price and Quality Changes

Table A.30. Parameter Estimates for $\ln P = \sum_{i=1}^{n} \beta_i \ln x_i$: Major Manufacturers, 1950–1965

	Frigidaire	GE	Hotpoint	Kelvinator	Philco	RCA	Westinghouse
Z_1	0.9996	1.0774	0.8152	0.9918	0.7104	0.1672	0.3463
	(8.304)	(7.359)	(4.253)	(7.025)	(5.869)	(7.950)	(1.116)
Z_2	0.3907	0.3655	0.0276	0.0328	−0.1455	−0.3470	−0.1970
	(2.746)	(2.202)	(0.181)	(0.271)	(−0.937)	(−2.368)	(−0.716)
Z_3	−0.0249	−0.7482	0.5249	−0.1044	−0.1844	−0.2352	−0.1781
	(−0.095)	(−2.506)	(2.532)	(−0.637)	(−0.466)	(−1.325)	(−0.375)
Z_4	−0.30004	0.9070	0.5095	−0.8694	−0.3729	0.4206	0.8678
	(−1.179)	(2.136)	(1.195)	(−4.770)	(−0.783)	(2.170)	(1.793)
T	−0.0333	−0.0226	−0.0455	−0.0297	−0.0277	−0.0862	−0.0363
	(−7.787)	(−5.092)	(−5.889)	(−7.631)	(−2.786)	(−6.193)	(−2.881)
$D1$	0.0345	0.0350	0.2082	0.0953	0.1386	0.1977	−0.0044
	(1.222)	(1.260)	(3.634)	(2.843)	(2.016)	(2.350)	(−0.046)
$D8$	0.0832	0.2235	0.0108	0.1356	0.1764	0.1483	0.1530
	(2.347)	(5.686)	(0.133)	(2.547)	(2.090)	(0.782)	(1.216)
$D13$	0.1676	−0.1333	0.0566	0.0348	−0.0090	−0.0219	0.1873
	(5.077)	(4.412)	(0.973)	(1.020)	(−0.130)	(−0.516)	(1.920)
$D19$	0.1539	0.2456	0.0876	0.1726	0.3186	0.3240	0.1391
	(2.701)	(5.228)	(0.820)	(3.341)	(3.662)	(3.985)	(1.003)
$D20$	0.2485	0.3022	0.2993	0.3423	0.1584	0.3649	0.3669
	(7.002)	(5.804)	(2.626)	(5.073)	(1.871)	(5.550)	(1.873)
$D21$	0.4549	0.4575	0.2827	0.4295	0.2205	0.4462	0.2497
	(9.273)	(7.005)	(2.069)	(4.947)	(1.775)	(4.508)	(1.144)
$D22$	−0.0254	0.0599	−0.0562	−0.0500	0.0608	−0.0129	0.0034
	(−0.631)	(1.152)	(−0.499)	(−0.714)	(0.826)	(−0.218)	(0.018)
Const	−1.0793	−0.3583	6.7669	−3.0548	−11.1499	−3.0163	−8.0081
	(−1.554)	(−0.356)	(2.770)	(−2.887)	(−2.572)	(−1.504)	(−1.824)
SDev	0.1112	0.1234	0.1611	0.1140	0.1034	0.0800	0.2155
R^2	0.9135	0.9042	0.7504	0.9101	0.9107	0.9566	0.6808

Table A.31. Coefficients Implied for *CF*, *FCF*, *H*, *W**, and *D* by Regression of Table A.30: Major Manufacturers, 1950–1965

	CF	FCF	H	W*	D
Frigidaire	0.2112	0.0588	0.3670	0.5854	−0.3198
GE	0.1365	0.1087	−0.2529	0.8871	−0.2376
Hotpoint	0.3306	0.1741	−0.1930	−0.0767	−1.5570
Kelvinator	−0.0349	0.1234	0.4297	0.6834	0.0693
Philco	0.0389	0.0742	1.3009	1.2455	0.7621
RCA	0.3903	0.0556	2.0207	−0.1885	−1.1214
Westinghouse	0.1613	−0.1220	2.1798	0.4135	−0.4123

Table A.32. "Pure Price" and "Quality" Components of Observed (Mean Log) Price Change

	1953	1957	1961	1962	1963	1964
			Manufacturer 1			
Mean Char.						
Z_1	2.6090	3.0520	1.5550	1.3790	1.3540	1.4660
Z_2	−1.3250	1.5620	0.8370	0.7380	0.7710	0.9640
C	0.5940	0.8620	0.8760	0.8110	0.9240	0.6430
DOR	0.4690	0.3540	0.1460	0.2160	0.2000	0.2620
ATR	0.2500	0.3230	0.2130	0.2300	0.1530	0.1190
PS	—	0.1080	0.1010	0.1220	—	—
Const	1.0000	1.0000	1.0000	1.0000	1.0000	1.0000
Mean log						
price	3.1070	3.2400	3.2460	3.2670	3.2790	3.2300
c_j, 1961	−0.6221	1.1196	—	−0.1481	−0.2102	−0.0738
$\bar{c}_j$, 1961	0.4833	−1.1256	—	0.1691	0.2432	0.0578
c_j^*, 1961	−0.1390	−0.0060	—	0.0210	0.0330	−0.0160
d_j, 1961	−0.7284	−1.6934	—	−0.1597	−0.2423	−0.0309
$\bar{d}_j$, 1961	0.8674	1.6874	—	0.1807	0.2753	0.0149
			Manufacturer 2			
Mean Char.						
Z_1	—	—	2.7230	1.9210	2.1940	2.0580
Z_2	—	—	2.2700	1.7120	2.3460	1.4630
C	—	—	0.5430	0.4900	0.5200	0.5680
DOR	—	—	0.3430	0.3730	0.3800	0.3410
ATR	—	—	0.0290	0.0200	0.0200	0.0230
Const	—	—	1.0000	1.0000	1.0000	1.0000
Mean log						
price	—	—	3.1130	3.0990	3.0830	3.0870
c_j, 1961	—	—	—	−0.3286	−0.1488	−0.3248
$\bar{c}_j$, 1961	—	—	—	0.3426	0.1188	0.2988
c_j^*, 1961	—	—	—	−0.0140	−0.0300	−0.0260
d_j, 1961	—	—	—	−0.4775	−0.2233	−0.2685
$\bar{d}_j$, 1961	—	—	—	0.4635	0.1933	0.2425
			Manufacturer 3			
Mean Char.						
Z_1	3.2170	4.2110	2.3660	2.7420	2.6370	2.3370
Z_2	1.7450	3.3520	1.8280	2.3600	2.3860	2.0230
C	0.4000	0.7500	0.6320	0.5850	0.6070	0.6560
DOR	0.1670	0.2810	0.2210	0.2260	0.1960	0.2500

Price and Quality Changes

Table A.32. (*continued*)

ATR	0.4000	0.1880	0.0150	0.0190	0.0180	0.0160
Const	1.0000	1.0000	1.0000	1.0000	1.0000	1.0000
Mean log price	3.1670	3.2110	3.1260	3.1140	3.1250	3.1090
c_j, 1961	0.6314	0.8082	—	0.1206	0.0551	−0.0549
$\bar{c}_j$, 1961	−0.5904	−0.7232	—	−0.1326	−0.0561	0.0379
c_j^*, 1961	0.0410	0.0850	—	−0.0120	−0.0010	−0.0170
d_j, 1961	0.6997	1.4123	—	0.1864	0.1359	−0.0043
$\bar{d}_j$, 1961	−0.6587	−1.3273	—	−0.1984	−0.1369	−0.0127

Table A.33. "Pure Price" and "Quality" Components of Observed (Log Mean) Price Change

Log mean price	1953	1957	1961	1962	1963	1964
			Manufacturer 1			
	3.2035	3.2846	3.2935	3.3277	3.3421	3.2908
c_j, 1961	−0.6223	1.1196	—	−0.1481	−0.2102	−0.0736
$\bar{c}_j$, 1961	0.5323	−1.2086	—	0.1823	0.2588	0.0711
c_j^*, 1961	−0.0900	−0.0880	—	0.0242	0.0486	−0.0027
d_j, 1961	−0.9574	−1.7764	—	−0.1465	−0.2267	−0.0176
$\bar{d}_j$, 1961	0.8674	1.6874	—	0.1807	0.2753	0.0149
			Manufacturer 2			
	—	—	3.1410	3.1213	3.1025	3.1183
c_j, 1961	—	—	—	−0.3286	−0.1488	−0.3248
$\bar{c}_j$, 1961	—	—	—	0.3089	0.1103	0.3021
c_j^*, 1961	—	—	—	−0.0197	−0.0385	−0.0227
d_j, 1961	—	—	—	−0.4438	−0.2318	−0.2652
$\bar{d}_j$, 1961	—	—	—	0.4635	0.1933	0.2425
			Manufacturer 3			
	3.2250	3.2517	3.1330	3.1246	3.1251	3.1184
c_j, 1961	0.6314	0.8082	—	0.1206	0.0551	−0.0549
$\bar{c}_j$, 1961	−0.5394	−0.6895	—	−0.1290	−0.0630	0.0463
c_j^*, 1961	0.0920	0.1187	—	−0.0084	−0.0079	−0.0146
d_j, 1961	0.7507	1.4460	—	0.1900	0.1290	−0.0019
$\bar{d}_j$, 1961	−0.6587	−1.3273	—	−0.1984	−0.1369	−0.0129

Appendix B to Chapter 4

In this appendix we shall explain the nature of the homogeneity test applied in section 3 and motivate the use of R^{*2} in making (judgmental) comparisons regarding the goodness of fit of various functional forms. Thus, suppose we have at our disposal s samples, and we wish to test the hypothesis that all of them belong to the same regression process. To this effect, suppose

$$(1) \qquad y_{\cdot i} = X_i \beta_{\cdot i} + u_{\cdot i} \quad i = 1, 2, \ldots, s$$

gives the model pertaining to the ith sample. In (1) $y_{\cdot i}$ is a vector of T_i observations pertaining to the dependent variable, X_i is a $T_i \times m_i$ matrix of observations on the explanatory variables, $\beta_{\cdot i}$ is the m_i element vector of coefficients to be estimated, and $u_{\cdot i}$ is the T_i element vector of error terms, all pertaining to the ith subsample. Notice that we allow for different number of observations for each sample. Of course, since the hypothesis to be tested is that

$$(2) \qquad \beta_{\cdot i} = \beta^* \quad i = 1, 2, \ldots, s,$$

it is clear that we must have the same number of elements in the vectors $\beta_{\cdot i}$, say m.

To properly formulate the test we need some assumption on the random vectors; thus suppose

$$(3) \qquad u_{\cdot i} \sim N(0, \sigma_{ii} I), \quad \mathrm{Cov}(u_{\cdot i}, u_{\cdot j}) = \delta_{ij} \sigma_{ii} I,$$

where δ_{ij} is the Kronecker delta. Let

$$(4) \qquad X = \begin{bmatrix} X_1 & & 0 \\ & \ddots & \\ 0 & & X_s \end{bmatrix}, \quad X^* = \begin{bmatrix} X_1 \\ X_2 \\ \vdots \\ X_s \end{bmatrix}$$

and note that

$$(4a) \qquad X^* = X \begin{bmatrix} I \\ I \\ \vdots \\ I \end{bmatrix},$$

where the matrix multiplying X in the right member of (4a) consists of

Price and Quality Changes

s identity *matrices* each of order m. If we put

(5) $$y = \begin{bmatrix} y_{\cdot 1} \\ y_{\cdot 2} \\ \vdots \\ y_{\cdot s} \end{bmatrix}, \quad \beta = \begin{bmatrix} \beta_{\cdot 1} \\ \beta_{\cdot 2} \\ \vdots \\ \beta_{\cdot s} \end{bmatrix}, \quad u = \begin{bmatrix} u_{\cdot 1} \\ u_{\cdot 2} \\ \vdots \\ u_{\cdot s} \end{bmatrix},$$

then the s samples in (1) can be expressed compactly as

(5a) $$y = X\beta + u.$$

The efficient estimator of the vector β can be obtained as

(5b) $$\hat{\beta} = (X'X)^{-1}X'y.$$

Suppose now we wish to test the hypothesis that *all* the s samples were obtained from the same universe. This implies that

(5c) $$\beta_{\cdot i} = \beta^*, \quad \sigma_{ii} = \sigma^2, \quad i = 1, 2, \ldots, s.$$

If, in fact, the hypotheses in (5c) are correct, then the pooled sample can be written as

(6) $$y = X^*\beta^* + u,$$

and the efficient estimator of β^* is given by

(6a) $$\hat{\beta}^* = (X^{*\prime}X^*)^{-1} X^{*\prime}y.$$

How can we now conduct a test of the hypotheses in (5c)? We note that the residuals from the regression in (6) can be written as

(6b) $$y - X^*\hat{\beta}^* = y - X\hat{\beta} + X\hat{\beta} - X^*\hat{\beta}^*.$$

Hence

(6c) $$(y - X^*\hat{\beta}^*)'(y - X^*\hat{\beta}^*) = (y - X\hat{\beta})'(y - X\hat{\beta}) \\ + (X\hat{\beta} - X^*\hat{\beta}^*)'(X\hat{\beta} - X^*\hat{\beta}^*).$$

Now

(7) $$y - X\hat{\beta} = [I - X(X'X)^{-1}X']u$$

(7a) $$X\hat{\beta} - X^*\hat{\beta}^* = X(X'X)^{-1} X'X\beta \\ + X(X'X)^{-1} X'u \\ - X^*(X^{*\prime}X^*)^{-1} X^{*\prime}X\beta \\ - X^*(X^{*\prime}X^*)^{-1} X^{*\prime}u.$$

Under the null hypothesis (5c), we notice

(8) $\quad X^*(X^{*\prime}X^*)^{-1}X^{*\prime}X\beta = X^*(X^{*\prime}X^*)^{-1}X^{*\prime}X \begin{pmatrix} I \\ I \\ \vdots \\ I \end{pmatrix} \beta^* = X^*\beta^*.$

Also,

(8a) $\quad X\beta = X \begin{pmatrix} I \\ I \\ \vdots \\ I \end{pmatrix} \beta^* = X^*\beta^*.$

Thus, (7a) becomes

(9) $\quad X\hat{\beta} - X^*\hat{\beta}^* = [X(X'X)^{-1}X' - X^*(X^{*\prime}X^*)^{-1}X^{*\prime}]u.$

The matrices in the right members of (7) and (9) are easily shown to be idempotent, so that we can write

(10) $\quad (y - X\hat{\beta})'(y - X\hat{\beta}) = u'[I - X(X'X)^{-1}X']u$

(10a) $\quad (X\hat{\beta} - X^*\hat{\beta}^*)'(X\hat{\beta} - X^*\hat{\beta}^*) = u'[X(X'X)^{-1}X'$
$\qquad\qquad\qquad\qquad\qquad\qquad\qquad\qquad - X^*(X^{*\prime}X^*)^{-1}X^{*\prime}]u.$

In view of the assumptions on the error vector u, we thus conclude

(11) $\quad \dfrac{u'[I - X(X'X)^{-1}X']u}{\sigma^2} \sim \chi^2_{r_1},$

$\qquad \dfrac{u'[X(X'X)^{-1}X' - X^*(X^{*\prime}X^*)^{-1}X^{*\prime}]u}{\sigma^2} \sim \chi^2_{r_2}$

where

(12)
$r_1 = \text{rank}[I - X(X'X)^{-1}X'] = \sum_{i=1}^{s} T_i - sm$

$r_2 = \text{rank}[X(X'X)^{-1}X' - X^*(X^{*\prime}X^*)^{-1}X^{*\prime}] = sm - m$

To show the independence of the two quadratic forms in (11) it is sufficient

Price and Quality Changes

to show that the two matrices there are mutually orthogonal. But

$$(13) \quad X(X'X)^{-1}X'[X(X'X)^{-1}X' - X^*(X^{*\prime}X^*)^{-1}X^{*\prime}]$$

$$= X(X'X)^{-1}X' - X(X'X)^{-1}X'X \begin{pmatrix} I \\ I \\ \vdots \\ I \end{pmatrix} (X^{*\prime}X^*)^{-1}X^{*\prime}$$

$$= X(X'X)^{-1}X' - X^*(X^{*\prime}X^*)^{-1}X^{*\prime}$$

and the conclusion follows immediately from (13).

Thus, under the null hypothesis

$$(14) \quad \frac{(y - X^*\hat{\beta}^*)'(y - X^*\hat{\beta}^*) - (y - X\hat{\beta})'(y - X\hat{\beta})}{(y - X\hat{\beta})'(y - X\hat{\beta})} \cdot \frac{\sum_{i=1}^{s} T_i - sm}{m(s-1)}$$

$$\sim F_{m(s-1),\ \sum_{i=1}^{s} T_i - sm}$$

and a test of the latter can easily be based on the central F-distribution. Perhaps it will be simpler to grasp the nature of the test in a different notation. Let Q_T be the sum of squares of residuals from the regression of the pooled sample. Let Q_i be the sum of squares of the residuals from the regression using *only* the ith subsample. Then we can rewrite (14) as

$$(14a) \quad \frac{Q_T - \sum_{i=1}^{s} Q_i}{\sum_{i=1}^{s} Q_i} \cdot \frac{\sum_{i=1}^{s} T_i - sm}{m(s-1)} \sim F_{m(s-1),\ \sum_{i=1}^{s} T_i - sm}.$$

It is clear that we reject the null hypothesis in (5c) if the computed statistic is "too high," given the level of significance of the test.

In Section 3 we also had occasion to test the hypothesis that the constant terms among manufacturers are different, but the coefficients of the other variables are the same. In terms of the theoretical framework above, this test necessitates little change. Thus, consider all variables in (1) as deviations from their respective sample means. The sample representation in (1) would be the same except for the error term, which should now read

$$(15) \quad w_{\cdot i} = \left(I - \frac{ee'}{T_i}\right) u_{\cdot i}$$

This is so since the error term after sample means have been subtracted becomes $u_{ti} - \bar{u}_i$. But

$$(15a) \quad \bar{u}_i = \frac{e'u_{\cdot i}}{T_i}, \quad e = (1, 1, 1, \ldots, 1)',$$

and (15) follows immediately.

In this scheme the arguments leading to (10) and (10a) remain valid except that now they involve the vector

(16) $$w = \begin{pmatrix} w_{.1} \\ w_{.2} \\ \vdots \\ w_{.s} \end{pmatrix}$$

Let*

(16a) $$S_i^* = \frac{ee'}{T_i}, \quad S = \text{diag}\,(S_1^*, S_2^*, \ldots, S_s^*)$$

so that S is a block diagonal matrix of order $\sum_{i=1}^{s} T_i$. It is obvious that

(17) $$w = (I - S)u.$$

It is also apparent that since the elements of the X_i are now centered observations about (the relevant) sample means, we have

(18) $$SX = 0, \quad SX^* = 0.$$

Thus, the quadratic form corresponding to the right member of (10) now becomes

(19) $$u(I - S)[I - X(X'X)^{-1}X'](I - S)u$$
$$= u'[I - S - X(X'X)^{-1}X']u.$$

In view of (18) the quadratic form $(X\hat{\beta} - X^*\hat{\beta}^*)'(X\hat{\beta} - X^*\hat{\beta}^*)$ remains exactly as exhibited in the right member of (10a). Now, the matrix $[I - S - X(X'X)^{-1}X']$ is easily shown to be idempotent. Since

(20) $$\text{rank}\,[I - S - X(X'X)^{-1}X'] = \sum_{i=1}^{s} T_i - s - sm,$$

we conclude that in this scheme, under the null hypothesis,

(21) $$\frac{(y - X\hat{\beta})'(y - X\hat{\beta})}{\sigma^2} \sim \chi^2_{\sum_{i=1}^{s} T_i - s(m+1)}$$

To show that the two quadratic forms corresponding to (10) and (10a), in the present context, are mutually independent, it is sufficient to show that $[I - S - X(X'X)^{-1}X']$ and the matrix of the quadratic form in (10a) are mutually orthogonal. But this obvious in view of (13) and (18).

---

* In equation (16a), as well as in (15a), one should really write e_i to indicate that e_i is a T_i element vector of unities. We omit the subscript for the sake of economy of notation.

Price and Quality Changes

Thus, to test the hypothesis that the slope coefficients in the s subsamples are the same, but the constant terms may differ, we may proceed as follows. Let Q_T be the sum of squared residuals in the pooled regression —allowing for variation in the constant terms. Let Q_i be the sum of squared residuals from the regression using *only* the ith subsample. Then

$$(22) \quad \frac{Q_T - \sum_{i=1}^{s} Q_i}{\sum_{i=1}^{s} Q_i} \cdot \frac{s(T - m - 1)}{m(s - 1)} \sim F_{m(s-1),\, \sum_{i=1}^{s} T_i - s(m+1)}.$$

We should remind the reader that here m refers to the number of bona fide variables, i.e., excluding the fictitious variable unity whose coefficient is the constant term of the equations.

In the previous derivation m did include this fictitious variable.

Turning now to the problem of choice among functional forms, it should first be remarked that insofar as the choice between semilog and double log forms, there is some pertinent literature due to Cox (1961, 1962). The test formulated by Cox is asymptotic in nature and essentially involves comparison of the residual variances from the relevant regression; the test statistic is asymptotically normal. The variance of this asymptotic distribution is typically a somewhat complicated function of unknown parameters and thus will have to be estimated separately.

In this study we have chosen to eschew this complicated test and rely instead on an informal criterion based on the interpretation of the coefficient of determination of multiple regression as a correlation coefficient between observed and "predicted" values of the dependent variable.

Let us illustrate this aspect before we give an account of the criterion actually employed. Consider the general linear model

$$(23) \quad y = X\beta + u,$$

where now X is $T \times n$, β is $n \times 1$, and are respectively the matrix of observations on the explanatory variables and the vector of parameters to be estimated. Suppose that all observations are stated as deviations from the relevant sample means. The ordinary least squares estimator is given by

$$(24) \quad \hat{\beta} = (X'X)^{-1}X'y;$$

the predicted values of the dependent variable are given by

$$(25) \quad \hat{y} = X\hat{\beta};$$

and the sample correlation between predicted and actual values of the dependent variable is given by

(26) $$r = \frac{y'\hat{y}}{(y'y)^{1/2}(\hat{y}'\hat{y})^{1/2}}.$$

But

(27) $$y'\hat{y} = y'X\hat{\beta}, \quad \hat{y}'\hat{y} = \hat{\beta}'X'X\hat{\beta}.$$

The square of r in (26) is thus

(28) $$r^2 = \frac{(y'X\hat{\beta})(y'X\hat{\beta})}{(y'y)(\hat{\beta}'X'X\hat{\beta})}$$

Since

(29) $$y = X\hat{\beta} + \hat{u}, \quad \hat{u} = y - X\hat{\beta},$$

we see that

(30) $$y'X\hat{\beta} = \hat{\beta}X'X\hat{\beta} + \hat{u}'X\hat{\beta}.$$

But

(31) $$\hat{u}'X\hat{\beta} = 0.$$

Thus, we conclude

(32) $$r^2 = \frac{\hat{\beta}'X'X\hat{\beta}}{y'y},$$

which is of course exactly the expression for the coefficient of determination of multiple regression (R^2) unadjusted for degrees of freedom.

Now suppose we wish to decide as to which of the following two forms "fits" the data better:

(33) $$\ln P_t = \sum_{i=1}^{n} \alpha_i x_{ti} + u_t$$

or

(34) $$P_t = \sum_{i=1}^{n} \beta_i x_{ti} + w_t.$$

Suppose, further, that regression yields

(35) $$\ln P_t = \sum_{i=1}^{n} \hat{\alpha}_i x_{ti}$$

where of course P_t is price and x_i are the various characteristics of the

Price and Quality Changes

models as explained in Section 3. The predicted value of price, $\hat{P}_t$, may be obtained by exponentiation as

$$\hat{P}_t = e^{\ln P_t}. \tag{36}$$

The (square of the) correlation coefficient between the predicted and actual price is

$$R^{*2} = \frac{[\sum_{t=1}^{T} (P_t - \bar{P})(\hat{P}_t - \bar{\hat{P}})]^2}{[\sum_{t=1}^{T} (P_t - \bar{P})^2][\sum_{t=1}^{T} (\hat{P}_t - \bar{\hat{P}})^2]}. \tag{37}$$

where $\bar{P}$, $\bar{\hat{P}}$ are, respectively, sample means of the actual and predicted values of the dependent variable. This statistic is then directly comparable to the coefficient of determination one obtains when the regression in (34) is carried out.

We term R^{*2} the antilog R^2 and give it routinely in the tables of Appendix A.

5.

Irving B. Kravis and Robert E. Lipsey
International Price Comparisons by Regression Methods

This report on the use of regression analysis as a technique for comparing prices in different countries is an outgrowth of a National Bureau of Economic Research study of comparative prices and price trends in the United States and foreign countries. The study was designed to develop new methods of measuring price competitiveness in international trade, including measures of both price levels and price trends. Regression-based index numbers are only one of a number of types of price comparison used in the larger study, and the indexes for automotive diesel engines described in this paper are an example of our use of regression methods. The other regression-based indexes are described briefly in the appendix to this paper.

The study was financed in large part by grants to the National Bureau of Economic Research from the National Science Foundation. For a statement of its nature and purpose, see Irving B. Kravis and Robert E. Lipsey, *Price Competitiveness in World Trade* (New York: National Bureau of Economic Research, 1971). In preparing the present paper the authors have greatly benefited from discussions with Phoebus J. Dhrymes, Lawrence R. Klein, Robert Summers, and Paul R. Trumpler and suggestions from Stanley Diller, F. Thomas Juster, and James Kindahl. Joaquin P. Pujol was responsible for many of the computations, and Rita Bank rendered statistical assistance. Several companies in the diesel manufacturing industry were helpful in providing data and reviewing the manuscript. A shorter version of this paper was published in the *International Economic Review*, June 1969. The present version, with minor changes, is chapter 5 of *Price Competitiveness in World Trade*.

Irving B. Kravis is Professor of Economics, University of Pennsylvania, and a member of the Senior Research Staff of the National Bureau. Robert E. Lipsey is Professor of Economics, Queens College, City University of New York, and Vice President-Research of the National Bureau.

International Price Comparisons

Regression methods are applicable to many commodities that are difficult or impossible to price by traditional methods. They were first applied to domestic price indexes, and we have used them for intertemporal international price indexes in a number of commodity classifications. We have also extended their use to international price comparisons, where they have not been used before, and we dwell on this application here. However, our tests of the effect of alternative techniques on the final price measurement should be relevant to domestic price measurement as well.

The basic problem in international price comparisons, whether their purpose is to compare the purchasing power of currencies or to measure price competitiveness in international trade, arises from international differences in product specifications. Not only are many products highly differentiated among the producers within each country, but there are often significant international differences in the characteristics of products that serve the same general purpose. As a result, it is frequently impossible to find identical products in two countries, even though products performing the same function are manufactured in both countries.

A similar problem of comparability over time has troubled compilers of domestic price indexes. In recent years the problem has mainly taken the form of a suspected upward bias in price indexes due to insufficient accounting for improvements in quality. It has been suggested that the failure to measure quality change adequately is the most important defect in existing price indexes (*Price Statistics* 1961, p. 35). Although the Bureau of Labor Statistics, the producer of the official U.S. price indexes, makes a large number of ad hoc adjustments to take account of changes in quality of the products priced, it does not endorse any general method of dealing with quality change.

The construction of "hedonic" price indexes, using multiple regression, was suggested by Andrew Court (1939), but it was neglected for many years and only recently revived by Richard Stone, Zvi Griliches, and others.[1] The method has now been applied not only to automobiles, as originally proposed by Court, but also to farm tractors, electrical generating and transmission equipment, and single-family house prices.

The Rationale of Regression Analysis in Price Comparisons

The application of regression analysis to price measurement rests on the hypothesis that price differences among variants of a product in a particular market can be accounted for by identifiable characteristics of these

---

1. For a bibliography of such studies see Griliches 1967.

variants.[2] Each of these characteristics is regarded as an element of a complex product; variations in the mix of the elements produce product differentiation at a moment in time and changes in product quality over time. By fitting a regression equation to observations on the price and characteristics of commodity variants, typically in a cross section for a market at a given time, we can learn which characteristics are associated with the price of the commodity, and what the relationship is, and, if we have properly identified the relevant characteristics, the coefficients of the equation can be interpreted as prices for the characteristics. These prices are then used in comparisons among markets or among time periods, in which the commodity differs in quality (i.e., has different specifications or combinations of elements). Court, for example, computed regressions of automobile prices against weight, wheelbase, and horsepower in order to measure price changes over time.

Cost versus utility

Most discussions of the meaning of price indexes derived by regression methods—and the very name, "hedonic," that is applied to them—have stressed measures of utility to the consumer. Court, for example, spoke of "the potential contribution of any commodity . . . to the welfare and happiness of its purchasers and the community" and of "establishing an objective composite measure of usefulness and desirability" (1939, p. 107).

The Bureau of Labor Statistics and other producers of major price indexes rely on production relationships rather than on consumption relationships. The BLS "finds equivalence of quality in equal production cost" (*Price Statistics* 1961, p. 37).

The adoption of production cost rather than utility as a measure of quality does not preclude the use of regression methods, since valuation in terms of production cost and valuation in terms of utility may be viewed as alternative means of assessing the relative qualities and hence the relative prices of variants of a complex product each having a different mix of elements.[3] On a single market in competitive equilibrium, the two

---

2. See Stone 1956, chap. 4. For the extension of the theory of consumption to deal with the conception of goods as bundles of characteristics see Lancaster 1966.

3. See the Stigler Committee position on producers' goods (*Price Statistics* 1961, p. 37). Regression analysis, it may be added, can be regarded as providing a method of inferring statistically the prices of elements of a product for which the total price is determined by what is sometimes referred to as unit or component pricing. In component pricing, which may be found in industries as different as men's apparel and residential construction, the costs (assumed constant) of particular units of work (such as making a

International Price Comparisons

valuations should be identical. As Adelman and Griliches have pointed out, if the ratio of the marginal rates of substitution between two quality dimensions is smaller than the ratio of the costs exacted for them, both price and consumer purchases will adjust until equilibrium is reached, provided that price is not administered. "If prices are administered, and therefore not free to vary, equilibrium between the marginal rates of substitution and the cost of the quality dimensions will be reached by a decline in the ratio of Q_r to Q_s," by a change in the ratios of quantities purchased (Adelman and Griliches 1961, p. 547).[4]

Thus, for purposes of the regression analysis of prices, we may formulate the elements entering into a complex product either in terms of the cost of characteristics such as horsepower and fuel economy or in terms of their utility to consumers at a particular place and time.

The use of regression coefficients for price measurement

In a regression in which price is taken as the dependent variable, the coefficient of each element (that is, each independent variable) shows its price (that is, the cost per unit for additional units) in the mix of elements included in the complex product.[5] These regression coefficients may tend to change over time. To the extent that such changes reflect economic

---

buttonhole or providing and installing a window frame) are used to build up the cost and price of a particular product (such as a suit or house).

It would, however, be unduly confining to restrict regression analysis to the variables that form the building blocks used in industrial price formation. These are sometimes difficult to discover, and in any case performance characteristics may sometimes provide a better explanation of price differences, particularly in cases in which given characteristics may be attained through the use of different physical components by different producers.

4. As between two situations at different times, however, the cost and utility approaches, as they are sometimes defined, will yield different results when there are cost-free improvements in the second situation that were not present in the first. This outcome depends on the assumption that costs may be defined in terms of the physical characteristics of a product independently of the utility the product yields. The issues raised in this connection are not a special problem connected with regression methods and will not be pursued here.

5. To estimate the price of a specific product, the quantity of each element embodied in it must be multiplied by the price of that element. If there is more than one element, these products must be summed. To the product or sum of products must be added the constant of the equation. The existence of the constant term presumably reflects the fact that the assumption of linearity in element prices, even where it is satisfactory within the range of observation, does not apply outside it, particularly near the zero level. The explanation might be that there are elements in the product (including overhead costs) which we did not try to account for in the equation.

rather than statistical factors, they may be interpreted in the same way as the changes shown by other kinds of prices. For example, the lowering of the price of power over time accompanied by a shift towards more powerful machines that we have found in regressions for such products as railway locomotives and aircraft engines may be interpreted either as supply-based changes or as demand changes under conditions of decreasing supply price.[6]

International differences in the regression coefficients may also be expected, particularly if each country's market is isolated from the others. They could arise, for example, from differences in relative factor prices which would produce interspatial differences in the relative prices of the elements unless the factor mix required for increments in each quality element did not vary from one element to another in any of the countries.

In the case of diesel engines, for example, additions to weight (taken either as an element of cost or as a proxy for durability and/or reliability) might require a high material content, while additions to horsepower might require a relatively high labor content. In these circumstances we would find the ratio of the U.S. to U.K. coefficient or "price" for weight smaller than the ratio for horsepower. If, on the other hand, it took more labor to build a sturdier engine, and high weight were achieved through high labor content, the difference might be in the opposite direction. Or the relative prices might differ, again, if one country's industry specialized on a narrow range of the product (e.g., low horsepower) while another produced a wide range.

If there were truly competitive and frictionless international markets, we would not expect to find international differences in product prices, and if quality elements could be varied independently of each other, with no interdependence in utilities or costs, we would not expect to find international differences in their prices either. Any price that was out of line would bring a fall or rise in market share, changing cost, and price until price equality was established.

International markets for most products probably fall between the extremes of complete national isolation and complete international integration. For many products, transport costs, tariffs, and other isolating factors are sufficiently strong to permit the production in different countries of the same products or elements of products at different costs and their sale at different prices.

---

6. An illustration of a supply-based change is the reduction in the price of horsepower in automobile engines, which has been attributed to engine redesign (Fisher, Griliches, and Kaysen 1962, pp. 441–442).

International Price Comparisons

Specification differences and regression strategies

Some of the problems encountered in comparing prices in two situations are set out in a series of pictorial cases below. The examples are very simple ones, involving only one quality variable, and omit the complexities arising from the use of several variables, such as those from intercorrelations among quality characteristics and interactions between them. These illustrations, however, serve as an introduction to, and catalogue of, some of the problems referred to later.[7]

The simplest case for price measurement is one in which the price of the product is uniformly higher or lower in situation II than in situation I, over the whole range of the quality characteristic. The slope of line II, in other words, is equal to that of line I (see Fig. 1).

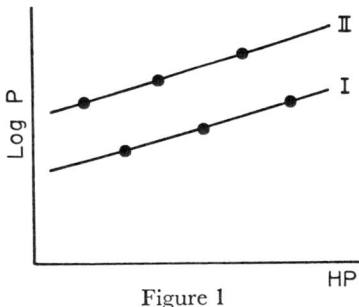

Figure 1

If there are observations at the same level of the characteristic, say horsepower (HP), in both situations, the price difference can be measured in the traditional way by comparing identical engines in the two places or two years.

If the same range of engines is produced in both situations, but not any pair identical in horsepower, the conventional method, relying on identical specifications, is useless, because there are no comparable items produced in both situations. Producers of index numbers probably meet this difficulty (if they do not drop the commodity from their indexes) by interpolating between two observations in situation I, for example, to estimate a price for the item produced in situation II. The method is a very crude version of the regression technique, involving fitting equations to individual pairs of points rather than to the whole set. It could give erratic results if the points were scattered around the line instead of being on one line as in Figure 1.

---

7. For an exploration of these problems in a different context see Morgan and Sonquist 1963.

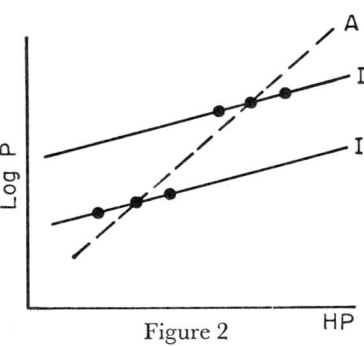
Figure 2

A more typical case, particularly if the years are some distance apart or the places very different, is one in which the bulk of the observations of the characteristic fall in different ranges in the two situations. Although there is usually some overlapping of the HP observations of the two situations, let us consider for the moment the extreme case shown on Figure 2, in which there is none. Here again, conventional methods would find no identical products to compare and could not, therefore, produce an index.

If a regression equation were fitted to each set of observations, the regression line for II would be above that for I, and we would calculate that prices were higher in II. The same result would follow from fitting a line to pooled data for I and II, with a dummy variable for II.

If we fitted a single equation to pooled data (A) and measured the price level in each situation by comparing actual prices with the equation, we would calculate that there was much less price difference. In the extreme case, when the line passed through the means of the two groups, we would make a finding of no price difference ($P_{II}/P_I = 1.00$).

All the examples up to this point have had one characteristic in common: the identity of slopes in the two situations are being compared. There is no index number problem, because all prices have changed, or differ, by the same amount. Thus if there are any overlapping observations, both conventional methods and regression analysis can easily cope with the measurement problem.

If the slopes differ in the two situations, an index number must be arrived at by selecting particular points within the range of the characteristic and measuring the price relationship for those points. The simplest case to picture is that of Figure 3, where the range of observations is the same for both countries but the slopes differ.

In this case, if the data were pooled and a single regression line were fitted, it would come out as equation III. The conclusion would be that situation I and situation II do not differ in price if an index were calculated

International Price Comparisons

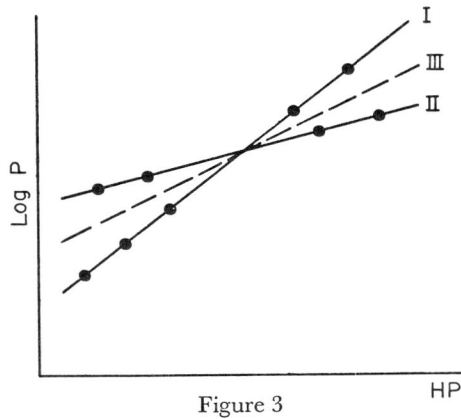

Figure 3

from the coefficient of a dummy variable representing one of the countries, since neither country is consistently above or below line III. The same inference would be drawn, provided each observation were given equal weight, if the equation were fitted without dummy variables and the index measured from each country's residuals, or if price difference were estimated from separate equations for I and II. However, an index calculated by weighting each price comparison by the importance of the engine to which it referred would depend upon the product mix.[8] If smaller engines were more important, situation I would be considered lower in price; if larger ones predominated, situation II would be lower. For purposes of measuring export price competitiveness, for example, the weights would be determined by the relative importance in international trade of engines of different horsepower.

The same results as would be derived in this way from separate equations for I and II could be obtained from a single equation pooling the data for the two situations but adding variables to differentiate for the level (i.e., intercept) and slope of situation II as compared to the level and slope of situation I.[9]

A more difficult case is that represented by Figure 4 and the following figure, in which the fitting of the equation or equations involves additional assumptions about the nature of underlying, but incompletely observed, relationships.

One assumption, represented by Figure 4, is that there are two price-HP relationships for the two situations, as I and II in Figure 3, but that all

---

8. Assuming that the regression were not also weighted.
9. This method is discussed further below. Other examples of this technique are given in Ben-David and Tomek 1965.

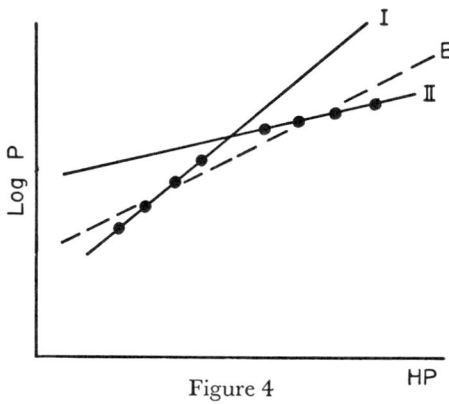

Figure 4

the engines for which prices are known for situation I are below the mean HP and all those for situation II are above. Such a case might evolve from Figure 3 if each country specialized in that HP range in which it was superior, and drove the other from the market in that range.[10] The outcome of the calculation here would again depend on the weighting of the different HP sizes. In a weighting based on that of one of the two situations (one country's exports or production, for example) that situation would be found to have the lower prices.

If a single equation (B) were fitted to the data of the case represented by Figure 4, with price indexes calculated from residuals or from country dummy variables, but with no country-slope interaction terms, the conclusion would be biased towards finding that there was no price difference between situation I and situation II. This would be true even if the price comparisons used only the horsepowers observed in one of the two situations, because the regression line would tend to pass near the means of the observations of each of the situations. However, the introduction of an intercept and slope interaction term would restore the conclusions derived from I and II.

As long as we restrict our consideration to linear functions, the estimation of separate equations or the use of country and slope interaction terms seems clearly superior to the fitting of a single function. Once this restriction is lifted, the possibility that the two situations lie on the same price-horsepower function must be considered. If such were the case, as in Figure 5, we would have to conclude that there was no price difference

---

10. It might be noted here that the collection of offer prices, in addition to transactions prices, might fill out the other end of the range for each country.

International Price Comparisons

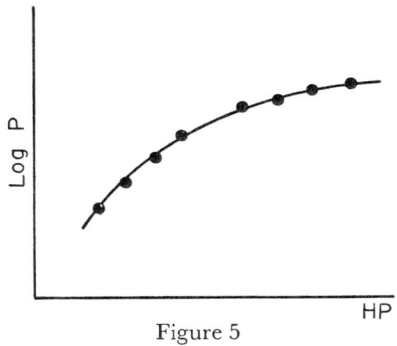
Figure 5

between I and II whether we compared prices on I's products, II's products, or a combination of both of them. However, when there is no overlapping, the data give us no guidance as to whether one function (as in Figure 5) or two functions (as in Figure 4) should be fitted. In these circumstances, it would be necessary to call upon other information about the nature of the shape of these functions. Fortunately, such extreme cases in which there were no overlapping observations have proved to be rare.

We are thus left with the alternatives of estimating separate equations or, what will yield the same price comparisons, using pooled regressions with situation (intercept) and slope dummies. A compromise between these two alternatives, which retains advantages of each, is "flexible pooling." In this technique we begin by estimating an equation in which there is a dummy variable for each situation[11] and a situation-interaction term for each combination of situation and characteristic. If situation I is taken as the base, the situation dummy variable distinguishes the intercept of situation II from that of situation I; the interaction term distinguishes the slope in situation II from the slope in the base situation. By dropping the dummy and interaction terms that do not prove to be significant and retaining those that do, we use the whole size and range of the combined sample for the two situations to estimate the coefficients which seem to be common to them while permitting the estimation of separate coefficients for the two situations where these appear to be warranted.

In order to simplify the foregoing outline of alternative regression strategies, we have posed the pricing problem in terms of a single independent variable. In fact, of course, it is necessary to take into account

---

11. Actually, a dummy variable is used for each situation except the base situation. See Suits 1957.

more than one product element in explaining the price differences between two situations. Indeed, for a complex product such as an automobile or even a diesel engine, product differentiation between models, brands, times, and places turns upon a very large number of elements. However, most of these tend to be highly intercorrelated, so that it is frequently possible to account for 90 percent or more of the price variation by including as few as three or four elements as independent variables.

It should be mentioned that both our purpose and the price data we employ differ in several ways from the simple examples described above and from those of other experiments with regression techniques. One difference is that the data relate to several different markets connected, to some degree, by international trade. They can, therefore, contain price differences for whole commodities and for particular quality characteristics which we would not expect to find within a single market. Another point is that the list of specifications could not be enlarged to take account of the regression results. Ideally, such an analysis should provide opportunities to test more thoroughly the effects on price measurements of alternative combinations of independent variables. We could also have examined more closely the cases in which such results as negative coefficients for features apparently useful and costly to produce suggested that the variables were acting as proxies for others not covered. However, the fact that the data were originally collected for conventional price comparisons meant that we were obliged to do as well as we could with the variables that seemed important in advance.

It should be emphasized that our main purpose was not to analyze the economic factors underlying price changes or to account for differences in price levels. For that reason we had no real interest in the element coefficients themselves. The price indexes, and therefore the country dummy variables from which they were derived, were the object of the experiment. The other coefficients were of importance only as they affected the price estimates.[12] Our major question in connection with the use of regression methods was whether the price indexes which they produced would be sensitive to choices among equally justifiable alternative equation forms and explanatory variables. Indexes computed by more traditional methods

---

12. Since we are not interested in the coefficients themselves, it has been suggested that factor analysis or principal components analysis would have been appropriate techniques for dealing with the problem of multicollinearity. The drawback to the use of these methods is the loss of identity of the independent variables. It is then impossible to impose any criteria for the reasonableness of the relationships. For an application of principal components analysis see Dhrymes 1967.

International Price Comparisons

are not immune from similar problems, but there has been little discussion of the relative merits of the two approaches with respect to the ranges of indeterminacy involved.

Automotive Diesel Engine Price Regressions

Data on 1962 price, horsepower, revolutions per minute, engine displacement, and weight were obtained for 73 automotive diesel engines produced in 4 countries (see Table 5.1). What we refer to as the "average" engine has the mean specifications (unweighted) of the 73 engines. The specifications of the "export" engine were derived by weighting each country average by the relative importance of that country in automotive diesel engine exports.

Table 5.1. Summary of Data for Automotive Diesel Engines, 1962

	U.S.	U.K.	Ger.	France[a]	Total or Average	"Export" Engine[b]
No. of producers	4	6	5	1	16	
No. of engines	22	22	23	6	73	
Averages						
Price ($)	3,470	1,593	2,023	2,394	2,360	2,250
Horsepower	190	147	163	184	168	164
RPM	2,182	2,191	2,367	2.050	2,232	2,217
Displacement (cu. in.)	517	539	488	590	520	524
Weight (lbs.)	2,117	1,531	1,509	2,123	1,749	1,715

[a] In addition, information was available on price, horsepower, and revolutions per minute, but not on weight and displacement for 5 engines of 2 other French producers. The averages for all 11 French engines were: price—$2,147; horsepower—166; and RPM—2,273. Only the 6 engines for which complete information was available were included in the pooled regressions; all 11 were included in the separate regressions for France.

[b] The "export" engine is the average of country averages weighted by the estimated share of each country in automotive diesel exports. The weights used were: U.K.—50 percent; U.S.—30 percent; Germany—18 percent; and France—2 percent.

NOTE: The U.K., German, and French data were supplied by an American firm; the U.S. data came from that firm and three others.

Prices are mainly those charged to distributors in the country of manufacture, but include also some on sales directly to truck manufacturers.

The American firm that was the main source of information had gathered the data in a market survey, presumably including the variables considered important. We had no opportunity to enlarge the list of specifications, even though a longer list would have been desirable for our purposes.

The specification of the relationship

The main utility sought by the purchaser of a diesel engine is power. The concomitant considerations include durability, frequency and ease of repair, fuel economy, and smoothness of operation. These qualities may also be viewed as being related to components of the total cost per unit of freight delivered (for a truck) such as driver time, repair and fuel costs, and costs of delayed delivery.

The variables at our disposal—horsepower (H), displacement (D), revolutions per minute (R), and weight (W)—are summary variables in the sense that they are determined by other elements such as the number and size of cylinders, inlet pressure and temperature, fuel-air ratio, and spark advance. Neither our summary variables nor the more detailed specifications behind them directly measure the various facets of delivery costs which may be important to the buyer. Indeed, only one of the variables—H—is a direct measure of a major utility to the diesel engine consumer. The others act as proxies for performance characteristics we are unable to measure.

Of the variables we have, three—H, D, and R—are parts of an engineering relationship that may be expressed as follows:

$$H = \frac{M \times D \times R}{k}$$

where M is mean effective pressure (the amount of pressure that operates on each cylinder) and k is a constant.[13] While M was not specifically included in our data, it is obvious that we can easily calculate it since we know the values of the other variables in the relationship.

The relationship indicates that a given horsepower can be achieved by means of different combinations of M, D, and R. Each has its advantages

---

13. The constant is 792,000 for a four-stroke-cycle engine and 396,000 for a two-stroke-cycle engine. See Rogowski 1953 p. 53 and Jennings and Obert 1944 p. 40. All of the engines in our sample are, to the best of our knowledge, four-stroke-cycle engines.

International Price Comparisons

and disadvantages. For example, given two engine designs with the same H, the one with the higher R will be smaller and may cost less because it uses less materials. On the other hand, it may vibrate more, thus requiring more servicing, and may have poorer combustion, thus consuming more fuel.

The relation of weight to the other variables is more difficult to specify. On the one hand an engine that is too light may not be durable; indeed, one industry source suggested that in a cross section of engines at any one time weight could be taken as a rough guide to the reliability and durability of an engine. On the other hand, weight per se is a disadvantage, and costly effort such as more careful casting may be undertaken to keep down weight.[14] Furthermore, since W is highly correlated with D and (inversely) with R, it may be expected to add little to the explanation of price variation. In fact $\bar{R}^2$ was significantly reduced when weight was eliminated and there were some substantial differences in the price relatives. The possible contribution of weight to the value of an engine in terms of its durability and the statistically significant role weight plays in the explanation of price variation are clear grounds for preferring the equations that include it.

To explain the variation in diesel engine prices, W and any three of M, H, D, and R can be taken, but not all four, because any three of them determine the fourth. We have chosen to retain M, D, and R and to eliminate H, partly because H is more highly correlated than M with the other variables and partly because the coefficients of the other variables make more sense when M is used. H is the one variable we are certain represents a utility to the purchaser of diesel engines. Leaving H out of the function permits us to measure the value of additions to the other elements when they result in additions to horsepower. Including H produces coefficients of the other variables whose meaning is ambiguous because an addition to any other variable, holding H constant, involves a subtraction from whichever variable is omitted (M, D, or R). For example, if H is used, the coefficient for D represents the price of an addition to displacement that does not add to horsepower, and therefore involves a reduction in M. It is difficult to say what sign such a coefficient should logically have. On the other hand, if M is used, the coefficient for D represents the price of an addition to displacement which does add to horsepower, clearly implying a positive sign.

---

14. The relationship of weight to utility may be positive across models at a given time but negative over time.

The relation between an equation in M, D, and R and one in H, D, and R can be expressed as follows:

$P = aH^b D^c R^d$ implies, given $H = \dfrac{MDR}{k}$, that

$$P = \frac{a}{k^b} M^b D^{b+c} R^{b+d}$$

The coefficients in this formulation represent the price of additions to horsepower through additions to each of the other variables. Since weight is not included in the function, the addition to displacement and horsepower will probably involve an increase in weight, too, and thus represent essentially the value of a larger engine minus the drawbacks attendant on increased size. However, if weight is included in the function, the D coefficient represents the price of increased horsepower through greater size without any weight penalty, presumably through the use of lighter materials or other engineering changes. We would expect this D coefficient to be larger than the one which allows for increased weight, since higher power is more desirable if it does not bring greater weight.

Alternative formulations might involve including both H and M but excluding D or R. If R were excluded, the H coefficient would represent the price of increased horsepower achieved by raising R, the M coefficient would represent the price of substituting M for R at a given horsepower, and the D coefficient would measure the price of substituting D for R.

The results presented below are based on regressions in which W, M, D, and R are the main independent variables,[15] but these, it should be remembered, only imperfectly and incompletely represent the desired performance characteristics of a diesel engine. Because of our uncertainty as to the relation of the missing factors to the proxies used, we can only speculate as to whether the coefficients are logical. We must depend on the assumption that their relation to the true utility elements does not differ substantially among the countries or on the assumption that if it does, the differences do not affect the price comparisons.

The mathematical form

Linear, semilog, inverse semilog, and double log regressions were fitted to the data in all the alternative combinations of variables and regression methods we tried. However, the double log regressions were considered

---

15. The statistical results from using other combinations of independent variables, including $(D \times R)$ as a composite variable, were generally inferior to those of the $MDRW$ equation.

International Price Comparisons

the preferable ones for several reasons. The arithmetic and semilog forms were rejected on the ground that the factors that underlie the international differences in price—whether profit margins, labor or material costs, better technology, or more skillful management in one country as compared with another—are more likely to result in a fixed percentage difference between prices for all variants of an engine—large and small, weak and powerful, and so on—than in a fixed, absolute dollar difference.[16]

The inverse semilog and double log forms possess the advantage that they estimate percentage rather than absolute price differences between countries, and it is percentage differences that we wish to express by index numbers. Each of the other forms yields a single absolute difference in price between each pair of countries for all engines, small or large, cheap or expensive.

The choice between the inverse semilog and double log forms was not as clear. The double log form was preferred because it incorporated the character of the technical relationships among the independent variables described in the previous section—a multiplicative rather than an additive relationship.

The type of regression

Three types of regression analysis were tried, each in several variants differing in the choice of variables and mathematical form. One type involved pooling all data under the assumption of equal element prices in all countries (additive dummy variables). The equation was

$$P = F(M, D, W, R, k, g, f)$$

where

P = price of engine
M = mean effective pressure
D = displacement
W = weight
R = RPM
k = dummy variable for U.K. engine
g = dummy variable for German engine
f = dummy variable for French engine

---

16. A related factor is that the equations in which arithmetic price is the dependent variable are fitted by minimizing squares of absolute deviations from actual prices, while the inverse semilog and double log forms are fitted in terms of percentage deviations. The latter seems more desirable because a larger absolute error is acceptable in estimating the price of a $5000 engine than in estimating the price of a $1000 engine.

A second approach was to fit a separate regression for each country:

$$P_u = F_u(M, D, W, R)$$
$$P_k = F_k(M, D, W, R)$$
$$P_g = F_g(M, D, W, R)$$
$$P_f = F_f(M, D, W, R)$$

where

P_u the U.S. price
P_k the U.K. price
P_g the German price
P_f the French price

A third technique was to pool all data but to allow for international differences in the prices of quality elements (additive and multiplicative dummy variables):

$$P = F'(M, D, W, R, k, g, f, kM, kD, kW, kR,$$
$$gM, gD, gW, gR, fM, fD, fW, fR).$$

The last of the three, which we refer to as "flexible pooling," was chosen as the most appropriate. It provided the advantages of pooling in that where there were no significant differences among countries in element prices, the size of the sample and its range were enlarged. On the other hand, it did allow for differences in element prices where they appeared to be statistically significant.

Pooling without allowances for differences in element prices requires the assumption that the relative prices of the different elements making up the product mix are the same in the different situations involved in the price comparison. This may be a questionable assumption even when the situations involve two different points in time referring to the same country; it seems quite unlikely when prices are being compared for two or more different countries. There are obvious and important differences in relative factor prices from one country to another, and these may affect the prices of the elements in our equations for diesel engines. U.S. labor costs are high relative to those of Europe, but the prices of alloys or certain castings requiring advanced technology are low. Since the factor mix required to produce the various elements that make up the product mix is unknown to us and cannot be assumed to be identical in each country from element to element, it seems desirable to use a regression method which does not impose the requirement that all price differences be summarized by a single intercept dummy.

International Price Comparisons

We present, first, the results from our application of flexible pooling, since these are the ones we accepted for use in the larger price study. These results are then compared with the outcomes of the other two methods.

Pooling with International Differences in Prices of Elements

The pooled regression, in this approach, includes as independent variables not only the several engine characteristics and the dummy variable for each foreign country, but also a dummy for each foreign country for the slope of each continuous variable. In the case of the weight variable, for example, this is accomplished by retaining a basic weight variable and adding a weight slope variable for each foreign country, which reflects the country-weight interaction. If the relationship between price and weight in a foreign country is the same as in the U.S., the weight *slope* coefficient will be zero or at least insignificantly different from zero. If intercept and slope dummies were included for all variables, the results would be the same as those obtained by fitting a separate regression for each country, using the same mathematical form and the same independent variables.

These regressions are based on 67 observations for the U.S., the U.K. and Germany, and contain 14 independent variables.[17] In view of our earlier discussion, we confine ourselves to the inverse semilog and double log forms.

The following rules were adopted to govern the retention and elimination of dummy variables from the equation finally used to compare prices.

1. The slope dummy coefficient for a country was not retained unless the coefficients for both that country and the base country conformed to a priori economic and technical considerations. For example, the slope dummy for U.K. mean effective pressure taken in conjunction with the base coefficient implied a negative relationship between price and pressure in the U.K. and was therefore rejected.

2. No intercept or slope dummy was retained unless it was at least as large as its standard error (S.E.). This choice of a 1-S.E. test in preference to the frequently used 2-S.E. test raises the issue of priority among the independent variables. We prefer to assign priority to quality characteristics in partitioning the observed variation in international prices into

---

17. If we included all four countries in such a regression there would be 19 independent variables, 4 basic ones for the engine characteristics, and 1 intercept and 4 slope dummies for each of the three foreign countries. Since we have only six complete observations for France, there is little point in including France in a regression which would require five additional independent variables.

quality differences on the one hand and country-to-country differences in prices (for given qualities) on the other hand. This might imply that the variables which measure price differences (the country and slope dummies) should be retained only when highly significant—i.e., when they meet the 2-S.E. test. However, this policy would rule out an observed difference in international prices unless the odds were overwhelming (20 to 1) that the difference would not be produced by chance. At the other extreme, by retaining all slope coefficients, however insignificant, we would forego the advantages of pooling.[18]

3. Even if significant in these terms, a slope dummy variable was not retained if its addition to the equation caused the corresponding element variable to lose its statistical significance.[19] The retention of the dummy variable under these circumstances would have had the effect of depriving the base situation of the advantages of pooling in cases in which the unpooled coefficient for that variable was not significant in the base situation.

4. When more than one equation (each with a different set of dummy variables) satisfied these three conditions, the one with the highest R^2 was chosen.

5. If, for a given foreign country, no combination of dummy variables met the above conditions, all the slope dummy variables were dropped and the coefficients of the intercept dummies were taken as the best measure of the price difference in preference to the alternative of reading the result as representing no price difference.

The "best" double log equation, selected by these criteria, has an intercept dummy for the U.K. and has German slope dummies for displacement and weight; it yields price relatives of 70 and 85 for U.K./U.S. and Germany/U.S., respectively. In Table 5.2, these results are compared with those based on alternative criteria for the retention of dummy variables. The U.K./U.S. relative ranges from 68 to 70 and the Germany/U.S. relative from 83 to 85 in those equations which do not contain negative coefficients for pressure.

The "best" inverse semilog equation yields price comparisons of 81 and 93 for U.K./U.S. and Germany/U.S., respectively.[20] There is thus a

---

18. The 1-S.E. criterion, if carried through consistently, would produce the highest level of $\bar{R}^2$. See Haitovsky 1969.

19. If the t-ratio for the basic variable was 2 or more prior to the addition of the slope dummy, the dummy was not retained if with its presence the t-ratio of the basic variable was less than 2. If the original t-ratio was between 1 and 2, the dummy was retained if its addition was not accompanied by a reduction in the t-ratio to a level below 1.

20. Unlike the case of the double log form in which only one set of dummy variables met all of the first three conditions given in the text, seven different sets of dummy variables satisfied these conditions in the inverse semilog form. They produced U.K./U.S. price relatives ranging from 76 to 84 and German/U.S. relatives ranging from 90 to 94.

International Price Comparisons

notable difference between the results from the two forms. Statistical criteria such as the $\bar{R}^2$'s and tests for heteroscedasticity[21] do not point to a decisive advantage of one form over the other, but we opt for the double log form on the grounds mentioned earlier.

Table 5.2. Price Comparisons for Automotive Diesel Engines Based on Alternative Criteria for Pooling; Double Log Equations

Criteria Met	Dummy Variables[a]	$\bar{R}^2$	U.K./U.S.[b]	Ger./U.S.[b]
1. All using 1 S.E.	$k\ g_d\ g_w$	0.911	70	85
2. All (1 S.E.) except third criterion (significance of basic variable)[c]	$k\ k_d\ g_w$	0.914	69	83
3. All using 2 S.E.	$k\ g$	0.909	68	85
4. All (2 S.E.) except third criterion (significance of basic variable)[c]	$k\ k_d\ g$	0.913	69	84

[a] k and g without subscripts refer to country (intercept) dummies for the U.K. and Germany, respectively. With the subscripts d and w, they refer to slope dummies for displacement and weight, respectively.

[b] Dropping criterion (1) produced price level indexes of 61 and 62 for the U.K. and 81–84 for Germany.

[c] See text.

There is one other complication in taking double log results of the flexible pooling approach. An equation yields different price indexes for each engine specification whenever one or more slope dummies is retained, because the slope dummy implies that there is not a single price difference attributable to country of origin but also differences in the prices of individual characteristics. One way of dealing with such situations is by pricing the "export" engine, which represents an export-weighted average of the average specifications for each of the four countries.[22] Averages obtained in this manner for displacement and weight enter, for example, into the computation of the estimate of 85 for the Germany/U.S. price relative selected as the preferred result of flexible pooling (Table 5.2, first line).

---

21. Each form meets the test performed.

22. The average specifications for each country are shown in Table 5.1. It should be noted that these averages refer only to the engines in our sample, and that we do not know precisely what the true averages are for each country's exports.

An alternative solution to the problem posed by the fact that there are different country-to-country price level indexes for different types of engines is to make a series of binary price comparisons—one for each country's average engine—and then to average the estimates with the use of export weights. We set out in Table 5.3 the German/U.S. price comparisons[23] based on the average specifications of each country (rows 1–4) and export weighted averages of the relatives in row 7.

Table 5.3. German/U.S. Price comparisons

Engines with specifications of	German/U.S.
1. U.S.	81
2. U.K.	87
3. Germany	85
4. France	82
5. Average	84
6. Export	85
7. Weighted average of relatives	85

SOURCES: Rows 1 to 6: See Table 5.1 for specifications. Row 7: Average of rows 1 to 4 weighted by relative importance of each country in exports.

The rationale for the export-weighted average of relatives is that the average engine of each country is regarded as representing a particular product variant whose importance in international trade is proportionate to the country's share in diesel engine exports. However, the alternative methods of averaging (rows 5–7) do not, in this and in other cases we have examined, produce very different answers.

A troublesome feature of these data is that in some instances the U.S.-type engine seems to be relatively cheaper in Germany than any of the European-type engines. Either the German producers are foregoing a significant market opportunity, or, what is more probable, if they actually began to make engines with U.S. specifications in larger volume, the coefficients of the German regression would shift so as to make the U.S.-type engine relatively more expensive, compared to U.S. prices, than the

---

23. The preferred equation contained no slope dummies, but only a country dummy for the U.K. The U.K./U.S. relative thus is 70 for all specifications of engines.

International Price Comparisons

average type engines now being produced in Germany. Actually our estimates of German prices of U.S.-type engines are based on relatively few observations and are probably misleading. Under these circumstances the smaller price differences suggested by the comparisons based on German-type engines might be a better approximation to the true relationship. Another possibility is that we have overlooked some quality elements which make U.S. engines more desirable at the larger end of the scale. In any case, the low Germany/U.S. ratio for U.S.-type engines represents a defect in our analysis. Fortunately, the lighter and lower horsepower German- and U.K.-type engines take up most of the weight in the average, and the export-weighted averages would therefore not be very different if the U.S.-type engine were excluded.

Other types of regression

In order to test the extent to which our choice of flexible pooling as a method determined our relative price estimates we ran regressions based on the two other methods described earlier.

Pooling the data without allowance for differences in element prices produced equations which fit the data well in inverse semilog and double log forms (Table 5.4) and considerably less well in arithmetic and semilog forms. The price comparisons calculated from equations in the two preferable forms were as follows:

	U.S. = 100		
Form of equation	France	Germany	U.K.
Inverse semilog (log-arith)	79	93	77
Double log (log-log)	72	85	68

The opposite extreme from this pooling is the use of separate country regressions, which use no information from one country in the estimate for another of the relation of price to quality characteristics.

If we try to base each comparison on a set of identical elements, we are faced with the difficulty that elements which explain a very high percentage of price variation in one country may explain only a low percentage in another. If we use, for each country, all the variables that are significant for any country, the $\bar{R}^2$ for a particular country, corrected for degrees of freedom, may be less than with a smaller number of variables. A frequent concomitant of this defect will be the presence of regression coefficients

Table 5.4. Regression Coefficients for Automotive Diesel Engine Prices: Pooled Equations with No Allowance for Country Differences in Element Coefficients (figures in parentheses are standard errors)

	Inverse Semilog[a]	Double Log[a]
1. Pressure (M)	0.4418	0.9110
	(0.0773)	(0.1444)
2. Displacement (D)	0.00059	0.5045
	(0.00021)	(0.1260)
3. Weight (W)	0.00038	0.4856
	(0.00006)	(0.1297)
4. RPM (R)	−0.00021	−0.2831
	(0.000095)	(0.2111)
5. France	−0.2414	−0.3243
	(0.0805)	(0.0794)
6. Germany	−0.0681	−0.1676
	(0.0578)	(0.0567)
7. U.K.	−0.2663	−0.3802
	(0.0620)	(0.0611)
8. Constant	6.5312	2.9133
	(0.3348)	(1.9512)
9. Standard Error as Percent of Mean	3.18	3.16
10. $\bar{R}^2$	0.910	0.912
11. $\bar{R}^2$ (transformed data)[b]	0.919	0.911

NOTE: Price in dollars, displacement in cubic inches, RPM in units, weight in pounds. M obtained by dividing horsepower by product of displacement and RPM and multiplying by 10,000. The logs are natural logs.

[a] In the inverse semilog equation the dependent variable (price) is logarithmic and the independent variables are arithmetic, while in the double log equation all variables are logarithmic.

[b] Correlation between antilogs of actual and predicted prices.

which seem unlikely on economic grounds. The use of such a coefficient would imply that an element which has a positive value in one country has a negative value in another.

This difficulty is illustrated by the equations for each country using M, D, R, and W in Table 5.5, where the separate regressions produce

International Price Comparisons

Table 5.5. Regression Coefficients for Automotive Diesel Engine Prices: Pooled and Individual Country Equations
(figures in parentheses are standard errors)

	Mean Effective Pressure	Displacement	RPM	Weight	Constant
Inverse Semilog (log-arith)					
a. Pooled	0.4418	0.00059	−0.00021	0.00038	6.5312
	(0.0773)	(0.00021)	(0.00010)	(0.00006)	(0.3348)
b. U.S.	0.5282	0.00076	0.00047	0.00046	4.6334
	(0.1066)	(0.00027)	(0.00031)	(0.00008)	(0.8105)
c. U.K.	−0.2795	0.00165	−0.00046	−0.00007	7.8716
	(0.3664)	(0.00075)	(0.00013)	(0.00027)	(0.7290)
d. Germany	0.6469	0.00165	−0.00016	−0.00006	6.1799
	(0.1808)	(0.00063)	(0.00020)	(0.00022)	(0.7605)
Double Log (log-log)					
a. Pooled	0.9110	0.5045	−0.2832	0.4856	2.9134
	(0.1445)	(0.1260)	(0.2111)	(0.1297)	(1.9512)
b. U.S.	0.9973	0.4649	0.2033	0.5652	−1.2311
	(0.2598)	(0.1780)	(0.7250)	(0.2149)	(6.2515)
c. U.K.	−0.2622	0.7988	−0.6544	0.2635	5.4689
	(0.4706)	(0.4294)	(0.2954)	(0.4644)	(3.2322)
d. Germany	1.4020	1.1116	0.1523	−0.1172	−0.1592
	(0.3338)	(0.3287)	(0.5605)	(0.3024)	(5.3910)

NOTE: Prices in dollars, displacement in cubic inches, RPM in units, weight in pounds. Mean effective pressure obtained by dividing horsepower by product of displacement and RPM and multiplying by 10,000.

some striking differences in the coefficients.[24] In particular, the U.K. coefficient for pressure is negative and not significantly different from zero while those of the other two countries are positive and significant (at the

---

24. We will drop further reference to French prices in this section, because it does not seem worth computing separate regressions for the six engines for which complete information is available. It would greatly add to the number of alternative results (all of them inferior) that we would have to present for the other countries if we based comparisons on equations including only H and R, the two variables for which there are 11 French observations.

0.05 level) in both the inverse semilog and double log equations. The most likely explanation for the negative U.K. coefficient is the extent of multicollinearity among the four engine characteristic variables.

A major difference between the U.K. and the other two countries is in the narrower range of observation of mean effective pressure,[25] and, to a lesser degree, of displacement. Because the U.K. coefficients of M and D are calculated over relatively narrow ranges, we can place less confidence in their values than in those for other countries. Similar problems arise when other combinations of independent variables are employed in U.K. regressions.[26]

Conclusions

The preferred results from double log equations produced by each method can be summarized as follows:

	U.S. = 100	
	U.K.	Germany
Flexible pooling (4 types)	68–70	83–85
Pooled regressions	68	85
Separate country regressions		
$MDRW$	–	81
$HDRW$	–	81

Depending upon decisions with respect to the choice between separate country regressions and pooling, independent variables, and the specifications to be priced—but leaving aside regressions rejected on grounds of goodness of fit, unreasonable coefficients (such as some zero or negative coefficients), or heteroscedasticity in the residuals—the U.K./U.S. price

---

25. The ranges for the U.K., U.S., and Germany for $H/DR \times 10,000$ were 1.14–1.48, 1.20–2.48, and 1.07–2.64, respectively.

26. One way to deal with these country differences would be to base the comparisons on *unlike* equations—that is, to fit a different equation for each country, using those variables and that mathematical form which produced the closest explanation of price. Prices for engines of given specifications could then be estimated from each country's "best" equation and compared.

The derivation of indexes from unlike equations is based on the assumption that we are warranted in comparing the prices of diesels in terms of a different set of elements in each country. It involves the questionable assumption that a variable not significant over the range of variation present in the sample for country A would not be significant—that is, would have a zero price—over the wider range found in country B, if country A produced that wider range of products.

International Price Comparisons

relatives ranged from 68 to 70 and the German/U.S. relatives from 81 to 85. We do not list the U.K./U.S. coefficients for separate country regressions, because they contained negative coefficients for variables which had significant positive coefficients in equations of other countries.

Use of the inverse semilog form yielded a range of 77–81 for the U.K. and 87–93 for Germany, the range being wider and the level higher than the results from the preferred double log equations.

The application of regression analysis to diesel engine prices in this paper was necessarily along simple lines in keeping with the resources of our study and its need to cover a very broad range of products. An obvious extension would be to take account of more engine characteristics, some of which might be continuous variables and others, such as power transmission, might be on an included-or-not basis (i.e., represented by dummy variables).

A more difficult extension of the work would be to aim at variables which reflect utilities to the consumer. The proxies we have been obliged to use represent these performance characteristics very imperfectly. We are therefore unable in many instances to judge whether the coefficients obtained are logical from an economic standpoint. Indeed, we cannot be certain that we have not omitted some key characteristic that accounts for a significant part of the observed difference in price in the two situations. Thus, it has been suggested to us that in the case of diesel engines the "quality" of the U.S. diesels is higher than that of European makes, so that the real difference in price is smaller than our estimates indicate. We cannot rule this possibility out, even though the industry itself competes in world markets with specifications set out mainly in terms of the elements we have used.

The regression analysis of automotive diesel engine prices described here is only one of several used in the study *Price Competitiveness in World Trade*. The others are outlined briefly in the appendix to this chapter, to give the reader an idea of the range of products and the types of equations used.

We have placed considerable stress in this paper on the extent to which the estimates of price changes or of price differences depend on decisions with respect to such matters as independent variables, mathematical form, and pooling. Regression-based indexes have been subject to criticism with respect to this indeterminacy. It is important to realize, however, that the range of indeterminacy in results based on regression methods is not inherently different from that which is embedded in the results of more traditional methods. The difference is rather that the indeterminacy is made explicit by regression methods whereas it tends to be concealed but not avoided or eliminated by the more conventional approach.

Indeed, the latter often turns out to be the equivalent of crude regression techniques such as the arithmetic interpolation of prices for a few models on the basis of one or two independent variables. Many of the decisions in such cases about the alternative methods or assumptions are made at disaggregated levels in ways that are difficult, if not impossible, to summarize and present to the users of the indexes. An important advantage of the regression technique is that the choices among methods and their results can be described and presented clearly and systematically.

Aside from making explicit the methods and the unavoidable indeterminacy of result, regression techniques also permit the use of a much wider range of product varieties in price measurement, and make possible price comparisons between different times and places for complex, differentiated products which are usually omitted from price indexes because of the difficulty of applying traditional methods of price measurement to them.

Thus, although much experimentation is still needed to put price measurement by regression methods on anything like a routine basis, even in the present embryonic stage regression methods provide an important and useful tool in the making of price indexes.

Appendix to Chapter 5

Other Applications of Regression Methods

This appendix gives a brief description of the main applications of regression analysis to products other than diesel engines in the volume on *Price Competitiveness in World Trade* (Kravis and Lipsey, 1971). The chapter references are to that book.

In the case of aircraft engines (appendix to chap. 12), it was not possible to find American and British engines of identical characteristics, from which conventional price comparisons could be made, although the two countries produced engines in the same weight and power range. Regression equations were fitted to data on 20 engines, relating their prices to take-off thrust, weight, and country of origin. The resulting price comparisons varied within a range of four percentage points, and the $\bar{R}^2$

International Price Comparisons

ranged from 0.85 to 0.95. The regressions we ran were a simpler version of one performed by a leading aerospace company, on essentially the same data, for the purpose of predicting the price of new engines.

Another set of place-to-place comparisons were performed by multiple regression for outboard motors (appendix to chap. 12). About 100 observations from 6 countries were available for each of 2 years, all gathered in a market survey by a large producer. The equations related price to horsepower, country of origin, market of sale, and the presence of an electric starter. The equations produced high levels of $\bar{R}^2$, all over 0.95, and the price comparisons, for the most part, were similar (within 5 percentage points) in arithmetic and logarithmic forms.

A U.S. price index for tractors, 1953–1964, was constructed from data for 61 tractor prices, obtained from 6 U.S. manufacturers (appendix to chap. 12). Information for all years was pooled, and the price index was estimated from year dummy variables. Price was related to horsepower, weight, and a dummy variable for type of tractor, as well as the year of sale. The $\bar{R}^2$ were extremely high for both arithmetic and logarithmic equations but lower for mixed equations. The logarithmic equations, however, showed a more rapid price increase in both types of tractors, by 9 to 12 percentage points over the 11 years (1953–1964). Almost all the difference was accounted for by the first period (1953–1957), when the sample was extremely thin, and the 1957–1964 period showed differences of only 3 percentage points.

In the case of power transformers (appendix to chap. 13), there were virtually no time series data on prices. Our prices were from reports by buyers, who would rarely purchase the same product twice, and from bidding documents, which were usually for unique products. The method chosen to calculate price changes over time was to fit regressions to the lowest prices bid by U.S. companies on approximately 150 power transformers. We used only capacity as a quality variable, and included as dummy variables the year in which the bidding took place and the location of the project (U.S. or foreign). Slope dummy variables allowed for differences among the years in the slope of the price-capacity relationship. All the logarithmic equations produced high levels of $\bar{R}^2$ (0.93–0.94), but there were some substantial differences in the resulting estimate of price movement depending on which intercept and slope dummies were retained. The price change was taken directly from the intercept coefficients for the years except for 1963–1964, in which case the slope dummy indicated that the price movements differed significantly with the size of transformer.

The regression, crude as it was, produced price indexes quite similar to others for U.S. domestic prices, which were derived by much more elaborate regressions and by other methods involving the use of a greater number of variables. The price change was calculated for several different sizes, and these were then weighted by the importance of each, as estimated from the bidding data.

For railway locomotives, a regression-based index was calculated for the U.S. time-to-time index but was not used except as a check on the conventionally calculated index (appendix to chap. 14). The number of categories available for equation fitting was small, and there were some erratic changes in the coefficients. The method used in this case was to fit a separate regression for each year and to price the 1963 set of locomotives produced in the United States in each year's equation.

A Japanese ship price index was computed from data for 205 contracts for ships built in Japanese yards (appendix to chap. 14). The logarithmic equation finally selected included continuous variables for the tonnage and horsepower of ships, and dummy variables for type of ship (bulk carrier, cargo vessel, or tanker) and for the year of purchase, using pooled data for all years. The indexes computed from this logarithmic equation were similar to those from a semilogarithmic equation and from an arithmetic equation using 1963 ship specifications. The logarithmic equation also produced the best fit, and the price indexes calculated from it were not sensitive to the addition of other marginal variables to the equation.

Regression-based index numbers were used in place-to-place comparisons for truck prices in the United States and the United Kingdom (chap. 14). Separate regressions were computed for diesel and gasoline-powered trucks. Gross vehicle weight, wheelbase, and displacement were used as continuous variables in both cases with the addition of dummy variables for cowl and forward control.

Both time-to-time and place-to-place indexes for automobiles were derived by regression techniques (chap. 15). This was the only group in which such extensive use was made of this method and virtually none of conventional price indexes. The basic data consisted of over 1000 domestic list price observations for U.S. cars and 700 for five foreign producing countries, covering the six years of the study (1953, 1957, 1961 1962, 1963, and 1964). The listed makes of car included in the comparisons accounted for 95 percent or more of national output in every case. The specifications included weight, length, horsepower, engine displacement, number of cylinders, the presence of automatic transmission, number of doors, and volume of production, but not all of them were used in the final regression equations.

International Price Comparisons

The regression equations were calculated by pooling data for pairs of years, permitting coefficients for the two years to differ where the difference was statistically significant (the method of flexible pooling described earlier in this chapter). The price index was derived from a time dummy variable or that variable in combination with others in cases where the characteristic coefficients differed between the two years.

In the time-to-time equations, the average $\bar{R}^2$ for the whole period, based on various combinations of explanatory variables, ranged from 0.85–0.88 for the U.S. and Japan (the lowest proportions explained) to 0.94–0.97 for Italy and Germany. The range of variation in the alternative estimate of price movements was highest in 1953–1957, when there were several instances of 5 and 6 percentage point differences. After that there were only 3 cases out of 24 in which the range among the price changes calculated from the variants of the equation was greater than 3 percentage points.

The place-to-place indexes for 1964 were calculated in two ways. The same domestic price data as in the time-to-time indexes were used to calculate equations matching pairs of countries (U.S. with each other country) instead of pairs of years. The $\bar{R}^2$ ranged from 0.892 to 0.967, but the price relatives, in every case, differed widely by type of car, with foreign prices always very high for U.S.-type cars and comparatively low for foreign-type cars. These price level comparisons were subject to serious problems stemming from wide differences in the type of car produced in different countries. U.S. cars were, of course, larger and more powerful than European cars, and the ranges for some variables hardly even overlapped. The worst instance is the comparison of the U.S. with France. Because of these wide differences, price comparisons were made for five classes of cars and then averaged on the basis of estimates of the importance of each type in world trade.

In addition to these comparisons of home market prices, comparisons were made of prices in four specific markets, based on a total of over 400 observations and using the same method of flexible pooling. The pattern of comparative advantage appeared much the same as in the comparison of home market prices, with the U.S. the lowest priced seller of large cars and the highest-priced seller of small cars.

6.

Jack E. Triplett
Quality Bias in Price Indexes and New Methods of Quality Measurement

Most previous discussion of quality problems in index number construction has proceeded from the premise that the question which should be investigated takes the form: "To what extent does undetected quality change bias existing price indexes upward?" The presumption has always been that quality changes are probably undetected (or, at least, inadequately allowed for), and it has popularly been believed that pricing agencies pay little attention to quality change and take no action to control it. An example of this point of view is the widely noticed footnote inserted in the Price Statistics Review Committee's report (*Price Statistics* 1961, p. 36) by one of its members:

> Richard Ruggles believes that the current practice of *ignoring* quality improvement and new products is arbitrarily assuming these elements to be zero . . . He believes further that an arbitrary allowance for quality change should be put into the CPI . . . [emphasis supplied]

This paper was sponsored by the Federal Reserve Board Price Committee. A shortened version (consisting of most of Part I) was read at the August 1969 meeting of the Business and Economic Statistics Section, American Statistical Association. Part of the material was gathered while the author was on the staff of the Office of Prices, Bureau of Labor Statistics, during the summer of 1968. Permission to use unpublished data and internal memoranda has been granted by the Bureau of Labor Statistics, but none of the analysis or conclusions contained in this paper represents an official view of the BLS or the Board of Governors of the Federal Reserve System, nor should it be interpreted as necessarily coinciding with opinions of the staff of the Office of Prices or the F.R.B. Price Committee. The author would like to thank Zvi Griliches and members of the staff of the Office of Prices for comments on earlier drafts.

Jack E. Triplett is Assistant Professor of Economics, Washington University, St. Louis.

Quality Bias and New Methods

The Ruggles orientation leads to the comforting assertion—now firmly ensconced in a number of our basic undergraduate textbooks—that we need not worry excessively about mild inflation because the alleged upward quality bias in existing price indexes causes them always to rise more rapidly than the true rate of inflation. I believe this is of doubtful validity and that it is an extremely dangerous proposition for policy makers to accept. The widespread currency of the idea doubtless contributed to the lassitude with which the mild beginnings of the current inflation were viewed, a response which, amplified by the appropriate lagging mechanisms that seem to characterize the inflationary process, had something to do with the magnitude of the inflation we have recently experienced.

Section I of the present paper is intended to demonstrate that even if the quality of products improves over time, imperfect methods for adjusting for quality change will not *necessarily* result in upward bias in price indexes. At least for some components of the indexes, and over some time periods, quality errors will produce indexes that understate the degree of inflation. The second section of the paper outlines approaches (with particular reference to research on the "hedonic" proposals for measuring quality change) that are likely to be most fruitful in solving these problems.

I. Quality Errors in BLS Price Indexes
A. *The BLS Pricing Procedure*

We begin by defining some terms. The definitions adopted are for the purposes of the present paper only, and are not generally consistent with usage in BLS published materials. We start with the concept of a "good" or "product," which terms we will treat as synonyms. The ambiguity of the concept of a product is well known, but we continue as if everyone understood clearly what is meant (as indeed we do, intuitively). An "item" is a particular good chosen for pricing in a price index. Goods are available in different "varieties," by which we mean there are a number of quality levels, and the quality level of a particular variety can (in principle) be determined by reference to the amounts of the "characteristics" of the product embodied in the particular variety. The concept of a "characteristic" has been developed more precisely elsewhere,[1] so for present purposes we simply end the chain by defining it tautologically as an element

---

1. Lancaster 1966 uses the term in exactly the same way as it is employed here, and a discussion of its meaning for an investigation of quality is contained in Triplett 1971.

or attribute of the product which is an important determinant of its quality. Note that different *brands* of a product may constitute the same variety (if they are the same quality level), and there may be more than one variety available under a single brand name.

Next, it is necessary to describe current BLS pricing procedures. Because of the wide variety of situations encountered in price gathering, a short description usually sacrifices either clarity or generality; the following applies more to the CPI than the WPI, and is written with the consumer-durables items of the indexes most closely in mind, although as a general description of current practice, it applies to many other components of the indexes as well.

For most of the items in the indexes (76 percent of the expenditure weight in the CPI), what is known internally as a "specification" is drawn up to guide pricing agents in selecting product varieties for pricing. In most cases, this "specification" is actually a *range* of product specifications — that is, there is a range of quality which is acceptable for the index.

Specifications for some products are drawn rather broadly; for others, the permissible quality range is narrower. The Stigler Committee expressed concern that specifications too narrowly drawn would make it difficult to locate varieties meeting the specification in retail outlets. In the intervening period, the BLS has chosen to extend the practice of establishing what we will here call "subspecifications" within the main specification. In effect, the range of quality covered by the specification is broken up into smaller segments. Although any variety falling within the limits of the full specification may be selected for pricing, once a selection has been made the agent is instructed to gather future prices only for varieties which fall into the same subspecification as the initial selection. Any observation belonging to a different subspecification is regarded as noncomparable for the index. Subspecifications permit the main specification to be wider, thus enlarging the range of quality that may be priced. In some cases (appliances, for example), the brand name becomes part of the subspecification, so that once a brand is selected in a retail outlet, future prices are to be collected only for models of the same brand.[2]

Pricing by specification does not eliminate quality variation from the index. The specification performs three functions: (1) it designates attributes of the product which are major quality characteristics; (2) it

---

2. For a fuller discussion of the methods used in setting up the specification, see U.S. Department of Labor 1955, pp. 7–13. A sample specification is reproduced as an appendix to the present paper.

Quality Bias and New Methods

determines which product varieties, among the range of those available in the market, are appropriate for pricing for the CPI (or WPI); (3) it attempts to establish limits on the quality error permitted in direct comparisons used for the indexes.

We turn now to a discussion of quality errors which may occur under the specification pricing procedure. We may distinguish, according to the impact on the index, four types.

1. Although the specification is drawn so that conforming varieties are normally available in volume in retail outlets, sometimes no variety meeting the specification can be found in an outlet. In this case, prices of any other product varieties which may be available are not collected.[3] The effect of this is to reduce the number of observations on which the index is based, and the index is subject to error because the probability sample of outlets is upset.

2. There are, in many specifications, subspecifications. Any subspecification may be priced, but price quotations referring to product varieties in different subspecifications are never compared directly. If a price corresponding to a change in subspecification is obtained, then for the month in which the price is *first* reported, the quotation is discarded.[4] These deletions have the same effect on the index as the first type of error—the number of observations is reduced, and any price change occurring in the retail outlet deleted is lost. The only difference is that when the deletion is caused by a substitution, a price is available for subsequent index comparisons (providing the new variety continues in the retail outlet), and the price quotation *exists* for use in the current period if some way is found to allow for the quality difference.

3. A price quotation may be obtained on a variety which differs from the one priced in a previous period; if both meet the specification and subspecification, the difference in quality is ignored and the two prices

---

3. Except that frequently a "major deviation" is declared and prices for it carried along as if the variety met the specification. This is in effect an ad hoc widening of the specification, which may serve as a prelude to a formal adjustment of the specification limits. The BLS staff maintains that the increased utilization of major deviations has substantially reduced the number of cases in which no price is collected.

4. In some BLS literature this is referred to as "linking" or "linking without overlapping prices," apparently because the new variety is linked into the index (in subsequent quarters, not the current one). I have avoided using this terminology, because it is confusing: "linking" is frequently used synonymously with "splicing" to designate the technique of moving from one variety to another so that a price differential at a common point in time provides the quality adjustment.

are compared directly.[5] Although it is conventionally presumed that direct comparison of substitutions leads to a positive error in the index, there is no reason for supposing that substitutions always involve shifts to higher quality levels; lower quality varieties do supplant higher quality levels in some index comparisons, and in these cases the failure to adjust for quality difference leaves the index standing too low, relative to the true course of price movement. We will return to this matter at a later point.

4. Finally, there may be more or less invisible changes made by the manufacturer on what is ostensibly the same product variety. This type of quality error creeps into the index primarily in cases where quality change occurs in some characteristic which is not incorporated into the BLS specification. The specification is drawn only on a limited number of quality characteristics—those which, in the judgment of commodity specialists, are the ones most important in the determination of product quality. The judgment of commodity specialists is not infallible,[6] and, moreover, in practice the composition of the specification is also governed by the feasibility of identifying characteristics, of quantifying or obtaining information on some of them, and of determining exactly how they influence the level of quality.

B. *Quality Problems Explicitly Associated with Specification Pricing*

Most of the literature on the quality problem in price indexes has focused almost exclusively on what we have designated "type 3" and "type 4" quality error. In this literature, it has often been supposed that the quality error in the indexes can be inferred from information about the extent and rapidity of quality change for products. As the Stigler Committee (*Price Statistics* 1961, p. 35) put it, most economists believed that "the failure of the price indexes to take full account of quality changes . . . introduces a systematic upward bias in price indexes—that quality changes have on average been quality improvements."

---

5. There are exceptions to this statement. For some items, even if the substitute variety falls within the same subspecification, the observation will be deleted if the change in one or more characteristics exceeds some magnitude. For example, the specification for "dresser and chests" in the furniture item designated "bedroom suite" contains a 4-inch variation in length, but no more than 2 inches of length variation were permitted for direct comparisons in the index (Hoover 1961), p. 1179. Also, although the volume range in the refrigerator specification is fairly broad (13.5 to 16.5 cubic feet), only 0.4 cubic feet difference in volume is permitted in direct comparisons (Rothwell 1964), p. 13. Since these controls are not, typically, written into the formal BLS specification, examining pricing specifications gives an exaggerated idea of the amount of quality variation permitted in direct comparisons.

6. More formal ways for identifying and testing for appropriate characteristics for the pricing specification would be of great assistance to operating agencies, a point developed at greater length in Part II.B.1 of this chapter.

Quality Bias and New Methods

It is, of course, true that some economists have questioned the premise (that the trend of quality change has been upward), pointing to widespread reports of quality deterioration in services, among other things. The present paper, however, challenges not the facts of the premise, but rather the logic of the proposition that the sign of the quality error in the indexes is determined by the sign of the quality change that takes place in the market. In fact, information on the course of quality change for a product is nearly irrelevant for determining the direction of the quality error in the indexes.

We can best illuminate the nature of quality errors in the indexes by concentrating attention on situations producing price indexes which accumulate negative quality error. Within the specification pricing procedure, two situations are of sufficient importance to command attention. One arises because of deletions in the index (types 1 and 2 quality error); the second occurs when direct comparison (type 3 quality error) involves movement to lower quality levels.

1. *Quality Error Arising from Deletion of Price Quotations*

If substitutions within the specification[7] are necessary, some of these will be handled by deleting the price quotation. Deletion implicitly assumes that the price change recorded for identical varieties can be taken as an estimate of price movement in retail outlets where substitution is encountered. However, during a period of rising prices, if a price change and a change in the varieties in retailers' stocks are both imminent, sellers at all levels are likely to try to arrange both changes to coincide, rather than putting them into effect separately. If this occurs, prices of unchanged varieties are not moving parallel to those of the new varieties encountered. Because price increases coincide with substitution, deletion of the price quotation misses some of the true price change. Thus, when prices are rising, this method of handling quality change tends to bias the index downward.

When prices of the product are falling, however, the effect may very well not be symmetrical. Price declines, in manufactured goods, probably initially take the form of increasing discounts or concessions from the list or posted price. There is little basis, in the case of falling prices, for asserting that the pure price change in cases where substitution is encountered is different from the price movement measured from observations

---

7. We do not discuss explicitly type 1 error (deletion of the outlet because nothing meeting the specification is available there), primarily because the BLS staff argues that, under present procedures, it occurs very infrequently. It is readily observed in older worksheets, however; see footnote 12, below.

on identical varieties (that is, there seems to be no particular incentive for manufacturers or retailers to attempt to mask price declines). Thus, when the price of the product is falling, I do not see that any a priori argument can be made about the probable sign of the bias attributable to handling quality change by deleting the observation. The direction of the quality error caused by deletion can only be determined, in the case of falling prices, if one had a method for factoring out the value of the quality change.

It is probably feasible (with a little more work on the specifications of hedonic quality functions for certain products) to go back over worksheets, adjust deleted prices for the value of quality changes involved, and form an estimate of the direction and extent of the bias introduced by substitution. Such an analysis has never been carried out.[8] And we do not presently have data appropriate for comparing the magnitude of type 2 (or deletion) quality error with types 3 or 4, in order to form an estimate of the relative importance of the various types. However, information from several BLS studies of substitution within the CPI does indicate something of the empirical importance of error introduced by deletion of price quotations when quality differences are encountered.

One of these studies (Rothwell 1966) examined all prices gathered for the index in the month of April 1966, analyzing more than 36,000 individual price comparisons. This was supplemented by an analysis of all reported price quotations for nonfood items for two large cities for the full year 1965. Partial summaries of the tabulations are recorded in Tables 6.1 and 6.2.

Table 6.1. Substitutions in the CPI, April 1966

	Nonfood Items	Food Items
Total number of price comparisons	20,911	15,534
Total number of substitutions	1,778	699
Substitutions handled by		
(1) Direct comparison	1,051	272
(2) Deletion of price quotation	643	91
(3) Linking (overlapping prices available)	37	—
(4) Explicit size or quality adjustment	47	336

SOURCE: Rothwell 1966, p. 10.

---

8. It is considerably more difficult than it appears at first glance.

Quality Bias and New Methods

Table 6.2. Substitutions in the CPI, Selected Components, Two Large Cities, Full Year 1965

	All Nonfood Items	Apparel	Furniture	Appliances	Recreational Goods
Total number of price comparisons	8,364	2,251	421	372	805
Percentage of substitutions	10.4	18.6	14.9	23.1	18.4
Percentage of substitutions handled by					
(1) Direct comparison	6.4	13.2	10.2	13.7	7.5
(2) Deletion of price quotation	3.5	4.6	4.5	9.1	10.7
(3) Linking (overlapping prices available)	0.5	0.8	0.2	0.3	0.2
(4) Explicit quality adjustment	a	a	a	a	a

SOURCE: Rothwell 1966, Table III.
a None reported.

It is clear from the two tables that the incidence of substitution in the CPI is high, approaching 10 percent overall. Not surprisingly, it presents more problems in some components of the index than in others. The four components with the highest proportion of substitutions to price comparisons are listed in Table 6.2. Two of these—apparel and furniture—are components where styling differences are frequently encountered, and this is the probable cause of most substitutions in these components of the index. Toys account for much of the substitution encountered in the recreational goods component. The highest percentage of all occurs in the appliance component.

Unfortunately, tabulations were prepared only for rather broad components, such as appliances or apparel; some individual appliance items undoubtedly show higher incidences of substitution than the average for the appliance component as a whole. It would be useful to know the index weight of individual items which show high rates of substitutions.

The tables do indicate rather clearly that in components where the proportion of substitutions to total price quotations is high, deletion is frequently used to avoid price comparisons between different quality levels, and therefore type 2 quality error is a problem in precisely those index components where quality variation presents the greatest difficulties. Thus, we cannot dismiss the possibility that the impact on the index is substantial; the probable direction of the bias is downward.

2. Quality Error Arising from Direct Comparisons

Tables 6.1 and 6.2 indicate that direct comparison of the prices of substitutions is practiced somewhat more frequently than deletion. We can infer, from consideration of BLS procedures, that the price and quality differences involved are greater, where deletion is practiced, than when prices are compared directly. Tables 6.1 and 6.2, however, provide no direct information on the relative magnitude (as opposed to frequency of occurrence) of type 2 compared with type 3 quality error.

A second study of substitution in the CPI (U.S. Department of Labor n.d.) involved the analysis of an individual index component over an extended period of time. The technique employed was to recompute a CPI component after eliminating all direct comparisons from the index. When a particular variety disappears and a price quotation is obtained for a substitute variety which meets the specification (is approximately the same quality level), the price for the substitute is normally compared directly with the old (introducing type 3 error into the index); in the recomputation, price comparisons were restricted to cases where the identical variety was available in both periods. Comparison of the two indexes will tell us whether prices of substitutions *which were compared directly* moved differently from prices recorded for identical varieties.[9]

The study used prices for refrigerators in a midwest city and men's suits in an eastern city (see Table 6.3). Although Table 6.2 shows that the apparel components of the indexes are subject to extensive substitution, the recomputed index of Table 6.3 indicates that direct comparison of substitutions is not much of a factor in the index for men's suits. Additional data on the men's suits component is contained in an unpublished study by Thomas Gavett (1967b), who adjusted actual WPI price quotations for quality change using the hedonic quality measurement technique. His index rose somewhat less, over the 1958–1966 interval, than either the WPI or CPI suits component (see Table 6.4), but Gavett concluded that the difference was probably not significant and that existing measures for controlling quality change were working fairly well for this component. Since the quality adjustment technique routinely used in the suits component is essentially splicing and matching of quotations, Gavett's finding appears consistent with the indexes for men's suits in Table 6.3.

Men's suits, however, are hardly very indicative of the quality problems to be found in the apparel components of the indexes. Women's clothing

---

9. The recomputed indexes are not necessarily more accurate than the originals, as type 3 quality error has been replaced with type 2.

Quality Bias and New Methods

exhibits far greater variety in construction, style, and material, and is more subject to styling and other changes from year to year, making it particularly difficult to retain the same variety of an item in the index for successive periods.

Table 6.3. Alternative Price Indexes[a] (year-to-year percentage changes)

Year and Quarter	Refrigerators, Midwest City		Men's Suits, Eastern City	
	Actual CPI	Recomputation	Actual CPI	Recomputation
1953, IV–1954, IV	2.7	−2.8	−0.3	−0.3
1954, IV–1955, IV	−24.1	−14.5	1.7	0.0
1955, IV–1956, IV	−17.1	−11.7	4.7	2.7
1956, IV–1957, IV	−9.6	−4.5	0.0	0.0
1957, IV–1958, IV	1.5	−3.9	0.0	−1.5
1958, IV–1959, IV	−2.2	−6.5	0.9	1.0
1959, IV–1960, I	0.5	−0.6	—	—
1953, IV–1959, IV	—	—	7.2	1.9
1953, IV–1960, I	−41.6	−37.4	—	—

SOURCE: U.S. Department of Labor n.d. Data taken from tables labeled "Summary of Alternative . . . Indexes for Electric Refrigerators . . ." and "Summary of Indexes for Men's Suits, A–114 . . ."

[a] For description of the Indexes, see text.

Table 6.4. Alternative Measures, Year-to-Year Price Changes for Men's Suits (year-to-year percentage changes)

Year	Suits, CPI	Suits, WPI	Suits, with Hedonic Quality Adjustments
1958–1959	0.69	0.78	−0.13
1959–1960	2.61	5.17	6.28
1960–1961	2.71	−0.95	0.10
1961–1962	0.79	0.88	0.28
1962–1963	3.29	6.24	5.25
1963–1964	4.27	0.42	0.24
1964–1965	3.37	5.03	5.05
1965–1966	4.35	2.89	1.00
1958–1966	24.25	22.07	19.27

SOURCE: Gavett 1967b, Part III, p. 11a.

Appliances also show high incidence of substitution in the enumeration in Table 6.2. When the city index for refrigerators was recomputed to eliminate substitution (Table 6.3), a substantial divergence from the actual CPI component was created. With July 1953 as the base, by January 1960 the actual CPI component[10] for this product and city had fallen by more than 40 percent (to 58.4), while the recomputed component stood at 62.6. The difference in the movement of the two indexes is intriguing. The actual CPI calculation for this city fell by an astonishing amount between 1954 and 1957 (from 102 to 58), but then remained more or less constant at that level through 1960; the recomputed index dropped less precipitously between 1954 and 1957, but fell continuously through the whole period.

Thus, over this period, when some varieties of refrigerators disappeared from retail outlets the varieties which replaced them were, on balance, *cheaper* ones,[11] implying that substitution in the index involved movement to *lower quality* varieties. Although this appears paradoxical during a period in which we know there were numerous innovations in refrigerators, information at hand on the nature of substitutions encountered for this product makes it seem probable that direct comparisons frequently result in movement to lower quality levels.

Understanding the nature of substitution in the indexes requires devoting attention to certain aspects of the marketing of major appliances, as they affect the gathering of prices for the indexes.[12] Much of the discussion on the quality problem has been conducted with the automobile

---

10. Indexes for a product in a particular city are normally not published (which is the reason we have not identified the city in this paper), but computing a city price relative for a product is the first step in the computational procedure, and so it is correct to refer to the refrigerator index for a city as a component of the CPI.

11. Of course, this statement applies only to those substitutions which were originally compared directly in the indexes, not to those for which the price quotation was deleted in the original computation.

12. The following few paragraphs are based on two blocks of information gathered by the author. The first, contained in Appendix A of Triplett 1966, was a by-product of a retail price survey, undertaken to obtain cross-section prices for hedonic quality functions for major appliances. This was supplemented by an examination of BLS tabulation sheets for the same products for three to five large cities, each for several years. The incidence of substitution in major appliance components of the CPI is fully as high as indicated for appliances as a whole in Table 6.2, but similar tabulations for individual items have not been prepared. There is considerable quarter-to-quarter variation in the number of substitutions encountered, and for much of the period considerable evidence of "type 1" error was observed in the worksheets.

Quality Bias and New Methods

in mind; but in many respects the automobile is anything but representative of the kinds of quality problems that occur elsewhere in the indexes.

Both automobiles and major household appliances are offered in a large number of different models. But whereas various items of optional equipment are offered with a clearly defined price tag on automobiles, for most major appliances the addition of special features or items of equipment to the basic machine results in a different model designation. There are, therefore, a large number of different models sold by most manufacturers. Moreover, two or more years' models are frequently found side-by-side in outlets, and the total number of models observed at the retail level is increased still further by the practice of producing "special" models for some establishments, which differ in detail, trim, or equipment from machines available in rival stores. The result of all these practices is that a rather small proportion of the possible selection of appliance models will be found in any particular retail outlet at any given point in time, and because models in retail stocks appear to rotate in some random way there is a not insignificant probability that the same model will not appear in a retailer's floor stock in successive quarters.

The specification for major appliances is drawn in such a way that several models from each manufacturer fall within the specification (and, as noted earlier, for these items each brand is considered a subspecification). When the model priced in one quarter is not found in the same retail outlet in the following quarter, quality error is introduced into the index, the type depending on which machines are discovered in the retail outlet in the second pricing period, and whether the change is handled by direct comparison or by deleting the observation.[13]

In automobiles, substitution in the index is identified with the annual model changeover, and, since this is normally the time quality changes are made, this determines the quality problem for this component. In major appliances there are also annual model changes, but these are of less importance for the index.[14] Substitution in the appliance components

---

13. In some cases, if a model disappears *and the retailer expects to stock it again in the next pricing period*, a hypothetical price (what the dealer would have charged for the appliance had he offered it for sale at the time pricing was carried out) may be collected.

14. In appliances, quality change seems to occur through the addition of completely new models to a manufacturer's line and progressive deletion of older ones. The refrigerator in this year's line that is comparable to a given model of last year's usually is very comparable indeed (they may often be found in the same store, where it takes an experi-

of the CPI is largely a consequence of retailing practices, and a certain proportion of these substitutions introduces quality deterioration into the index even if the quality of appliances available in the market is improving over time. Examination of BLS price sheets for major appliances reveals many instances of substitution to lower quality levels, although we have not been able to ascertain the net impact of substitution on the index (whether substitutions of lower quality in the index component outweigh substitutions toward higher quality varieties of the product).

It is possible, however, to describe a situation in which quality improvement may cause a downward quality bias in the index. Consider a major appliance on which a significant innovation occurs. "No frost" freezers, "thin wall" construction, and automatic ice makers have appeared on refrigerators in the recent past; suppose a similar innovation occurs in the future—perhaps a method for cooling drinks very rapidly. Such innovations are usually heralded in the trade journals, or reports may come to BLS directly from manufacturers, so that BLS commodity specialists will be in a position to write a subspecification for the "fast drink cooler" by the time it appears in retail outlets. Hence, price comparisons will not be made between the new variety and previous ones, and a shift in pricing, in retail outlets, from one to the other involves no upward quality bias, if the commodity specialists handle it correctly.[15]

So much for the changeover. But what of subsequent pricing periods? Usually, in appliances, an innovation will appear initially on the "top of the line" machines. That is, the manufacturer produces (or the dealer stocks) only "fast cooling" refrigerators which also were equipped with all of the myriad special features which, taken one by one, distinguish one closely related model from another within a manufacturer's line. But if the

---

enced eye to tell them apart, and the older one will probably be selling at no discount). Less frequently, the manufacturer revamps his entire line, and the quality problem in these instances more nearly resembles the automobile annual model changes.

15. Of course, in the absence of explicit quality adjustments, the procedure employed would be to delete the observation from the index at the time the innovation was first priced in each outlet, creating type 2 quality error. We do not know the direction of the error, although if prices are generally rising, it probably biases downward. Note that there are potential problems at this stage that are ignored in the present discussion: (1) the new subspecification might not be written promptly, so that prices for machines carrying the new feature might not be collected until well after they had appeared in volume in retail outlets; (2) if the new subspecification *is* set up promptly, the innovation might not be accepted by the market as a quality improvement, in which case an error may be put into the index because an implicit adjustment was made for a quality change that was not validated by the market. The latter situation would pose even more serious problems if explicit quality adjustments (through use of manufacturer's cost data, or the hedonic technique) were made.

Quality Bias and New Methods

new feature proves very popular with buyers, it will be offered on progressively more "stripped" machines. And when these machines appear in retail outlets, if the individual deleted features do not warrant a subspecification, there will be a substitution in the index, for which prices are compared directly. For a series of substitutions of this type, the price index would be biased *downward*.

To put the matter another way, we admit that there is quality improvement in the product. But we *control* for quality, in the index comparisons, by holding constant a particular feature, or a group of features, which seem the most important quality determinants. At some future time, the range of quality available—among machines that exhibit the controlled characteristics—will be extended downward. Some of the lower quality varieties appearing in the subspecification will be selected for pricing, thus biasing the index downward.

Substitution of this kind has occurred in the appliance components of the index. The magnitude and pervasiveness of it and whether it has been strong enough over any time period to result in *net* downward bias are unknown. However, the continual decline in the appliance components over a protracted period (see the indexes of Table 6.5) is in itself a signal for more attention for these components of the index.

In Part I.B. we have shown that the mere fact of product improvement is insufficient, by itself, to prove that price indexes are biased upward. Even when substitute varieties are introduced into the index by direct

Table 6.5. Selected Durable and Appliance Components, Consumer Price Index, 1953–1968 (1957–1959 = 100)

	Household Durables[a]	Appliances	Refrigerators	Washing Machines
1953	103.8	116.3	147.3	108.1
1955	98.3	105.9	129.0	102.6
1957	99.6	101.1	102.4	101.4
1959	100.2	99.5	98.6	98.4
1961	98.9	96.5	95.3	93.0
1963	98.5	91.5	90.6	89.2
1965	96.9	87.1	86.2	86.8
1967	98.2	83.8	82.7	86.6
1968	101.4	84.8	83.8	88.6

Source: U.S. Department of Labor, *Consumer Price Index*.
[a] Before 1964, "Durables, less cars."

comparison (with the entire difference in quality ignored), the index may be biased downward because the substitutions that are compared directly in the index may be substitutions to lower quality varieties. Therefore, knowledge of the extent and direction of quality changes for individual products is insufficient information to assess whether there is quality error in the indexes or to ascertain the direction of the bias.

C. *Other Quality Problems in the Indexes*

In addition to quality errors associated with the specification pricing procedure, there are some other index errors attributable to quality variation in the market. All of them must be considered when forming an assessment of the direction and magnitude of quality bias in price indexes.

1. In a few components of the indexes the specification pricing procedure is not employed, and no measures for control of—or adjustment for—quality variation exist. Foremost among these in recent years has been the used car component of the CPI. Because of its weight in the CPI and its rather questionable behavior, it has been the object of attention from the Bureau, resulting in several recent changes.[16]

Prior to 1969, prices of used cars were not gathered by the BLS. Instead, average prices "for four age groups and two makes of standard-size used cars" were taken from used car price books published by the National Automobile Dealers Association (U.S. Department of Labor, 1967). Beginning in November 1966, limited adjustments were made for options whose prices (on used cars) were reported separately, with weights according to an estimate of the proportion of cars originally equipped with the option.[17]

Since the NADA data are gathered from new car dealers and are intended for use by car dealers in determining prices of used cars, their reliability as a measure of the change in used car prices is questionable, particularly since very little information exists about how the averages are compiled. It is even less clear whether the "book" option allowances

---

16. Prices of new and used cars must be related, because the commodities are obviously close substitutes. Under the circumstances, it seems hardly possible, let alone likely, for prices of late-model used cars to rise by 20 percent in a 4-year period, during which new car prices were *falling* (CPI: 1960, used cars = 101.6, new cars = 102.5; 1964, used cars = 121.6, new cars = 101.2). On the behavior of the new car component of the CPI during these years, see Triplett 1969 and Hall, "The Measurement of Quality Change from Vintage Price Data" (in this volume).

17. A more detailed explanation of procedures used in computing the used car component of the CPI is contained in U.S. Department of Labor 1967.

Quality Bias and New Methods

represent anything more than a rule of thumb, and in any case the small adjustments made in the used car component for changing amounts of optional equipment on used cars are a fraction of the quality adjustments routinely carried out in the new car components of the CPI and WPI.

In an attempt to base the used car component on data which are legitimately market prices, the BLS has begun using prices from used car auctions. Details have not yet been published, but two points are worthy of note: auction prices do nothing to ameliorate the quality problem in the used car component of the CPI, and they are wholesale, not retail, prices.

In view of the weight of the used car component in the CPI, used car prices should be gathered directly from retail sources, as the BLS does for other commodities. Such a change would be expensive, but the inadequacy of other expedients makes it essential.

It is interesting that the BLS adjusts for the age of used cars (and of housing purchases) while ruling out similar adjustments for age in new cars (and rental housing). Much of the difference in price between a new car at the beginning of the model year and the price for the same car toward the end of the year is attributable to the fact that the latter is so much closer to being "last year's car" at the time of purchase. The staff of the Office of Prices argues that this represents a change in the value of an asset and should not receive an adjustment in the CPI; but the imminence of the annual model change for new cars also affects the behavior of used car prices, so it is doubtful that one can attribute the decline, through the automobile model year, in the price for a specified age of used car solely to the fact that that particular car has less useful life remaining.

2. The fear has been expressed, from time to time, that prices of the varieties priced by the BLS might move differently from prices of varieties not priced, or that the varieties selected for pricing might not be representative. It is of course true that error can arise from such sources. Unfortunately, there is not much relevant data, despite some ingenious use of mail-order catalogs.

One example was Burstein's (1961) study of refrigerators. From mail-order catalogs Burstein constructed a price index for those refrigerator models which conformed to the BLS specification and compared it with an index computed from prices of all refrigerators listed in the catalogs. The "conforming" index stood *below* the index for all varieties, leading to the conclusion that the CPI refrigerator component was biased downward—probably, Burstein explained, because the prices of refrigerators chosen for pricing by the BLS fell relative to the prices of refrigerators as a group. Burstein's conclusion, however, rests entirely on his assertion that the index he compiled from mail-order catalogs for refrigerators meeting the BLS specifications (his "conforming" index) was *superior* to the actual CPI component as a measure of price change for this size of refrigerator. For even though the "all varieties" index rose more than the "conforming" index, both of the indexes computed from mail-order catalogs rose *less* than the published CPI refrigerator component. No adequate explanation for the substantial divergence between the "conforming" index and the CPI refrigerator component has been offered. It is not warranted to assume from the fact of divergence alone that it must be the CPI that is wrong.

Another use of mail-order catalogs is in a study by Rees (1961). Rees constructed price indexes for ten different non-durables,[18] in each case preparing an index for all varieties of the product listed in the catalog and a separate index number for those varieties which conformed to the BLS specification for the product. Perhaps the major point which emerges from this exercise is how difficult it is for an outside investigator to duplicate BLS indexes: in only three cases out of ten does Rees's index for varieties conforming to the CPI specification coincide with the relevant CPI component. For one of the seven cases where the "conforming" index diverged from the CPI, Rees was able to compare the procedure he employed in computing his "conforming" index with that actually used in the computation of the CPI. For this case, "inspection of the [BLS] worksheets revealed serious errors in following the BLS specifications" (Rees 1961, p. 168). In several of the seven cases in which the "conforming" index diverged from the CPI, Rees's "all varieties" index proved to be a better approximation to the actual CPI component than his "conforming" index (this duplicates Burstein's experience).

It is true that for the three cases in which the "conforming" index approximated closely the CPI components, the "all varieties" index was in every instance lower. However, considering all ten indexes computed, some of the "all varieties" indexes rose less, some more, and some the same as comparable CPI components. Rees's "conforming" indexes failed to duplicate the CPI components very well, so the source of the divergences between his "all varieties" indexes and actual CPI components cannot be identified uniquely with differences in the price movements of different product varieties. It is possible that prices of mail-order houses may not change by the same percentage as prices in conventional outlets; if not, mail-order price indexes may differ from CPI components mainly because price movements differ in various types of retail outlets.

---

18. Six clothing items, three from the house furnishings components (mattresses, rugs and carpets, and blankets), and automobile tires.

Quality Bias and New Methods

Other information on the problem is scanty. The BLS has claimed that the estimates of sampling error which have been published for the CPI indicate something of the error associated with pricing different varieties (Wilkerson 1964). However, the sampling error could not possibly give any information about error stemming from unrecorded price movements of varieties outside the specification, because none of these will be priced for the index.[19] The most the replicated sample could provide is an estimate of sampling error arising out of the fact that only certain of the varieties that fall *within* the specification are priced.

Unfortunately, an estimate of the error associated with pricing different varieties within the BLS specification has not been made public; the claim that it is reflected in the overall estimate of the sampling error is no substitute for an explicit estimate of this component of the sampling error. Such an estimate would not give an answer to the question of whether prices of varieties falling outside the specification move differently from prices of varieties falling within the specification; but at the moment we have very little information on the variance of price movements among different varieties of a product, and data from the BLS replicated sample could tell us something about this. Studies of the sampling error connected with the varieties selected for pricing should be carried out by the BLS and the results made public.

3. It is well known that the BLS makes quality adjustments in automobile prices on the basis of production cost data supplied by manufacturers. The same data is used as the basis for the adjustment in the CPI and WPI.

Aside from automobiles, explicit quality adjustments in the CPI consist mainly of adjustments for changes in the size of packages in food items in the index.[20] However, the collection of manufacturer's cost data as the basis for quality adjustment has spread, in the WPI, from autos to include other vehicles and industrial and agricultural machinery.

One could scarcely contend, on the whole, that we were not better off with the production cost data than without it. But the use of such data poses certain problems.

Some manufacturers, when supplying data to the BLS, report in effect that they never change a price without an equivalent quality change and that all quality changes are always fully transmitted into price changes. Even in cases where manufacturers are not so obviously trying to "justify"

---

19. Except that sometimes a "major deviation" will be accepted and carried along in the index; see above, note 3.
20. See the tabulation in Table 6.1. A number of examples of explicit quality adjustments in the CPI are given in Rothwell 1964.

price there is some tendency toward overstatement of the cost of quality changes. The BLS does not always use the full claimed value of quality changes. But from what information can be obtained, it appears that disallowing or modifying reported cost figures occurs in relatively few of the cases for which reports are filed, and the reductions are usually small. It may be significant that in autos (where more experience has accumulated with the use of cost information as quality adjustments) the cost estimates are subjected to more stringent surveillance before use in the indexes. In all cases, however, there is no systematic procedure for evaluating the cost data. If conflicting information is at hand, there will probably be editing of the cost figures before they are used to prepare the quality adjustment; otherwise they are accepted at full value.

My judgment cannot be backed up by many firm figures, but I believe that where the full requested cost information is provided by manufacturers, the result is probably quality adjustments that are too large. On the other hand, with the exception of automobiles, in components of the WPI where cost-based quality adjustments are currently employed the BLS does not yet receive quality reports for every price report, so there are some quality improvements for which no adjustment is made. This would usually offset, to some extent, over-adjustment for quality changes in other reports.

However, the situation promises to worsen as more cooperation is obtained for reporting the cost of changes. The appropriate conception for use in compiling cost information is not easy to convey to respondents. We want to compare the cost of producing last year's quality level with the cost of this year's quality level, with scale of output and factor prices constant over the period of comparison. It is fairly certain that what we frequently obtain from manufacturers is a cost change attributable to various sources—technical change in production, changing output levels and input prices—and is only partly caused by pure quality change. In other words, we get a comparison of the cost of producing this year's quality level this year with last year's quality level last year. This is not appropriate comparison for the index. The frequent published references to product changes reported as "increased quality at lower cost" indicate the problem arises frequently (see, e.g., Stotz 1966 and Gavett 1967*a*).

Whether a reported change can legitimately be regarded unambiguously as a quality change sometimes poses difficulties. An example is provided by adjustments to cover the cost of increased warranty provisions on new cars. Repairs under warranty substitute in production for the cost of inspection for defects during the manufacturing process. Some *increases* in warranty costs may represent quality *deterioration*, because the warranty

Quality Bias and New Methods

repairs reflect some other changes in production that increase the frequency of repairs. To use as a quality adjustment for the indexes data on the cost of servicing warranties, the costs should be standardized to eliminate any changes in the incidence of repairs required, leaving an adjustment that reflects only changes in the length of time over which free repairs will be made, or changes in the coverage and terms of the warranty agreement. One should note that warranties is an area where the BLS has frequently not accepted the full claimed value of the changes submitted by the manufacturers, and furthermore that the Bureau itself has been aware that making quality adjustments for changes in warranty terms poses unusual and difficult problems.

4. A traditional method for handling the quality problem in index numbers has been to convert it into the (supposedly) more tractable product-mix problem: different varieties are treated as if they were different products and carried along in the index separately. In the WPI, for example, prices may be collected for several varieties of an item of machinery and separate components published for each of them. Then, when the quality of machines improves, it may be possible to allow for the change by shifting the weights attached to each of the separate subcomponents.

For some products, data on sales by different varieties are not available.[21] But when market shares data are available, in the past there has been more than one method employed to reflect them into the index. The best is the most obvious and straightforward: simply shift the weights to reflect new data as soon as data becomes available.

The less desirable alternative is represented by the farm tractor component of the WPI. Some of the subclasses of farm tractors consist of groupings by horsepower (horsepower is taken as the principal quality characteristic, a practice confirmed by a hedonic study of quality in farm tractors; see Fettig 1963). The latter half of the 1950's brought a rapid shift toward the larger sizes of ordinary wheeled farm tractors, and the BLS adjusted for this only partly by adjusting the weights of the several individual tractor series carried in the index; it also shifted the limits of the horsepower size classes used, "linking" shifts in the index when they occurred.

Because of the way the size classifications were shifted, the published indexes for varieties of farm tractors have little meaning. For example, the

---

21. The reader is reminded that "varieties," in this paper, means quality levels; see beginning of Part I.A.

Table 6.6. Wholesale Price Indexes, Farm Tractors (1947–1949 = 100)

Code Number	1952	1960
11–11 (farm tractors)[a]	117.7	140.6
11–11–01	114.9	143.8
11–11–02	114.2	132.0
11–11–03	120.4	139.9
11–11–04	120.5	131.7

Source: Data taken from various BLS publications and releases on the WPI, converted to a common base, and checked against BLS tabulation cards.

[a] Sometimes labeled "farm and garden tractors." There are several other subcomponents besides the four listed in this table.

wholesale price of all farm tractor varieties rose by 19 percent from 1952 to 1960 (see Table 6.6). During the same interval the component identified by code number 11–04 rose by only 9 percent. We would like to conclude from this information that prices of one size of tractors fell relative other sizes. But code 11–04 was subjected to no less than seven changes in definition between 1954 and 1961. It actually consists of several indexes, each reporting price changes for some tractor variety for some relatively short time period, with all of them spliced together end-to-end to give the final index. Although an index for code 11–04 was published for the entire period, it has no meaning as an index of a variety of tractor because sometimes it represents one thing, sometimes another. A comparison of the movement of code 11–04 with, perhaps, code 11–03 cannot be given *any* interpretation.

One would like to have the basis for establishing how much of the observed shift to larger tractors in the late 1950's was attributable to falling price differentials for larger tractors, as opposed to other considerations such as larger farms, changing capital-labor ratios (increased mechanization), different growing and harvesting methods, and so forth. It would also be useful to compare the WPI tractor component with an index adjusted for quality change by hedonic methods, such as that constructed by Fettig (1963); in this case, it is essential to estimate what part of the divergence between the two was caused by quality drift (substitution) within the individual subspecification, as opposed to the impact of the changing mix of tractors. The way the WPI farm tractor index was put together, analysis of these and other questions is virtually impossible.

5. There will always be human error in any index. In addition to the possibility of mistakes in identifying product varieties, recording prices,

Quality Bias and New Methods

transcription, and so on, the commodity specialists no doubt occasionally err in deciding when substitutions are to be deleted or compared directly, and in the application of explicit quality adjustments (where they exist). It seems to me that the less time the commodity specialist has to make these decisions the more likely it is that he will make incorrect ones, and so the pressure to get the index out by an established date increases the quality errors (as well as other kinds of errors) in it. For this reason, the Administration's recent order[22] to all agencies to speed up the release of statistical series may purchase a gain of one or two days in the release of the CPI and WPI at the expense of a decline in their accuracy. In view of the pressure for more rapid reporting, the Stigler Committee's proposal that the indexes come out in preliminary form so that mistakes subsequently discovered can be corrected in the final published figure deserves additional consideration.

D. *Summary*

The conventional position on the quality error in price indexes is an argument of the form:

Premise (1) — the quality of products improves over time;
Premise (2) — no quality adjustments, or inadequate quality adjustments, are carried out by the pricing agencies;
Conclusion (1) — the quality of varieties actually priced by the BLS increases so that direct comparisons involve positive quality errors;
Conclusion (2) — this means that the CPI is biased upward because of quality change.

In Part I of this paper, we have shown that conclusion (1) cannot be derived from the two premises; even if the quality of products is improving, those substitutions in the indexes for which direct comparisons are made may involve movement to lower quality varieties. And even if direct comparison involves quality improvement, conclusion (2) does not follow because some substitutions are handled by deleting the price quotation from the index when the new variety is first observed, rather than by comparing directly, and also because quality variation in the market leads to a number of other errors—some of which are indicated in Part I.C—in the indexes. Evaluating the net quality error in any index component requires examination of all the kinds of quality errors that may be present, and cannot be accomplished solely on the basis of information about the extent of quality improvement in the market.

---

22. See *Statistical Reporter*, February 1969, p. 126.

II. New Measurement Techniques

Several new methods for measuring quality change have been proposed in recent years. Foremost are the hedonic technique (see Griliches 1961 and 1967, and Court 1939), and the vintage-price method suggested by Burstein (1961) and explored empirically by Cagan (1965) and Hall ("The Measurement of Quality Change from Vintage Price Data," included in this volume). Both of these were originally proposed in the hope that they would lead to improvements in price indexes. Except for the Commerce Department's relatively new house construction index (see U.S. Bureau of the Census 1968, pp. 17–24), however, neither has been put to any use in existing indexes. Part II of this paper explores problems of making the new techniques operational within the present indexes. It has not been recognized that the existing empirical research on new quality measurement techniques has produced little that is directly useful for the quality problems that arise in the indexes as they are now constructed.

A. *Estimating Quality Change for a Product*

Of the existing quality studies using the hedonic or the vintage price techniques, most have attempted to form an estimate of the extent of quality change for a particular product. This objective may be perfectly proper within certain contexts.[23] But, as indicated in Part I, it will be of little value in existing price indexes. For the question that needs answering is not: "What is the extent of quality change for, e.g., appliances?", but rather: "What undetected quality errors remain in the appliance components of the indexes?" Although it has sometimes been thought that an answer to the first question will also provide an answer to the second, the two questions do not amount to the same thing at all, and information on the one may say little or nothing about the other.

Furthermore, the investigator may not be able to answer the second of the two questions by seeking the answer to yet a third: "How much quality change has occurred in the product varieties actually selected by the BLS for pricing?"[24] The answer to this question will only indicate the degree of quality error in the index component if all substitutions in the indexes are compared directly (no deletion or explicit quality adjustments), and this will seldom be the case.

---

23. However, the meaning of a statement such as "The quality of gadgets has been improving" is more ambiguous than first appears.

24. Quality indexes for product varieties priced for the CPI were computed in Griliches 1961 and Triplett 1969.

Quality Bias and New Methods

B. *Improving the Pricing Specification*

A major, though so far unappreciated, avenue for using the hedonic technique to improve price indexes is its potential for improving the pricing specification. Currently, specifications are drawn up according to the judgement of BLS commodity specialists, who must decide if a particular attribute or feature of a product "significantly" influences its quality. The hedonic technique provides a means for carrying out a formal test[25] on the significance of variables thought to be quality determinants, imposing a testing stage between the point at which the commodity specialist's judgment is exercised and the point at which the specification is written.

Studies on the validity of BLS pricing specifications offer particularly promising opportunities for the outside investigator: something very similar must be done as the first step in any hedonic quality study, and the data and information requirements for evaluating the pricing specification are considerably less formidable than for other objectives which investigators have usually set for themselves.

The first step in any hedonic study is a cross-section analysis which seeks to isolate variables that are quality characteristics of the product. This always requires a careful study of the product in order to determine the appropriate disaggregation.[26] A good starting point is the BLS specification. The initial hedonic results may therefore be used to test the validity of specifications and subspecifications currently employed by the BLS and to isolate additional variables which should be incorporated into existing specifications in order to provide closer control over quality variation in the index.

Owing to the degree of multicollinearity which afflicts most hedonic studies, it may be necessary to employ proxy variables in some cases, rather than the quality characteristics that are really desired. The use of proxies is not unique to the hedonic method for deriving pricing specifications. The current pricing specifications already employ proxy variables in some instances, precisely because of the kind of structural relationships among variables that give rise to the multicollinearity problem in its classic form. In these cases, the BLS uses

> associations of quality characteristics whenever possible. If a hidden quality factor . . . is associated with another quality factor which can

---

25. By applying the standard t-test of significance to a regression coefficient.

26. The hedonic technique may be interpreted as a disaggregation of products into the characteristics that enter the utility function. This is spelled out in Triplett 1971.

be observed or is known by price reporters, both are included in the specification by defining the one which can be observed. [Hoover 1961, p. 1179]

On the other hand, in seeking to improve the pricing specification, care must be exercised lest unperceived technical relationships among the variables chosen invalidate the results. As an example, one of the ways that the quality of refrigerators has improved in recent years has been the so-called "thinwall" construction—improved insulation that results in less waste space taken up by the refrigerator walls. In Dhrymes' studies of refrigerators (1967, and "Price and Quality Changes in Consumer Capital Goods," included in this volume), internal volume was introduced as a quality variable, but also thrown into the regression were the external height, width, and depth dimensions. This resulted in puzzling signs, leading to the conclusion that quality was inversely related to width. However, the "thinwall' attribute pertains to the relation between internal and external volume. A negative sign on the coefficient of an external dimension such as width indicates that holding net refrigerated volume and other dimensions constant, the narrower the refrigerator, the higher its quality; but, of course, if internal volume is held constant, the exterior dimensions can only be made smaller by making the walls thinner. This result is just an indication that the thinwall feature is a quality characteristic.[27]

A study which is designed explicitly to test the validity of pricing specifications surmounts, in many instances, the most formidable data requirement for hedonic quality studies—acquiring a set of market prices for a sufficiently broad range of different varieties. It is clear that the "quality" or appropriateness of the price data used for the regression's dependent variable becomes a serious problem if one's task is to estimate a set of implicit prices for quality characteristics (these are the regression coefficients), and even more so if one wishes to estimate the "pure" (or adjusted for quality change) price change.

But a variety of sources of cross-section prices might be employed if the objective is to isolate a set of quality characteristics. List, or suggested, prices (retail or wholesale) are available for many durable goods, or they may be collected from distributors or retailers. An array of list prices for different quality levels would usually provide an adequate indicator of the quality spread among the different quality levels found in the market,

---

27. A "thinwall" variable was tested directly in my own refrigerator study (Triplett 1966) and found significant.

Quality Bias and New Methods

unless the relation between the list price and the actual market price is related in some way to the quality characteristics used in the hedonic quality function (in other words, if discounts from list or posted price are conditional upon the purchaser's accepting or specifying certain features or attributes, or combinations of them). Gavett, in his study of washing machines (1967b), made use of suggested retail buying prices, put out by one of the consumer advisory organizations. Suggested prices have been published for a number of products and would also be an acceptable source of cross-section prices, if the objective was to evaluate the pricing specification (even though they would be questionable as the basis for a measure of price change over time). Also it may be possible for an independent investigator to gather a set of prices for one or two years or periods only. This would have serious shortcomings if the results were to be applied in any way to time series data. But using one or two cross-sections to evaluate the BLS pricing specification might produce valuable results.

C. Designing Improved Quality Adjustment Techniques for Use within the Indexes as Presently Constructed

To be useful in this context, a hedonic quality function, or any other new quality measurement technique, must be capable of reducing the four types of quality error associated with the specification pricing procedure (these errors are described in Part I.A, above). This requires quality adjustments that can be used to factor out specific quality changes observed when substitution occurs in pricing—either accurate estimates of the quality of each of the product varieties involved in the substitution, or implicit prices for the individual quality characteristics in which the two observations differ.

Suppose an investigation into the quality of a particular product yields a quality function of the general form

$$P = a_0 + a_1 X_1 + a_2 X_2 + \cdots + a_k X_k + \cdots + a_n X_n + u,$$

where the first k variables are those already included in the pricing specification, and the next $n-k$ are newly discovered quality characteristics, not incorporated into the specification. The a's are all interpreted as implicit prices for the quality attributes.

By adding $n-k$ quality characteristics to the pricing specification, the hedonic quality function would reduce the incidence of quality error resulting from direct comparison (types 3 and 4), whether or not any use is made of the implicit prices. But a reduction of direct-comparison error will normally only be purchased by an increase in deletion error (type 2): to reduce the latter, values of the a's are required.[28] Then, when quality change involves any of the characteristics X, the pricing agency can simply factor out the value of the changes in characteristics (evaluated by the implicit prices, the a's) from the recorded price change.

Unfortunately, the existing hedonic quality studies have produced few estimates of implicit prices for characteristics that can be used for quality adjustments in the indexes. In part, this may simply reflect the fact that most of them were preliminary, or, at least, subject to additional refinement. But the idea that hedonic studies will necessarily increase the BLS control over quality depends on success in adding quality variables to those presently controlled and forming precise estimates of implicit prices for all variables controlled. In components where pricing specifications are currently employed, I am not convinced that hedonic quality measures are likely to achieve dramatic reductions in reducing quality error in the indexes.

One problem is multicollinearity. Multicollinearity in most of the hedonic functions so far estimated has made interpretation of the coefficients somewhat less than straightforward. On the other hand, the distinction drawn by Greenberg (1969) between multicollinearity arising from structural relations in the system as opposed to that originating in the sample strikes an optimistic note. Some of the multicollinearity observed in hedonic studies may reflect stable technological relationships in the product, or in production, so that one of the collinear variables never changes without changes in the others. For these cases, one need not worry about the interpretation or value of *one* of the coefficients; quality adjustments will always involve the set of coefficients for the collinear variables. More work on the nature, source, and interpretation of the multicollinearity in hedonic quality functions is needed.

Secondly, there is a certain amount of conflict between the principles usually associated with sound econometric research and the task of deriving adjustments for all of the kinds of changes actually observed among the various product varieties. Ordinarily, an econometric investigation will be designed to accomplish its explanatory goal with as few variables as possible, partly because of the specter of multicollinearity, but also because explanation requires abstraction from the detail of reality. Pricing specifications for more complex products, on the other hand, are already written on numerous quality attributes. For example, the current pricing specification for refrigerator-freezers (reproduced in the appendix) contains

---

28. Also, the a's may be employed when a range of values of the X's is permitted in direct comparison, though this range is normally small. See above, note 5.

Quality Bias and New Methods

approximately 14 quality variables.[29] It is unlikely that further research will produce a *well-behaved* hedonic quality function containing all the 14 variables of the current pricing specification, plus any significant number of new ones. If anything, a perfected hedonic quality function for this product will undoubtedly indicate that fewer than 14 quality attributes are adequate for explaining the range of prices observed for different varieties of refrigerators.

The point at issue can be stated in two ways: (1) if a few variables are all that are required to account for quality variation, should the BLS control only for these in the pricing process? Or (2) will controlling for quality using characteristics isolated by the hedonic technique reduce the error presently accepted in direct comparisons? The answers require recognition that not only the present system, but also the new quality measures, contain error.

To get information on the size of direct comparisons of substitutions when a well-developed specification is employed, substitutions in the refrigerator-freezer component of the CPI were examined for one large city for the years 1961–1964. The mean price change,[30] among substitutions handled by direct comparison, was $15.61 or 5.4 percent. Substitutions involved both price increases and decreases with about the same frequency and magnitude for each (the net effect of price changes of substitutes compared directly was an increase of 0.4 percent). Along the same line, Rothwell (1966, pp. 11–12) noted that, in a sample of CPI price comparisons, 75 percent of the substitutions handled by direct comparison involved price differences of less than 5 percent in the prices compared. On the other hand, there were undoubtedly cases in my own computation, and in the study cited by Rothwell, where substitution brought with it quality change but no recorded price change. But even so, the 5.4-percent figure is probably a considerable overstatement of the size of type 3 quality error.

---

29. I arrived at this figure by counting the elements in the specification which could be employed as independent variables in a hedonic quality function (some attributes would be coded in the form of dummy variables).

30. For each substitution (which was compared directly), the work sheets record the price of the model priced in the first of the two periods and also the price of the (different) machine selected in the second pricing period. The statistic computed is the mean of the absolute value of the difference between the two prices. Not all the recorded price change when substitution took place can be attributed to quality changes. Some of the substitution recorded I am reasonably sure involved little or no quality change yet contributed price change to the total. For example, a number of the substitutions consisted merely in changes in the manufacturer's code for the model year, and there was almost no change in the machines themselves; where these substitutions were accompanied by price changes, all of it is "pure" price change.

As further information bearing on the size of the quality error permitted in direct comparisons, specifications of the leading brands of refrigerator-freezers were checked against the BLS pricing specification for that product.[31] Taking the machines that conformed to the specification, list prices (where available) were examined for those which would be compared directly if one was substituted for another. Taking all possible direct-comparison type substitutions (for which list prices were available), the mean value of the (absolute) difference in price that would be accepted was 7.7 percent. Of course, prices entering the CPI are not list prices, but since we are dealing with percentage differences in price, I do not think the estimate is defective for that reason.

The 7.7-percent figure is, again, somewhat of an overstatement, partly because we could control only imperfectly for one or two of the variables of the pricing specification (so some of the larger price differences entering into the computation represent refrigerators which would not in fact be compared directly for the CPI). The 7.7-percent estimate from list prices is higher than the 5.4-percent price change computed from the actual work sheets, which probably indicates that actual substitutions occur more frequently between machines closest together in quality.

Set against these figures, which indicate something of the size of type 3 quality error, is the error which would be associated with a quality estimate derived from a hedonic quality function. A natural measure of error for the function is the standard error of estimate. In my own study of household appliances, the standard error of estimate for refrigerator-freezers was around 6 percent, for washing machines and dryers 3–4 percent (Triplett 1966, p. 137a, col. II, and p. 146a). Griliches (1961, p. 181) reported around 8 percent for his study of automobiles (in my automobile study it was a little lower). To my knowledge, none of the other hedonic studies has reported this valuable statistic.

An alternative measure of error, appropriate in some cases, is provided by the standard errors of the regression coefficients. If two varieties differ only with respect to one (or a few) of the quality characteristics, then the pricing agency need only evaluate the value of the changed characteristic,

---

31. I used specifications for 1965 refrigerator-freezers because that is the only year for which I have an array of list prices for this product. Starting with 130 refrigerator models from 9 manufacturers, 45 models met all the elements of the pricing specification (except that almost all of them deviated from the specified interior and exterior finish). From the CPI tabulation sheets, it would appear that "major deviations" are frequently permitted for refrigerators with bottom freezers, but these were not included in the computation reported here.

Quality Bias and New Methods

not the quality levels of the two varieties,[32] and one need be concerned only about the size of the standard error of the regression coefficient (or those of a subset of the full set of coefficients). However, for most of the products on which hedonic studies have been carried out, the kinds of quality changes for which direct comparison is current practice in the index do not correspond to the set of variables isolated by the hedonic quality function. It seems to me likely that this will also be the case as more studies are completed.

D. *Other Approaches*

1. Greater room for improvement exists in components of the index that are not priced by specification, since in these it is more nearly true that quality changes are ignored.[33] These components offer a fertile field for the outside investigator, as the problems involved are often conceptual ones, and producing practical improvements does not require familiarity with intricacies of present practice. Indeed, it is easier to make a case for scrapping present procedures in favor of new computational techniques or other radical restructuring.

2. Most of the existing hedonic quality studies estimated a price index number directly from a regression,[34] or, alternatively, some kind of quality index was constructed, which could be used to adjust a price index. None of the early investigators argued that these were the *only* ways for using the hedonic results, but the fact that the regression coefficients provided explicit adjustment factors for specific quality changes was often overlooked by others.[35] In any event, the idea of replacing existing computational procedures with an index estimated in some other way has seemed appealing.

An index number estimated directly from a regression containing hedonic variables (likewise one estimated by the vintage price method) has

---

32. That is, for varieties j and k, the agency need evaluate only $a_i\,(X_{ij} - X_{ik})$ rather than $\hat{p}_j - \hat{p}_k$, where $\hat{p}_k = \sum_i a_i X_{ik}$ and $\hat{p}_k = \sum_i a_i X_{ik}$.

33. Rothwell 1966 notes that these items "present particularly difficult pricing problems . . . Many of [the prices] come from secondary sources and represent realized prices for broadly defined qualities." But better ways for handling quality may facilitate improvement in other respects.

34. By adding a dummy variable for time to a hedonic quality function and running it simultaneously on cross-section data for two or more years or periods. The procedure is spelled out in Griliches 1961.

35. In part because the variables isolated in the early hedonic studies did not coincide with the specific changes observed in index comparisons.

usually been based on a larger number of varieties than the existing indexes. Thus it has sometimes been thought that replacing existing computational techniques by one of the new methods will eliminate at the same time the quality error from direct comparison and also the possible error (discussed in Part I.C, above) that might arise because only a restricted number of product varieties are priced for the index.

However, it is budgetary considerations, rather than the form of the index, that now limits the number of varieties priced. Estimating a price index by the adjacent-year method would require a tremendous increase in the number of prices to be gathered, if we are not to lose—because of increased sampling error from other sources—as much as we gain in reducing quality error. For example, one source (Rothwell 1966) indicates that an average of about 40 price quotations are gathered each pricing period for each make of car priced for the CPI, or about 320 in all (for the 8 models now priced). My own automobile sample for 1965 contained 118 separate models of four-door sedans, without any provision for other body types, "sporty" type cars or foreign cars, and it is very likely that close to 300 different models and varieties of car could be identified for pricing. Clearly, for a given budget we can trade more prices per car for more cars in the index, but in order to get a sample which was comprehensive in varieties the number of prices gathered per car would decline. If the budget were expanded, we could price more cars without giving up the accuracy of the present sample size. But if these prices were collected they could be used in a conventional index number, so the proposal to increase the number of varieties in the index has nothing to do with the way the index is computed.

There are additional difficulties (beside the cost) in obtaining an appropriate set of market prices in order to estimate an index number directly from a regression. All evidence shows enormous store-to-store price variation. Some of this price variation is undoubtedly attributable to differences in the amounts or the quality of retailing services provided, some of it to other influences. Thus, the model of pricing is:

$$P = a_0 + a_1 X_1 + a_2 X_2 + \cdots + a_k X_k + a_m X_m + u,$$

where the variables $X_1 \ldots X_k$ are the quality characteristics (including a time dummy variable, since the regression is to be run on two years' data) and X_m is retailing services specific to an outlet or brand, or some other feature which varies over the sample, but is not related to the quality hypothesis. We estimate only the first k coefficients, as the X_m are not known precisely. By an argument similar to that advanced by Griliches

Quality Bias and New Methods

(1967) on "left-out" quality characteristics, we conclude that if there is any change in the constitution of the sample between the two years, then the estimate of the index number (the coefficient of the time variable) is biased, unless the change in the sample does not change the values of X_m between the two years.

The CPI sample is always changing. Over a period of one or two years there are a sufficient number of changes that the use of an adjacent-years estimating procedure must be questioned. The changes are fewer between quarters; although the samples may be similar enough that an adjacent-period estimate could be taken from the regression without serious bias,[36] computing these regressions every quarter implies a tremendous expansion in the amount of data for the index. If reliable hedonic quality functions can be estimated, adjustment for quality can be made just as well by using the regression coefficients from single-year cross-section regressions, so there is not much of a case to be made for changing the present computational procedure of the indexes just to introduce better quality adjustments.

It may also be true that variation in the X_m's will cause difficulties in estimating quality adjustment factors from data collected at a single point in time—for example, the value of X_m might be related to the quality variables $X_1 \ldots X_k$. This is not unreasonable; discount stores do carry different varieties of products from prestige department stores (i.e., the level of retail services provided is related to the quality of the goods stocked), and where discounts are given, the size of the discount may be related to the quality of the variety purchased. I am less convinced that this kind of retail price variability will invalidate the single-year cross sections, for reasons that need not be explored here; but continual changing of the sample means that it presents greater problems for estimates of price change using two or more cross sections in the same regression.

In the WPI, a somewhat wider range of prices is now gathered for most items, so gathering cross-section prices will be less costly. Also, the problem of different amounts of services provided with the sale is probably less important, making the use of an adjacent-year regression more feasible than in the CPI. In fact, the only hedonic studies to make use of

---

36. Currently, changes in outlets, brands within an outlet, or type of merchandise carried by a reporting outlet are handled by deleting the observation when the change is first reported. This procedure fails to capture any price change that occurs at this time (an error analogous to type 2 quality error described in Part I.A of this chapter). The longer the period of the comparison, the larger the number of such changes and the greater the error.

actual BLS quotations[37] were based on prices gathered for the WPI. In principle, the index computed from the regression should give the same result as the conventional summation and division method, so the question of the form of the computation is not very interesting.

The hedonic results, or the vintage-price method, may be used to compute alternative estimates of price change as a check on conventional procedures. This is most valuable, and probably justifies continuing to do research on both methods in the way it has been done in the past, even if the results cannot immediately be integrated into the indexes.

Further Research

We conclude this paper on a noncontroversial note—a call for more research. Above (Part II.B), we noted the need for hedonic tests of the validity of a large number of the BLS pricing specifications. We also need more studies of the type undertaken in the past—studies which produce quality functions for various products and attempt to make comparisons of the results with appropriate CPI and WPI components. We need them even if they are based on list prices or some other not entirely suitable data, even if they employ unusable proxy variables as quality characteristics, even if the variables are the same as those controlled in the pricing specification, or the quality adjustments proposed are clearly factored out by the BLS, or the data not comparable with the CPI or the WPI for some other reason. We need such studies, and can learn from them, largely because they raise issues and provoke thought and discussion about the admittedly unsatisfactory ways that quality change is handled in the current indexes. The studies will be better and more useful, and will come closer to being relevant as quality adjustments, if their authors do try to come to grips with the actual problems in a particular component; but it is often difficult for an outside investigator to inform himself sufficiently to be able to make his quality measures relevant (or know if they are going to be), and it would indeed be unfortunate if the present paper were interpreted as an injunction against research under other than ideal conditions.

Having said this, however, it is also imperative to add one last caution about the interpretation of hedonic (and vintage price) quality studies: just because an economist produces an index that differs from an official index, this does not necessarily imply that it is the official index that must be the incorrect one.

---

37. On carpets and men's suits, by Gavett 1967*b*.

Appendix to Chapter 6

Sample CPI Pricing Specification for Refrigerators

APPLIANCES

23-387
REFRIGERATOR-FREEZER: Electric; two doors; 13.5 to 16.5 cu. ft. capacity

HOUSING

STYLE:
> Semi-deluxe model
> 2 outside doors
> True (zero degree) freezer
> Exclude: Single-door refrigerator-freezers and models with bottom or slide out "drawer type" freezer

FINISH:
> White baked enamel exterior
> Porcelain enamel interior
> Size:
>> * 13.5 to 16.5 cu. ft. net capacity overall (including freezer)
>
> Freezer Compartment:
>> Separate full-width top freezer
>> Freezer capacity approximately.
>> * 100 to 185 lbs. frozen food or 3.0 to 5.7 cu. ft. net capacity
>> 2 to 4 ice trays
>> Freezer door equipped with rack or shelf

TYPE OF FREEZER DEFROST:
> A. Automatic (frost-free)
> B. Manual

REFRIGERATOR COMPARTMENT:
> 2 to 4 shelves
> 2 crispers or hydrators, (may have 1 if full width)

A new method of estimating quality changes in automobiles is explored here. Because automobiles are an important item in consumer expenditures and installment credit, their quality has a general interest as well as a special importance to price indexes. The main reason for focusing on automobiles here, however, is that secondhand prices are available for them, which the new method requires. Because of that requirement, the method has practical limitations preventing its universal application, but it provides a valuable independent check on other methods which are more practical but whose accuracy is open to question.

A. Standard Methods of Handling Quality Changes

Methods now used to adjust for quality changes select a few relevant and known physical characteristics of the product and hold these constant over time or adjust for changes in them.[2] Compilation of the Consumer Price Index follows that procedure, though to a very limited extent. Such characteristics might be size or weight of durable goods, BTU.'s of heating fuels, nutrient content of fertilizers, and so on. Such adjustments, if carefully done, can be extremely useful. They have the obvious deficiency, however, of measuring quality by an arbitrary list of factors, not necessarily those given most weight by the public. Moreover, they can be hopelessly outmoded in dealing with a radically new product.

A more sophisticated variant of the approach is the "hedonic" price index used by Court (1939) and recently revived by Stone (1956) and Griliches (1961). Although here the physical characteristics of the product are preselected, their relative weights are determined by cross-section regressions using the prices of different varieties of the product at each point in time. That lets market conditions determine the weights. In his application of the method to automobiles, for example, Griliches regressed the price of new automobiles of each model year on their length, weight, horsepower, and other properties. The regression coefficients served as weights to compute an average price change from one year to the next after adjustment for changes in those characteristics. Theoretically, any number of characteristics could be included, with the regression determining their relative importance, though in practice data can usually be obtained for only a few. A source of error here is that many engineering improvements and alterations in design, as well as the quality of workmanship, cannot be readily quantified. The regressions will give inaccurate estimates if the included and the relevant excluded quality changes are not

---

2. For recent commentaries on the problems of this procedure and suggested improvements, see *Price Statistics* 1961. See also Brady 1966.

Quality Changes and the Purchasing Power of Money

closely related. Also, list prices set by the manufacturers may not accurately reflect quality differences, though that deficiency could be rectified by using the discounted prices at which the cars are actually sold (if available) or secondhand prices compiled from used-car dealers.

Barring serious errors, the hedonic price index can in practice be used to adjust for quality changes in a wide range of products and even services. Before we can have confidence in it, however, some check on its reliability is needed. The next subsection presents another method.

B. An Alternative Method

One widely accepted way to measure the quality difference between two varieties of a product, and the most direct approach, is to compare their open-market selling prices at the same point in time. If the prices quoted reflect the free play of supply and demand (and no distress selling), we are justified in viewing the price differential as the market's overall estimate of the quality differences, including any difference due to marketing and advertising as part of the package.[3] Two special obstacles often stand in the way of such comparisons, however: (1) Prices of manufactured goods may be set by the producer (and so far as published price quotations go, often are), with the amount supplied adjusted to the amount demanded at the price set. Such prices do not always represent the market's estimate of quality. (2) The old variety of the product may be discontinued when the new variety is introduced, so that the two are not sold concurrently. A new product might be sold for less or more than its predecessor, depending among other things upon manufacturing and marketing costs and sales strategy. If the price of a new product undercuts its predecessor, does the decline reflect lower costs of production or cheapened quality? The answer is seldom obvious.

Secondhand prices offer a way out of this difficulty (see Bailey, Muth, and Nourse 1963, and Burstein 1961). For all practical purposes, secondhand quantities are fixed, and selling prices in a broad market reflect the free play of demand and hence the public's estimate of relative qualities. Since manufacturers usually discontinue the old product when offering a new one, the two varieties differ not only in quality but also in age. If the depreciation rate of the product is known or can be estimated, quality

---

3. At first, it might seem desirable to exclude differences in price due to marketing and advertising factors and to measure only changes in the inherent quality of products. But the distinction appears impossible to define unambiguously. Methods of estimating quality by physical characteristics seem to exclude marketing factors, but they do so only by disregarding buyers' preferences as reflected in market prices. Disregarding preferences can introduce serious errors.

differences can still be obtained. This is the method described here and applied to automobiles. The depreciation rate and the quality of new cars are estimated from their secondhand prices, which assumes of course that quality improvements endure to benefit subsequent owners and are reflected in secondhand prices.[4] (Estimating the depreciation rate presents certain problems which are discussed later.) The method is perfectly general and would apply to the introduction of new versions of any durable good, so long as the new and the old are sold secondhand with quoted prices for an extended period of time before being scrapped. Once we measure the quality difference, the prices of the product when new can be adjusted to give a "pure" price index over time.

It goes without saying that this approach measures, as seems appropriate, the market's estimate of quality, not solely that of engineers, product-testing laboratories, or self-styled social critics. More specifically, the "market" here pertains to buyers of the product secondhand, not the original purchasers. The two groups may appraise quality differently, but secondhand buyers are likely to be somewhat less influenced by ephemeral fads and to pay more attention to innovations of enduring importance. The method captures elusive changes in style and workmanship as well as obvious engineering improvements, and captures in addition all the minor but collectively important changes affecting quality, which a specified list cannot hope to cover in full. In short, any difference (real or fancied) in the characteristics of two secondhand cars (aside from age) that leads the average buyer to pay more for one is recorded as a difference in quality. This is far more inclusive than measures like the hedonic index can possibly be. Depending upon one's definition of "quality" and the purposes intended, this may or may not be more inclusive than is desired.

C. Quality and Changes in Tastes

The quality of a product can be viewed as reflecting a set of different characteristics. The public attaches different weights or prices to each of them, depending upon tastes and preferences that vary over time. Since

---

4. The method implicitly assumes also that any quality improvement (or decline) depreciates in value at the same rate as the rest of the car, so that the value of the quality change remains proportional to the market price over the life of the car. (That would not be true, however, of longer warranties that expire after a certain mileage.) Alternative assumptions that might be made are more complicated and, at this stage, less appealing.

One might argue that secondhand prices merely reflect new prices, adjusted only for depreciation. That implies, however, that buyers, contrary to all suppositions about rational consumer behavior, make no independent assessment of quality but simply accept the manufacturer's indication of quality as given by relative prices set on the products when new. In that event, assumed here to be rare, any kind of adjustment for quality is questionable and, indeed, may be unnecessary.

Quality Changes and the Purchasing Power of Money

the method here compares the secondhand prices of two successive model years at the *same point in time*, the same tastes determine the prices of both models at that time, and the estimate of quality change holds tastes constant. At another point in time the comparison may involve different tastes, so that the quality index derived does not hold tastes constant over time even though each year-to-year change in the index does.[5] The method therefore resembles a chain-link price index, in which the weights of components of the index are held constant from one period to the next but are allowed to change for successive links of the index.[6]

Even though the year-to-year comparisons hold tastes constant, changes in tastes can still affect the resulting index of quality. The public may attach a different weight to various characteristics at one time than at another. Or dramatic changes may occasionally occur with special consequences: When manufacturers produce new models catering to the new tastes, secondhand buyers who usually bought old models to save money may instead buy the newer ones to satisfy their new preferences. This shift in demand will depress the used prices of the older models and reduce our measure of their quality. In the same way, the newer models will show an equal increase in quality, apart from any other quality changes in the new models. The introduction of compacts in 1960, for example, satisfied a desire for smaller cars, which many buyers preferred (for a while, anyway). As a result, the full-size, six-cylinder 1960 models sold for less on used-car lots in subsequent years than the 1960 compacts did.[7] Such short-period fluctuations due to changes in tastes can affect the estimates, but they will tend to cancel out in the total change for a number of years combined, because the induced shifts in demand tend to be reversed in subsequent years and then produce the opposite effects. That will also be

---

5. It should be added that, while the present method compares the prices at a point in time, the year-to-year changes in the index are averages of such comparisons in different years. Thus, year-to-year changes in the index actually hold average tastes for several years constant.

6. In the hedonic index, weights for all specified components of quality may be obtained for every year. In one version of the index the same set of weights (obtained from a regression for one particular year) is used for all years. In another version (which seems more appropriate) a different set of weights is used for each year-to-year change, to produce a chain-link index. The latter is the kind reported later for automobiles in Table 7.4.

7. The hedonic index would, in principle, give the same result here if it were based on used-car prices and not list prices, which do not fully reflect shifts in demand. In the example cited, the hedonic regression would attach a negative weight for that year and those models to the size of cars. (For all cars, such a regression would probably still give a positive weight to size because of the heavy influence of very expensive cars. The result would still approximate the present method if both were based on the same set of cars.)

true of the effects on secondhand prices of large differences in the relative number of cars originally produced, and of temporary imperfections in the secondhand market. The figures for an extended period are therefore likely to be more reasonable than those for individual years.

Because appealing style changes will affect market estimates of quality, the present method might still include a spurious increase in quality for the following reason: If the public, because it liked variety, were always willing to pay a premium for the newest style, years with style changes would always register quality improvements, even though at the end of a period of years the latest style might be generally viewed as no better than a half-forgotten style of many years earlier. In that event, styles might go through long cycles, continually bringing a premium merely because they appeared new compared with the preceding few years. (The increases would not be absorbed by the depreciation rates, because those rates, as explained later, are estimates for years of slight model change which would receive no premium.) Premiums paid for variety cannot be attributed to quality improvements by any conventional meaning of the term, and ideally they should be excluded. Such premiums are probably small in the used-car market, however, and of minor importance. Buyers comparing 2-, 3-, and 4-year-old cars probably pay little extra for the newer styles which by then have largely lost their novelty.

D. *Limitations of the Method*

The use of secondhand prices, of course, imposes a severe practical limitation on this method. The estimates are always out of date, and so mainly help to reappraise historical price trends for clarification of current policy. In addition, such prices are readily available only for automobiles, though machine tools, commercial airplanes, real estate, and certain consumer appliances are also traded secondhand, and some data on prices are available. The method also tends, as noted, to be overly inclusive, and there are difficulties in estimating depreciation rates. Yet, despite its limitations, the method appears worth exploring to provide an independent check on the accuracy of the hedonic index, which has a potentially wider application. The hedonic index also has severe drawbacks. Comparison of the two is useful because their respective drawbacks are quite different.

Section II describes the new method in detail, and section III presents some data. The method gives an average quality increase of 1.9 percent per year for automobiles from 1954–1960, which is nearly half the 4.4-percent per year rise in list prices.

… 221

Quality Changes and the Purchasing Power of Money

2. Description of the Method

A particular car line, such as a standard low-priced six-cylinder Chevrolet, generates over the years a matrix of prices; the price vectors represent each model year over its lifetime. Let P_t^i denote the secondhand price of a low-priced Chevrolet or Ford for model year i at time t. We can obtain from used car price lists the following open-ended matrix:

$$\begin{array}{ccccccc} & & & \cdots & \cdots & & \\ & & & P_{t+2}^{i+2} & P_{t+3}^{i+2} & P_{t+4}^{i+2} & \cdots \\ & & P_{t+1}^{i+1} & P_{t+2}^{i+1} & P_{t+3}^{i+1} & \cdots \\ & P_t^i & P_{t+1}^i & P_{t+2}^i & \cdots & & \\ \cdots & \cdots & & & & & \end{array}$$

The element P_{t+2}^{i+1} might be (say) the the price of the 1956 model in 1958. The matrix starts from the bottom with any model year we choose—here year i—and with each year spreads upward and rightward, a particular row ending when that model is no longer actively traded on the used car market. Reliable quotations of secondhand prices do not become available until about a year after a model is first introduced. (Before that, the number of trade-ins is small.) Hence P_{t+k}^{i+k} is the first price on model $i + k$ at time $t + k$, about a year after the model was first sold.

A. Quality Changes

For our purposes, the secondhand price can be viewed as composed of three elements: (1) a pure price index representing the general purchasing power of a dollar at time t and assumed applicable to all cars (and other products) sold at that time, p_t; (2) a quality index for cars, q_i, representing the merits of the ith year model relative to the first (base) year model being measured; and (3) a depreciation factor $d_{i,k}$, representing the value (excluding general price changes) of model i at any age k as a fraction of its value when first entered in the matrix. Hence, $1 - (d_{i,k})^{1/k}$ is the average annual rate of "pure" depreciation from the time of first quotation to age k. The price vector for two successive model years may thus be represented as follows:

$p_{t+1}q_{i+1} \quad p_{t+2}q_{i+1}d_{i+1,1} \quad p_{t+3}q_{i+1}d_{i+1,2} \quad \cdots$

$p_i q_i \quad p_{t+1}q_i d_{i,1} \quad p_{t+2}q_i d_{i,2} \quad \cdots$

Quality q is assumed to remain constant over the represented life of the model. In these terms, the price of a particular model changes from year to year because of general price changes and depreciation.

Unless all the d's are equal, which is unlikely, a count of known quantities and unknown variables indicates that the latter exceed the former, not allowing a determinant solution. An additional assumption must be introduced. One with considerable appeal is that the depreciated values for a particular car, while they no doubt have random variations, approximate a certain average rate of decline over a period of years. We might therefore specify that the expected value of $\log (d_{i,k})^{1/k}$ is the same for all model years. Hence:

(1) approximates D to the power
$$\prod_{k=1}^{L} (d_{i,k})$$

$$\sum_{1}^{L} k$$

for L not too small. If D is known, we can then solve for the price and quality factors, as follows. Ratios of the prices of two successive model years in each of L consecutive time periods,

$$\frac{p_{t+n} q_{i+1} d_{i+1,k-1}}{p_{t+n} q_i d_{i,k}}, k = n = 1, \ldots L,$$

have the geometric mean:

(2) $$\frac{q_{i+1}}{q_i} \left(\frac{d_{i+1,1} d_{i+1,2} \cdots d_{i+1,L-1}}{d_{i,1} d_{i,2} d_{i,3} \cdots d_{i,L}} \right)^{1/L}$$

(By definition $d_{i,0}$ is unity for all i.) The factor in parentheses by assumption approximates

$$\left(\frac{D^{\sum_{}^{L-1} k}}{D^{\sum_{}^{L} k}} \right)^{1/L} = \frac{D^{(L-1)/2}}{D^{(L+1)/2}} = \frac{1}{D};$$

hence (2) approximates

(3) $$\frac{q_{i+1}}{q_i D}.$$

With a value for D, we can solve for the quality change and, setting $q_0 = 1$, compute a quality index for the years following $t = 0$. (The derivation of D is discussed shortly.)

Quality Changes and the Purchasing Power of Money

Note that the assumption that underlies this solution implies that the value of a model over time (apart from changes in the general price index p) approximates a declining exponential curve, $e^{-(1-D)t}$, with percentage deviations from the curve averaging zero. The assumption does not say that the decline in real value of a car from one year to the next, $d_{i,k+1}/d_{i,k}$, averages D. That statement would imply that the geometric mean of the yearly rates of decline in real value,

$$\left(d_{i,1} \frac{d_{i,2}}{d_{i,1}} \frac{d_{i,3}}{d_{i,2}} \cdots \frac{d_{i,L}}{d_{i,L-1}}\right)^{1/L} = (d_{i,L})^{1/L},$$

approximates D. In that event, the best estimate of quality change would be the single ratio:

$$\frac{p_{t+n} q_{i+1} d_{i+1,L-1}}{p_{t+n} q_i d_{1,L}}$$

for the largest L rather than the geometric mean as above. But the geometric mean will generally be far more reliable, because the prices of very old cars do not accurately reflect differences in quality over their full life.

B. Depreciation

The method requires accurate estimates of D. It is perhaps not necessary to point out that the frequently used procedure of fitting a curve to prices of used cars of successive ages is unacceptable. Such curves, if based on a cross section of prices at a point in time, confound quality differences with depreciation, and if based on a time series of prices of the same model year over time, confound changes in the value of money with depreciation. In principle, one might estimate "pure" depreciation from survival rates of cars, derived from car population data, but extensive experimentation with that approach convinces me that it is much too imprecise.

The simplest practical estimate is provided by two successive model years in which the product line does not change (or only slightly), so that we may set $q_i = q_{i+1}$. Then D can be derived from (2) and used for all other model years. Although two successive model years of American cars are seldom identical (since minor changes are invariably made and, even if not, changing qualities of workmanship may enhance or lessen the likelihood of "bugs" in a car), many models are produced with little change for two years in a row. The calculations reported in the next section are based on the evaluation of the magazine *Consumer Reports* to determine whether, from the point of view more of intelligent consumers than of sophisticated engineers, two model years were essentially the same. If quality always improves ever so slightly even between years with no apparent differences, our quality index will have a small downward bias. The index can be viewed as giving a minimum estimate of quality improvements.

3. The Empirical Results

Formula (2) was computed for the low- and middle-line of 4-door sedans of various makes for the period 1947–1960. Prices were compiled from the *Official Used Car Guide* of the National Automobile Dealers Association for Middle Western states in February, May, August, and November, pertaining to prices of the preceding months, respectively. The geometric means of the price ratios cover 16 quarters, except for 1959–1960, which covers only 15, and begin with August of the model year in the numerator. Sixteen quarters, or four years, was the longest period for which price quotations were available for all cars covered. Using a multiple of four quarters avoids any seasonal variation in the prices, though none was observed in the data. Means for 20 quarters were also computed for some cars. They gave similar results for the most part, though sizable differences occurred in some cases. Such differences, depending upon the length of period L used in the geometric mean, are a source of ambiguity in the method, which further refinement may help to lessen.

The chart graphs the geometric means of the price ratios for the middle-line, six-cylinder sedans. The low-line sixes and the eights (not shown) display similar patterns. The calculation of the means may be described as follows: For the 1956 Ford, for example, its secondhand price in August 1956 was taken as a ratio to the secondhand price in the same month of the 1955 Ford, and similar ratios were taken for the two cars in 15 subsequent quarters. The geometric mean of those ratios is the figure shown in the chart for Ford in 1956/55. Corresponding calculations were made for other years and other makes. The mean ratios all exceed unity by the average amount of a year's depreciation in the older car, times any quality change. There is undoubtedly a certain amount of measurement error in these ratios which largely cancels out in average ratios for a group of cars.

A. *Estimates of Depreciation*

The ratios all rise substantially during the late 1940's and early 1950's. For many of those years in which the quality change was undoubtedly

Quality Changes and the Purchasing Power of Money

Chart
Mean Price Ratio of Current to Preceding Model Year, 1947–1960
Medium Line of Six-cylinder Sedans*

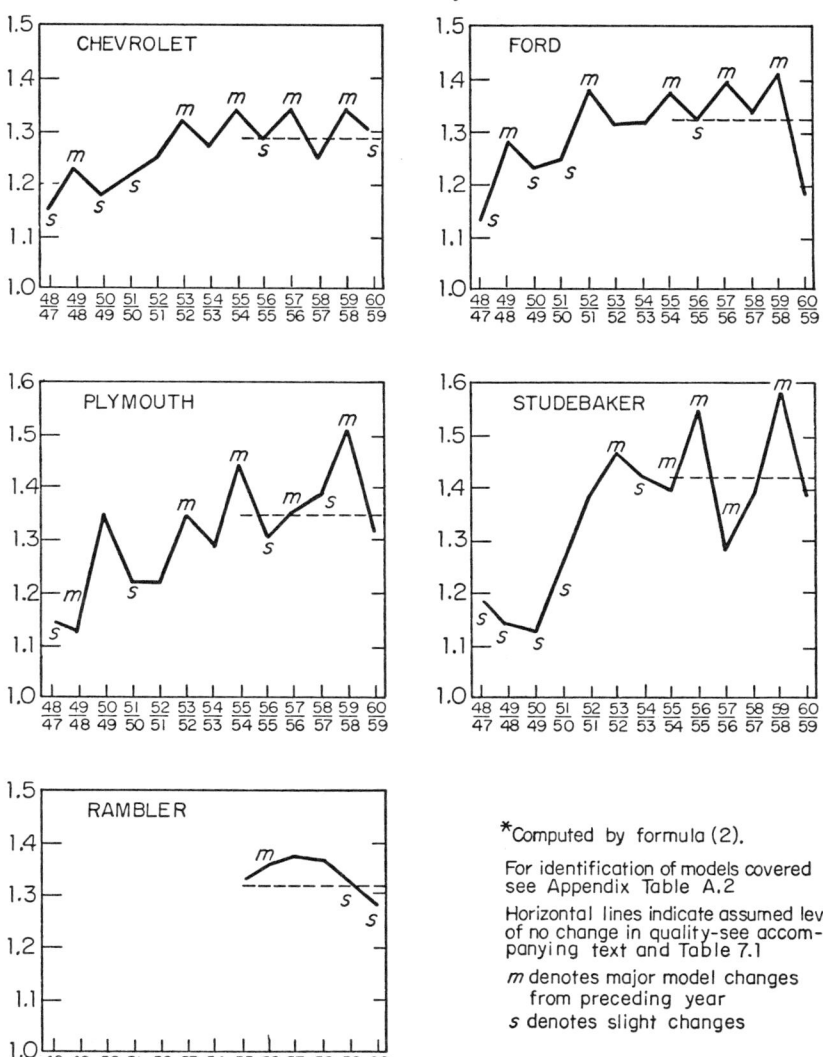

*Computed by formula (2).

For identification of models covered see Appendix Table A.2

Horizontal lines indicate assumed level of no change in quality—see accompanying text and Table 7.1

m denotes major model changes from preceding year
s denotes slight changes

small, the rise in the ratio most likely reflects a rise in depreciation rates.[8] Apparently the absence of 1942–1945 cars on secondhand lots created an unusually heavy demand for the relatively new used cars, holding up their prices. During those earlier years, the shortage may also have induced owners to maintain their cars in especially good condition, though most likely that was of secondary importance producing low depreciation rates. There was also some increase in average miles traveled per year for cars during the early 1950's, but not enough to explain the entire rise in the ratios.[9] For present purposes, it seems best to ignore the years up to 1954, by which time most effects of the early postwar car shortage should have passed.

While no substantial changes in depreciation rates appear to have occurred after 1954, it is not clear that the rates were precisely constant year after year. Even small changes could affect estimates of quality change. Unfortunately, we do not have many years in which model changes were slight in the period to reveal the trend of average depreciation rates. According to the evaluations of *Consumer Reports* (indicated in the chart), there are only two such years for Chevrolet after 1954 for which the mean price ratios have practically the same level, indicating no change in depreciation rates. For Plymouth, after 1954 there are also two such years, and they indicate a moderate rise in depreciation. For Ford after 1954 there is but one. Such meager evidence is inconclusive. Data for future years in which no model changes occur will help to clarify the time trend of depreciation.[10] In the meantime, we may select the years of least apparent change in quality to compute depreciation rates (by formula [3], as indicated above.) Those are the years that determined the level of the horizontal lines drawn on the chart, except for Plymouth, for which an average of 1955–1956 and 1957–1958 was used. For other years in the period 1954–1960, points above the line imply quality improvements, below the line quality declines.

---

8. The average age of cars of successive model years might not differ by exactly one year, which introduces a small error into the estimate of annual depreciation rates. No attempt was made to adjust for average ages.

9. The average mileage traveled per year by passenger cars (see Automobile Manufacturers Association 1963, p. 46) fell 9 percent from 1946 to 1950, then rose 4 percent to 1952, and remained virtually unchanged thereafter until 1956, after which it rose slightly to 1960. If changes in depreciation rates because of varying degrees of car use from 1948 to 1952 or 1953 model years were proportional to changes in average mileage over the life of those cars, the implied effect on depreciation is slight: the decline in average mileage from 1946 to 1950 just about cancels the subsequent rise to 1952.

10. A method (not used here) for estimating changes in depreciation rates is discussed in the appendix.

Quality Changes and the Purchasing Power of Money

The depreciation rates implied by those lines are presented in Table 7.1. The rates vary among the cars, but cluster around 25 percent per year. The generally low rates for Chevrolet apparently reflect its strong sales organization and favorable trade-in market, and probably not a lower rate of physical depreciation. The estimates of its rates may appear too low here, but by other considerations they are not. Given the data, higher rates would imply smaller quality improvements in the other years, which already appear low for Chevrolet compared with Ford and Plymouth.

Table 7.1. Estimated Average Depreciation Rates[a] $(1 - D)$
(percent per year)

	Sixes		Eights		
	Low-Priced	Medium-Priced	Low-Priced	Medium-Priced	High-Priced
Chevrolet	25.2	22.0	22.7	21.0	
Ford	25.2	24.3	22.9	21.4	
Plymouth	27.6	25.4	26.4	23.5	
Rambler	25.8	24.8		24.6	
Ambassador				26.3	25.1
Studebaker	28.4	29.8		26.4	

[a] Reciprocal of geometric means subtracted from one $(1 - D$ calculated from formula (2) with $L = 16$); 1955–1956 for Chevrolet and Ford, average of 1955–1956 and 1957–1958 for Plymouth, 1958–1959 for Rambler, 1956–1957 for Ambassador, and 1953–1954 for Studebaker.

B. Quality and "Pure" Price Changes

Multiplication of the price ratios by D for each car line, the complement of the depreciation rate, gives the estimated quality changes from year to year (see formula [3]). These changes from 1954–1960 are shown in Table A.1 in the appendix to this chapter for low- and medium-priced sixes and eights of Chevrolet, Ford, Plymouth, Rambler, and Studebaker, except where a model line could not be followed consistently, in which case substitutions or sometimes duplications were made, as indicated in Table A.2 in the appendix. For 1960, the "compacts" of the Big Three were linked to the corresponding sixes of 1959 and are shown separately.

The quality of an individual line may go up or down, not only because of engineering innovations or unplanned declines in workmanship, but also because of intentional upgrading or downgrading of the line accompanied by corresponding price changes. When various price lines are continually introduced and discontinued, it is not always clear how a particular line should be specified in certain years. In 1958, Chevrolet introduced a low-priced line called the Delray which was dropped the next year. The Delray had lower quality as well as lower price than the middle line (the Biscayne), also introduced in 1958 and continued thereafter as the low line. The tables show quality changes for Chevrolet in 1958 both including and excluding the Delray. The two treatments give quite different quality changes for 1957–1958 and 1958–1959 individually, though naturally much less difference for the two years combined. Otherwise, all car lines were fairly easy to identify. Where there was doubt, lines were specified according to list price, the low line being lowest priced, and the middle line the next to lowest priced. Ambiguities of specification make less difference if we relate the quality change to the price change, also included in Table A.1. It would be desirable to use the average discounted price at which cars were sold, but in the absence of such data we may use the advertised price of 4-door sedans including Federal taxes and handling charges, but excluding all optional equipment, freight, and state or local taxes. If the degree of discounting does not vary greatly from year to year, the list prices give percentage changes with reasonable accuracy.

In addition to a comparison with prices, the quality changes of the different lines need to be weighted by the share of each in total sales. Weighted averages of the lines for each make are also shown in Table A.1. The data used for sales were not as detailed as might be desired. It was necessary to take an unweighted average of the low- and medium-priced lines in the two cylinder groups; that assumes the two lines have roughly equal sales, which is inaccurate for many years. The data do allow a weighted average of the six- and eight-cylinder groups for each car, and for 1959–1960 allow us to give the compacts a separate weight.[11] In a more detailed study, weighted averages should be computed for each make and line of car, including particularly the high-priced lines not included here at all that account for a substantial part of total sales. In the absence of

---

11. The sales data give total registrations of each make in a calendar year, without regard to the model year, and so are not entirely appropriate for use here. Insofar as new models are introduced before the first of the year, the data mix together the sales of part of two successive yearly models. (Sales data are from *Automotive News*, annual *Almanac* edition.)

Quality Changes and the Purchasing Power of Money

Table 7.2. Average Quality and Price Changes[a] (percent)

Model Years	Quality	List Price	Price/Quality
1954–1955	5.2	2.5	−2.5
1955–1956	−0.2	6.0	6.3
1956–1957	4.2	10.5	6.1
1957–1958	0.1	5.3	5.3
1958–1959	5.7	5.9	0.4
1959–1960	−3.3	−3.1	0.4
1954–1960	11.9	29.7	16.7
Per Year	1.9	4.4	2.6

[a] An average of figures in the last column of Table A.1, weighted by the share of each manufacturer in total sales. The third column plus 100 may not equal the second column plus 100 divided by the first column plus 100 because of rounding.

Table 7.3. List Price Changes per Unit of Quality[a] (percent)

Model Years	Chevrolet	Ford	Plymouth	Rambler	Studebaker	All Cars Weighted Average
1954–1955	−1.6	−1.9	−6.2	0.6	−5.7	−2.5
1955–1956	5.7	6.4	9.3	4.8	−3.7	6.3
1956–1957	7.2	1.9	9.9	6.4	12.4	6.1
1957–1958	8.6 (7.7)[b]	1.6	2.7	−0.8	10.7	5.3 (4.8)[b]
1958–1959	4.4 (5.9)[b]	−2.1	−6.7	2.5	−14.2	0.4 (1.1)[b]
1959–1960	−1.1	3.5	−3.7	5.8	2.6	0.4
1954–1960	25.0	9.5	4.0	20.7	−0.5	16.7
Per Year	3.8	1.7	0.9	3.2	−0.1	2.6

[a] Price changes divided by quality changes, weighted as in Tables A.1 and 7.2.
[b] Biscayne is used instead of Delray in 1958 for the low-priced line, and Bel Air is used instead of Biscayne for the medium-priced line. The figures in parentheses were not used for the 1954–1960 total as shown, though their inclusion gives practically the same total figure.

that detail, the weighted averages in Table A.1 for each make have been combined into an industry average, weighted by the relative number of total cars sold by each company. These summary figures are shown in Table 7.2, and the weighted averages of price changes divided by quality changes—the "pure" price index—are shown in Table 7.3.

C. Summary of Results

In terms of the combined figures for all cars during the period 1954–1960, shown in Table 7.2, quality declined in two years, was virtually constant in one, and rose by 4 to 5 percent in three. The increases coincide with the years of substantial model changes (see the chart), except for 1959–1960 when quality declines accompanied the introduction of compacts, mentioned earlier. The net result for the period was an increase of almost 12 percent or nearly 2 percent per year, that is, roughly two-fifths the corresponding change in list prices, so that prices adjusted for quality rose 17 percent over all or 2.6 percent per year, less than three-fifths of the unadjusted price increase. In timing as well as magnitude, the figures seem plausible, though the total increase in quality is lower than the hedonic index shows (see below). Whether this half decade was typical of earlier or later years is difficult to say. It included extensive design changes; engineering improvements were continual and collectively substantial, though not radical.

4. Reliability of the Estimates and Possible Improvements

While the overall estimates appear credible and the method avoids many of the arbitrary assumptions inherent in other measures of quality change, there is reason for viewing the results as exploratory and tentative. Two extensions of the data are available but were not used here in order to keep down the compiling job. (1) Including quality estimates for every line of automobiles in the average and weighting them according to sales would give more reliable results; the coverage here accounts for only about half of total sales. Monthly rather than quarterly prices would also improve accuracy, though probably not by much. (2) Monthly sales data, on the other hand, would allow a needed adjustment, not made here, for deviations from one year in the average age of cars of successive model years. Since production scheduling differs from year to year, the average difference in age of successive models may be a few months more or less than one year, requiring an adjustment in the estimated annual depreciation rate. The absence of such adjustments could produce errors of one, or at most two, percentage points in the quality estimates, however, and the error is not cumulative but tends to cancel out over a period of years.

The most serious source of error is undoubtedly in the estimates of depreciation, even apart from changes in average age. To estimate depreciation, some model year has to be assumed in each car line not to differ in quality from the previous year. The method offers no way to avoid error if that assumption is not entirely correct. A slight error here cumulates over model years, since it makes the estimate of quality change too high or too low in every year. We need two successive years in which the models are identical. Model changes were slight for the years noted in the chart and used here to estimate depreciation, but some change did occur, introducing an unknown error. If no change occurs, choices between the two models by used-car buyers would focus mainly on workmanship. Although they might find it has sometimes improved and sometimes deteriorated, the finding would normally vary among car lines, thus canceling out in the overall figures. Coverage of a longer period will provide a better selection of years to satisfy this requirement.

In addition to errors in estimating the depreciation rate, there is also a problem of drift in the rate. Models of the same line produced in different years may not depreciate at the same rate. Such drift may partly account for the wide variation in price changes adjusted for quality, summarized for the full period in Table 3. Most of those differences are due to the quality estimates; list prices usually moved quite closely, at least for the Big Three. Two possible techniques for handling depreciation drift have been mentioned. One, discussed in the Appendix, is to estimate changes in depreciation rates from changes in the price ratios over time. That technique has certain difficulties, however, and requires further refinement before it can be used. Another technique is to interpolate depreciation rates, which requires a longer period than was used here to provide several benchmark rates based on years in which model changes were slight. How much difference such corrections would make in the overall figures is unclear, and until improved the present results should be viewed as highly tentative.

5. Comparison with Hedonic Index and Consumer Price Index

A. Hedonic Index

As stated at the outset, one purpose of developing new estimates of quality change is to evaluate the hedonic index, which in practice can be applied to a wide range of products and services, but which has a questionable reliability. The new method is not necessarily more accurate; it has certain deficiencies of unknown importance and needs refinement. Nevertheless, the two methods are independent and have quite different deficiencies; each can be assessed by the other.

The hedonic index has been applied to automobiles by Griliches, as noted (1961 and 1963). He regressed a cross section of list prices on various preselected specifications of automobiles in successive years. With the regression coefficients as moving weights, he calculated the quality change from year to year based on the specifications in one of each pair of years for three lines of Chevrolet, three of Ford, and two of Plymouth. His estimates of quality changes for 1954–1960, shown in Table 7.4, are based on six-cylinder models to 1956 and V-8's thereafter. Table 7.4 also shows

Table 7.4. Estimates of Quality Change in Chevrolet, Ford, and Plymouth[a] (percent)

Model Years	Hedonic Index[b] (Griliches)	Present Estimates Based on Secondhand Prices[c]
1954–1955	5.7	5.2
1955–1956	2.9	−0.7
1956–1957	4.8	4.4
1957–1958	3.4	3.8
1958–1959	1.4	4.9
1959–1960	0.3	−3.2
1954–1960	19.9	15.0

[a] Sixes to 1956 and eights thereafter.
[b] From Griliches 1963, Table 7, p. 396.
[c] For two lines of sixes or eights from Table A.1; each line is weighted $\frac{3}{16}$ for Chevrolet and Ford and $\frac{1}{8}$ for Plymouth.

a comparable weighted average derived from the figures in Table A.1 in the Appendix. Table A.1 covers only two lines of Chevrolet and Ford, so each of these four lines was weighted by $\frac{3}{16}$, and each of two lines of Plymouth by $\frac{1}{8}$, to be comparable with Griliches' figures. The two indexes are still not entirely comparable for the more important reasons that Griliches used list, rather than secondhand prices, and his regression weights were derived from a larger cross section of cars than the ones to which the weights are applied here. Nevertheless, until more comparable indexes are available, these can serve for judging the degree of similarity.

There is considerable similarity between the two indexes despite their different derivations and lack of common coverage. Although some of the

Quality Changes and the Purchasing Power of Money

years show divergent movements, the increases for the full period have the same order of magnitude. If a longer period did not produce any larger difference, the percentage difference would decline, and the two would give for an extended period a range for the total quality change in which we could place some confidence. The results justify further research on both methods.

B. Consumer Price Index

Aside from throwing light on the much-disputed quality of new cars, the main purpose of this study is to clarify the accuracy of our price indexes and suggest a way of improving them. It is widely contended that

Table 7.5. Price Changes of New Cars (percent)

Model Years	Consumer Price Index[a]	List Prices[b]	List Price Adjusted for Quality[c]
1954–1955	−3.5	2.0	−2.5
1955–1956	2.8	6.3	6.3
1956–1957	5.3	10.3	6.1
1957–1958	3.2	5.6	5.3
1958–1959	4.3	6.0	0.4
1959–1960	−1.4	−0.6	0.4
1954–1960	10.8	33.1	16.7

List Prices of Big Three[d]
Sixes 1954–1960 and Eights 1955–1960

	Chevrolet		Ford		Plymouth	
	Sixes	Eights	Sixes	Eights	Sixes	Eights
Low line	37.9	32.6	34.3	34.6	32.4	30.7
Middle line	37.7	32.7	28.9	29.6	31.6	30.7

[a] New cars, *Monthly Labor Review* and Bureau of Labor Statistics, Bulletin No. 1256.

[b] Two lines each for Chevrolet, Ford, and Plymouth, unweighted average; sixes to 1956, eights thereafter. Compacts are excluded for 1960 to be comparable with CPI (see footnote 12).

[c] From Table 7.2 for all cars, weighted.

[d] From Table A.1, excluding compacts.

a major reason why the Consumer Price Index has continued to rise 1 to 2 percent a year, even when inflationary pressures seem absent, is that it fails to adjust for quality improvements. To judge the validity of that criticism, reliable estimates of quality change are essential.

Table 7.5 compares the automobile component of the Consumer Price Index with corresponding list prices and the "pure" price index of Table 7.2. The CPI covers only sedans of the Big Three and only V-8's since 1956.[12] The table suggests that the CPI is not biased upward and may even overcorrect for quality improvements in automobiles. How that happened is not clear. The comparatively small rise in the CPI does not reflect any quirk of weighting. The price increases over the period in individual lines of the Big Three, shown in the bottom half of the table, are all around 30 percent, which is three times the rise in the CPI. Those list prices exclude major changes due to optional equipment like automatic transmissions, which are excluded from the CPI. The CPI has apparently also been corrected for some quality changes, though in a manner that published sources do not explain in detail. One discussion states:

> Where the quality change involves the the addition or deletion of features which have an established retail price, prices are adjusted to eliminate their influence. [However,] only recently has it been possible to adjust automobile prices for some of these changes in automobile construction [and longer warranties, using cost information from the manufacturers].[13]

That implies some quality adjustment, though presumably not much. While the CPI also solicits actual prices charged, it is hard to believe that discounting rose enough to offset a large part of the overall increase in list prices, though whatever discounting did occur should also be incorporated into the quality-adjusted index. Only if the average discount had risen 6 percent or more from 1954–1960 would the present index after adjustment for discounting show a smaller rise than the CPI does.

This surprising result makes the need for reliable estimates of quality change all the more imperative. It has commonly been thought that price indexes are biased upward, with only the amount in doubt. The comparison here throws even the direction of bias into question. To be sure, it seems unlikely that the CPI similarly overcorrects for quality changes in other durable goods; yet any correction based on costs rather

---

12. Compacts were linked into the index in 1960, but in such a way as not to affect the change from 1959 to 1960. See Larsgaard and Mack 1961.

13. From Larsgaard and Mack 1961, pp. 522–523.

Quality Changes and the Purchasing Power of Money

than open market prices will contain errors of uncertain size. The purpose of this study is not to criticize the capability or integrity of the CPI compilers, who face a very difficult task, but to suggest the importance and feasibility of expanding and improving our estimates of quality change.

Appendix to Chapter 7

A Proposal for Estimating Depreciation Drift

Depreciation drift is the tendency for the average rate of depreciation of successive model years to change slightly. Rates drifted upwards during the postwar years until about 1953 or 1954, and the data also suggest that the rates were not completely constant thereafter. The present method of estimating quality change requires an accurate estimate of average depreciation rates, making it desirable to be able to take account of any drift. The method below provides a theoretical framework for studying depreciation drift, but must overcome certain practical difficulties (as explained) before it can be successful.

In recognition of differences in depreciation rates between model years, we need to place a factor $R_i^{A(i)+k}$ in front of every $d_{i,k}$ of formula (2). The power of R_i, $A(i) + k$, is the age of the ith model in the kth year; $A(i)$ is a fraction of a year accounting for differences in the time of year when the average car of each model year was produced and sold. For simplicity in what follows, however, let us assume that the $A(i)$ are equal for all i. Then they can be omitted. The matrix of prices is then represented as follows:

$$p_{t+1}q_{i+1}R_{i+1} \quad p_{t+2}q_{i+1}R_{i+1}^2 d_{i+1,1} \quad p_{t+3}q_{i+1}R_{i+1}^3 d_{i+1,2} \cdots$$
$$p_t q_i R_i \quad p_{t+1}q_i R_i^2 d_{i,1} \quad p_{t+2}q_i R_i^3 d_{i,2} \cdots$$

The conversion factor R affects differently the slope and the initial level of the declining curve of prices for each model year as it ages. Hence, it is possible to estimate differences in average depreciation by the slope of the price ratio curve and quality changes by its initial level.

This can be done by regressing on k the logarithm of the price ratios for model years i and $i + 1$:

(A1) $$\frac{p_{t+n}q_{i+1}R_{i+1}^k d_{i+1,k-1}}{p_{t+n}q_i R_i^{k+1} d_{i,k}}, \quad k = 1, \ldots L.$$

In the resulting regression function

(A2) $$\log_e \frac{q_{i+1}R_{i+1}^k d_{i+1,k-1}}{q_i R_i^{k+1} d_{i,k}} = a + bk,$$

the slope estimates the difference in depreciation, and the intercept estimates the logarithm of formula (2). To prove this, first note that, by assumption (1),

(A3) $$\frac{d_{i+1,k-1}}{d_{i,k}} \quad \text{approximates} \quad \frac{1}{D},$$

since the two depreciation factors do not differ in level (by assumption that difference is absorbed by the conversion factors R) but only by random variations which cancel out in fitting the regression equation. Hence we may treat the approximation (A3) as an equality. Make that substitution of D and differentiate equation (A2) with respect to k:

(A4) $$\log_e \frac{R_{i+1}}{R_i} = b, \quad \text{for } i \text{ and } i+1.$$

The estimate of a is found by averaging the regression line over k. If we make the substituion for b of (A4), we have:

(A5) $$\log_e \frac{q_{i+1}}{q_i R_i D} = a.$$

For two successive years in which quality is assumed constant, we may estimate $R_i D$. Then $R_i D$ for all i can be found from successive estimates of b for other pairs of years and thence the quality changes from successive estimates of a.

This method was tried on the data, but it was unsuccessful and was put aside. The price ratios (A1) for many model years display fluctuations that throw off the estimates of slope (A4) and produce patently inaccurate results. Experiments with various smoothing devices did not succeed. The price ratios are apparently affected at certain times by special developments. It might be possible to adjust for them in various ways, but this requires a careful study of the car market and has not been done.

It should be noted that depreciation rates affect quality. The estimate of quality change of the car when new,

$$\frac{q_{i+1}}{q_i},$$

Quality Changes and the Purchasing Power of Money

should be multiplied by the present discounted value of the series:

$$\frac{R^k_{i+1}}{R^k_i}, \quad k = 0, 1, \ldots$$

A model will decline in value at a different rate than its predecessor if these ratios are not all unity. Depreciation, after all, affects the value of a car over time, and the present value of any difference in depreciation rates affects the "true" worth of the car to the first purchaser, assuming the difference represents durability and not upkeep. This is in addition to differences in relative purchase prices. We can, in principle, make this adjustment in our quality index. Although a higher or lower depreciation rate shows up in the future and will not ordinarily be recognized at the time of purchase, such drift in rates represents differences in quality that should be counted.

Table A.1. Quality and Price Changes of 4-Door Sedans, 1954–1960[a] (percent)

| | Sixes | | | | Eights | | | | | |
| | Low-Priced | | Medium-Priced | | Low-Priced | | Medium-Priced | | Average[b] | |
Model Years	Qual.	List Price	Qual.	List Price	Qual.	List Price	Qual.	List Price	Qual.	List Price
CHEVROLET[c]										
1954–1955	4.6	2.9	4.4	2.7					4.5	2.8
1955–1956	—	6.2	—	5.6	—	5.9	—	5.3	—	5.7
1956–1957	3.4	11.6	4.6	13.2	5.5	11.1	4.1	12.6	4.5	12.0
1957–1958	−3.6	5.2	−3.2	5.3	−2.9	5.3	−2.9	5.4	−3.1	5.3
	(3.7)	(11.8)	(3.7)	(12.2)	(4.2)	(11.6)	(3.8)	(12.0)	(3.9)	(11.9)
1958–1959	−0.7	6.8	4.2	6.6	1.2	6.9	4.5	6.7	2.3	6.8
	(−7.7)	(0.5)	(−4.1)	(0.0)	(−5.6)	(0.9)	(−3.4)	(0.4)	(5.1)	(0.5)
1959–1960	−1.5	0.7	1.2	−0.1	1.3	0.2	2.1	−0.5	−0.6	−1.7
Corvair										
1959–1960	−10.3	−11.4	−10.1	−13.8						
FORD										
1954–1955	5.9	3.1	3.6	2.9	7.3	4.3	5.1	4.0	6.0	4.0
1955–1956	—	6.5	—	6.9	—	6.2	—	6.5	—	6.4
1956–1957	8.4	9.4	5.2	9.4	8.2	8.9	5.6	8.9	6.9	9.0
1957–1958	4.9	3.3	1.0	5.9	6.2	5.3	2.8	6.7	4.1	5.6
1958–1959	6.1	7.8	6.7	5.5	7.7	6.0	9.6	5.0	8.1	5.8
1959–1960	−12.0	0.5	−11.9	−4.1	−9.2	0.0	−8.1	−4.2	−8.7	−5.6
Falcon										
1959–1960	−6.9	−13.2								
PLYMOUTH										
1954–1955	6.3	0.6	7.6	0.1					7.0	0.4
1955–1956	−2.7	6.4	−3.0	6.0	−4.4	6.0	−1.8	5.7	−3.0	6.0
1956–1957	1.6	10.0	0.9	11.5	−2.0	9.3	2.0	10.8	0.3	10.2
1957–1958	2.9	5.5	2.9	5.1	3.1	5.7	1.9	5.2	2.6	5.4
1958–1959	12.7	5.3	12.8	5.9	12.3	5.5	14.7	6.1	13.3	5.7
1959–1960	−3.7	1.2	−2.1	0.0	−3.9	1.1	−1.2	0.0	−0.8	−4.6

Table A.1. (continued)

	Sixes				Eights				Average[b]	
	Low-Priced		Medium-Priced		Low-Priced		Medium-Priced			
Model Years	Qual.	List Price	Qual.	List Price	Qual.	List Price	Qual.	List Price	Qual.	List Price
Valiant										
1959–1960	2.0	−10.1	1.4	−12.7						
RAMBLER										
1954–1955			−0.4	0.2					−0.4	0.2
1955–1956	1.2	5.9	2.1	6.0					1.2	6.1
1956–1957	3.9	9.2	2.7	11.4					3.2	9.7
1957–1958	3.6	4.4	2.1	4.2			2.7	4.0	3.7	3.3
1958–1959	—	2.5	—	2.5			—	2.4	−0.1	2.3
1959–1960	−5.8	0.0	−4.7	0.0			−6.3	−0.5	−5.3	0.1
Rambler Ambassador[d]										
1955–1956					−2.5	6.5	−3.2	7.8		
1956–1957					—	−4.6	—	−5.8		
1957–1958					−14.7	−8.3	14.5	−9.3		
1958–1959					−2.3	0.0	−1.9	0.0		
1959–1960					−7.2	0.0	−6.6	0.0		
STUDEBAKER										
1954–1955	1.6	−1.0	−2.4	−1.7			1.7	−7.6	0.8	−5.0
1955–1956	16.8	11.8	8.7	5.7			9.7	5.3	11.1	6.9
1956–1957	−14.2	−6.0	−10.0	2.8			−9.7	2.5	−11.3	−0.2
1957–1958	−8.8	0.0	−2.7	10.0			1.8	9.4	−4.2	6.0
1958–1959	25.4	6.5	11.0	−3.5			12.9	−2.9	16.5	0.1
1959–1960	−0.6	2.6	−2.7	1.0			0.6	0.9	−0.8	1.6

[a] Method of computation: By formula (2) for 16 quarters (only 15 for 1959–1960). Basic data are displayed in the chart, depreciation rates in Table 7.1. Dashes indicate years of assumed no-change in quality. Big Three compacts for 1950 were linked to corresponding full-size sixes of 1959.

[b] Low- and medium-priced lines of each cylinder group were averaged with equal weight, and the averages for these two groups were then averaged with weights given by sales of sixes and eights of that make in each calendar year (from *Automotive News Almanac*). Big Three compacts were treated as a separate cylinder group and included in averages for 1959–1960, weighted by their sales in 1960. Rambler average includes Ambassador.

[c] See Table A.2 for identification of figures in parentheses.

[d] Medium-priced and high-priced lines, respectively.

Table A.2. Model Lines Used in Computing Price Ratios

	Sixes		Eights		
Model Years	Low-Priced	Medium-Priced	Low-Priced	Medium-Priced	High-Priced
CHEVROLET					
1947–1948	Stylemaster	Fleetmaster			
1949–1952	Styleline Special	Styleline Deluxe			
1953–1954	"150"	"210"			
1955–1957	"150"	"210"	"150"	"210"	
1958[a]	Delray (Biscayne)	Biscayne (Bel Air)	Delray (Biscayne)	Biscayne (Bel Air)	
1959–1961	Biscayne	Bel Air	Biscayne	Bel Air	

Quality Changes and the Purchasing Power of Money

Table A.2. (*continued*)

	Sixes		Eights		
Model Years	Low-Priced	Medium-Priced	Low-Priced	Medium-Priced	High-Priced
Corvair					
1960	Standard	Deluxe			
1961	"500"	"700"			
FORD					
1947–1948	Deluxe	Super Deluxe	Deluxe	Super Deluxe	
1949	Deluxe	Custom	Deluxe	Custom	
1950–1951	Deluxe	Custom Deluxe	Deluxe	Custom Deluxe	
1952–1956	Mainline	Customline	Mainline	Customline	
1957	Custom	Custom 300	Custom	Custom 300	
1958–1960	Custom 300	Fairlane	Custom 300	Fairlane	
1961	Fairlane	Fairlane 500	Fairlane	Fairlane 500	
Falcon					
1960–1961	Falcon 6				
PLYMOUTH					
1947–1950	Deluxe	Special Deluxe			
1951–1953	Cambridge	Cranbrook			
1954	Plaza	Savoy			
1955–1958	Plaza	Savoy	Plaza	Savoy	
1959–1961	Savoy	Belvedere	Savoy	Belvedere	
Valiant					
1960–1961	V-100	V-200			
RAMBLER					
1954		Super			
1955–1956	Deluxe	Super			
1957	Deluxe	Super		Super	
1958–1960	Deluxe	Super		Rebel Super	
1961	Classic Deluxe	Classic Super		Classic Super	
Rambler Ambassador					
1955–1961				Super	Custom
STUDEBAKER					
1947–1949	Champion Deluxe	Champion Regal Deluxe			
1950	Champion Custom	Champion Deluxe			
1951–1952	Champion Custom	Champion Deluxe		Commander Regal	
1953–1955	Champion Custom	Champion Deluxe		Commander Deluxe	
1956[b]	(Champion)	Champion		Commander	
1957	Scotsman	Champion Custom		Commander Custom	
1958	Scotsman	Champion		Commander	
1959–1961	Lark Deluxe	Lark Regal		Lark Regal	

[a] In 1958 Delray was the lowest-priced Chevrolet, followed by Biscayne and then Bel Air; in 1959 Delray was discontinued.
[b] Since there was only one line of Studebaker six in 1956, the Champion was used for both lines.

8.

Robert E. Hall
The Measurement of Quality Change from Vintage Price Data

1. Introduction

Under some circumstances, the quality of a capital good can be measured unambiguously by a single numerical index. When this is possible, and when the type of capital good under consideration is traded in a secondhand market, it is natural to look for a method for deducing the relative qualities of capital goods of different vintages or model years from the corresponding relative prices in the secondhand market. This proposal is made particularly attractive by the fact that if the price of each vintage is observed N times, its ratio to the price of the next earlier or later vintage is observed $N - 1$ times. This permits the calculation of the relative quality of two successive vintages as an appropriate average of the $N - 1$ separate observations. Something can then be said about the statistical properties of the resulting quality index, and formal statistical tests of hypotheses about quality change can be carried out.

The only difficulty with this proposal is that the difference between the prices of two capital goods of different ages is determined not just by the difference in their inherent qualities but also by a pure age effect, namely depreciation. Comparison between prices observed at different times can eliminate the depreciation effect, but only at the cost of introducing the influence of the changing price level. In order to measure quality change from secondhand market data, some method for disentangling it from the effects of depreciation and changes in the price level is needed.

This paper is devoted to the theoretical and empirical study of the problem just mentioned. In Section 2, some theoretical aspects of the behavior of secondhand markets are discussed. Conditions for the existence

---

Robert E. Hall is Associate Professor of Economics, Massachusetts Institute of Technology.

Measurement of Quality Change

of an overall measure of capital efficiency are mentioned, and the definition of a quality index as a special restriction on the efficiency index is proposed. The quality index (or index of embodied technical change) is shown to be unambiguously defined except for its trend or average rate of growth, which cannot be measured from secondhand market data in the absence of additional information.

In Section 3 the regression equation developed in Section 2 is applied to data on the prices of used pickup trucks. The trend in quality change is arbitrarily set to zero, so only departures from a constant rate of growth are measured. The results are in close accord with Triplett's findings for automobiles (1966), although based on an entirely different method; they suggest that the rate of quality improvement was much higher from 1955 to 1960 than from 1961 to 1966. Various hypotheses about the path of quality change and the relation between the two makes studied (Chevrolet and Ford) are tested. The hypothesis of geometric or declining balance depreciation is tested and rejected.

In Section 4, two methods for estimating the trend of quality change are discussed and tested. The first is due to Cagan (1965)[1] and consists in identifying vintages that are apparently functionally identical and adjusting the trend of the quality index so that it has the same value for these vintages. The second is to express the quality index as a function of observed characteristics and to estimate the parameters of that function from the price data. It is essentially the well-known hedonic method applied to the matrix of prices for a single make in place of the vector of prices of many makes. The results of both of these methods are quite similar; the quality index rises rapidly from 1955 to 1960 and falls slightly from 1961 to 1966, again in conformity with Triplett's results for automobiles.

Finally, in the last section the quality-corrected price index for pickup trucks derived in this study is compared to various other related indexes. The suggestion is made that the index derived from the secondhand market may measure actual transaction prices for new trucks more satisfactorily than does the list price or the Wholesale Price Index for trucks. The quality-corrected index of this study shows a steady upward movement from 1963 to 1966, while the official index and the list price remain roughly constant. No support is given in this study to the hypothesis that the upward movement in the unit price of pickup trucks from 1961 to 1967 was the result of quality improvement rather than inflation.

---

1. In many respects the whole of the present paper can be regarded as a formalization and refinement of Phillip Cagan's work.

2. The Behavior of Secondhand Markets for Capital Goods

The natural starting point in our discussion of secondhand markets is the familiar hypothesis that the price of a capital good is equal to the present value of its future services:

$$(2.1) \qquad p_{t,\tau} = \sum_{s=0}^{N-\tau-1} \left(\frac{1}{1+r}\right)^s x_{t+s,\tau+s}.$$

Here $p_{t,\tau}$ is the price at time t of a capital good of age τ, r is the interest rate (assumed to remain constant over time), and $x_{t,\tau}$ is the value at time t of the services of a capital good of age τ. The implications of this hypothesis, without any further restrictions, were studied many years ago by Harold Hotelling in an important paper (1925).

Our goal here is to construct a restricted form of equation (2.1) with the property that the familiar parameters of capital measurement—deterioration and technical change—appear in it explicitly. We begin by separating the value of the services of a capital good into a price and a quantity:

$$(2.2) \qquad x_{t,\tau} = \hat{p}_t z_{t,\tau}.$$

Here $\hat{p}_t$ is the rental price of one unit of capital services, and $z_{t,\tau}$ is the number of units of capital services provided by a capital good of age τ at time t. Separation in this way does not impose any mathematical restriction on $x_{t,\tau}$, and can be done in any number of arbitrary ways. A leading question in capital theory is whether or not there is a natural method for separating the value of capital services into a price and a quantity. By a natural method we mean a method for measuring the quantity of capital services that permits the calculation of a meaningful total quantity of the services of capital goods of all ages. Furthermore, we require that the quantity of services attributed to a particular capital good be independent of the circumstances in which it is used in production; in particular, it should be independent of the quantity of other factors employed and of the quantity of capital goods of different ages available. In other words, the index $z_{t,\tau}$ should be a purely technical measure of the relative efficiency of capital goods, unaffected by economic variables.[2]

---

2. The conditions under which a capital aggregate can be formed have been studied very intensively at the theoretical level; see Fisher 1965 for a definitive treatment and a bibliography of previous work. In vintage production functions with constant returns to scale, the basic theorem of capital aggregation establishes that a capital aggregate exists if and only if the marginal product of capital of age τ at time t has the fixed ratio $z_{t,\tau}/z_{t,0}$ to the marginal product of new capital at time t. This can be extended to intertemporal

Measurement of Quality Change

If we suppose that such an index exists, it has a strong implication for the behavior of rental prices at any point in time; since the services of old and new capital goods are perfect substitutes, the rental prices of capital goods must stand in the fixed proportions dictated by their relative efficiencies. In this case, there is a well-defined measure of rental per unit of capital, independent of the age of the capital supplying the services. The separation of price and quantity expressed in equation (2.2) was written with this in mind; $\hat{p}_t$ does not depend on age, τ.[3]

The index $z_{t,\tau}$ combines the influence of deterioration (decline in efficiency as capital ages), embodied technical change (increasing efficiency for later vintages of capital), and disembodied technical change (increasing efficiency of all capital as time passes). Implicit in most discussions of quality change and capital measurement is the assumption that these processes take place independently, so that it is sensible to speak of an index of deterioration, say Φ_τ, an index of embodied technical change, b_t, and an index of disembodied technical change, d_t. The hypothesis of independence is expressed mathematically by putting the efficiency index $z_{t,\tau}$ equal to the product of the three indexes:

$$(2.3) \qquad z_{t,\tau} = \Phi_\tau b_{t-\tau} d_t.$$

This is a strong restriction and one that can be tested with the data available.

At this point a grave difficulty arises. The comprehensive efficiency index $z_{t,\tau}$ is a characteristic of the production function and could be measured to any degree of accuracy by a suitable set of experiments. But even if it were known exactly, and if it obeyed the independence assumption stated earlier, it would not be possible to deduce the indexes Φ_τ, b_v, and d_t from it. The difficulty is the following: Suppose it is true that

$$(2.4) \qquad z_{t,\tau} = \Phi_\tau b_{t-\tau} d_t.$$

Then it is also true that

$$(2.5) \qquad z_{t,\tau} = \Phi_\tau^* b_{t-\tau}^* d_t^*,$$

---

comparisons by considering the (hypothetical) problem of aggregating new capital of different vintages. By the same theorem, this can be done if and only if the marginal product of capital of vintage t has the fixed ratio $z_{t,0}$ to the marginal product of capital of the first vintage. The latter is normalized at 1: $z_{1,0} = 1$. Taken together, these conditions imply the existence of $z_{t,\tau}$.

3. The relation between capital aggregation and the rental price of capital was studied by the present author in an earlier paper (1968). Much of what follows in this section is adapted from that paper.

where the indexes with *'s are different from their counterparts in equation (2.4) in every period other than the base period. In other words, there is an ambiguity in separating the total change in efficiency into components of deterioration, embodied technical change, and disembodied technical change. The precise form of the ambiguity is the following: If $\Phi_\tau b_{t-\tau} d_t$ is one way to write $z_{t,\tau}$, then equally valid alternatives are provided by

(2.6) $$\Phi_\tau^* = B^\tau \Phi_\tau$$

(2.7) $$b_{t-\tau}^* = B^{t-\tau} b_{t-\tau}$$

and

(2.8) $$d_t^* = B^{-t} d_t,$$

where B is any positive number.[4] So in spite of the fact that the unrestricted efficiency index $z_{t,\tau}$ is an unambiguous measure, the conventional factorization of the efficiency index into deterioration, embodied technical change, and disembodied technical change contains a serious ambiguity. Information from the production function (all the relevant information is contained in $z_{t,\tau}$) can be used to find indexes Φ_τ, b_v and d_t, but it cannot distinguish between these and the alternatives given in equations (2.6), (2.7), and (2.8). For B taken to be greater than one, these equations show that slower deterioration, faster embodied technical change, and slower disembodied technical change are an equally valid description of the characteristics of the production function. In a world in which embodied technical change takes place smoothly over time at a constant rate of growth (that is, b_v is an exponential function of v), the notion of embodiment can be dispensed with altogether by an appropriate choice of B. In Hall 1968 I suggested that the appropriate way to eliminate the ambiguity in the conventional view of deterioration and technical change is to adopt an arbitrary normalization of any of the three indexes by setting it to 1 at a second point. The easiest such normalization for our present purposes is to set the index of embodied efficiency to 1 at the end of the period of observation as well as at the beginning. From the point of view of the study of production functions, this normalization is inconsequential since it does not affect $z_{t,\tau}$. On the other hand, the quality-corrected price index we derive below is seriously affected by the choice of normalization. If it is to have any meaning, something better than an arbitrary distinction between embodied and disembodied technical change must be found.

---

4. For a proof that this is the only ambiguity, see Hall 1968. There, B is written e^β.

Measurement of Quality Change

This raises the question of whether there is additional information available that might allow us to make the distinction.[5] We have already established that no information about how capital is used in production will allow us to escape the ambiguity—all such information is contained in the index $z_{t,\tau}$, and that is not enough. However, there is another source of information that we have not drawn upon so far. If embodied technical change is associated with change in the characteristics of the capital goods, then information about those characteristics can be brought to bear on the problem of separating embodied from disembodied technical change. The prospects for empirical success in such a procedure are quite good, since this information is used to estimate only a single parameter, namely the undetermined coefficient B in equations (2.6), (2.7), and (2.8).

Returning now to the basic present value relationship thought to characterize markets for secondhand capital goods, we have, after substituting the proposed restriction on rental values,

$$(2.9) \qquad p_{t,\tau} = \sum_{s=0}^{N-\tau-1} \left(\frac{1}{1+r}\right)^s \Phi_{\tau+s} b_{t-\tau} d_{t+s} \hat{\rho}_{t+s}.$$

This assumes foresight with respect to the future behavior of disembodied technical change, d_{t+s}, and the rental price, $\hat{\rho}_{t+s}$. An alternative assumption, perhaps more realistic and certainly more convenient, is that all participants in the market have static expectations about d_{t+s} and $\hat{\rho}_{t+s}$.[6] Then

$$(2.10) \qquad p_{t,\tau} = b_{t-\tau} d_t \hat{\rho}_t \sum_{s=0}^{N-\tau-1} \left(\frac{1}{1+r}\right)^s \Phi_{\tau+s}.$$

The separate components of the product $d_t \hat{\rho}_t$ are not econometrically identifiable in this equation. In economic terms, disembodied technical change has no differential effect on capital goods of different ages at the same point in time. Its effect over time cannot be distinguished from the effect of changes in the rental price over time. In short, nothing about disembodied technical change can be deduced from secondhand market data. We can, however, estimate the product, $\rho_t = d_t \hat{\rho}_t$, and interpret

---

5. At this point we depart from Hall 1968.
6. The errors made in assuming a constant interest rate and static expectations for $\hat{\rho}_t$ are self-canceling to the extent that departures are caused by pure inflation. The assumptions here are equivalent to assuming a constant *real* interest rate and static expectations for $\hat{\rho}_t$ in real terms.

it as the rental price of capital services uncorrected for disembodied technical change.[7] Then we have

$$(2.11) \qquad p_{t,\tau} = b_{t-\tau} \rho_t \sum_{s=0}^{N-\tau-1} \left(\frac{1}{1+r}\right)^s \Phi_{\tau+s}.$$

This is our basic behavioral equation, stated in terms of the parameters of capital measurement. A change of variables puts it in an alternative form in terms of the parameters of price measurement. We let

$$(2.12) \qquad \bar{p}_t = \rho_t \sum_{s=0}^{N-1} \left(\frac{1}{1+r}\right)^s \Phi_s;$$

this is a price index for new capital goods corrected for quality change (embodied technical change). Second,

$$(2.13) \qquad D_\tau = \frac{\sum_{s=0}^{N-\tau+1} \left(\frac{1}{1+r}\right)^s \Phi_{\tau+s}}{\sum_{s=0}^{N-1} \left(\frac{1}{1+r}\right)^s \Phi_s};$$

this is an index of *depreciation*, the decline in the price of a secondhand capital good as it ages. Under the special hypothesis of geometric deterioration,

$$(2.14) \qquad \Phi_\tau = (1-\delta)^\tau, \qquad N = \infty,$$

D_τ has the same geometric form, $(1-\delta)^\tau$, so the deterioration index and the depreciation index are identical. In every other case, however, the distinction between deterioration and depreciation is an important one. The failure to make this distinction has led to a certain amount of confusion in the literature on capital measurement.

In the new parametrization, our behavioral equation is

$$(2.15) \qquad p_{t,\tau} = \bar{p}_t b_{t-\tau} D_\tau.$$

That is, the observed price of a used capital good is the underlying quality-corrected price index $\bar{p}_t$, adjusted for quality as given by the index $b_{t-\tau}$ and depreciation as given by the index D_τ. We should note that this very simple relationship holds only under the assumption of

---

7. This is a sensible quantity to measure in its own right, since it excludes changes in efficiency due to changes in the method of using capital and includes changes attributable to the capital good itself.

Measurement of Quality Change

static expectations. Investigation of more sophisticated hypotheses about expectations could only be carried out in the original present value equation.

For convenience in estimation, we assume that a random disturbance enters equation (2.15) multiplicatively, so that by taking logs, we get

(2.16) $$\log p_{t,\tau} = \log \bar{p}_t + \log b_{t-\tau} + \log D_\tau + u_{t,\tau}.$$

The regression coefficients are the logs of the three indexes, and all of the right-hand variables are dummy variables. Two index normalizations are required; we use $D_1 = 1$ and $b_0 = 1$, implying that depreciation is measured relative to one-year-old capital goods and that quality is measured relative to the quality of vintage 0. In addition, we require a second normalization on the quality index; we use $b_{T-1} = 1$, where $T - 1$ is the last vintage observed, so that no net change in quality takes place over the period of observation.

An example may be useful to clarify this procedure. If $T = 3$ and $N = 4$, and price data from the secondhand market, $p_{t,\tau}$, are available for $\tau = 1, 2, 3$ and $t = 1, 2, 3$ (i.e., the prices of new capital goods are not available, as is the case in the present study), and if the observation matrix is stacked by rows to form a column vector, then the matrix of right-hand variables is

(2.17)
$$X = \begin{array}{ccccccccc} \bar{p}_1 & \bar{p}_2 & \bar{p}_3 & D_2 & D_3 & b_{-2} & b_{-1} & b_1 & b_2 \\ 1 & 0 & 0 & 0 & 0 & 0 & 0 & 0 & 0 \\ 1 & 0 & 0 & 1 & 0 & 0 & 1 & 0 & 0 \\ 1 & 0 & 0 & 0 & 1 & 1 & 0 & 0 & 0 \\ 0 & 1 & 0 & 0 & 0 & 0 & 0 & 1 & 0 \\ 0 & 1 & 0 & 1 & 0 & 0 & 0 & 0 & 0 \\ 0 & 1 & 0 & 0 & 1 & 0 & 1 & 0 & 0 \\ 0 & 0 & 1 & 0 & 0 & 0 & 0 & 0 & 1 \\ 0 & 0 & 1 & 1 & 0 & 0 & 0 & 1 & 0 \\ 0 & 0 & 1 & 0 & 1 & 0 & 0 & 0 & 0 \end{array}$$

Above each column is indicated the parameter whose log is the regression coefficient corresponding to that column. The normalizations are imposed simply by excluding the columns for the parameters normalized at unity, since their coefficients are zero. The excluded column for b_2 is shown just to the right of the matrix. It is useful to show that it is a linear combination of the columns of X, so that its inclusion in an attempt to measure the trend in quality change would cause the regression calculation to break down If $X(\bar{p}_1)$ is the column corresponding to $\bar{p}_1$, $X(D_2)$ to D_2, and so forth, then

(2.18) $\quad X(b_2) = \frac{1}{2}[X(\bar{p}_2) + 2X(\bar{p}_3) - X(D_2)$

$\qquad - 2X(D_3) + 2X(b_{-2}) + X(b_{-1}) - X(b_1)].$

This shows that the trend is not identified in this regression, confirming the analysis of the first part of this section.

3. Estimates of Efficiency Parameters for Half-Ton Pickup Trucks— Unrestricted Quality Change

Pickup trucks are well-suited to the kind of analysis just described. They are a standardized product traded in an active, competitive second-hand market, with relatively low transactions costs. In the period studied, 1955 to 1966, they underwent a number of minor design changes of the sort presumably described by our notion of quality change, but none was so major as to cast serious doubt on our capital-aggregation assumption that the services of old trucks are perfect substitutes for the services of new trucks.

Data for the average market prices in April of used pickup trucks were obtained from the National Automobile Dealers Association *Official Used Car Guide*[8] for the years 1961 to 1967, covering model years 1955 to 1966. Two makes were studied: Chevrolet (model 3104 for 1955 to 1959, Cl404 for 1960 to 1966) and Ford (model F-100 in all years). For both makes, the older style pickup body (Stepside for Chevrolet, Flareside for Ford), the 6-cylinder engine of 230- to 250-cubic-inches displacement, and the 110- to 115-inch wheelbase were studied. Prices for models of the six previous years are published in the *Guide* and are reproduced in Table 8.1. Apparently because the market in very new trucks is quite thin, prices for trucks of the current model year are not available in April (The 1968 *Guide* was not used at all because the latest model reported was 1966). Consequently, this study does not cast any light on the important question of how much a truck depreciates in its first year.

Our first set of results is for the simplest reasonable specification. We assume that $b_v = 1$ for all vintages. In view of the normalization requirement, we can see that this restriction is compatible with smooth exponential quality change at any positive or negative rate. The improvement in

---

8. I am grateful to Zvi Griliches for making his back copies of the publication available to me.

Measurement of Quality Change

Table 8.1. Prices of Used Pickup Trucks

	Chevrolet					
	Age (years)					
Model Year	1	2	3	4	5	6
1961	$1575	$1260	$1040	$ 910	$690	$500[a]
1962	1640	1375	1070	865	710	545
1963	1640	1350	1110	850	670	510
1964	1720	1405	1185	1010	745	550
1965	1625	1400	1185	1020	875	655
1966	1765	1415	1205	1005	850	700
1967	1575	1420	1205	1000	820	710
	Ford					
1961	$1550	$1230	$1065	$870	$670	$525
1962	1660	1340	1075	860	700	520
1963	1630	1345	1095	885	715	550
1964	1710	1405	1150	995	765	585
1965	1655	1385	1150	985	815	640
1966	1745	1470	1210	1005	820	685
1967	1600	1440	1210	1000	825	700

[a] Average of two models.

the fit that we obtain later in the study by estimating parameters of quality change is attributable to the presence of nonexponential quality change, that is, to changes in the trend in quality change.

Results for this simple specification are given in Table 8.2. Twelve parameters are estimated: 7 prices and 5 points on the depreciation function. These results suggest, not surprisingly, that the view is close to the truth that capital depreciation is the principal determinant of prices in the used truck market. The standard errors of the regressions are 6.0 percent for Chevrolets and 4.2 percent for Fords. The size of the standard errors of the estimates of the parameters suggests that they are measured with considerable accuracy. The covariances of the estimates of the prices are all positive in both regressions, so that differences between the rental rates have standard errors only slightly larger than those of the estimates themselves. As a result, relatively powerful tests of hypotheses about changes in the prices can be made. The most interesting of these is the test for inflation over the whole period. The null hypothesis of no inflation

Table 8.2. Regression Results for Constant Rate of Quality Change

Year	Price Index Chevrolet $\log \bar{p}_t$	Chevrolet $\bar{p}_t$	Ford $\log \bar{p}_t$	Ford $\bar{p}_t$	Age (years)	Depreciation index Chevrolet $\log D_\tau$	Chevrolet D_τ	Ford $\log D_\tau$	Ford D_τ	Summary statistics	Chevrolet	Ford
1961	7.318 (0.032)	$1508	7.314 (0.022)	$1501	1	0	1.000	0	1.000	Standard error	0.060	0.042
1962	7.355 (0.032)	1564	7.345 (0.022)	1549	2	−0.181 (0.032)	0.834	−0.184 (0.022)	0.832	Sum of squared residuals	0.10638	0.05243
1963	7.334 (0.032)	1532	7.364 (0.022)	1577	3	−0.367 (0.032)	0.693	−0.373 (0.022)	0.688	R^2	0.980	0.990
1964	7.419 (0.032)	1667	7.428 (0.022)	1683	4	−0.552 (0.032)	0.576	−0.561 (0.022)	0.571			
1965	7.467 (0.032)	1749	7.444 (0.022)	1710	5	−0.771 (0.032)	0.463	−0.780 (0.022)	0.459			
1966	7.489 (0.032)	1788	7.487 (0.022)	1785	6	−1.027 (0.032)	0.358	−1.016 (0.022)	0.362			
1967	7.466 (0.032)	1747	7.473 (0.022)	1760								

Measurement of Quality Change

in that case is $\bar{p}_7/\bar{p}_1 = 1$ (i.e., $\log \bar{p}_7 - \log \bar{p}_1 = 0$); the alternative hypothesis is $\bar{p}_7/\bar{p}_1 > 1$. For Chevrolets, estimated inflation, $\bar{p}_7/\bar{p}_1$, is 14.7 percent with standard error 3.4 percent. The corresponding t-statistic is 4.3, causing us to reject the null hypothesis at any reasonable level of significance. The estimate of inflation for Fords is 15.9 percent with standard error 2.4 percent, so the null hypothesis is even more emphatically rejected. Our conclusion is that if there has been no quality change in pickup trucks over the period 1955 to 1966, there certainly has been inflation in their prices between 1961 and 1967.

Since the depreciation function is also estimated in these regressions, any amount of smooth exponential quality change is compatible with the results just presented. If B^v is the true index of quality, then our estimates can be restated to take account of that fact in the following way: Estimated prices should be $\bar{p}_t/B^t$ and estimated depreciation should be $B^\tau D_\tau$, where $\bar{p}_t$ and D_τ are the estimates from the regressions just presented for the normalization of no quality change. Thus our conclusion that $\bar{p}_7$ is greater than $\bar{p}_1$, initially thought to indicate inflation in the cost of pickup trucks, might alternatively be attributable to quality change. This is the familiar claim that the observed inflation in many products actually reflects quality improvement. As long as we restrict our attention to data on the *efficiency* of capital goods, we are unable to test this optimistic view of inflation, exactly because we cannot separate changes in efficiency unambiguously into embodied and disembodied components. Information about the *characteristics* of capital can test this view, however. We shall return to this point in section 4; evidence presented there indicates fairly strongly that the optimistic view is incorrect and that a substantial amount of inflation took place over the period.

In the results presented above, the arbitrary normalization $bT = 1$ was imposed. In addition, a substantive restriction was imposed on b_v, namely that $b_v = 1$ for all vintages. Our next set of results relaxes the second restriction while keeping the normalization.[9] Departures of the estimates of $\log b_v$ (for $v = -4, \ldots, 0, 2, \ldots, 6$) from zero indicate *nonexponential* quality change. The results, shown in Table 8.3, suggest that quality change in pickup trucks has been far from exponential. In 5 out of 10 years for Chevrolets and 8 out of 10 for Fords, the estimated coefficient of the log of quality is more than two standard errors smaller or larger

---

9. The reader should be warned that the quality coefficient for the 1966 model is estimated from a single observation in these and all subsequent results. Since that observation was a year of distress in the market for used cars and trucks (1967), the quoted standard error probably understates the true standard error.

than zero. The null hypothesis that each coefficient is zero (purely exponential technical change) can be tested against the alternative hypothesis that some are different. The resulting F-statistic[10] is 6.1 with 20 and 40 degrees of freedom; the critical point in the F-distribution at the 0.05 level of significance is 1.8, so the null hypothesis is rejected decisively for both makes considered together (it is also rejected for each make separately). We conclude that in the microeconomic data under consideration, quality change does not proceed smoothly with the same upward trend over time, in spite of the fact that it is generally thought to do so in the aggregate.

The results in Table 8.3 suggest that the pace of quality change slowed substantially after 1960. The arbitrary normalization requires that no quality change take place between 1960 and 1966, so no statement can be made about its overall rate. A striking difference between the results in Table 8.3 and those in Table 8.2 is that the strong evidence of inflation in the earlier results is not supported at all when the restriction of purely exponential technical change is relaxed. As we shall see in section 4, there is some evidence that the normalization used in these estimates (that the efficiency of a one-year-old 1966 truck was the same as the efficiency of a one-year-old 1960 truck), actually overstates the trend of quality change. Note that the rate of quality change between 1960 and 1965 appears to have been significantly positive; it is a sudden drop in estimated efficiency in the 1966 models that makes the estimates meet the arbitrary normalization.

An indirect test of the validity of these results is provided by the reasonable assumption that Chevrolets and Fords are essentially perfect substitutes. If this is so, their prices should move in fixed proportion. The ratio between the two prices is shown in Table 8.3. There it appears that Chevrolets have become progressively cheaper per unit of capital over the period, in comparison to Fords. But this is not consistent with our assumption—the unit of capital is the one-year-old 1960 model in both cases, so every year after that (if the correction for technical change is

---

10. Tests of this and succeeding hypotheses are based on the statistic

$$F = [(N - 1)T - k_1][Q_1 - Q_0]/[(k_1 - k_0)Q_0]$$

where Q_0 is the sum of squared residuals from the regression without the restriction, k_0 is the number of parameters estimated in the restricted regression, and k_1 is the number of parameters in the unrestricted regression. This statistic has the F-distribution with $k_1 - k_0$ and $(N - 1)T - k_1$ degrees of freedom, under the null hypothesis. In the absence of constraints across makes, Q_0 and Q_1 are calculated as the total sum of squared residuals for the corresponding separate regressions. Implicit in this procedure is the assumption that the variances of the disturbances are the same for both makes.

Measurement of Quality Change

correct) the prices should stand in the same proportion. This suggests that it would be useful to set up a model in which the constraint is imposed that Chevrolets and Fords are perfect substitutes. This is particularly interesting because it permits us to estimate the quality of Fords of every vintage, including those coefficients previously normalized at unity. The resulting index gives the quality of Fords relative to the quality of the 1960 Chevrolet. An arbitrary normalization for the 1966 Chevrolet is retained; since the 1966 Ford is treated as a perfect substitute for the Chevrolet of that year, the quality coefficient for the 1966 Ford measures

Table 8.3. Regression Results for Unrestricted Quality Change and Unrestricted Depreciation (master model)

	Index of quality			
	Chevrolet		Ford	
Vintage	$\log b_v$	b_v	$\log b_v$	b_v
1955	−0.352 (0.061)	0.703	−0.245 (0.043)	0.783
1956	−0.236 (0.047)	0.790	−0.219 (0.033)	0.803
1957	−0.186 (0.038)	0.830	−0.140 (0.026)	0.869
1958	−0.177 (0.030)	0.838	−0.105 (0.021)	0.900
1959	−0.100 (0.025)	0.905	−0.061 (0.017)	0.941
1960	0	1.000	0	1.000
1961	0.024 (0.020)	1.024	0.024 (0.014)	1.025
1962	0.021 (0.023)	1.021	0.028 (0.016)	1.029
1963	0.033 (0.028)	1.034	0.044 (0.020)	1.045
1964	0.029 (0.034)	1.029	0.059 (0.024)	1.061
1965	0.077 (0.041)	1.080	0.071 (0.029)	1.074
1966	0	1.000	0	1.000

Table 8.3 (*continued*)

	Price Index				
	Chevrolet		Ford		
Year	$\log \bar{p}_t$	$\bar{p}_t$	$\log \bar{p}_t$	$\bar{p}_t$	Ratio
1961	7.420 (0.025)	$1670	7.385 (0.017)	$1612	0.966
1962	7.395 (0.022)	1627	7.372 (0.016)	1590	0.978
1963	7.331 (0.023)	1527	7.349 (0.016)	1554	1.020
1964	7.379 (0.026)	1602	7.382 (0.018)	1607	1.003
1965	7.392 (0.031)	1623	7.371 (0.021)	1589	0.979
1966	7.385 (0.036)	1611	7.392 (0.025)	1623	1.007
1967	7.362 (0.036)	1575	7.378 (0.025)	1600	1.016

	Depreciation index			
	Chevrolet		Ford	
Age	$\log D_\tau$	D_τ	$\log D_\tau$	D_τ
1	0	1.000	0	1.000
2	−0.167 (0.020)	0.846	−0.175 (0.014)	0.839
3	−0.317 (0.022)	0.729	−0.339 (0.015)	0.712
4	−0.470 (0.026)	0.625	−0.499 (0.018)	0.607
5	−0.651 (0.031)	0.521	−0.680 (0.022)	0.507
6	−0.854 (0.038)	0.426	−0.877 (0.026)	0.416

Measurement of Quality Change

Table 8.3 (*continued*)

	Summary statistics	
	Chevrolet	Ford
Standard error	0.036	0.025
Sum of squared residuals	0.02576	0.01256
R^2	0.995	0.998

its quality relative to that of the 1966 Chevrolet. Thus the arbitrary normalization for Chevrolet carries over to Ford, in the sense that only the trend of quality change of Fords relative to the trend in Chevrolets can be estimated. The overall trend remains unmeasurable.

A second hypothesis of interest on the relation between Chevrolets and Fords is that they have the same depreciation index. There is no strong economic reason to believe that this is true, but it is worth investigating for the purpose of economizing on parameters.

The two hypotheses just mentioned are linear restrictions on the parameters of the master model presented in Table 3.3. We consider the following two F-statistics: (1) for testing the hypothesis of perfect substitutability against the master model, and (2) for testing the hypothesis of equal depreciation indexes against the master model restricted to perfect substitutability. If Q_0 is the sum of squared residuals for the master model, Q_1 is the sum of squared residuals for the regression with only the constraint of perfect substitutability imposed, and Q_2 is the sum of squared residuals with both constraints imposed, then the statistics are $\frac{1}{5}(Q_1 - Q_0)/\frac{1}{40}Q_0$ and $\frac{1}{5}(Q_2 - Q_1)/\frac{1}{45}Q_1$. If in fact both constraints are true, these statistics both are distributed as F. Further, it is known that they are independent (Hogg 1961). This establishes a rigorous basis for separate tests of the two hypotheses.

The F-statistic for the hypothesis of perfect substitutability against the master model with no constraints across makes is 0.68 with 5 and 40 degrees of freedom. The corresponding critical F at the 0.05 level is 2.45. We conclude that there is no strong evidence against perfect substitutability, and, since there are reasonably persuasive economic arguments in its favor, we proceed by imposing the constraint in the remainder of this work.

The value of the F-statistic for the hypothesis of identical depreciation functions is 0.18 with 5 and 45 degrees of freedom; the critical F at the 0.05 level is 2.43. This suggests that it is not unreasonable to impose the

Table 8.4. Regression Results for Unrestricted Quality Change and Perfect Substitutability between Makes

Vintage	Index of quality				Price index (constrained equal for both makes)			Depreciation index (constrained equal for both makes)			Summary statistics	
	Chevrolet		Ford									
	$\log b_v$	b_v	$\log b_v$	b_v	Year	$\log \bar{p}_t$	$\bar{p}_t$	Age	$\log D_\tau$	D_τ		
1955	−0.354 (0.047)	0.702	−0.305 (0.047)	0.737	1961	7.416 (0.017)	$1663	1	0.000	1.000	Standard error	0.029
1956	−0.237 (0.037)	0.789	−0.275 (0.037)	0.760	1962	7.393 (0.015)	1625	2	−0.168 (0.012)	0.846	Sum of squared residuals	0.04351
1957	−0.190 (0.030)	0.827	−0.185 (0.030)	0.832	1963	7.346 (0.016)	1550	3	−0.321 (0.015)	0.726	R^2	0.996
1958	−0.180 (0.024)	0.836	−0.144 (0.024)	0.866	1964	7.384 (0.019)	1609	4	−0.474 (0.019)	0.623		
1959	−0.100 (0.020)	0.905	−0.096 (0.020)	0.909	1965	7.381 (0.023)	1605	5	−0.651 (0.024)	0.522		
1960	0 —	1.000	−0.027 (0.017)	0.973	1966	7.384 (0.027)	1610	6	−0.848 (0.029)	0.428		
1961	0.023 (0.017)	1.023	0.005 (0.017)	1.005	1967	7.362 (0.030)	1575					
1962	0.021 (0.019)	1.022	0.015 (0.019)	1.015								
1963	0.037 (0.023)	1.038	0.034 (0.023)	1.035								
1964	0.035 (0.027)	1.035	0.055 (0.027)	1.056								
1965	0.078 (0.033)	1.081	0.079 (0.033)	1.082								
1966	0 —	1.000	0.016 (0.042)	1.016								

Measurement of Quality Change

constraint, especially since the rather good fit of these regressions makes the test quite powerful.

The regression results for the model with both constraints are presented in Table 8.4. The quality coefficients for Chevrolet are essentially unchanged from their values in Table 3.3. The quality coefficients for Ford are also essentially unchanged, except they are renormalized to have a steeper trend. The arbitrary normalization used in the previous regression is replaced by the normalization, deduced from the data, that the 1960 Ford was 2.7-percent less efficient than the Chevrolet of the same year, but that the 1966 Ford was 1.6-percent more efficient than the 1966 Chevrolet. In other words, the trend in the relative price observed in Table 8.3 can be explained as an improper normalization for Ford. If, on the other hand, there had been substantial variations in the relative prices in Table 8.3 that could not be explained by renormalizing the Ford quality coefficients, then the null hypothesis of perfect substitutability would have been rejected.

The quality coefficients in Table 8.4 have been brought fairly close to each other by the renormalization, suggesting that it might be interesting to test the hypothesis that they are, in fact, the same. The F-statistic for this restriction on the results of Table 8.4 is 0.90 with 12 and 50 degrees of freedom, compared to the critical point of 1.96 at the 0.05 level. There is no strong evidence against this hypothesis, which amounts to holding that Chevrolets and Fords are identical in every respect. On the other hand, there is no convincing reason to believe that it is true, and it has the disadvantage that it is inconsistent with the hypothesis to be investigated in the next section.

The logs of the depreciation coefficients in Table 8.4 lie quite close to a straight line. They would lie exactly on it if depreciation were of the geometric or declining balance form. Since this form of depreciation corresponds to geometric deterioration or radioactive decay of capital, and that model of deterioration has such an important role in empirical capital measurement and in capital theory, it is of some interest to test the geometric restriction against the more general model of Table 8.4.[11] The constrained regression gives a rate of depreciation (or deterioration) of 0.1653 with standard error 0.0062, very close to the value implicit in the results of Table 8.4. Nonetheless, the null hypothesis is rejected; the F-statistic is 3.59 with 4 and 50 degrees of freedom, compared to a critical F at the 0.05 level of 2.57. Again, this test has quite high power; the proper

---

11. This is the only interesting null hypothesis about the deterioration function that can be stated as a linear restriction on the depreciation function.

interpretation of rejection of the geometric hypothesis is that while depreciation is almost certainly not geometric, the geometric function is probably a reasonable approximation for many purposes. Certainly, there are no grounds for believing that any very serious error has been committed by using a geometric deterioration function in calculating capital stock. On the other hand, the regressions of the present study should properly contain the unrestricted depreciation variables.

4. Estimates of Quality Change under the Assumption That It Is a Function of the Characteristics of Capital Goods: A Modified Hedonic Method

So far we have dealt with quality change as if it were a mystery to be measured but not explained. Except for the inability of our method to measure the overall exponential trend in quality change, its application to measuring the efficiency of pickup trucks has been relatively successful. Nevertheless, the trend is the single most interesting part of the quality index and of the quality-corrected price index, and it would leave things in rather an unsatisfactory state for it to remain unmeasured.

The measurement of the exponential trend in embodied technical change requires the development of a framework of capital measurement in which the notion has an unambiguous definition. As we have seen, if our framework is restricted to consideration of the *efficiency* of capital in use, the trend is ambiguous, and it would be senseless to try to estimate it. An alternative to this view is to suppose that embodied technical change, far from being a mystery, can be explained in terms of changes in the observed *characteristics* of capital goods. By characteristics we mean size, weight, power, and other information of an engineering nature. This hypothesis might be formulated as

(4.1) $$b_v = H(x_{v1}, \ldots, x_{vM}),$$

where $x_{v1}, \ldots, x_{vM}$ are the values of M variables measuring the characteristics of the capital good of vintage v.[12] This view can immediately remove the ambiguity in the definition of the trend in embodied technical change. When only the efficiency of capital in use was considered, an upward trend in efficiency could be attributed equally well to a trend in the efficiency of the use of capital goods (disembodied technical change) or

---

12. The depreciation index may also depend on the characteristics, but this possibility is not considered in the present paper.

Measurement of Quality Change

to a trend in the efficiency of capital itself. Any restriction on the b_v index that reduces its dimensionality by 1 eliminates this one-parameter ambiguity. As long as the number of unknown parameters in H is less than $T + N - 2$, the hypothesis of equation (4.1) is likely to eliminate the ambiguity.

The mere statement that a functional relation exists between a set of characteristics and the quality index may be enough to make it possible to estimate the trend in quality. If all of the characteristics are the same for two different vintages, then the existence of the functional relation requires that the quality index be the same for those two vintages. This fact can be used to replace the arbitrary normalization with a factual one and to identify the trend in embodied technical change.

Suppose it were known that two successive vintages had exactly the same embodied efficiency. Then the dummies for the separate vintages could be collapsed into a single variable with the value 1 for both vintages. The usefulness of this procedure lies in the fact that it would then be possible to add the dummy variable for vintage T that was previously outlawed. The hedonic information that two vintages have the same efficiency embodied in them is exactly a normalization of the kind needed to estimate an index of embodied technical change or quality for all vintages. The significant advance is that it is no longer an *arbitrary* normalization, so the resulting estimates include the exponential trend of quality change as well as departures from it. This method is properly attributed to Phillip Cagan, since he introduced it in a somewhat different framework in an important paper on the measurement of quality change from the prices of used automobiles (1965). Briefly, Cagan's method is the following. Under the assumption of geometric depreciation, it is possible to estimate the rate of depreciation from the ratios of the prices of two successive vintages known to have the same quality coefficient. For example, if the 1958 and 1959 models are the same, then $1 - \delta$ can be estimated as the average of the ratio of the price of the 1958 model to the price of the 1959 model in 1960, 1961, and subsequent years. Then the ratios between the quality coefficients of successive vintages can be estimated as the averages of the ratios of the prices of the models in the secondhand market, corrected for depreciation as calculated previously.

Two objections to Cagan's procedure can be raised. First, it is not explicitly econometric; that is, it does not attempt to calculate statistically optimal estimates starting from an assumption about the nature of the random disturbances. This is a relatively minor shortcoming, but it does mean that there is no indication of the reliability of Cagan's estimates. The econometric method mentioned earlier in this section could be used to carry out an econometric version of Cagan's method; it does not seem likely that the results could be very different from the application of his original method.[13]

Cagan himself raises a much more fundamental objection to his method: It is sensitive in the extreme to errors in the choice of identical vintages. Any departure of the actual rate of growth in efficiency from vintage v^* to vintage $v^* + 1$ from its assumed value of zero is automatically manifested as an error of the same magnitude in the rate of growth of efficiency in every vintage. The result is that the overall trend in efficiency is estimated with great unreliability, although, once again, relatively accurate estimates of departures from the trend can be obtained.

Since information on the characteristics of capital seems to provide the most likely approach to identifying the trend in quality change, either by something like Cagan's method or by parametrizing the function H, it is useful to examine the data at hand on the characteristics of pickup trucks. In Table 8.5 we present data on seven characteristics published in the *Used Car Guide*. The first two characteristics, wheelbase and shipping weight, are general indicators of change from one model to the next. The next four characteristics refer specifically to the engine. The first of these, displacement, changes only when a completely redesigned engine block is introduced—there were only two such changes for Chevrolet and one for Ford in the entire period. The second engine characteristic, the ratio of bore to stroke, measures the modernity of the engine design; in only one year did it decrease, and that was for the 1966 Chevrolet, which does rather badly no matter what specification is used. The rated horsepower and torque are also given; these change much more frequently than the characteristics of block design. The final characteristic is tire width.

A variant of Cagan's method is suggested by these data on characteristics. For both makes, there are at least two pairs of vintages that are apparently identical. Putting two constraints on the quality index for each make will go far to meet the second objection to Cagan's method. The constraints chosen are $b_{1956} = b_{1957}$ and $b_{1961} = b_{1962}$ for Chevrolet, and $b_{1957} = b_{1958}$ and $b_{1962} = b_{1963}$ for Ford. Relative to the model of Table 8.4, this involves one substantive constraint on the Chevrolet quality index (one of the constraints replaces the arbitrary normalization) and two on the Ford quality index. The data of Table 8.5 suggest additional constraints for both makes, but it is perhaps most interesting to

---

13. Actually, no new regressions would have to be run to do this. The results of section 3 could simply be renormalized so that $b_{v^*} = b_{v^*+1}$ instead of $b_T = 1$, where v^* and $v^* + 1$ are vintages known to have the same quality coefficient.

Measurement of Quality Change

Table 8.5. Characteristics of Half-ton Pickup Trucks

Year	L	W	D	B	H	Q	T
			Chevrolet				
1955	115	3137	233.5	0.905	118	204	6.00
1956	114	3217	233.5	0.905	140	210	6.70
1957	114	3217	233.5	0.905	140	210	6.70
1958	114	3273	233.5	0.905	145	215	6.70
1959	114	3260	233.5	0.905	135	217	6.70
1960	114	3395	233.5	0.905	135	217	6.70
1961	114	3390	233.5	0.905	135	217	6.70
1962	114	3385	233.5	0.905	135	217	6.70
1963	114	3190	230.0	1.192	125	210	6.70
1964	114	3175	230.0	1.192	125	210	6.70
1965	114	3190	230.0	1.192	140	220	7.75
1966	115	3195	250.0	1.096	155	235	7.75
			Ford				
1955	110	3080	223	1.008	118	195	6.00
1956	110	3070	223	1.008	133	202	6.70
1957	110	3110	223	1.008	139	207	6.70
1958	110	3110	223	1.008	139	207	6.70
1959	110	3098	223	1.008	139	207	6.70
1960	110	3105	223	1.008	139	203	6.70
1961	114	3129	223	1.008	135	200	6.70
1962	114	3244	223	1.008	135	200	6.70
1963	114	3254	223	1.008	135	200	6.70
1964	114	3220	223	1.008	135	200	6.70
1965	115	3170	240	1.257	150	234	7.75
1966	115	3260	240	1.257	150	234	7.75

L = Wheelbase, inches.
W = Shipping weight, pounds.
D = Displacement, cubic inches.
B = Ratio of bore to stroke.
H = Horsepower.
Q = Torque, pound-feet.
T = Tire width, inches.

look at results for a small number of constraints. These results are presented in Table 8.6. The quality indexes for both makes are similar to those in Table 8.4, except that the upward trend is much less pronounced,

Table 8.6. Regression Results with Constrained Quality Index for Apparently Identical Vintages

Vintage	Index of quality				Year	Price Index (constrained equal for both makes)		Age	Depreciation Index (constrained equal for both makes)		Summary statistics	
	$\log b_v$	b_v	$\log b_v$	b_v		$\log \bar{p}_t$	$\bar{p}_t$		$\log D_\tau$	D_τ		
1955	−0.250 (0.063)	0.779	−0.202 (0.063)	0.818	1961	7.415 (0.017)	$1661	1	0.000	1.000	Standard error	0.029
1956	−0.138 (0.040)	0.871	−0.192 (0.049)	0.826	1962	7.413 (0.020)	1658	2	−1.188 (0.016)	0.829	Sum of squared residuals	0.04636
1957			0.111 (0.031)	0.895	1963	7.388 (0.027)	1616	3	−0.361 (0.025)	0.697	R^2	0.996
1958	−0.139 (0.029)	0.870			1964	7.446 (0.035)	1712	4	−0.535 (0.035)	0.586		
1959	−0.080 (0.021)	0.923	−0.075 (0.021)	0.928	1965	7.463 (0.046)	1742	5	−0.734 (0.044)	0.480		

Measurement of Quality Change

Year									
1960	0.000	1.000		0.973	1966	7.486	1784	6	−0.950	0.387
	—					(0.056)			(0.054)	
1961	−0.008	0.992	−0.027	0.985	1967	7.485	1781			
	(0.022)		(0.017)			(0.067)				
			−0.016							
			(0.020)							
1962	−0.025	0.975	−0.027	0.974						
	(0.037)		(0.030)							
1963	−0.048	0.954	−0.027	0.973						
	(0.048)		(0.048)							
1964	−0.024	0.976	−0.023	0.977						
	(0.059)		(0.059)							
1965	−0.123	0.884	−0.107	0.898						
	(0.073)		(0.073)							
1966										

and in fact disappears after 1960. As suggested in Section 3, the arbitrary normalization used in the earlier regressions appears to have *overstated* the true trend in quality change, if the present results are to be trusted. As a consequence of the much lower rate of quality improvement (essentially zero for the 1960–1965 models), the quality-corrected price index in the second part of Table 8.6 shows evidence of a positive true rate of inflation.

Since the present regression is a constrained version of the regression of Table 8.4, it is possible to carry out a formal test of the hypothesis that the apparently identical vintages have the same quality coefficients. The F-statistic for this test is 1.09 with 3 and 50 degrees of freedom, compared to the critical F at the 0.05 level of 2.80. There is thus no strong evidence against the hypothesis.

If we are willing to make stronger assumptions about the function H, then estimates of the quality coefficients can be obtained that are substantially better than those just presented, provided the assumptions are true. This requires a departure from the nonparametric character of the earlier parts of this study. Thus our remaining discussion of estimation under the "hedonic"[14] view of embodied technical change is carried out under the assumption that a log-linear functional form is a satisfactory approximation to the function, H. Since b_v is still an index, we need to restrict the elasticities, say, $\alpha_1, \ldots, \alpha_M$ to values that guarantee that $b_1 = 1$. This can be done by measuring all of the x-variables as ratios to their base-year values:

(4.2) $$\hat{x}_{vj} = x_{vj}/x_{1j}, \quad j = 1, \ldots, M.$$

The H-function obtained is

(4.3) $$\log b_v = \alpha_1 \log \hat{x}_{v1} + \cdots + \alpha_M \log \hat{x}_{vM}.$$

Our previous unrestricted specification of Section 3 is a special case of this one, in which each x-variable is a dummy variable having the value 1 for one vintage and the value 0 for all other vintages. For Chevrolet, there is one dummy variable for each vintage except vintage 1 and vintage T, or $M = N + T - 3$ in all. In the regression of Table 8.6, two of the dummies have the value 1 for two successive vintages, for both Chevrolet and Ford.

Now we proceed to a consideration of the full hedonic specification, in which engineering variables (rather than dummy variables) appear in

---

14. "Hedonic" is hardly the right term in dealing with ordinary pickup trucks, but its use is suggested by the related body of literature on automobiles.

Measurement of Quality Change

the expression for b_v. Both Cagan and Griliches (in his survey of hedonic methods, 1967) refer to Cagan's method as an alternative or supplement to the ordinary hedonic method. Our proposal is essentially to combine the two approaches in a single econometric equation. Note that this requires a slight formal modification of the traditional hedonic view, since that view relates the characteristics of a capital good directly to the price of the capital good when new. In our view, characteristics determine the efficiency of capital goods, and the present value of future efficiency determines the prices of new and used capital goods.

Although most of our right-hand variables are engineering measurements in our full hedonic method, it should be recognized that many of them serve as dummy variables as well. Our interest is directed more toward the derived estimates of b_v than toward the regression coefficients $\alpha_1, \ldots, \alpha_M$. If, as seems inevitable, some important characteristics are omitted from our x-variables, the α-coefficients may be seriously biased, but as long as some of the included variables are highly correlated with the omitted ones, the estimates of b_v may be fairly close to the truth. Since engineering changes frequently occur together, there is reason to hope that the omitted variables are fairly highly correlated with the included ones.

Our method may be viewed as a substantial generalization of Cagan's method. Instead of taking a single pair of vintages and constraining their embodied efficiencies to be equal, the embodied efficiencies of *every* pair of vintages with similar characteristics are constrained to be equal. This fact alone makes the method significantly less arbitrary than Cagan's. Furthermore, we make the not unreasonable assumption that the contribution to efficiency of each characteristic is proportional to the departure of the characteristic from its base year value. This constrains the estimated efficiencies in years with only small changes in the characteristics to be close together. This feature is entirely absent from Cagan's method. The consequence of the imposition of these constraints is to reduce the number of right-hand variables from the number of vintages to the number of characteristics, with a corresponding improvement in the quality of the estimates, provided the constraints are true.

Experimentation with a variety of hedonic specifications indicated that it was probably useful to include three dummy variables in the regressions in addition to the variables measuring characteristics. These were (1) a dummy variable with value zero for Chevrolet and 1 for Ford, to measure any constant difference in quality between the two makes; (2) a dummy variable for the 1955 Chevrolet, because of a mid-year model change, and (3) a dummy variable for the 1966 Ford, because of a change in the front suspension that is not covered by the measured characteristics.

Table 8.7. Regression Results for the Hedonic Specification

Price index (constrained equal for both makes)			Coefficients of characteristics			Depreciation index (constrained equal for both makes)			Summary statistics	
Year	$\log \bar{p}_t$	$\bar{p}_t$	Characteristic	Chevrolet	Ford	Age	$\log D_\tau$	D_τ		
1961	7.410 (0.015)	$1652	Wheelbase	—	2.25 (0.77)	1	0.000	1.000	Standard error	0.0292
1962	7.410 (0.013)	1653	Weight	1.82 (0.41)	−0.51 (0.46)	2	−0.189 (0.013)	0.828	Sum of squared residuals	0.04959
1963	7.387 (0.014)	1615	Ratio of bore to stroke	0.01 (0.17)	2.40 (0.66)	3	−0.366 (0.015)	0.693	R^2	0.995
1964	7.450 (0.016)	1720	Horsepower	−0.88 (0.25)	3.95 (0.75)	4	−0.542 (0.018)	0.581		
1965	7.470 (0.019)	1754	Torque	−0.20 (0.52)	−3.26 (0.88)	5	−0.745 (0.022)	0.475		
1966	7.495 (0.024)	1798	Tire width	0.77 (0.32)	−3.19 (0.84)	6	−0.964 (0.027)	0.381		
1967	7.495 (0.028)	1799	1955 dummy	−0.13 (0.05)	—					
			1966 dummy	—	−0.07 (0.04)					
			Ford dummy	—	−0.022 (0.015)					

Measurement of Quality Change

Further, the displacement variable was excluded for both makes; its coefficient was essentially zero for Chevrolet and the variable was linearly dependent on the other characteristics for Ford.

Results for the hedonic specification are given in Table 8.7. The quality-corrected price index presented in the first part agrees quite closely with the index in Table 8.6, except that it is slightly (but not significantly) more inflationary than the earlier results. There is a compensating increase in the rate of depreciation, as can be seen by comparing the third parts of the two tables.

The coefficients of the characteristics and vintage dummy variables are given in the second part of Table 8.7. These can be interpreted as the elasticities of quality with respect to the various characteristics. Two disturbing features of these estimates are immediately apparent. First, many of the coefficients are surprisingly large, especially in the case of Ford. Second, there is complete disagreement between the coefficient for the same characteristic for Chevrolet and Ford. The latter is completely inconsistent with the basic hypothesis of previous hedonic work, in which the contribution of characteristics has been measured in a cross section of different makes. The hypothesis that the hedonic coefficients are actually the same is emphatically rejected in the results of Table 8.7. The F-statistic is 13.69 with 5 and 58 degrees of freedom, compared to a critical F of 2.38 at the 0.05 level. This seems to be strong evidence that the measured characteristics are seriously incomplete and are serving as dummy variables for important changes in unmeasured characteristics.

The quality index implicit in the hedonic regression can be calculated by applying the coefficients to the matrix of characteristics. In addition, the standard errors of the quality coefficients can be calculated by the usual method for the sampling properties of a linear combination of regression coefficients. These are presented in Table 8.8. The quality indexes for both makes are quite similar, except that, as mentioned earlier, the rate of quality change here is slightly lower than in the indexes in Table 8.6. The standard errors are substantially smaller for the hedonic indexes than for the earlier ones, exactly because additional information in the form of the hedonic constraints is used in the hedonic indexes.

The hedonic model is to a very close approximation a constrained version of the model of Table 8.6. The approximation arises because the weight of the Chevrolet dropped by 5 pounds between 1961 and 1962, and that of the Ford increased by 10 pounds between 1962 and 1963. In both cases the small change was ignored in the earlier results, but appears in the results of Table 8.8. The latter coefficients fail to meet the constraint of the earlier model by 0.002 in both cases, presumably an amount small

Table 8.8. Quality Index Calculated from Hedonic Regression Results

Vintage	Chevrolet		Ford	
	$\log b_v$	b_v	$\log b_v$	b_v
1955	−0.231	0.794	−0.182	0.834
	(0.043)	0.794	(0.043)	
1956	−0.124	0.884	−0.175	0.840
	(0.026)		(0.033)	
1957	−0.124	0.884	−0.087	0.917
	(0.026)		(0.017)	
1958	−0.128	0.880	−0.087	0.917
	(0.019)		(0.017)	
1959	−0.074	0.929	−0.085	0.919
	(0.017)		(0.018)	
1960	—	1.000	−0.022	0.978
	—		(0.015)	
1961	−0.003	0.997	−0.013	0.987
	(0.001)		(0.014)	
1962	−0.005	0.995	−0.031	0.969
	(0.001)		(0.014)	
1963	−0.036	0.965	−0.033	0.968
	(0.018)		(0.015)	
1964	−0.045	0.956	−0.027	0.973
	(0.018)		(0.013)	
1965	−0.033	0.968	−0.032	0.969
	(0.030)		(0.030)	
1966	−0.134	0.875	−0.117	0.889
	(0.037)		(0.040)	

enough to ignore. The approximate F-statistic for testing the hedonic constraint (exact except for the difficulty just mentioned) is 0.74, with 5 and 53 degrees of freedom, compared to the critical F of 2.40 at the 0.05 level.

5. The Uses of Secondhand Market Data in Price Measurement

The results of the previous two sections are sufficiently encouraging to suggest that secondhand market data are potentially a rich source for price measurement. We have demonstrated, implicitly, two uses of these

Measurement of Quality Change

data. First, the relative qualities of different vintages can be inferred from their relative prices, except that identification of the trend in quality change requires the use of additional information. The hedonic method of Section 4 was a not entirely successful attempt at this. Second, a price index can be calculated as a suitably adjusted average of the prices of all of the vintages observed in each year. The adjustments required for price measurement are for both quality change and depreciation. Even if the price index sought is not to be corrected for quality change, it is essential to take account of quality change in calculating it. We will give an example of the need for this below. Both of these uses of secondhand data appear implicitly in our regressions; the distinction between them is logical rather than practical.

To compare the results of our calculations with those based on other methods, we present in Table 8.9 a set of price indexes for pickup trucks

Table 8.9. Various Price Indexes

Year	Pickup trucks, quality-corrected, this study[a] (1)	Ford pickup trucks, index of (1) without quality correction[b] (2)	Ford pickup trucks, no allowance for quality change, this study[c] (3)	WPI, motor trucks[d] (4)	CPI, new cars[e] (5)	CPI, used cars[f] (6)	List price, Fords[g] (7)
1961	1.000	1.000	1.000	1.000	1.000	1.000	1.000
1962	1.001	0.983	1.032	0.998	0.996	1.141	1.007
1963	0.978	0.959	1.051	0.989	0.986	1.190	1.018
1964	1.041	1.026	1.121	0.985	0.992	1.238	0.999
1965	1.062	1.043	1.139	0.995	0.947	1.289	1.000
1966	1.088	0.980	1.189	0.998	0.945	1.212	1.052
1967	1.089	—	1.173	1.014	0.946	1.217	1.118

[a] $\bar{p}_t$ from Table 8.7, converted to index
[b] $\bar{p}_t b_t$ for Ford from Tables 8.7 and 8.8, converted to index
[c] $\bar{p}_t$ for Ford from Table 8.2, converted to index
[d] Wholesale Price Index, motor truck component, Bureau of Labor Statistics (April of given year)
[e] Consumer Price Index, new car component, BLS (March of given year)
[f] Consumer Price Index, used car component, BLS (March of given year)
[g] Advertised delivered price, Ford pickup, *Used Car Guide*.

and related capital goods. The first column is the set of price estimates, $\bar{p}_t$, from Table 8.7, reduced to an index based in 1961. The second column gives the price per new truck estimated from the same regression; it is calculated as the price per unit of efficiency, $\bar{p}_t$, multiplied by the efficiency of a new truck, b_t. This is the price index not corrected for quality, mentioned above. The third column is the set of $\bar{p}_t$ coefficients from Table 8.2, reduced to an index. This index is not only not corrected for quality change, but the existence of quality change was ignored in calculating it. The fourth column gives the Wholesale Price Index for motor trucks, the most detailed index available from the Bureau of Labor Statistics for pickup trucks. The fifth column is the well-know Consumer Price Index for new automobiles, incorporating significant corrections for quality change; the sixth column is the used car price index from the same source. Finally, the seventh column is an index of the list price of new Ford pickup trucks.

The quality-corrected price index from the present study, column 1, shows inflation beginning in 1964, while the list price index (column 7) is stable until 1966, and the WPI is stable through 1967 (it moves upward sharply in 1968). Under our basic hypothesis of perfect substitutability between new and used trucks, column 1 can be interpreted as an index of the actual transaction price for new trucks. Thus, if the hypothesis is even approximately correct, the comparison of our index with either the list price index or the WPI suggests a substantial reduction in the difference between list and transaction prices for the early years of the recent economic expansion. The Wholesale Price Index behaves more like the list price index than like our estimate of the actual price. If our results were assumed to be representative of all durable goods, a significant reinterpretation of the aggregate pattern of inflation since 1964 would be in order, since the current evidence is derived from the WPI. No such claim is made here, however.

In spite of the fact that pickup trucks and automobiles are probably fairly close substitutes in production, there is no observable connection between the quality-corrected index for pickups in column 1 and the quality-corrected index for automobiles from the CPI in column 5. The CPI does not show any response at all to the inflationary pressure of the years after 1963. Furthermore, it has a slight downward trend of just under 1 percent per year, while our index rises at a rate of over 1 percent per year. Either automobiles are becoming 2-percent per year less expensive to produce than pickup trucks, or the quality corrections in one or both indexes are systematically biased. Again, no strong claims in favor of the method of this study are sustained by the evidence.

Measurement of Quality Change

Finally, we note that the index calculated from Table 8.2 (column 3) and the CPI for used automobiles behave in very much the same way. The first index is essentially an average over all surviving vintages of prices in the secondhand market, adjusted for depreciation but not for differences in quality. The CPI is probably calculated in much the same way. Both appear to suffer from the same error: Quality improved rapidly in the late fifties and remained roughly constant in the early sixties, for both pickups and automobiles (on the latter, see Triplett 1966). In each succeeding year in the sixties, a price observation for a low-quality vintage of the fifties is dropped from the calculation of the average price over vintages, and a sixties-quality observation is added. The result is a false inflationary bias as long as low-quality vintages are being dropped. This can be seen in both columns 3 and 6—they rise sharply during the noninflationary years 1961–1964, and then remain roughly constant after 1964. The appropriate way to calculate a price index without quality correction from secondhand price data is to adjust each vintage price for its quality relative to the quality of the current new unit. This is the method used in calculating column 2, which is substantially different from (and more reasonable than) the index of column 3, although it is derived from the same data.

Bibliography and Index

Bibliography

Part I of the bibliography, "Price Indexes and Quality Change," lists the important books and papers in this field. Most of the works are cited by author and date in this volume. Part II, "Other Works Cited," lists other works referred to in the book.

I. Price Indexes and Quality Change

Adelman, Irma. 1960. "On an Index of Quality Change." Paper given at the August 1960 meeting of the American Statistical Association, Stanford, Calif.

Adelman, Irma, and Griliches, Zvi. 1961. "On an Index of Quality Change." *Journal of the American Statistical Association* 56:535–548.

Administered Prices, see U.S. Senate.

Allen, R. G. D. 1963. "Price Index Numbers." *Review of the International Statistical Institute* 31:281–297.

Arrow, K. J. 1958. "The Measurement of Price Changes." In *The Relationship of Prices to Economic Stability and Growth*, U.S. Congress, Joint Economic Committee, pp. 77–88. Washington: Government Printing Office.

Bailey, M. J., Muth, R. F., and Nourse, H. O. 1963. "A Regression Method for Real Estate Price Index Construction." *Journal of the American Statistical Association* 58:933–942.

Barzel, Y. 1964. "The Production Function and Technical Change in the Steam Power Industry." *Journal of Political Economy* 72:133–150.

——— 1969. "Productivity and the Price of Medical Services." *Journal of Political Economy* 77:1014–1027.

Becker, G. S. 1965. "A Theory of the Allocation of Time." *Economic Journal* 75:493–516.

Bibliography

Brady, Dorothy S. 1966. "Price Deflators for Final Product Estimates." In *Output, Employment, and Productivity in the U.S. after 1800*, Studies in Income and Wealth, Vol. 30, pp. 91–116. New York: National Bureau of Economic Research.

Brown, S. L. 1964. "Price Variation in New Houses, 1959–1961." Staff Working Paper in Economics and Statistics, No. 6. Washington: Bureau of the Census. Mimeographed.

Burstein, M. L. 1961. "Measurement of Quality Change in Consumer Durables." *Manchester School of Economics and Social Studies* 29:267–279.

Cagan, Phillip. 1965. "Measuring Quality Changes and the Purchasing Power of Money: An Exploratory Study of Automobiles." *National Banking Review* 3:217–236. (Reprinted in this volume.)

Chow, Gregory C. 1967. "Technological Change and the Demand for Computers." *American Economic Review* 57:1117–1130.

Court, Andrew T. 1939. "Hedonic Price Indexes with Automotive Examples." In *The Dynamics of Automobile Demand*, pp. 99–117. New York: General Motors Corporation.

Cowling, Keith, and Cubbin, John. 1970. "Price, Quality and Advertising Competition: An Econometric Investigation of the U.K. Car Market." St. Louis: Department of Economics, Washington University. Mimeographed.

Cowling, Keith, and Rayner, A. J. 1970. "Price, Quality, and Market Share." *Journal of Political Economy* 78:1292–1309.

Cramer, J. S. 1966. "Een prijsindex van nieuwe personenauto's, 1950–1965." *Statistica Neerlandica* 20:215–239.

Dacy, Douglas C. 1964. "A Price and Productivity Index for a Nonhomogeneous Product." *Journal of the American Statistical Association* 59:469–480.

——— 1965. "Productivity and Price Trends in Construction since 1947." *Review of Economics and Statistics* 47:406–411.

Davidson, J. B., McCuen, G. W., and Blasingame, R. U. 1933. *Report of an Inquiry into Changes in Quality Values of Farm Machines between 1910–1914 and 1932*. St. Joseph, Michigan: American Society of Agricultural Engineers.

Dean, C. R., and DePodwin, H. J. 1961. "Product Variation and Price Indexes: A Case Study of Electrical Apparatus." *Proceedings of the Business and Economic Statistics Section*, pp. 271–279. Washington: American Statistical Association.

Denison, E. F. 1957. "Theoretical Aspects of Quality Change, Capital Consumption, and Net Capital Formation." In *Problems of Capital Formation*, Studies in Income and Wealth, Vol. 19, pp. 215–226. New York: National Bureau of Economic Research.

Dhrymes, Phoebus J. 1967. "On the Measurement of Price and Quality Changes in Some Consumer Capital Goods." *American Economic Review* 57:501–518.

Fettig, Lyle P. 1963. "Adjusting Farm Tractor Prices for Quality Changes, 1950–1962." *Journal of Farm Economics* 45:599–611.

Fisher, Franklin M. 1965. "Embodied Technical Change and the Existence of an Aggregate Capital Stock." *Review of Economic Studies* 32:263–288.

Bibliography

Fisher, Franklin M., Griliches, Zvi, and Kaysen, Carl. 1962. "The Costs of Automobile Model Changes since 1949." *Journal of Political Economy* 79:433–451.

Fisher, Franklin M., and Shell, Karl. 1967. "Taste and Quality Change in the Pure Theory of the True Cost-of-Living Index." In *Value, Capital, and Growth: Essays in Honour of Sir John Hicks*, ed. J. N. Wolfe. Edinburgh: University of Edinburgh Press. (Reprinted in this volume.)

——— 1970. "The Pure Theory of the National-Output Deflator." Working Paper No. 59. Cambridge, M.I.T. Mimeographed.

Gainsbrugh, M. R., and Backman, Jules. 1966. *Inflation and the Price Indexes*. New York: National Industrial Conference Board. Also printed as Joint Committee Print, 89th Congress, 2nd Session, Washington: Government Printing Office.

Gavett, Thomas W. 1967a. "Quality and a Pure Price Index." *Monthly Labor Review* 90:16–20.

——— 1967b. "Research on Quality Adjustments in Price Indexes." Unpublished Bureau of Labor Statistics memorandum, Washington.

Gordon, R. A. 1961. "Differential Changes in the Prices of Consumers' and Capital Goods." *American Economic Review* 51:937–957.

Gordon, R. J. 1970. "Recent Developments in the Measurement of Price Indexes for Fixed Capital Goods." *Proceedings of the Business and Economic Statistics Section*. Washington: American Statistical Association.

——— 1971. "Measurement Bias in Price Indexes for Capital Goods." *Review of Income and Wealth*, Series 17(2).

Griliches, Zvi. 1961. "Hedonic Price Indexes for Automobiles: An Econometric Analysis of Quality Change." In *The Price Statistics of the Federal Government*, General Series, No. 73, pp. 137–196. New York: National Bureau of Economic Research. (Reprinted in this volume.)

——— 1964. "Notes on the Measurement of Price and Quality Changes." In *Models of Income Determination*, Studies in Income and Wealth, Vol. 28, pp. 301–404. Princeton: National Bureau of Economic Research.

——— 1967. "Hedonic Price Indexes Revisited: Some Notes on the State of the Art." *Proceedings of the Business and Economic Statistics Section*, pp. 324–332. Washington: American Statistical Association. (Reprinted in revised form in this volume.)

Hall, Robert E. 1968. "Technical Change and Capital from the Point of View of the Dual." *Review of Economic Studies* 35:35–46.

Hanoch, Giora. 1965. "Personal Earnings and Investment in Schooling." Ph.D. dissertation, University of Chicago.

Hofsten, Erland von. 1952. *Price Indexes and Quality Changes*. Stockholm: Bokforlaget Forum AB.

Hoover, Ethel D. 1961. "The CPI and Problems of Quality Change." *Monthly Labor Review* 84:1175–1185.

Houthakker, H. S. 1951–1952. "Compensated Changes in Quantities and Qualities Consumed." *Review of Economic Studies* 19:155–164.

Jorgenson, D. W., and Griliches, Zvi. 1967. "The Explanation of Productivity Change." *Review of Economic Studies* 34:249-283.

Knight, Kenneth E., and Barr, James L. 1966. "Micro Measurement of Technological Change in the Computer Industry." Unpublished paper, presented at the Inter-University Committee Conference on Micro-Economics of Technological Change in Philadelphia, March 24, 1966.

Kravis, Irving B., and Lipsey, Robert E. 1969. "International Price Comparisons." *International Economic Review* 10:233-246. (Reprinted in revised form in this volume.)

——— 1970. *Price Competitiveness in World Trade*. New York: National Bureau of Economic Research.

Lancaster, K. 1966. "A New Approach to Consumer Theory." *Journal of Political Economy* 74:132-157.

Larsgaard, O. A., and Mack, Louis J. 1961. "Compact Cars in the Consumer Price Index." *Monthly Labor Review* 84:522-523.

Levine, L. S. 1960. "A Small Problem in the Analysis of Growth." *Review of Economics and Statistics* 42:225-228.

Mack, Louis J. 1955. "Automobile Prices in the Consumer Price Index." *Monthly Labor Review* 72:5.

Magnusson, Bjorn, and Aberg, Carl Johan. 1961. "Kbalitetsvariationer och Produktblandning vid Prisindexberakningar [Quality Variations and Product-Mix in Price Index Computations]." *Ekonomisk Tidskrift* [Swedish Journal of Economics] 43:201-208.

Malmquist, S. 1953. "Index Numbers and Indifference Surfaces." *Trabajos de Estadistica* 4:209-242.

Musgrave, J. C. 1969. "The Measurement of Price Changes in Construction." *Journal of the American Statistical Association* 64:771-786.

Muth, R. F. 1966. "Household Production and Consumer Demand Functions." *Econometrica* 34:699-708.

Nicholson, J. L. 1967. "The Measurement of Quality Changes." *Economic Journal* 77:512-530.

Price Statistics of the Federal Government, The. 1961. General Series, No. 73. New York: National Bureau of Economic Research. Also published as U.S. Congress, Joint Economic Committee, *Government Price Statistics, Hearings*, 87th Congress, 1st session, Part 1, Jan. 24, 1961. Washington: Government Printing Office. (Cited as *Price Statistics* 1961.)

Rayner, A. J. 1968. "Price Quality Relationships in a Durable Asset." *Journal of Agricultural Economics* 19:231-249.

Rayner, A. J., and Cowling, Keith. 1967. "Demand for a Durable Input: An Analysis of the U.K. Market for Farm Tractors." *Review of Economics and Statistics* 49:590-598.

Rees Albert. 1961. "Alternative Retail Price Indexes for Selected Nondurable Goods, 1947-1959." In *The Price Statistics of the Federal Government*, General Series, No. 73, pp. 137-172. New York: National Bureau of Economic Research.

Bibliography

Richter, M. K. 1966. "Invariance Axioms and Economic Indexes." *Econometrica* 34:749–755.

Rothwell, Doris P. 1964. "The Consumer Price Index: Pricing, and Calculation Procedures." Unpublished paper. Partially incorporated in chapters 9 and 10 of *The Consumer Price Index: History and Techniques*, Bureau of Labor Statistics Bulletin, No. 1517, Washington: Government Printing Office.

——— 1966. "Quality Adjustment in CPI." Unpublished Bureau of Labor Statistics memorandum, Washington.

Stone, Richard. 1956. *Quantity and Price Indexes in National Accounts*. Paris: Organization for European Economic Co-operation.

Stotz, Margaret S. 1966. "Introductory Prices of 1966 Automobile Models." *Monthly Labor Review* 89:178–185.

Triplett, Jack E. 1966. "The Measurement of Quality Change." Ph.D. dissertation, University of California.

——— 1969. "Automobiles and Hedonic Quality Measurement." *Journal of Political Economy* 77:408–417.

——— 1970. "The Quality Problem: A Survey of Empirical Studies Relating to Quality Bias in Price Indexes." St. Louis, Washington University. Mimeographed.

——— 1971. "The Theory of Hedonic Quality Measurement and Its Use in Price Indexes." BLS Staff Paper 6. Washington: U.S. Department of Labor, Bureau of Labor Statistics.

U.S. Congress, Joint Economic Committee. 1961. *Government Price Statistics*, Hearings, 87th Congress, 1st session, Part 2, May 1–5, 1961. Washington: Government Printing Office. (For Part 1, See *Price Statistics* 1961.)

U.S. Department of Labor. 1955. *Average Retail Prices: Collection and Calculation Techniques and Problems*. Bulletin No. 1182. Washington: Government Printing Office.

——— 1966. *Bureau of Labor Statistics Handbook of Methods for Surveys and Studies*. Bulletin No. 1458. Washington: Government Printing Office.

——— 1967. "Seasonal Demand and Used Car Prices." *Monthly Labor Review* 90:12–16.

——— n.d. "Specification Pricing in General." Unpublished Bureau of Labor Statistics memorandum.

U.S. Senate, Subcommittee on Antitrust and Monopoly. 1958. *Administered Prices*, Hearings, 85th Congress, 2nd session, Part 7: *Automobiles* (Appendix). Washington: Government Printing Office. (Cited as *Administered Prices*.)

Wilkerson, Marvin. 1964. "Measurement of Sampling Error in the Consumer Price Index: First Results." *Proceedings of the Business and Economic Statistics Section*, pp. 220–230. Washington: American Statistical Association.

Yoshihara, K., Furuya, K., and Suzuki, T. 1970. "The Problem of Accounting for Productivity Change in the Construction Index." SEAS Discussion Paper No. 5, Kyoto University. Mimeographed.

II. Other Works Cited

Arrow, K. J., and Enthoven, A. C. 1961. "Quasi-concave Programming." *Econometrica* 29:779-800.

Automotive Industries. Philadelphia: Chilton Company. Various issues.

Automobile Manufacturers Association. 1963. *Automobile Facts and Figures.* Detroit.

Ben-David, S., and Tomek, W. G. 1965. "Allowing for Slope and Intercept Changes in Regression Analysis." Agricultural Economics Report 179. Department of Agricultural Economics, Cornell University, Ithaca, N. Y. Mimeographed.

Box, G. E., and Cox, D. R. 1964. "An Analysis of Transformations." *Journal of the Royal Statistical Society* (B), 26(2):211-252.

Chow, Gregory C. 1960. "Tests of Equality between Sets of Coefficients in Two Linear Regressions." *Econometrica* 28:591-605.

Cox, D. R. 1961. "Tests of Separate Families of Hypotheses." In *Proceedings of the Fourth Berkeley Symposium on Mathematical Statistics,* ed. J. Neyman. New York: Wiley.

——— 1962. "Further Results on Tests of Separate Families of Hypotheses." *Journal of the Royal Statistical Society* 24:406.

Graybill, F. A. 1961. *An Introduction to Linear Statistical Models,* Vol. 1. New York: McGraw-Hill.

Greenberg, Edward. 1969. "Multicollinearity Revisited Again." Washington University, St. Louis. Unpublished paper.

Haitovsky, Yoel. 1969. "A Note on the Maximization of $\bar{R}^2$." *The American Statistician* 23:20-21.

Hogg, R. V. 1961. "On the Resolution of Statistical Hypotheses." *Journal of the American Statistical Association* 56:978-989.

Home Appliance Trade-In Blue Book, 1966. Madison, Wis., National Appliance Publishing Co. Various issues.

Hotelling, Harold. 1925. "A General Mathematical Theory of Depreciation." *Journal of the American Statistical Association* 20:340-353.

Jennings, B. H., and Obert, E. F. 1944. *Internal Combustion Engines.* Scranton, Pa.: International Textbook Co.

Kendall, M. G. 1957. *A Course in Multivariate Analysis.* New York: Hafner.

Leontief, W. W. 1947*a*. "Introduction to a Theory of the Internal Structure of Functional Relationships." *Econometrica* 15:361-373.

——— 1947*b*. "A Note on the Interrelation of Subsets of Independent Variables of a Continuous Function with Continuous First Derivatives." *Bulletin of the American Mathematical Society* 53:343-350.

Mart. New York: Buttenheim Publishing. Various issues.

Mood, A. 1950. *Introduction to the Theory of Statistics.* New York: McGraw-Hill.

Morgan, James N., and Sonquist, John A. 1963. "Problems in the Analysis of Survey Data and a Proposal." *Journal of American Statistical Association* 58:415-434.

Bibliography

National Automobile Dealers Association. *Official Used Car Guide*. Washington. Various issues 1954–1960. (Cited as *Used Car Guide*.)

Red Book of Official Used Car Valuations. Chicago: National Market Reports, Inc. Various issues. (Cited as *Red Book*.)

Rogowski, A. R. 1953. *Elements of Internal-Combustion Engines*. New York: McGraw-Hill.

Samuelson, P. A. 1947. *Foundations of Economic Analysis*. Cambridge, Mass.: Harvard University Press.

Statistical Reporter. Washington, D.C.: Government Printing Office.

Strotz, R. H. 1955–1956. "Myopia and Inconsistency in Dynamic Utility Maximisation." *Review of Economic Studies* 23:165–180.

Suits, D. B. 1957. "Use of Dummy Variables in Regression Equations." *Journal of the American Statistical Association* 52:548–551.

U.S. Bureau of the Census. 1968. *Construction Reports, Housing Starts*, Series C20:68-5, May, 1968. Washington: Government Printing Office.

U.S. Department of Labor, Bureau of Labor Statistics, *Consumer Price Index: Price Indexes for Selected Items and Groups, Annual Averages*, 1935–1961 (issued September 1962) and various annual and quarterly supplements for later dates.

Used Car Guide, see National Automobile Dealers Association.

Ward's Automotive Reports. Detroit: Powers and Co. Various issues.

Index

Adelman, Irma, 4, 153
Administered Prices, 85, 86
Agricultural Marketing Service prices paid for automobiles index, 83
Aircraft engines, 176
American Statistical Association, Business and Economic Statistics Section, 180n
Apparel, 187, 188–190
Appliances, household, 190–192, 208. *See also* Refrigerators; Washing machines
Arrow, K. J., 25n, 39n, 40n
Automobiles, 3, 5, 8, 88, 89, 90, 178, 190–191, 208, 215–239; secondhand market prices, 8–11, 76–82; and BLS, 11, 191, 197; hedonic price indexes for, 55–87, 232; price and quality indexes for U.S., 69–76; official price indexes for, 82–87; evolution of quality of average model, 90–92; European manufacturers, 91; and identifiable characteristics, 93; and quality or pure price effect, 94–116 *passim*; substitution in the price index, 191; methods of handling quality changes, 216–218
Automotive Industries, 89

Bailey, M. J., 3, 217
Bank, Rita, 150n
Barr, James L., 4
Barzel, Y., 4
Base period, 38–40
Blair, John M., 86
Box, G. E., 6
Brown, S. L., 3, 5
Bureau of Labor Statistics (BLS), 11–12, 71, 75, 270; and quality change, 151; and production relationships, 152; Office of Prices, 180n, 195; quality errors in price indexes, 181–201; pricing procedure, 181–183; and used car market, 194; product-mix data, 199–200; and human error, 200–201; and new measurement techniques, 202–209; need for more research, 212
Burstein, M. L., 8, 195–196, 202

Cagan, Philip, 3, 8, 10, 11, 202, 241, 259–260, 265
Capital goods, consumer, 88–149, 242–248, 270; rental prices, 243–245; characteristics, 258–265
Chain-link index, 73–74, 219
Change, "costless," 15

Index

Characteristics, 4, 5; and prices, 5–6; quantity-of-characteristics index, 6; left-out, and construction of price index, 210–211; and quality index, 241; of capital goods, 258–265
Chow, Gregory C., 4
Commerce Department, U.S., 202
Comparisons, direct, 188
Computers, 4
Constraints, 19–20, 26; and new goods, 39–41
Consumer Expenditure Survey, 73
Consumer information, 24
Consumer Price Index (CPI), 11, 182; and U.S. cars, 71–76, 270–271; and list prices, 74–75; and shifting supply conditions and tastes, 79–81; new automobile component, 82–87; substitution in, 187; used car component, 194–195; and quality change, 216–218; and hedonic index, compared, 231–235
Consumer Reports, 223, 226
Consumption, satiation in, 39–40
Cost, and utility, 152–153
Cost-of-living index, 16–54; misinterpretation of theory, 17; and intertemporal comparisons of welfare, 18–24; interregional and international comparisons, 21n; and taste change, 24–38; and corner solutions, 38–42; and quality change, 42–54
Court, Andrew T., 7, 56n, 88, 93, 94, 152, 202, 216
Cox, D. R., 6, 95
Cramer, J. S., 3
Cross-sections, annual, 7–8

Dean, C. R., 3
Demand: functions, 24, 25; price elastic, 33, 35–36, 41; reservation prices, 40–42
Denison, E. F., 215

DePodwin, H. J., 3
Depreciation, 9, 10, 77, 217–218, 220, 223–224, 240; estimates of, 224–227; drift proposal for estimating, 235–239; and pickup trucks, 251–252, 255–258; and vintage-price method, 259
Deterioration, 243–244
Dhrymes, Phoebus J., 3, 5, 150n, 204
Diesel engines, 3, 150n, 154–160 *passim*; price regressions, 161–174
Diller, Stanley, 150n
Divisia indexes, 6
Dummy variables, 10

Electric apparatus, 3
Enthoven, A. C., 25n, 39n

Federal Reserve Board Price Committee, 180n
Fettig, Lyle P., 3, 199
Fisher, Franklin, 3, 4, 9, 13, 16n, 49n, 88, 93, 94
Furniture, 187

Gavett, Thomas, 4, 15n, 188, 198, 205
Goods, "disappearing," 380
Gordon, R. A., 215
Griliches, Zvi, 3, 4, 6, 15, 88, 93, 94, 153, 180n, 202, 208, 210–211, 216, 232, 265

Hall, Robert E., 4, 9, 10n, 11n, 202
Hanoch, Giora, 4
Hedonic (characteristics) approach, 4–15, 202, 209–212; and secondhand market prices, 10–11, 216–239; and relevant units, 15; and consumer satisfaction, 24; and quality change, 43n; and automobiles, 55–87, 216–217; and improving pricing specification, 203–205; and improved quality adjustment

Index

techniques, 205–209; and Consumer Price Index, compared, 231–235; and pickup trucks, 264–268
Hofsten, Erland von, 17, 40, 55
Home Appliance Blue Book, 89
Hoover, Ethel D., 184n, 204
House prices, 3; and purchaser's income, 5
Houthakker, H. S., 23

Indifference map, consumer's, 18, 19, 20n, 21n–22n; and new goods, 39
Inflation, 181, 264, 270
Innovation, 192–193, 227
International price comparisons, *see* Prices, international comparisons of

Jorgenson, D. W., 6, 15
Juster, F. Thomas, 150n

Kaysen, Carl, 3, 88, 93, 94
Kefauver Hearings, 85
Kendall, M. G., 97
Kindahl, James, 150n
Klein, Lawrence R., 150n
Knight, Kenneth E., 4
Kravis, Irving B., 3, 150n

Lagrange multiplier, 26, 40, 45
Lancaster, K., 4, 93
Laspeyres, index numbers, 6, 21–22, 23n, 35–36, 40, 41, 57, 59, 73
Leontief, Wasily, 50
Lipsey, Robert E., 3, 150n
List price, 204–205, 217
Lo, Fu-chen, 88n
Locomotives, 178

Manufacturers, homogeneity in price behavior of, 89; and quality corrected price indexes, 93, 115–117; in automobiles, 94–104, 116; in refrigerators, 105–110, 116–117
Market price, 204–205, 210–212

Mart magazine, 89
Musgrave, J. C., 3
Muth, R. F., 3, 4, 217

National Automobile Dealers Association, 11, 194–195; *Official Used Car Guide*, 224, 248, 260
National Bureau of Economic Research, 150
Nourse, H. O., 3, 217

Obsolescence, 10
Outboard motors, 177

Paasche index numbers, 6, 21–22, 23n, 35–36, 59; and new goods, 40–42
Packaging, 14n, 16; and quality change 42–43, 49–50
Pickup trucks, 241; parameters of quality change, 248–258; prices of used, 249–255; characteristics of, 258–264, 265; and price measurement, 268–271
Power transformers, 177
"Power" variable, 4, 5
Price Competitiveness in World Trade (Kravis and Lipsey), 175, 176
Price indexes, 3–4, 6; construction of pure, 6–7; for automobiles, 82–87; quality corrected, 93, 115–117, 241, 270; and human error, 200–201
Price-of-living index, 12–14
Price-quality equation, 60–61
Price Statistics, 17
Price Statistics Review Committee, 180
Prices: relationship to characteristics, 5–6; intertemporal comparisons, 18–21; elasticity, 37–38; and quality change, 42–54; automobile, 56–87, 94–116; in consumer capital goods, 88–149; and identifiable characteristics, 93, 100–101,

151–152; refrigerator, 105–116; international comparison, 150–176; diesel engines, 154–174; secondhand market, 216–239; pickup trucks, 249–255, 268–271
Pricing specifications, 203–205, 209
Product specifications, 151; and regression strategies, 155–161; of diesel engine, 162–174; and BLS, 182; functions of, 182–183; and quality errors, 183–184; and quality problems, 184–194
Production costs, 14–15
Production function, 13, 14
Pujol, Joaquin P., 150n

Quality change, 4, 7, 9, 10, 24, 42–54; in BLS statistics, 11, 151, 197–198; utility theory, 12–14; and production costs, 14–15; and true cost-of-living index, 16; and augmenting of enjoyment, 43–44, 50–54; and automobiles, 54, 55–87, 216; quantification of, 60–61; measurement of 60–61, 215–239; chain-link index, 73–74, 219; and consumer capital goods, 88–149; component of price movements, 110–115; upward trend, 181, 184–185; and errors in indexes, 194–195; defined, 215n; and taste change, 218–220; and secondhand market prices, 221–239; and pure price change, 227–230; measured from vintage price data, 240–271; and capital goods, 258–268
Quality error, 181–201, 208; from deletion of price quotations, 185–188; from direct comparisons, 188–194

Rees, Albert, 196
Refrigerators, 3, 43–44, 50–52, 88, 90, 188, 190, 195–196, 204; evolution of quality of average model, 92; increase in average price, 92; quality effect versus pure price effect, 105–116 *passim*; quality component of price movements, 110; pricing specifications, 206–207; and product specifications, 208
Regression analysis, 4, 6–8, 150–176, 209; rationale in price comparisons, 151–161; cost versus utility, 152–153; for price measurement, 153–154; and specification differences, 155–161; diesel engine price, 161–174; pooled with international differences in prices of elements, 167–171, 178; separate country, 171–174. *See also* Prices; Specific commodities
Richter, M. K., 6
Ross, Arthur, 11
Rothwell, Doris P., 184n, 186, 207, 210
Ruggles, Richard, 180–181

Sampling error, 196–197
Samuelson, Paul, 16n, 19n
Secondhand market prices, 4, 8–11, 240; to measure quality change, 10, 216–239; for automobiles, 61, 76–82, 194–195; and change in taste, 219–220; and capital goods, 242–268; and price measurement, 268–271
Shell, Karl, 4, 9, 13, 16n
Specifications, *see* Pricing specifications; Product specifications
Steam power generators, 4
Stigler Committee, 152, 182, 184
Stone, R., 56n, 216
Stotz, Margaret S., 11, 198
Strotz, R. H., 21n
Substitutions, in price index, 183–194, 207
Summers, Robert, 16n, 150n

Index

Taste change, 79–81; and pure cost-of-living index, 16–17, 22, 24–38; and intertemporal comparisons, 18–38; and income, 20–21, 23; and consumer information, 24; and goods' desirability, 24; parametization, 25; disembodied, 25; and quality, 218–220; and secondhand market prices, 221–239
Technical change, 243–245. *See also* Innovation
Technology, 91–92; and refrigerators, 92
Tractors, 3, 177, 199–200
Triplett, Jack E., 3, 5, 8, 190n, 208, 241, 271
Trumpler, Paul R., 150n

USDA (United States Department of Agriculture), Prices Paid by Farmers Index, 71, 82
Utility theory, 12–15; and true cost-of-living index, 17; and taste change, 18; and quality change, 43–45, 52–53; and cost, 152–153

Vintage-price method, 202–212; measurement of quality change from, 240–271; and capital goods, 258–260

Ward's Automotive Reports, 11, 89
Washing machines, 3, 205
Wholesale Price Index, 11, 70–71, 74, 182; passenger car component, 82–85; for trucks, 241, 270
Wilkerson, Marvin, 197

Yoshihara, K., 3